The Italian Venus

'Poi, ch'in terra Odio, e 'n Cielo lnvidia, e Ira
Scorse Venere bella, al santo Figlio
Rivolto il vago, e luminoso ciglio
Disse qual Donna, che d'amor sospira:
"Ergiti al Cielo omai, ch' odioso gira
Senza il tuo Foco, e 'l livido e 'l vermiglio
Lume rasserena; io della terra piglio
Cura, che senza noi piange e s' adira".
Obedi il Nato, alla pietosa e saggia
Onde il Ciel tosto d' amorosa face
S' accese che senti gl' orati Strali.
D' Amor la Terra, et di tranquilla pace
S' empié, fugato il reo di tutti i mali,
Scoprendo rose, e Fior per ogni Piaggia'.

[When Venus saw hate on the Earth and envy and wrath in the Heavens,
turning to her son (Cupid) she said, as a woman who sighs with love:
'Go up to Heaven, as without your fire hate prevails,
I'11 take care of the earth, that without us is filled with tears and war'.
Cupid obeys the wise and compassionate goddess, just as the heavens,
touched by his darts, are set aflame with a fire of love
and the earth with love and peace, making the one guilty of evil take flight,
and uncovering roses and flowers in every corner]

Sonnet by Agnolo BRONZINO, painter
between 1540 and 1550
– Sopra una Pittura d'una Venere -
(Sframeli, M. 'Il mito di Venere' 2003, p. 50)

...on peut dire de tout art qu'il provient d'une nostalgie,
du désir de vaincre l'absence,
de faire se survivre et se conserver pour soi,
ce qui bientôt sera loin ou ne sera plus.

[...we could say that all art comes from nostalgia,
from the need to conquer absence,
to help survive and to keep for oneself
what will soon be far away or not be at all.]

(Georges Rodenbach, 1892, quoted by Patrick McGuiness,
The Times Literary Supplement, December 22 & 29, 2006, p.17)

The Iconography of Venus
from the Middle Ages to Modern Times
Volume 1.1

The Italian Venus

A topical catalogue of sculptures, reliefs, paintings, frescos, drawings, prints and illustrations of identified Italian artists

Compiled by
K. Bender

2007

To C and all my friends who supported me

Cover : La nascita di Venere (The birth of Venus), engraving by Marco DENTE da Ravenna, c1516, after a drawing by Giulio ROMANO, probably preparatory for the fresco by the workshop of Sanzio RAFFAELLO, in 'La stufetta del Cardinale Bibbiena', Musei Vaticani, Roma.
Photo Istituto nazionale per la Grafica, Roma.

A hard copy and digital pdf version are available at www.lulu.com

Contents

Introduction

Numerous books and essays have been written about the iconography and the iconology of Venus and many art exhibitions were organized during the past decades, showing the continuing interest in the subject (see a list of exhibitions below). No other mythological personage than Venus has been so often *on stage*. The reader interested in the iconography of Venus (or Aphrodite), in the iconology and history of her perpetual ambivalent presence and attention in our society, may find a support in this catalogue, besides a selected up-to-date bibliography of the subject.

The aim of the **Topical[1] Catalogue** is to offer a comprehensive list of artworks with the subject 'Venus'. The ***catalogue entries*** are the artworks, ordered *by 18 main topics* and, - within a topic or subtopic - *listed chronologically*, giving essential details on the date, the artist, the title(s) of the work, the type of work and its size, the owner and the source(s) of information. The identification is based solely either on the Roman name 'Venus' (or her Greek counterpart 'Aphrodite') in the title of the work - given by its creator or used by the owner - or on the subject closely related to 'Venus', e.g. the story of the 'Judgement of Paris' or the "Tale of Psyche". In general, no attempt has been made to interprete artworks which seemingly refer to Venus but which do not bear her name in the title. In a few cases, however, such artworks are identified in this catalogue if the owner or art scholars explicitely refer to Venus in the description of the artwork. Works related to the paleo-historic so-called Venus are not considered.

This volume concerns only **works of identified Italian artists**. In principle only those artists born in Italy are catalogued, but some non-native artists are added because their work was solely or for the largest part made in Italy and is therefore often regarded as Italian artwork. The many Italian artists who worked abroad are included. The alphabetic ***Index of Artists*** gives succinct basic information about their whereabouts and lists the 'Venus'-topics that were sources of inspiration for their works. The ***Directory of Owners*** shows the worldwide dispersal of these works. Artworks considered in this catalogue are *sculptures, reliefs, paintings and frescos, drawings and prints (woodcuts, engravings, etchings, lithographs, silk-screens) and illustrations (illuminations, book-illustrations and ex-libris)* of identified artists, including works identified as "attributed to…" or "workshop/studio of…" or "circle of…" if the date of the work corresponds to the artist's period of activity. Artworks made by unknown artists and described "after…" or "follower of…" or "school of…" are not included.

As far as known, **Topical Catalogues for Venus** have never been made at the scale envisaged[2]. The catalogue lists 1840 identified artworks and many replicas and copies: it should be useful to the owners of the works for comparison reasons; to museums, galleries and auctioneers in order to help correct identification of works attributed to some artist and to improve the title and description of the work; to those studying mythology and iconology and to art historians: which are the 'Venus'-topics most popular in different periods and why? How did the iconography evolved over time? Which and how many topics were popular with a given artist? Future similar topical catalogues of artworks made by different groups of artists – e.g. French artists, artists of the Low Countries, etc. – could support correlation and relationship studies.

---

[1] Relating to a particular subject, arranged by topics.

[2] Rochelle (1991) and Reid (1993) published topical catalogues on general mythology: hence, their entries for Venus/Aphrodite are limited. The Photographic Collection Index of the Warburg Institute (2002) offers a list of topics similar to the one used in this catalogue, but the contents of the folders according to this index are not published.

The specificity of this catalogue should also guarantee the attention of other scientists, e.g. archaeologists who search for later copies or representations of ancient artworks; philologists who wish to link literary text to topics in artworks; scientists in philosophy, religion and sociology who are interested in the general subject 'Venus/Aphrodite' and its past and present aura in society. For these reasons, other types of art (i.e. ceramics, jewellery, tapestry, etc.), as well as works in literature, music and dance, theatre, films, or photographs, posters, cartoons, trivia, etc. could also be compiled. Last but not least, WEB-editors may find in this catalogue support to improve their specific information or to extend their image-databases.

Obviously, such a catalogue can never be complete (e.g. many artworks remain in private collections and have not been yet identified) or without errors. The readers are kindly encouraged to notify omissions, supply missing information or point out errors: they will be gratefully acknowledged in a revised version of this catalogue. Please send an E-mail to <bender@telenet.be>.

Some "Venus/Aphrodite" exhibitions in Europe [1]

"La Vénus de Milo ou les dangers de la célébrité" Ready Museum, Bruxelles 1971
"Venus te lijf – liefde en verleiding in de oudheid", Allard Pierson Museum, Amsterdam 1985
"Cyprus and Aphrodite", Allard Pierson Museum, Amsterdam 1989.
"Vénus et déesses mères, préhistoriques et antiques"Albi/Saint-Denis/Evreux 1990-1991
"Venus" Bettina van Haaren. Art Communication, Berlin 1991
"Venus re-defined - Sculptures by Rodin, Matisse and Contemporaries", Tate Gallery, Liverpool 1994
"Jim Dine's Venus", Civico Museo Revoltella, Trieste 1996
"El triunfo de Venus - La imagen de la mujer en la pintura veneciana del siglo XVIII", Museo Thyssen-Bornemisza, Madrid 1997-98
"Venus, Bilder einer Göttin», Wallraf-Richartz-Museum, Köln 2000/ Alte Pinakothek, München 2001
"Venus, vergeten mythe – Voorstellingen van een godin van Cranach tot Cézanne», Koninklijk Museum voor Schone Kunsten, Antwerpen 2001
"In den Gärten der Aphrodite » Institut für Klassische Archäologie der Freien Universität Berlin, 2001
« Reliquaire pour un culte de Vénus», Exposition itinérante de Jean-Jacques LEBEL, France 2001-02; Barcelona 2003 and in many other European cities.
« Venere e Amore : Michelangelo e la nuova bellezza», Galleria dell'Academia, Firenze 2002
«Tiziano - Rubens : Venus ante l'espejo», Museo Thyssen-Bornemisza, Madrid 2002
"Titian: Venus with a Mirror" Hermitage Museum, St. Petersburg 2002
«Pour l'Amour de Vénus», Donjon de Vèz, Vèz 2003
«Venus ontsluierd – de Venus van Urbino van Titiaan», Europalia, Bozar, Brussel 2003
«The Myth of Venus», Municipal Arts Centre, Nikosia 2003
«Le mythe de Vénus- de Titien à Rubens, chefs d'oeuvres des musées de Florence», Mairie du Vème arrondissement de Paris 2003
«Bella come una dea. Le seduzioni di Venere», Museo Ostiense, Ostia 2003-04
«Il Mito di Venere», Biblioteca per la Cultura e per le Arti , Bari 2004
«Pour l'Amour de Vénus -Vénus et l'Amour dans la peinture française, italienne, flamande du XVII ème et XVIII ème siècle», Musée des Beaux-arts , Nîmes 2004
"La Venere di Anzio", Museo Civico Archeologico, Anzio 2004
"La Nascita di Venere nel Trono Ludovisi: un'assenza rituale», Museo Altemps, Roma 2005
"Venus, Adonis y Cupido", Museo Nacional del Prado, Madrid 2005
"Nørgaard: Venus spejler - spejler Venus», Statens Museum for Kunst, Kopenhagen 2005
"Venus, Goddess of Love", National Gallery of Scotland, Edinburgh 2006
"La Venere di Sebastiano Ricci", Banca Popolare di Vicenza 2006-07.
"Canova e la Venere Vincitrice", Galleria Borghese, Roma 2007-08.

[1]Most of these exhibitions were accompanied by well-illustrated catalogs, but not all of them give full information about the artworks.

Guideline to the Topical Catalogue

All entries are found under 18 main topics .. Within a topic, subtopic or subdivision, artworks are listed chronologically. Each entry offers essential information about the work as explained hereafter. The information is the one found in the referred information sources, given without guarantee of correctness. It does not exclude more accurate information from other sources not yet consulted.

Topic

The choice of topics is based on well-established or well-known characteristics or stories of 'Venus'. The English names of the Greek or Roman mythological personages are used. If appropriate, references are made to the equivalent names. Thus, e.g. **Aphrodite→Venus**, **Venere→Venus**; **Eros→Cupid(o) ; Amo(u)r→Cupid(o); Ares→Mars**, etc. However, the personage's name in the title of the work is always preserved as given in the language of the owner. French accents are used in the titles but are not distinguished in the entries of the catalogue, thus **Vénus = Venus**, or **Pâris = Paris**.

In many cases, the given title of the work is too general and does not allow for a detailed topical cataloguing, or the number of works under a given topic is too large for a meaningful topical cataloguing. It is then necessary to split the **main topic** in **subtopics** and the subtopics in **subdivisions**. The following approach has been applied:

The main topic is always found in the title of the work as given by the present owner[1]. E.g. a work entitled "Venus and Adonis" is catalogued under main topic **Venus and Adonis**; "Venus and Cupid" under main topic **Venus and Anteros/Cupid**; but "The bath of Venus", "The crouching Venus" and "The toilet of Venus" are grouped under a common topic **Toilet/Bath of Venus/Venus crouching**. Similarly, "Birth of Venus", "Venus Anadyomene", Venus Marina" and other works with clear reference to the sea or to water are grouped under one main topic. Other groups are also created.

- **The subtopic is always the major ACTION** or **CIRCUMSTANCE** or **THIRD PERSONAGE depicted in the work**. E.g. ACTIONS: Adonis **meeting Venus**, Adonis **leaving Venus**, Adonis **dying**, etc. E.g. CIRCUMSTANCE: Venus **reclining, seated, standing** etc. E.g. THIRD PERSONAGE: Venus and Adonis together with **Cupid,** etc.; "Venus, Mars and Cupid" is entered under main topic **Venus and Mars** , and not under main topic Venus and Anteros/Cupid, but Cupid will be a subtopic under the main topic **Venus and Mars**.
    - **The subdivision** is created whenever the subtopic lists too many works. A similar approach as for the subtopics is followed, often with respect to the POSITION of Venus, e.g. Venus **reclining** or **seated** or **standing in the center, to the left, to the right**. In the case of "Venus and Anteros/Cupid", subdivisions are also created with the attributes of Cupid, i.e. arrow and bow, etc.

Whenever works could not definitely catalogued under a subtopic, they are listed at the beginning of the main topic.

Date of work

Under a given topic/subtopic/subdivision the works are listed chronologically by date, as given by the owner or derived from other sources. The letter **"c" (circa)** before the year indicates that style or other

[1] Often the title is a traditional one, not necessarily the original one, if known. In some cases more than one title is known and translated titles do not always correspond exactly to the original title.

evidence approximately established a date. Other letters used before the year are **"a"(after)** and **"b"(before).** The expression "xth century" has been always transcribed in the approximate year: e.g. "15th century" = c1450; "early 16th century" = c1525; "mid 18th century" = c1750; "late 19th century" = c1875, etc.

Artist's/creators' name(s)

The artist's name follows the date. The SURNAME (always in uppercase) and first name used are the most common ones in art history: e.g. Alessandro di Mariano Filipepi→ BOTTICELLI, Sandro. The **Index of Artists** gives details on the names given, the dates of birth, of main residence(s), if known, and of death. The total number of works catalogued is given, followed by the main topics where works of the artist are catalogued. There may be, *in italic,* also given some further information, e.g. a justification for entering a non-native artist in this list.

The following abbreviations BEFORE the artist's name are used:
(att) = attributed to <SURNAME>
(cir) = circle of <SURNAME>
(wor) = workshop/studio of <SURNAME>.
It is understood that 'circle' and 'workshop/studio' means that the artwork was made during the lifetime of the artist: therefore, these works are considered as 'identified'.
Works by unknown artists, described **"after (aft)" <SURNAME>** or **"follower (fol)" of <SURNAME>**, often with a later date, do not get an entry in this catalogue, nor get those works generally identified under the name **"School of..."** or **"Italian Art"**, but comments *in italic* may be added at the end of an entry of a similar or corresponding 'identified' work.

If the work is a **copy** made by an identified Italian artist of a work of another artist, this is indicated by (**aft** or **cop** <SURNAME>) between brackets following the title. But anonymous copies or copies made by non-Italian artists are not catalogued. However, the existence of such copies found is often mentioned at the end of the entry (see below).

In the case of 'prints' (woodcuts, etchings, engravings, etc.), there may be 4 or 5 creators known: the 'inventor', the 'drawer', the 'engraver' and the 'printer' or 'publisher/editor'. The 'engraver', who may be also the 'drawer', is likely considered as the creator: this name is generally used after the date of the work. The name(s) of the 'inventor' and/or 'drawer' is then indicated by **"aft" (after) <SURNAME>**, written between brackets following the title of the work.

In some cases the 'inventor' or 'drawer' is more commonly known as the main creator and the 'engraver' is indicated as **"eng"<SURNAME>** , if known, between brackets following the title of the work. This may be also the case where prints were made after a painting: if the painting is known and got an entry, the print does not get a separate entry, but the information is given in the *comments*. If known, the 'publisher/editor' or 'printer' is also given between brackets after the title of the work, but *in italic* with the letter symbol ***"pub"<SURNAME>.***
In the case of book-illustrations, the author ***"aut",*** and possibly also the title of the book may be added between brackets *in italic* after the title of the illustration. But if the 'drawer' of the illustration is not known, the 'author' may get the entry.
Surnames, not written in uppercase, are not included in the Index of Artists: i.e. surnames of non-Italian creators and some minor Italian artists (e.g. engravers or publishers/editors).

Title of work

The title of the work is generally given in the language of the owner, with an English translation between brackets if appropriate. If more than one title is known, they will also be given between brackets. For reasons of cataloguing, the "official" title may be adjusted with words *in italic*, which indicate the topic of the catalogue or describe more in detail the iconography. Occasionally, further comments are given *in italic* at the end of the entry. A question mark <(?)> indicates doubt about the identification or any other information given.The abbreviation (sic) indicates a manifest odd or wrong word in the title or in any other information item of the work, according to the author of this catalogue.

Type of work

The following uppercase letter symbols are used to describe the type of work, following its title

AS = assemblage
CL = collage
DR = drawing
FR = fresco
IL = illustration (print in books)
IM = illumination or miniature
MM = mixed media
OT = other
PA = painting
PR = print
RE = relief
SC = sculpture

If a drawing (DR) is obviously a preparatory study for a painting (PA) or sculpture (SC) by the same artist, this information is given *in italic* at the end of the entry and accounted for in the number of works in the Index of Artists and Directory of Owners.

Medium and material of support

The following lowercase letter symbols, following the uppercase letter symbols of the type of work, describe the medium and material of support

a = acrylic, plastic, synthetic resin, etc.
b = board (card, cardboard, millboard)
c = canvas
d = pen and ink, pencil, crayon, chalk, etc.
e = etching, engraving, woodcut
f = fabric other than canvas, e.g. silk
g = gouache
h = enamel
i = ivory
j = metal other than bronze or copper
l = lithograph, silkscreen
m = marble
o = oil
p = plaster or other cast or moulded material
q = terracotta
r = coloured
s = stone or mineral other than marble
t = tempera
u = watercolour, pastel
v = various
w = wood, panel
x = paper
y = copper
z = bronze

Drawings (DR) and prints (PR) are considered as made on paper (x) if no other information is available.

Dimension of work and series

Seizes, given after the medium of the work, are in centimeters *height x width*. Print sizes are generally for the size of the image. Sculpture seizes are given *height x width x depth*, or height only.
In cases where a series of identical copies of the work were made - e.g. PR (prints) and SC/z (bronze sculptures) - the serial number, if known, is given followed by the number of copies in the series between brackets: e.g. (45/300) means that there were 300 copies of the work made and the one described in this catalogue is n° 45 of the series.

Owner of work

The owner of the work is given by the city name and an abbreviation of the museum, institution, library, etc. listed in the **Directory of Owners**. A work in a private collection is indicated by the city name (if known) and the symbol **PrC**. If only the auctioneer is known, the auction date **(dd.mm.'yy)** is given, if known. A work for sale in a commercial gallery is indicated by the city name and the symbol **GAL**, with the name of the gallery in the Directory of Owners. A work for sale on Internet is indicated by **WEB,** followed by the shortname of the website. If the location of the work is unknown or if the work is lost, the letters **UN** and **LO** respectively are used., sometimes with information about the previous (**pre.**) owner or location.

Inventory number of work

The owner's inventory number, if known, is written as "**Inv.** #". If the owner is not known but the auctioneer is known, then the sales-lot numbers are given: "**Sl.**#-#", if known.

Source(s) of information about the work

The source(s) of information can be an exhibition (**exh**), a bibliographic reference, listed in the Selected Bibliography and/or it can be Internet (**IT**). Given the fleeting character of the latter, no URLs are given: search engines will generally offer a quick guide to the source, but a helpful reference or hint may be added.

Reference number of work

The reference number of the work in the author's database[1] is given as <**R**#.>, followed by an automatic sequence number of the work identified in this catalogue.

[1]Using the software programme ArtWorks-The Art Organizer. Version 1.2.20a. Copyright 2002-2005. Belgrave Park Pty. Ltd. (Australia). www.ArtWorksPro.com

Replicas, copies of work and comments

A work is a replica, resembling very closely the original, made by the artist (or his/her circle or workshop/studio) of the original. The information is given ***in italic*** at the end of the entry of the (supposed) original. A replica is counted for in the number of works. A work is a copy of the original if made by another artist, often not identified. Information *in italic* is given at the end of the entry about copies of the work made by non-Italian or unknown artists**.** If the artist of a copy is identified and is Italian, then the work has a separate entry and is thus accounted for in the number of works. Prints or illustrations made after an original painting or drawing, will be described *in italic* at the end of the entry describing the painting or drawing. Only prints or illustrations by identified Italian creators are accounted for in the number of works. Copies in series of prints or (bronze) sculptures are not accounted for, but *comments* about the owners may be added.

Example

Venus and Adonis

*The topic **"Venus and Adonis"** is described by four subtopics: **"Adonis meeting Venus**"; "**Adonis loving Venus**"; **"Adonis leaving Venus**"; **"Adonis dying**". Subtopic "Adonis leaving Venus", however, counts 41 entries; therefore two subdivisions are created describing the iconography in more detail: **'Venus reclining'** and **'Venus seated'**.*

- ### Adonis leaving Venus
  - #### Venus seated

c1555 TIZIANO, Vecellio: Venere e Adone con capello rosso (Venus and Adonis with the red hunter's cap)/ PA/ oc/ 187x134/ Roma, GNB/ Inv. 922/ Mochi Onori 2001, p.54-55, n°34/ R352.453. *Replica (or copy?): **c1555** (wor) (without Cupid in the picture) /PA/ oc/ 150x200/ London, SOT 10.7.'03/ Sl. L03031-4/ IT/ R5881.454.*

In full the entry reads:
*Topic: **Venus and Adonis;** subtopic: **Adonis leaving Venus**; subdivision: **Venus seated.***
Approximate date of the work is 1555; the creator is TIZIANO, Vecellio, listed in the Index of Artists ; the title of the work is given in Italian (language of the owner) with English translation between brackets; the type of work is a painting (PA); the medium is oil (o) and the material of support is canvas(c); its seizes are 187 cm height and 134 cm width; the owner (GNB) is the museum Galleria Nazionale d'Arte Antica, Palazzo Barberini in Roma, listed in the Directory of Owners; the inventory number Inv. of the owner is 922; the source of information is Mochi Onori 2001, p.54-55, n°34, listed in the Selected Bibliographical References; the reference numbers in the author's database and in this catalogue are respectivelys R352 and 453.
*Then follows **in italic** information about the auction in London by Sotheby's on 10 July 2003, sale L03031, lot number 4, of a replica (or copy?), painting, oil on canvas, dated approximately of the same time, from the workshop (wor) of TIZIANO, where Cupid is omitted in the picture, with sizes 150 cm height and 200 cm width; the information source is Internet(IT) and the reference numbers for this work are R5881.454. Since the work is identified as a replica (wor) (although it may be a copy), it has been accounted for in the number of identified works.*

List of abbreviations

a	acrylic, plastic, synthetic resin, etc.
a	after<YEAR>
a.	active in <YEAR(S)>
aft	after <SURNAME>
AS	assemblage
att	attributed to <SURNAME>
aut	author<SURNAME>
b	board (card, cardboard, millboard)
b	before<YEAR>
b.	born
c	canvas
c	circa <YEAR>
Cat.	Catalogue
cir	circle of <SURNAME>
CL	collage
Col.	collection
cop	copy of <SURNAME>
d	pen and ink, pencil, crayon, chalk, etc.
d.	died
DR	drawing
e	etching, engraving, woodcut, etc.
ed.	editor (bibliographic reference)
eng	engraver<SURNAME>
exh	exhibition
f	fabric other than canvas
f.	first<YEAR>mentioned
fig.	figure
fol	follower of <SURNAME>
FR	fresco
g	gouache
h	enamel
i	ivory
IL	illustration (print in books)
IM	illumination or miniature
Inv.	inventory number
IT	Internet
j	metal other than bronze or copper
l	lithograph, silkscreen
l.	last<YEAR>mentioned
LO	lost or looted
m	marble
MM	mixed media
nr/n°	number
o	oil
OT	other
p	plaster or other cast or molded material
p.	pagina
PA	painting
pl.	plate
PrC	private collection
PR	print
pre.	previously
pub	publisher or editor<*SURNAME*>
q	terracotta
r	coloured
R	reference number in database
RE	relief
s	stone or mineral other than marble
SC	sculpture
sic	odd or wrong word(s)
Sl.	sales-lot numbers
t	tempera
u	watercolour, pastel
UN	unknown location of work
v	various
V	image not provided/not on display
w	wood, panel
WEB	location on Internet
wor	workshop of <SURNAME>
x	paper
y	copper
z	bronze
Ǿ	diameter
?	missing or questionable information
#	unknown number

Table of topics and topic-index

Topic-index

Catalogue

1.Allegories

(Garden of Venus, Hymen, Love, Music, Spring)/ Planet Venus

1478 BOTTICELLI, Sandro : Primavera (Allegory of Spring)/ PA/ tw/ 203x312/ Firenze, GdU/ Inv. 8360/ Berenson 1963, p.34, pl.1079; Clark 1969, p.163; Levi d'Ancona 1992; Damisch 1997,p.238)/ R3158.1.
c1484 BOTTICELLI, Sandro : Un jeune homme présenté par Vénus (?) aux sept arts libéraux (A young man introduced by Venus to the seven liberal arts)/ FR/ / 237x269/ Paris, MdL/ Inv. R.F. 322/ Berenson 1963, p.37/ R555. 2.
c1490 MASTER of SANTO SPIRITO : Allegory of love (Venus seated left)/ PA/ ow/ 61.9x77.5/ London, WaC/ Inv. 556/ Anonymous 1989, Vol.I, p.418/ R10900. 3.
c1508 BAZZI, detto SODOMA, Giovanni Antonio : Vénus terrestre et Vénus céleste (Venus profane *with Eros* and Venus sacred *with Anteros*)/ PA/ ow/ Ø61/ Paris,MdL/ Inv.RF2107/ IT/ R2465.4.
1515 TIZIANO, Vecellio: Amor Sacro e Amor Profano (Geminae Veneres/ Twin Venuses; Sacred and Profane Love; Laura Bagarotto at the fountain of Venus) PA/ oc/ 118x279/ Roma, GaB/ Inv. 147/ Berenson 1958, p.196, pl.955-957 ; Clark 1969, T.I, p.200; Panofsky 1969, fig.108, pl..LIX; Tiziano 1995; Goffen 1997, p.44; Moreno 2004, p.394-95, n°3/ R358.5.
b1520 LOTTO, Lorenzo: Il trionfo della castita *(Venus?-with Cupid and dove-chased by Chastity)*/ PA/ ?/ ?/ Roma, PaRo/ Inv.#/ Berenson 1958, p.108, pl.775/ R9618.6.
1545 (att) BANDINELLI, Baccio: Combattimento tra Amore e Ragione (Combat of Ratio and Libido/Love *or Venus, Cupid and Vulcan against Apollo, Diana,a.o.)*(*eng Béatrizet, N.*)/ PR/ e/ ?/ Paris MdL/ Inv.#/ Panofsky 1969, pl.LVIII, fig.107; Seznec, 1961, p.110-13, fig.38/ R6027.7.
c1550 BORDONE, Paris: Venus, Mars and Cupid crowned (Matrimonial allegory)/ PA/ oc/ 115,5x174,5/ Wien, KHM/ Inv.120/ Panofsky 1969,pl. LXVI,fig.121; Mai ed. 2001, p.326-27, n°46/ R1614.8.
c1550 TIZIANO, Vecellio : Allégorie d'Alfonso d'Avalos (aft?)/ PA/ oc/ 129x100/ Montauban, MuI/ Inv. MI.843.3.4/ Panofsky 1969, p.160, fig. 118, pl. LXIV/ R8870.9. *See PR by MATTIOLI.*
c1555 MICHELI, Parrasio: Lute-playing Venus with Cupid/ PA/ oc/ 110x97/ Budapest, MFA/ Inv.#/ IT/ R1520.10.
c1565 BRONZINO, Agnolo: Allégorie de l'Hymen avec Vénus couronnée, et les Muses (Hymen, Venus crowned and the Muses)/ DR/ d/ 40x31,3/ Paris, MdL/ Inv.953recto/ Monbeig-Goguel 1972, p.39,n°12/ R3827. 11.
c1570 VERONESE, Paolo Caliari, detto : Epiphany of Venus (allegory 'Respect')/ PA/ oc/ 188x188/ London, Nga/ Inv. NG1325/ Wind 1980, p.272, fig.46/ R10428.12.
1590-92 VIANI, Antonio Maria : Allegorie auf die Thronbesteigung und glückliche Regierung von Maximilian I. von Bayern (*Venus, Amor, Minerva und Mars*)/ PA/ oc/ 119,5 x 147,5/ Wien, DOR 24.4.'07/ Sl. –485/ IT/ R9396.13.
1597-1604 CARRACCI, Agostino: Venere terrena e Venere celeste, particolare del 'Trionfo dell'unione dell'Amore celeste e dell'Amore terreno' (Venus profane and Venus sacred) /FR/// Roma, PaFa/ Inv.#/ Ginzburg Carignani 2000,n°60-61/ R3773.14.
c1625 (att) SAN GIOVANNI, Giovanni da: An allegory of the Arts: Painting, Sculpture and Architecture (*with gilt-bronze statuette of Venus by Giambologna*)/ PA/ oc/ 45,7x30,3/ London, CHR 8.12.'06/ Sl. 7290-250/ IT/ R8059.15.

c1625 VAROTARI, Alessandro: Venere, Cupido e una sposa (L'oracolo d'amore) (Psiche riceve da Venere il vaso)/ PA/ oc/ 155x111/ Milano, PCS/ Inv.298/ Tiziano, 1995, p.427,433-434,fig.147/ R4430.16.
c1625 VAROTARI, Alessandro: Allegory of Married life depicting the Gods Vesta, Hymen, Mars and Venus/ PA/ oc/ 95x127/ Wien, KHM/ Inv.#/ IT/ R8995.17.
c1627 CORTONA, Pietro da: Nozze Aldobrandini/ DR/ u/ ?/ Windsor, RCo/ Inv. RL19228/ Rodino 1997,p.70,n°2.3/ R3558.18.
1627 CAPITELLI, Bernardino(eng): Antique marriage ceremonies (aft CORTONA)/ PR/ e/ 25.2x99.9/ Roma, ING & Wien, ALB/ Bartsch 45(20,2) 1982, p.38-39,n°31(162); Rodino 1997,p.70/ R4983.19.
c1630-34 LANFRANCO, Giovanni: Venere che suona l'arpa (La Musica) (Venus playing the harp - Allegory of Music)/ PA/ oc/ 214x150/ Roma GNB/ Inv.2411/ Mochi Onori 2001, p.69, n°45/ R353.20.
c1631-37 TESTA, Pietro: Il giardino di Venere/ PR/ e/ 35,6x41,8/ Roma, ING/ Inv. FC122499/ Bartsch 45 (20,2) 1982, 148,n°26-II(222); Bartsch 45 C (20,) 1990, p.153,n°4506.026; Massari 1989, p.512-513,n°210/ R2593.21. *Also: NY, MMA/ Inv 1926 (26.70.3[44])/ IT/ R1644.21.;Lisboa, BNP/ Inv. E. 446 A; Lyon, BiM and elsewhere.*
1637 DELLA BELLA, Stefano *(aut Coppola, Giovanni Carlo : Le nozze degli dei)* : Terza Scena Giardino di Venere (third scene Garden of Venus *in The Weddings of the gods)*/ PR/ e/ 20x28,5/ Caen, MBA/ Inv.#/ Anonymous 1998,p.46-47, n°8-3/ R3826.22. *Also in Hanover, HMA/ Inv. PR.979.66.3.*
c1640 TESTA, Pietro: Venus submitting to the river Serchio, an allegory of the virtues of Lucca/ DR/ d/ 20x29,1/ Paris, MdL/ Inv. 1910, rect/ IT/ R8436.23. *Also in London, BMu/ Inv. 1943,0710.00015.*
1657 GALESTRUZZI, Giovanni Battista: Venere Celeste (with wings; from 'The Antique Figural Gems' Roma/ PR// 9,7x7,8/ Milano, BiA/ Inv.#/ Bartsch 46 (21,1) 1982, p.175,n°175(73); Bartsch 46 C 1985; p.214,n°4606.175/ R4989.24.
1674 BARTOLI, Pietro Santi: Aldobrandini wedding/ IL/ux/ ?/ Glasgow, ULi/ GUL 232063 Title MS GEN 1496 Plate XLI/ IT/ R7455.25.
c1700 MATTIOLI, Ludovico: Allegoria di Alfonso d'Avalos (aft TIZIANO)/ PR/ e/ 21.2x20.9/ Venezia, MuC/ Inv. D49-8/ Chiari 1982, p.160, nr.186/ R10406.26.
1776 CARLONI, Marco : Aldobrandinische Hochzeit/ PR/ e/ ?/ Roma, BiH/ Inv. #/ IT/ R10126.27.
c1790 APPIANI, Andrea : Venere e Imeneo piangente/ PA/ oc/ 75x60/ Pavia, MuM/ Inv.#/ Precerutti-Garberi 1970, p.23, n°8/ R9637.28.
c1800 BONATO, Pietro: Amor profano (aft TIZIANO)/ PR/ e/ 31x22.4 oval/ Roma, ING/ Inv. FC51277/ Catelli Isola 1976, p.72, nr.273/ R10486.29. *Venus, almost naked, is alone and called here 'amor profano'.*
c1800 REGONA, Antonio: Amor profano (aft TIZIANO)/ PR/ e/ 31x23.7 oval/ Venezia, MuC/ Inv.Molin339/ Chiari 1982, p.216, nr.293/ R10410.30. *Identical to BONATO's PR but Venus is dressed.*
1806 AGRICOLA, Luigi: Aldobrandinische Hochzeit/ PR/ e/ ?/ Roma, BiH/ Inv.#/ IT/ R10123.31.
1877 BARTOLO, Francesco di: Amor sacro e Amor profano (Sacred and Profane Love) (aft TIZIANO, Vecellio)/ PR/ e/ 47,5x81/ Roma, ING/ Inv.2208.2207/ Tiziano 1955, p.231,306, Cat.121/ R5551.32.

Planet Venus

1334 PISANO, Andrea : Allegoria del pianeta Venere/ RE/ m/ 86x59/ Firenze, OMF/ Inv.#/ Trottein 1993, p.23, fig.7: Pisano, Nino?/ R7719.33.
1365 GUARIENTO di ARPO : La Planète Vénus et la jeunesse/ FR// ?/Padova, ChE/ Inv.#/ Seznec 1961,p.204,n°85; Trottein 1993, p.21,n°6 ; Mai ed. 2001, p.83 n°2/ R7718.34.
1424-1440 MIRETTO, Zuan : Le Taureau et la Planète Vénus ou 'La Madone'/ FR// ?/ Padova, PdR/ Inv.#/ Trottein 1993, p.26-7, fig.8-9/ R7720.35.
1424-1440 MIRETTO, Zuan : La Planète Vénus/ FR// ?/ Padova, PdR/ Inv.#/ Trottein 1993, p.28-9, fig.10-11/ R7721.36.
c1460 BALDINI, Baccio : La Pianeta Venus (Planet Venus)/ PR/ e/ 32,8x21,9/ Pavia, MuC/ Inv.StMal1591/ Bartsch 24, p.113 n°2403(.005) ; Trottein 1993,p.92,fig.39 ; Dempsey 2001, p.84, fig.62 ; Lomartire 2003, p.106,n°42 ; /R3650.37.*Also in Coburg;, Firenze;,London, BMu; Paris, BnF;*
c1464 (att)BALDINI, Baccio : Vénus et ses Enfants (Planet Venus)/PR/ey/ ?/ London, BMu/ Inv.Hind A.III.5,b/ Trottein 1993,p.93,fig.40 ; Dempsey 2001, p.83, fig.61/ R7042.38.

1466-75 (att) PREDIS, Cristoforo de : Les Enfants de Vénus (*'Sphaera' Codex 1X.2.14 lat.209,fol9v & lat209f10r)/* IM/ Modena, BiE/ Trottein 1993, p.106-107/R 559 & R7742.39.

c1482 (cir) PINTURICCHIO, Bernardino di Betto, detto : Vénus et ses Enfants/ FR/ plafond Salle des Sybilles/ ?/ Roma, MuV (Appartements Borgia)/ Inv.#/ Trottein 1993, p.163, fig.68/ R7746.40.

c1500 PERUGINO, Pietro: La Planète Venus (*with chariot and doves*)/ FR//?/ Perugia, CdC/ Inv.#/ Trottein 1993, p.97, fig.43/ R1113.41.

c1510 (att) PERUZZI, Baldassare Tommaso : Venere (*with ram or goat*)/ FR//?/ Roma, ViF/ Inv.#/ IT/ R6052.42. *Also **c1511** (att) PIOMBO, Sebastiano: Venere nel segno del Capricorno...la dea Anadiomene ritta su una conchiglia, circondata delle colombe a lei sacre.*

a1536 GIOLITO de FERRARI, Gabriele: La planète Vénus/ PR/ e/ ?/ Paris, BnF/ Inv.#/ Trottein 1993, p.174, fig.77/ R7238.43.

c1540 CARUCCI, Jacopo (PONTORMO): Vénus au Capricorne (Venere e Cupido con i segni zodiacali del Capricorno e dell'Ariete)/ DR/ d/ 17,5x17,6/ Paris, MdL/ Inv. 10396recto/ Falletti 2002,p.216,n°38/ R4318.44.

1548 PRIMATICCIO, Francesco: Vénus avec l'Amour et les Parques et le signe du Taureau; étude pour la Galerie d'Ulysse (Fontainebleau)/ DR/ d/ 32x36/ Paris, MdL/ Inv. RF 1470/ Primatice 2004, n°146./ R2832. 45.

c1700 CRETI, Donato : Astronomical observation: Venus/ PA/ ?/ ?/ Roma, MuV/ Inv. #/ IT/ R9072.46.

2. Apotheosis/Sacrifice/Temple/ Triumph/Worship of Venus

c1335 (att) LORENZETTI, Pietro : Venustanius worshipping Venus (?) (Venustanius, the Roman Governor of Tuscany, trying to persuade Saints Sabinus, Marcellus and Exuperantius to worship a pagan statue, here apparently Venus)/ PA/ tw/ 37,5x33/ London, NGa/ Inv. NG1113/ IT/ R6547.47.
c1425 (att) MAÎTRE de la Prise de TARENTE: Le triomphe de Vénus vénérée par six amoureux légendaires (Achille , Tristan , Lancelot , Samson ; Pâris ; Troile)/ PA/ ow/ 51 polygonal/ Paris, MdL/Inv. RF 2089/ Clark 1969, T.I, p.159; Trottein 1993, p.33, n°12/ R2467.48. *Also*: ***c1360*** *(att) MAîTRE de SAINT MARTIN/* Eco 2004,p.162.
c1450 GIOVANNI di TOMMASO, Apollonio di : Giuliano in preghiera davanti a Venere/ ILL/ e/ ?/ Firenze, BNC/ Inv. E.6.4.84/ IT/ R11600.49.
c1469-70 COSSA, Francesco: Trionfo di Venere, particolare del mese di Aprile/ FR/ / 500x320/ Ferrara, PaS/ Inv.#/ Seznec 1961,p.207,n°89; Berenson 1968, p.131 ; Trottein 1993, p.119,125, n°48, 51; Zuffi 2001,p.66 ; Mai ed. 2001, p.49, n°1 and p.374, n°1/ R455, R7743.50.
1499 COLONNA, Francesco : Nymphs worshipping *Venus (Poliphilo's Dream about the Strife of Love/ pub Aldus Manutius)*/IL/ e/ 29x21,5/ NY, MMA/ Inv. 1923 (23.73.1)/ IT; Tiziano 1995, p.44, fig.19:' Venere e il sarcofago di Adone'/ R1638.51.
c1500 FRANCIA, Jacopo: Omaggio a Venere/ DR// 23,3x19,9/ Firenze, GdU/ Inv. 1171^{E}/ Faietti 1988, p.298-300,n°87/ R3539.52.
c1515 (wor) RAIMONDI, Marcantonio : Triumph of Venus/ PR// 11,7x17,7/ Wien, ALB/ Inv.#/ Bartsch 28 (15,1) 1985, p.51,n°7-I(8); Bartsch 28 C (15,1) 1995, p.38-39,n°2801.042/ R4837.53.
c1517 PORTA, Fra Bartolommeo della : Worship of Venus/ DR/ d/ 20,5x28,8/ Firenze, GdU/ Inv. 1269 E/ Goffen 1997, p.110,n°68/ R5542.54.
1519 TIZIANO, Vecellio : Worship of Venus (Culto di Venere) (from 'Imagines' of Philostratus, aft DR by Fra Bartolommeo della PORTA)/ PA/ oc/ 172x175/ Madrid, MNP/ Inv.419/ Berenson 1958, p.193, pl.959 ; Goffen 1997, p.112, fig.69; Mai ed. 2001, p.70, n°2; p.174, n°1/ R469.55.
Reverse PR by PODESTA, Giovanni Andrea/ R871.56.
c1526 ROMANO, Giulio: Venus and Cupid receive garlands/ DR/ d/ 27,8x40,8/ Haarlem, TMu/ Inv. A*48/ Mai ed. 2001, p.407,n°T13/R8478.57.
c1540 MAESTRO B nel Dado: Venus being worshipped on water/ PR/ ?/ ?/ WEB, Corbis/ Inv.#/ IT / R2694.58.
c1550 CAMBIASO, Luca: The triumph of Amphitrite or Venus, or Allegory of Fortune/ DR/ d/ 38,1x28,6/ LA, CMA/ Inv. AC1994.257.1/ IT/ R1083.59.
c1550 INDIA, Bernardino: Trionfo di Venere / DR/ d/ 11,7x38,2/ Venezia, FGC/ Inv.N.41/ IT/ R8425V. 60.
1555 GHERARDI, Cristofano: Offerte a Venere/ FR//254x183/ Firenze, PaV/ Inv. 531/ IT/ R8585.61.
1570 PALLADIO, Andrea : Temple of Venus and Rome, Rome/ *aut I quattri libri, book IV, pl.XXIII*/ ?/ Venezia/ McParland 1989, 131, p.97, fig.23/ R3201 & R11016.62.
c1600 VALERIANI, Giuseppe: Trionfi di Venere, Apollo e Mercurio/ DR/ d/ 47.5x102/ Venezia, FGC/ Inv. 84/ IT/ R10240V.63. *Preparatory for a FR.*
c1618 VAROTARI, Alessandro: Worship of Venus (aft TIZIANO)/ PA/ oc/ 175x178/ Bergamo, AcC/ Inv.#/ Bentini 2003, p.284, fig.205/ R8892.64.
1636 PODESTA, Giovanni Andrea: Venus with numerous putti (Worship of Venus) (aft TIZIANO, reverse)/ PR/ e/ 31,5x39,5/ Lisboa, BNP/ Inv. E. 873 A/ Bartsch 45 (20,2) 1982, p.65,n°8(173)/ R871.65. *Also in SF, FAM/Inv. 1993.63.4; Offerte a Venere/ Venezia, MuC/ Inv.1516/ Chiari 1982, p.140, nr.150/ Wien, ALB.*

c1650 (att) CODAZZI, Viviano: Rito in onore di Venere/ PA/ oc/ ?/ Roma, MuC/ Inv. E36392iccd/ IT/ R8919.66.

c1650 GRIMALDI, Giovanni Francesco : Paesaggio con omaggio a Venere (Landscape with homage to Venus)/ PA/ ?/ ?/ Roma, GAP/ Inv. E41859iccd/ IT; Cicinelli 1988, VOL.IV, p. 57./ R8531.67.

c1665 CARPIONI, Giulio: Festival of Venus/ DR/ d/ 47x60/ Milano, BiA/ Inv.F253 inf.n.1137/ IT/ R8716.68. *The drawing corresponds with some variation to Carpioni's painting of the same theme in the Berti di Oderzo Collection, datable to ca. 1665: replica of R8327.69?*

c1665 CARPIONI, Giulio: Feast of Venus/ PA/ oc/ 85x95/ Yerevan, NGA/ Inv.#/ IT/ R8327.69. *See comments R8716.68.*

1670-80 MARATTA, Carlo: Homage to Venus *(by Neptun)*(Birth of Venus)/ FR// ?/ Frascati, ViF/ Inv.#/ IT/ R11113V.70.

c1675 FRANCHI, Antonio : Temple of Venus/ PA/ oc/ 260 x 321/ London, SOT 5.7.'95/ Sl. ?-76/ IT/ R9061.71.

1678-79 CIGNANI, Carlo: Trionfo d'Amore (Triumph of Venus) (*in a chariot*)/ FR/ ?/ ?/ Parma, PdG/ Inv.#/ Miller 1991, p.16; Pellegrino and Poletti 2003,p.48/ R4433.72.

c1690 MAURO, Domenico: Gabinetto di Venere/ PR/ e/ 30.7x39.2/ Venezia, FGC/ Inv. N.66/ IT/ R11501V.73. *Scenograph eng by Lorenzi, Mattioli, Bonavera & Francia*

c1700 PELLEGRINI, Gianantonio: Venere trionfante/ DR/ d/ 23.5x17.8/ Venezia, MuC/ Inv. N.4/ IT/ R11481V.74.

1704 FRANCESCHINI, Marcantonio: The triumph of Venus *(in a chariot)*/ PA/ oc/ oval 90,5x117,5/ London, CHR 7.7.'06/Sl. 7254 –207/ Miller 1991, p.xi, pl.I; IT/ R6962.75.

c1713 RICCI, Marco & Sebastiano : Triumph of the (Marine) Venus (?) /PA/ oc/ 157x207/ LA, JPG/ Inv. 72.PA.29/ Mai ed. 2001, p.382,n°71/ R307.76.

c1720-1730 MAGNASCO, Alessandro : Triumph of Venus *(in a chariot)*/ PA/ oc/ 116x146/ LA, JPG/ Inv. 78.PA.2/ IT/ R308.77.

c1731-42 BEAUMONT, Claudio Francesco: Trionfo di Venere e Amore (Venus and Cupid enthroned among clouds)/ PA/ oc/ 73x58,7/ Torino, GaS/ Inv.#/ IT/ R3455.78.*Preparatory for FR/ Torino, PaR/ R8233V.*

c1742 BEAUMONT, Claudio Francesco: The triumph of Venus/ FR/ ?/ Torino, PaR/ Pinto 1957/ R8233V.79.

1748-52 PIRANESI, Giovanni: Tempio di Venere appresso il Circo Apollinare (Temple of Venus at the Circus of Apollinarius*) (pub Fausto Amidei: Varie vedute di Roma antica e moderna disegnate e intagliate da celebri autori)*/ PR/ e/ 11,3x18,4/ Roma, ING/ Inv.#/ Ficacci 2000, p.94, fig.61/ R11211.80. *Several editions. Also in Hanover, HMA/ Inv. PR.977.24.54D.*

1748-52 PIRANESI, Giovanni: Tempio di Venere e Cupido *(pub Fausto Amidei: Varie vedute di Roma antica e moderna disegnate e intagliate da celebri autori)*/ PR/ e/ 12,3x17,9/ Roma, ING/ Inv.#/ Ficacci 2000, p.95, fig.63/ R11212.81. *Several editions. Also in Hanover, HMA/ Inv. PR.977.24.47B.*

c1750 GUARANA, Jacopo: Venere trionfante/ DR/ d/ 33x44/ Venezia, MuC/ Inv. N.34/ IT/ R11482V.

c1759 TIEPOLO, Giambattista: Il trionfo di Venere (L'Olimpo)/ PA/ oc/ 87x61.5/ Madrid, MNP/ Rizzoli 1968, p.132, n°281; Llorens 1997, p.242-243, Cat.77; Pedrocco 2002, p.302, cat.263/ R8539.82. *Preparatory for PA , LO, one of four, sent to St. Petersburgh.*

1762 LEONARDIS, Giacomo : Offerta a Venere/ PR/ e/ 32,4x46,7/ Udine, PrC/ Succi 1983, p.199-200,n°227/ R3661.83.

1768 BOTTANI, Giuseppe: Trionfo di Venere/ PA/?/175x66/ Roma, PaBr/ Inv. MR 36457/ IT/ R3746.84. *A replica exist in Roma, PrC.*

c1770 TIEPOLO, Lorenzo: The Triumph of Venus (aft Giambattista TIEPOLO)/ PR: e/ 66,8x50,5/ London, CHR 29.11.'05/ Sl. 7096 –75/ Rizzoli 1968, p.132; IT/ R5194.85.

c1775 CUNEGO, Domenico : Temple of Venus (in Napoli ?)/ IL/ e/ 46,9x59,9/ SF, FAM/ Inv. 1963.30.37586/ IT/ R746.86.

c1775 FONTANESI, Francesco: Reggia di Venere/ DR/ d/ 21.1x41.8/ Venezia, FGC/ Inv. N.192/ IT/ R11502V.87.

c1775 GANDOLFI, Gaetano : The triumph of Venus/ DR/ d/ 32,5x38/ London, SOT 5.7.'06/ Sl. L06040-72/ IT/ R6850.88.
c1780 ZUCCHI, A.R.A & BORGNIS, Pietro Maria: Triumph of Venus (as part of a set of 18 decorations)/ PA/ocb/ v/ London, SOT 26.3.'04/ Sl. L04120-51/ IT/ R5876.89.
1789 GIANI, Felice : Trionfo di Venere/ FR// ?/ Roma, PaA/ Inv. E33160iccd/ IT/ R8915.90.
1798-1800 APPIANI, Andrea: Trionfo di Venere/ FR/ c/ 165,5x469,5/ Milano, PiA/ Inv. 1638/ IT/ R8509. 91.
c1800 (att) PEDRINI, Filippo : The Apotheosis of Venus/ DR/ du/ 28x22/ London, CHR 15.12.'00/ Sl.?-76/ IT/ R8014.92.
1830 BIGATTI, Tommaso: Temple of Venus at Baia/ IL/ u/ 9,7x9,8/ London, CHR 25.4.'07/ Sl. 5228-0376/ IT/ R9153.93.
1830-50 GAGLIARDI, Pietro: Apoteosi di Venere (o di Psiche)/ FR// 120x200/ Roma, PaBr/ Inv. MC 137/ exh/ R3759.94.
c1836 PODESTI, Francesco : Trionfo di Venere/ DR/ p/ ?/ Roma, PaBr/ Inv. MR 16984/ IT/ R3920.95. *Although this DR has the same title as the next PA, it is seemingly another design.*
c1836 PODESTI, Francesco : Trionfo di Venere/ PA/ ob/ ?/ Roma, MuC/ Inv. E41025iccd/ IT/ R8922.96.
1837 COTTAFAVI, Gaetano : Tempio di Venere a Roma *(sixteenth plate in the book, Raccolta delle principali vedute di Roma e suoi contorni / aut Tommaso Cuccioni)*/ IL/ e/ 21,2x28/ SF, FAM/ Inv. #/ IT / R1370.97.
1857 MUSSINI, Cesare: Trionfo di Venere/ FR//?/ Firenze, UFEC/ Inv.#/ IT/ R8600.98.
c1875 CASSIOLI, Amos : L'offerta a Venere/ PA/ ?/ ?/ Firenze, GAM/ Inv.#/ IT/ R11138V.99.
1876 SCIUTI, Giuseppe : Il tempio di Venere/ PA/?/ ?/ Roma, GAM/ Inv.1004/ IT fototeca/ R8501.100.
1973 PRADELLA, Vinicius: Il tempio di Venere/ PA/ oc/ 70x50/ UN/ Inv.#/ CELIT 1974 Vol 1, p.564/ R8678.101.
1983 LAUDANI, Gaetano: Scena per Aphrodite/ PA/ oc/ 50x40/ UN/ Inv.#/ CELIT 1988 Vol 12, p.8275/ R8663.102.
2006 NUNZIANTE, Antonio: La casa di Venere/ PR/ lc/ 60x50/ WEB, eBay 26.11.07/ IT/ R11389.103.

3. Attributes of Venus
(apple, chariot, doves, mirror, roses, swans, torch, tortoise)

1447-54 (att) PASTI, Matteo di Andrea: Venere *(Venus in a chariot drawn by swans)*/ RE/ m/?/ Rimini, TeM/ Inv.#/ Pope-Hennessy 1996, Vol. II, p.250-51, pl.237 / R7140.104. *Also (att) or (wor) Agostino di DUCCIO/ Reid 1993, p.114.*
c1500 BRESCIA, Giovanni da : Venus in her chariot drawn by doves. Illustrations to the Aeneid (aft RAIMONDI)/ PR/ 10,3x33,2/ Oxford, AMu/ Inv.#/ Bartsch 25 C (13,2) 1984,p.347,n° 2511.024/ R4802.105.
c1500 LIPPI, Filippino: Venus draped, sailing on a swan/ DR/ d/ 20,5x18/ Roma, Gci/ Inv. 128403/ Berenson 1938, Vol2. Catalogue, p.153 ; Vol.3 Illustrations, fig.254-1364A verso/ R3588.106.
c1510 MODENA, Nicoletto da: Venus (*with torch and mirror*)/ PR//19,8x13,8/ Paris, BNF/ Inv.#/ Bartsch 25 C (13,2) 1984, p.186-87,n°2508.027/ R4799.107.
c1510 MODENA, Nicoletto da: Venus (*with torch, mirror and Cupid*)/ PR//9,3x6,2/ Milano, BiA/ Inv.#/ Bartsch 25 C (13,2) 1984, p.225,n°2508.083/ R4800.108.
c1510 RAIMONDI, Marcantonio : Venus *(left, reclining in a landscape)* and Eros (*with torch)* (after ROMANO, Giulio)/ PR/ e/ 23,7x16,8/ London, BMu/ Inv.#/ Bartsch 26 (14,1) 1978, p.320,n°318(239)/ R4816. 109.
1514 VENEZIANO, Agostino: Venus *(reclining)* and Cupid *(with torch)* (aft ROMANO)/ PR/ e/ 22.9 x 16.8/ SF,FAM/ Inv. 1963.30.2796/ IT/ R11719.110. *Also in Firenze, GdU/ Inv.#/ De Witt 1938, p.70,n°495.*
1515 BELLINI, Giovanni: Venus with mirror (Naked young woman in front of the mirror; Venus of the Belvedere)/ PA/ oc/ 62x79/ Wien,KHM/ Inv.97/ Stillman 1898, p.3-8/ R517.111.
c1515 RAIMONDI, Marcantonio : Venus wounded by the rose's thorn (after RAFFAELLO)/ PR/ e/ 26,1x15,9/ London, BMu/ Inv.#/ Bartsch 27 (14 1978, p.12,n°321-II(241)/ R4833.112.
c1515 ROMANO, Giulio: Vénus enlevant l'Amour dans son char/ DR/ d/ 27,3x43,8/ Paris, MdL/ Inv.#/ Duboucher 1992, fig.81/ R7645.113.
c1516 DENTE, Marco: Venere punta dalla spina (La Venere Spinaria; Venus wounded by the rose's thorn) (aft ROMANO, G. or RAFFAELLO, S. workshop drawing for the fresco decoration of the Stufetta Bibbiena in the Vatican)/ PR/ e/ 26x17,3/ Roma, ING/Inv. FC30535/ Massari 1989, p.66-68, n°19b; Massari 1993, p.38-39,n°34/R1640.114. *Also Cambridge, FWM/ Inv. P.5363-R; Cleveland, MuA/ Inv. 1930.581; London, CHR 30.6.'94/ Sl. ?-53;NY, MMA/Inv. 1986.1180.213; SF, FAM/Inv. 1963.30.3149; Stockholm, NMK/Inv. NMG 86/1876; Washington, NGA/Inv. B. XIV, 241,321; Wien, ALB.*
c1525 PARMIGIANINO : Venus (*in chariot with doves*)/ DR/ d/ 9,7x15,3/ SF, FAM/ Inv. 1963.24.151/ IT/ R867.115.
1531 ALCIATO, Andrea : Venus, why is a turtle shown beneath your foot? *(with apple and doves, sun and tree)* (*Emblematum liber)*/ IL/ XCVII/ Leis 2000, p.131/R2571.116.
1531 ALCIATO, Andrea : Venus and the tortoise *(with apple and doves in interior)* (*Emblematum liber)*/ IL/ ?/ Seznec 1961, n°39, p.115 /R6028.117.
1531 ALCIATO, Andrea : Alma Venus with tortoise *(with Cupid in interior)* (*Emblematum liber)*/ IL/ 196/ IT/ R6049.118.
c1531-1578 MICHELI, Parrasio: Venus and Cupid *(with doves)*/ PA/ oc/ 186x102/ Kopenhagen, SMK/ Inv. KMSsp148/ IT/ R7564.119.
1532 DADDI, Bernardo: Venus wounded by the thorns of a rose (aft RAFFAELLO, Sanzio)/ PR/ e/ 19,2x16,3/ SF, FAM/ Inv. 1963.30.37156/ IT/ R748.120.

Also: ***1532*** *MASTER of the DIE/ PR/ e/ 19,1x16,8/ London, BMu/ Inv.#/ Bartsch 29 (15,2) 1982, p.173 n°16(194)/ R4849.121.; PR/ e/ 20x17,1/ Detroit, DIA/ Inv. 09.1S74/ IT; Cambridge, FWM/ Inv. P.113-1952;*
1532 *Meister mit dem Würfel: Venus verwundet von den Dornen einer Rose/ PR/ e/ 18,9 x 13,9/ Wien, DOR 17.10.07/ Sl. ?-23/ IT/ R11092.122.*
c1539 ROSSO FIORENTINO, Giovanni Battista: Vénus et Cupidon sur un char/ DR/ d/ 21,4x20,8/ Stockholm, NMK/ Inv.#/ Duboucher 1992, fig.111/ R7656. 123.
c1544 CARPI, Girolamo da : Venus von Schwänen gezogen (Venus drawn by swans)/ PA/ oc/ 144x267/ Dresden, SKS/ Inv.143/ Berenson 1968, p.189/ R7083.124.
1546 ALCIATO, Andrea : Veneris poma (*Emblematum liber, pub Manutius, Venezia)*/ IL/ CCVII/ IT/ R6046.125.
c1550 ABATE, Nicolo dell' : Une femme assise et plusieurs amours retenant un sanglier (*Venus in her chariot with cupids retaining a boar)*/ DR/ d/ 2,83x24,1 /Paris, MdL /Inv. 8748,recto / IT/ R8031.126. *A theme which is related to the death of Adonis.*
c1550 LICINIO, Bernardino: Venere con due colombi/ PA/ ?/ ?/ München, PrC forNemes)/ Inv.#/ Berenson 1958, p.100/ R9616V.127.
c1550 MASTER IOV: Venus in a chariot drawn by two swans (aft ROMANO, Giulio)/ PR/ e/ 29,8x46,2/ London, BMu/ Inv.#/ Bartsch 33 (16,2) 1979, p.273,n° 3(372)/ R4936.128.
c1550 SICIOLANTE, Girolamo: Venere della tartaruga/ PA/?/?/ Torino, GaS/ Inv. 973/ exh/ R350V.129.
c1554 TIZIANO, Vecellio: Venus at the mirror (Barbarigo Venus or Venus at her toilet)/ PA/ oc/ 125x106/ Washington, NGA/ Inv. 1937.1.34/ Mai ed. 2001, p.246, n°1/ R445.130.
Replicas: ***c1555*** *(wor) Venus vor dem Spiegel/ PA/ oc/ 118x101/ Köln, WRM/ Inv. 0332/ IT/ R10088.131.;*
c1575 *(wor) Venus, sich spiegelnd (without second cupid crowning Venus)/PA/ oc/ 115x100/ Dresden, SKS/ Inv.178/ Mai ed. 2001, p.250-51, n°12/ R8472.131.;*
(wor) Venus und Amor mit einem Spiegel/ PA/ oc/ 120x105/ Berlin, GSM/ Inv. 189/ IT/ R10062.132.;
c1555 *(wor)Venere allo specchio'(without cupids; the canvas was cut at the right and the mirror disappeared)/ PA/ oc/ 115x84/ Venezia, CdO/ Inv. D.38/ Duca 1966, p.404, fig.566/ R5347.133.;*
(with right hand before bossom)/ Firenze, PGC/ Inv.#/ Duca 1966, p.404, fig.565, / R5345.134.
1556 GHISI, Giorgio: Venus and the Rose (aft PENNI, Luca/ PR/ e/ 30,8x21,6/ LA, CMA/ Inv. M88.91.156/ Bartsch 31 (15,4) 1986, p.98,n°40; Bellini 1998, p.129-135,n°28/ R1095.135. *Also in: A'dam, RPK/Inv.#/Mai ed. 2001, p.428-29, n°G8; SF, FAM/ Inv. 1963.30.36704.*
c1560 AVIBUS (OSELLO): Venere punta dalle spine (aft GHISI, Giogio)/ PA/ t/ 14,1x10,1/ Modena, PrC/Inv.#/ Bellini 1998, p.129-135,n°86/R3655.136.
1564 AVIBUS (OSELLO), Gaspar ab : Venus and the Rose (aft GHISI, Giorgio ; aft.PENNI, Luca)/ PR/ e/ 30,5x21,3/ LA, CMA/ Inv. M88.91.155/ Bellini 1998, p.129-135,fig.88/ R1105.137. *Also in Cambridge, FWM/ Inv. 37.1-68 ; SF,FAM/Inv. 30.36832; Wien, ALB/ Bartsch 31 (15,4) 1986, p.100, n°40.*
c1617 GUERCINO, Giovane Francesco Barbieri: Venus and Cupid in a chariot/ DR/ d/ 25,5x39,4/ Cleveland, MuA/ Inv. 1925.1188/ IT/ R1492.138.
c1620 CORTONA, Pietro da: Carro di Venere (o Aurora)/ PA/ tc/ 106x238/ Roma, MuC/ Inv.223/ IT/ R700.139.
c1625 DOMENICHINO, Domenico: The repose of Venus *(with chariot in a landscape)*/ PA/ ?/?/ St. Petersburg, HMu/ Inv.#/ IT/ R1533.140.
c1650 MITELLI, Giuseppe Maria : Venus in her chariot (from *'Giuoco di carte con nuova forma di Tarocchini –Varignana 552*)/ PR// 26,9x35,4/ Bologna, CdR/ Inv.#/ Bartsch 42 (19,2) 1981, p.434,n°159(305)/ R4979.141.
c1650 (cir) ROMANELLI, Giovanni Francesco: Venere sul carro con colombe/ FR// ?/ Roma, PaLR/ Inv. E58460iccd/ IT/ R8935.142.
c1670 CIGNANI, Carlo: Venere e Cupido *(with doves)*/ PA/ ?/ ?/ Torino, GaS/ Inv.137/ exh/ R345V.143.
Replica: Vénus et l'Amour/ PA/ oc/ 95,2x74,2/ Valenciennes, MBA/ Inv. P.46.1.314/ IT/ R8781.144.; replica (att) Venus and Cupid./ PA/ oc/ 100.4 x78.7/ NY, SOT 26.1.'07/ Sl. N08282-204/ IT.
c1700 (att) CHIARI, Giuseppe: Venus creating the red rose/ PA/ ?/ ?/ Kopenhagen, SMK/ Inv. 4551/ Kerber 1968, p.79/ R11112V.145.

c1700 RUGGERI, Antonio Maria: Venus with the Golden Apple of the Hesperides/ DR (design for a ceiling)/ d/ 20,2x19,2/ Milano, BiA/ Inv. F 236 inf. N. 1393/ IT/ R8717.146.
1701 MATTIOLI, Ludovico: April (*Venus, putti, doves*) from'Fasti di Lodovico XIV.il Grande'/ PR// 18,6x13,3/ NY, PuL/ Inv.#/ Bartsch 43 (19,3) 1982, p.167,n°app.4-(4)(389)/ R4980.147.
1709 CARRIERA, Rosalba: Venus and Cupid/ PA/ i/ 10,3x8,5/ Kopenhagen, SMK/ Inv. KMS4837/ IT/ R7562.148.
c1725 PIAZZETTA, Gianbattista : Cocchio condotto da Venere/ DR/ d/ 52x36/ Venezia, FGC/ Inv. 49/ IT/ R10238V.149.
c1725 PIAZZETTA, Gianbattista : Venere su un cocchio/ DR/ d/ 27x37/ Venezia, FGC/ Inv. 50/ IT/ R10239V.150.
c1725 TIEPOLO, Giambattista: Venere allo specchio/ PA/ oc/ 38x48/ Milano, PrC Gerli/ Inv.#/ Rizzoli 1968, p.90,n°39 ; Pedrocco 2002, p.209, cat.53/ R4438.151.
c1760 CIPRIANI, Giovanni Battista: Venus in the Chariot of Love, attended to by cherubs/ DR/ du/ 22.8x26.6 oval/ London, CHR 3.7.'07/ Sl. 5120-0509/ IT/ R9690.152.
1785 CANOVA, Antonio: Venere con lo specchio (Venus with the mirror)/ PA/ oc/ 134x177/ Possagno, CdC/ Inv. 7/ Stefani 2004, p.33,165 nr.34/ R8316.153. *Preparatory **1782** DR/ d/ ?/ Bassano, MuC/ Inv. 1125. Several PRs by VITALI, P., Fontana, P. & Piroli, T.*
a1785 VITALI, Pietro Marco: Venere, fanciulla transtiberina (Giovane donna trasteverina sdraiata) *(with mirror)* (aft CANOVA)/ PR/ e/ 34,2x46/ Roma, PaBr/ Inv. MR 16324/ IT/ R8320.154.
1788 ROSASPINA, Francesco : Venere e Amore *(with doves)*/ PR// 43x30,6/ Parma, BiP/ Inv. BB.I.27053/ Mussini 2003, p.180-181,n°373/ R3644.155.
c1800 PEDRO, Francesco del: Il carro di Venere (aft Kauffmann, Angelica)/ PR/ e/ 13x18/ Roma, ING/ Inv. FN20067/ exh/ R3483.156.
1806 GHIGI, Pietro: Quadrijugis per inane Venus subvecta columbis (aft RAFFAELLO)/ PR/ e/ ?/ Roma, BiH/ Inv. #/ IT/ R10120.157.
1822 BISI, Michele: Venere e Amore *(with doves)* (aft APPIANI, Andrea)/ PR/ e/ 49,2x36,2/ Milano, PAB/ Inv.64/ Anonymous 1996, p.87,280,n°64/ R3529.158.
1830 HAYEZ, Francesco: Venere che scherza con due colombe (Ritratto della ballerina Carlotta Chabert)/ PA/ oc/ 183x137/ Trento, CRT/ Inv.#/ Stefani 2003, p.76 / R1650.159.
c1990 MANARA, Milo: Venus of Velasquez/ PR/c/ 50x70/ WEB, MiloManara/ Inv.#/ IT/ R1311.160.
1997 STANGALINO, Laura: Omaggio a Velasquez-La Venere allo specchio/ PA/ oc/ 100x150/ UN/ Inv.#/ CEDE 2001 Vol 16, p.11563/ R8650.161.
c2007 ANCILOTTI, Claudia: Venus/ PR/ ?/ 24x18/ UN/ Inv. #/ IT/ R9337.162.

4. Birth of Venus/Venus Anadyomene/ Venus Marina/dolphins/sea and shells/ fountains and water

c1450 (wor) PISANELLO, Antonio Pisano: Scenes from the myth of Venus *(Venus in a shell)*/ DR/ d/ 16,3x22/ Milano, BiA/ Inv. F 214 inf. n. 14 verso/ IT/ R8734.163.
c1475 LOMBARDO, Antonio : Venere Marina/ SC/ z/ ?/ Roma, PaV/ Inv. E37641iccd/ IT/ 8946.164.
c1485 BOTTICELLI, Sandro: La nascita di Venere/ PA/ tc/ 172x278/ Firenze, GdU/ Inv.878/ Berenson 1963, p.34, pl.204-205; Clark 1969, t.I,p.166, t.II, p.115 ; Gli Uffizi 1984 ; Levi d'Ancona 1992/ R377.165.
c1503 (1510-15) LOMBARDO, Antonio: Venus (*Anadyomene*): RE/ m/ 40x20x7/ London, VAM/ Inv. A.19-1964/ Goffen 1997, p.129, fig.76/ R5544.166. *Model for TIZIANO's Venus Anadyomene.*
c1506 RAIMONDI, Marcantonio : Venere sul bordo del mare (Venus wringing her hair)/ PR/ e/ 21,7x15,3/ Wien, ALB/ Inv. 1971-328/ Faietti 1988, p.144-146, n°28/ R3535.167. *Also in Boston, MFA; Cambridge, FWM/ Inv. P.5357-R.*
c1510 RAFFAELLO, Sanzio: Venus with Cupid on a sea monster/ FR (Stufetta del Cardinale Bibbiena)/ / ?/ Roma, MuV/ Inv.#/ IT/ R8519.168.
c1510 RAIMONDI, Marcantonio : Venus reclining on a dolphin *(with Cupid)* (aft RAFFAELLO)/ PR/ e/ 16,6x25,3/ London, BMu/ Inv.#/ Bartsch 26 (14,1) 1978, p.236,n°239(192)/ R4807.169.
c1515 DENTE, Marco: Venus und Amor auf Dolphinen (Venus and Eros carried by dolphins) (aft RAFFAELLO, S.)/ PR/ e/ 26,5x17,3/ Wien, ALB/ Inv. It.,I.21/ Oberhuber 1999, p.105,n°44/ R760.170. *Also in Cambridge, FWM/ Inv. P.5558-R ; Firenze, GdU.*
c1515 RAIMONDI, Marcantonio : Venere e Cupido sopra delfini (aft RAFFAELLO)/ PR/ e/ 26,8x17,5/ London, BMu/ Inv.#/ Bartsch 27 (14,2) 1978, p.16,n°324-I(244); Bellini 1998, p.308,n°F.31/ R3657.171. ***1515-27** : Venus and Eros arried by dolphins (aft DENTE, Marco) / PR/ e/ ?/ Cambridge, FWM/ Inv. P.5366-R.*
c1516 DENTE, Marco : Nascita di Venere (aft ROMANO, Giulio) /PR/ e/ 26,7x17,7/ Roma, ING/ Inv. FC30531/ Massari 1989, p.69-71, n°20; Massari 1993, p.34,n°31/ R3488.172. *Also: (aft RAFFAELLO, Sanzio)/London, BMu/ Bartsch 27 (14,2) 1978, p.15,n°323(243); Cambridge, FWM/ Inv. P.4145-R; Cleveland, MuA/ Inv. 1930.581 ; New Haven, YAG/ Inv. B. XIV, 243, 323 ;'Venus Anadyomene'/Wien, ALB/ Oberhuber 1999, p.106,n°45; Mai ed. 2001, p.426, n°G5.*
1516-17 (wor) RAFFAELLO, Sanzio : La nascita di Venere (in 'La stufetta del Cardinale Bibbiena)/ FR// ?/ Roma, MuV/ Inv.#/ Porcheron-Felsing 1983, p.24,61fig.9 / R8263.173.
*Also :**c1516** ROMANO, Giulio: Venere (Venus Anadyomene)/ DR/ d/ 24,3x14,6/ München, SGS/ Inv. 2459/* Massari 1989, p. p.69-71, fig.12 ; Mai ed. 2001 p.406-*7,n°T12/ R3489.174. ;*
'Venere'/ reverse DR or PR//?/ London, BMu/ Inv. 1939-2-1-1/ Massari 1993, p.35, fig.25/ R3547.175.
c1516 VENEZIANO, Agostino: Venere e Amore (Venus reclining on a dolphin with Cupid*)* (aft ROMANO, Giulio)/ PR/ e/ 17,2x25,8/ Roma, ING/ Inv. F.C.30761/ Massari 1989, p.48-49,n°13/ R626.176. *Replica aft RAIMONDI?*
c1519 VENEZIANO, Agostino: Amore e Venere sul mare (aft ROMANO, Giulio)/ PR/ e/ ?/ Roma, ING/ Inv. FC447/ Massari 1993, p.XVII, Tav.4/ R3543.177.
c1525 CORREGGIO, Antonio: The birth of Venus / PR/ e/ 14,8x16,9/ SF, FAM/ Inv. 1963.30.37159/ IT/ R745.178. *(att)Monogrammiste: Venus couronnee par les dieux/ Paris, BNF/ Inv.#/ Dunand & Lemarchand s.d., III p.781, fig.1242.*
c1525 RAIMONDI, Marcantonio: The birth of Venus/ PR/ e/ ?/ Washington, NGA/ Inv. 1941.1.66/ IT/ R8441V.

c1525 TIZIANO, Vecellio: Venus Anadyomene (Venus emerging or rising from the sea)/ PA/ oc/ 75.8x57.6/ Edinburgh, NGS/ Inv. NG 2751/ Berenson 1958, p.190, pl.971; Clark 1969, p.202; Goffen 1997, p.127, fig.73/ R471.179.
c1540 ROMANO, Giulio: Naissance de Vénus/ DR/ d/ 26,8x25,8/ Paris, MdL/ Inv.3483/ IT/ R2809.
1544-45 LUZZI, Luzzio detto ROMANO: Nascita di Venere/ FR// ?/ Roma, CSA/ Inv. E51466iccd/ IT/ R8918.180.
c1550 ALBERTI, Cherubino: Venus *on a shell with drapery fold above*/ PR/ e/ 20,9x14,2/ London, BMu/ Inv.#/ Bartsch 34(17,1)1982, p.210,#97(82) / R4954.181.
c1550 CARPI, Girolamo da : Venus Anadyomene/ PA/ ?/ ?/ Roma, GDP/ Inv.s103/ exh/ R370V.182.
c1550 MARCO da FAENZA: Venere/ FR/ tf/ ?x115/ Firenze, PaV/ Inv.#/ IT/ R8595.183.
c1550 MAZZONI, Giulio: Venere e Nettuno (L'Acqua)/ FR/ op/ ?/ Roma, PaS/ Inv. E68546iccd/ IT/ R8933.184.
c1550 (att) ROSSO FIORENTINO, Giovanni Battista: Birth of Venus/ PR// 34,6x49,5/ Paris, BNF/ Inv.#/ Bartsch 33 (16,2) 1979, p.350,n°75(406)/ R4945.185. *By MASTER IỌV after damaged stucco by ROSSO/ Beguin 1989, fig.32.*
c1550 SCHIAVONE, Andrea Meldolla, detto : Venere portata da un delfino a Citera/ PA/ ?/ ?/ Milano, CaS/ Inv. 55/ Berenson 1958, p.166, pl.1157/ R9624.186.
1555 VASARI, Giogio & Cristoforo GHERARDI detto il Doceno : Nascita di Venere/ FR// 515x684/ Firenze, PaV/ Inv.527/ IT ; Sframeli 2003, p.51/ R4022.187.
c1558 (att) BARBARO, Marcantonio: Venus on the Nymphaeum *with dolphin and Cupid)*/ SC/ s/?/ Maser, ViB/ Kolb 1997; Wundram 1988,p.128/ R5897.188.
c1560 CAMBIASO, Luca: Venere ed Amoro sul mare/ PA/ oc/ 102x95/ Roma, GaB/ Inv. 123/ Moreno 2004, p.246, n°17/ R368.189.
1570 DANTI, Vincenzo : Afrodite Anadiomene (Venere)/ SC/ z/ 98/ Firenze, PaV/ Inv.271/ Pope-Hennessy , Vol.III,1996, p.322,326-27,485-86, pl.306+307 ; Sframeli 2003,p.52/ R4021.190. *Or AMMANNATI, Bartolomeo: Venus/ Clark 1969,T.I,p.218,n°102 ; Encyclopédie de L'Art 2005,p.21.*
c1571 GIAMBOLOGNA: Afrodite Anadiomene/ SC/ z/ 125/ Firenze : VMP/ Inv.#/ Sframeli 2003,p.53./ R3069.191. *Copy: Venus and Cupid/ SC/ z/124,5/ Washington, NGA/ Inv. 1991.242.1/ IT/ R802.*
1574-75 ZUCCHI, Jacopo: Venere e Cupido trasformati in pesci per sfuggire a trifone (Venus and Cupid transformed in fishes in order to escape from a typhon)/ FR// ?/ Roma, PaFi/ Inv. E832iccd/ IT/ R8947.192.
c1575 CAMBIASO, Luca : Vénus et deux enfants, portés par un dauphin/ DR/ d/ 25.1x37/ Paris, MdL/ Inv. 9320, rect/ IT/ R10198.193.
c1575 (att) MOSCA, Francesco: Vénus accompagnée d'un Amour chevauchant un dauphin/ RE/ m/ 50x32/ Paris, MdL/ Inv. MR 1642/ IT/ R2420.194.
c1585 PEROLI, G.B.&F.: Venus o Anfitrite/ FR// ?/ El Viso, PaM/ Inv. vestibulo/ Navarrete 2005, p.47, fig.73/ R11017.195.
c1590-95 CARRACCI, Agostino: Venus or Galatea supported by dolphins/ PR/ e/ 14,9x10,5/ Washington, NGA/Inv.#/ (Bartsch 39 (18,1) 1980,p.171,n°129(108);Bartsch 39 C Part 1 (18,1 1995, p.325-27,n°3901.203)/R735.196.
Also in many other places; Berlin, BAS 29.11.07/ Sl. 090-5545.
Reverse copy exists/ Dunand & Lemarchand s.d., III p.796, fig.1263/R10754.197.
1597-1604 CARRACCI, Annibale: Venere condotta sul mare a una cerimonia nuziale (Venus and Triton)/ FR/ Roma, PaFa/ Inv.#/ Ginzburg Carignani 2000,n°66/ R7142.198.
c1600 (wor) ARPINO, Giuseppe Cesari detto il Cavaliere: The birth of Venus/ PA/ ow/ 134x89,5 oval/ London, BON 07.12.'05/ Sl 11914-72/ IT/ R6553.199.
c1600 (cir) ASPETTI, Tiziano: Venus Marina *(type Venus Fortuna)*/ SC/ z/ 55,5/ Wien, KHM/ Inv. pl.5885/ Mai ed. 2001, p.491,n°B8/ R8484.200.
c1600 (cir) ASPETTI, Tiziano: Venus Marina *(type Venus Medici)*/ SC/ z/ 30/ Bremen, KuH/ Inv. 391-1956-5/ Mai ed. 2001, p.492-93,n°B9/ R8485.201. ***c1650** aft ASPETTI, Tiziano : 'bronze door knocker Venus Marina'/ SC/ z/ 32/ London, SOT 7.7.'06/ Sl.L06231-75/ IT/ R6855. More replica or copies known.*
c1600 BOSCOLI, Andrea : Naissance de Vénus/ DR/ d/ 15,7x12,8/ Paris, MdL/ Inv. 12584/ Viatte 1988,p.50-51, n°62/ R3832.202.

c1600 (att-wor) CAMPAGNA, Girolamo: Venus marina/ SC/ z/ 47/ London, SOT 12.12.'03/ Sl. L03233-195/ IT/ R5780.203.

c1600 CARRACCI, Annibale : The birth of Venus and Cupid riding a dolphin (aft FR wor RAFFAELLO and eng DENTE)/ DR/ d/ 19.3x25.6/ Winsor, RCo/ Inv. 2290/ Wittkower 1952, p.156, Cat.422/ R10422V.204.

c1600 (att or aft) FANELLI, Francesco: Venus & Cupid sitting on dolphin/ SC/ z/ 8,9/ London, CHR 7.12.'06/Sl. 7288-174/IT/R8196.205.

c1600 ROMANELLI, Giovanni Francesco: Birth of Venus/ FR//?/ Roma, MuA/ Inv. #/ Cresti & Rendina 1998, p.180-181/ R9831.206.

c1600 VALESIO, Giovanni Luigi: Venere con delfino/ PR/ e/ 37x23,4/ Roma, BiH/ Inv.#/ Bartsch 40 C 1(18,2) 1987, p.82,n°4002.066/ R4970.207.

c1625 ALBANI, Francesco: Elemento dell'Aqua con Venere sul carro (The element Water with Venus on her chariot)/ PA/ oc/ 180x180/ Torino,GaS/ Inv.495/ Astrua & Spantigati, 2000, p.57/ R344.208.

1626 MALFATTI, Cesare : Venere nata della spuma del mare('Immagini degli dei delli Antichi' *aut Vincenzo Catari, pub Pietro Paolo Tozzi)*/ PR/ e/ 22.6x16.3/ WEB, eBay 19.12.07/ R11648.209.

1640-1660 DE ROSSI, Alessi : Nascita di Venere/ RE/ ?/ ?/ Roma, PaSC/ Inv. E530iccd/ IT/ R8948.210.

c1645 ALGARDI, Alessandro: Venus in her sea chariot suckling Cupid/ DR/ d/ 30x44,2/ LA, JPG/ Inv. 92.GB.39/ IT/ R304.211.

c1650 (cir)ALBANI, Francesco : Naissance de Vénus (Birth of Venus)/ PA/ oy/ 37,5x52/ Paris, DRO 30.06.'89/ Sl.14-14/ IT/ R5059.212.

c1650 DIAMANTINI, Giuseppe: Venus carried by dolphins/ PR/ e/ 21,8x16,1/ Wien, ALB/ Inv.#/ Bartsch 47 (21,2) 1983 p.405,#21(278)/R5001.213.

c1650 DIVINI, Cipriano: Aphrodite auf einem Delphin reitend/ DR/ d/ 23x34.5/ Köln, WRM: Inv. #/ IT/ R10106.214.

c1650 GUERCINO, Giovane Francesco : Venus rising from the sea/ DR/ d/ 36,8x45,7/ NY, PML/ Inv. IV,168i/ IT/ R8885V.215.

c1650 (att) ROMANELLI, Giovanni Francesco: Venere su conchiglia (Venus on a shell)/ PA/ oc/ ?/ Brescia : PTM/ IT/ R8181V.216.

1657 GALESTRUZZI, Giovanni Battista: Venere Marina (with myrtle twig; from 'The Antique Figural Gems' Roma/ PR// 8,5x10,5/Milano, BiA/Inv.#/ Bartsch 46 (21,1) 1982, p.234,n°294(80); Bartsch 46 C 1985, p.254,n°4606.294 S2/R4993.217.

1670 FALDA, Giovanni Battista: Fontana di Venere a Villa Pamphilj *(Li giardini di Roma)*/ IL/ e/ ?/ Roma, VDP/ Pocino 1996, p.386-387/ R10117.218. *Also in Cambridge, FWM/ Inv. PB 1675.1.77*

1686 GALESTRUZZI, Giovanni Battista: Venus Anadyomene (from ' Le gemme antiche figurate')/ PR// 12,9x9,4/ NY, PuL/ Inv.#/ Bartsch 46 C 1985; p.269-270,n°4606.338/ R4994.219. *Not etched by GALESTRUZZI.*

1687 VENTURINI, Giovanni Francesco: Fountain of Venus, Villa Frascati (from 'Le Fontane' *aut Giovanni Battista Falda **c1675***)/ IL/ e/ ?/ UN, PrC/ Inv.#/ IT/ R8994.220.

c1690 DELEVI, Giuseppe: Venere Marina (*with dolphin*)/ SC/ z/ ?/ Roma, PaV/ Inv. F14979iccd/ IT/ R8931.221.

c1690 DELEVI, Giuseppe: Venere Marina (*small, with dolphin*)/ SC/ z/ ?/ Roma, PaV/ Inv. F6491iccd/ IT/ R8932.222.

c1700 BARTOLI, Francesco : Antichi affreschi « da una stanza sotterranea » (*three 'lunettes' with Venus playing among attendants and cupids in the sea)*/ DR/ du/ Eton, ECL/Inv.Bn5:22-24/ Borea 2000, T.II:643-644, n°9-11/ R1771.223.

1705 GIULIANI, Giovanni : Venus Anadyomene/ SC/ q/ 47/ Wien, LMu/ Inv.#/ exh/ R7827.224. *Rather unusual title for a statue of Venus with a small Cupid at her side with her right hand on his shoulders and her left arm holding a drapery.*

1731 CAMPIGLIA, Giovanni Domenico : Venus Anadyomene *(Raccolta di 26. spintrie, Ricuate da stampe e camei antichi/ aut GORI, Giovanni Francesco/ Museum florentinum')*/ IL/ e/ ?/ Nordmann 2004, p.159-161,n°63/ R6260.225.

1739 (att) AMIGONI, Jacopo: Venere Anadiomene/ PA/ oc/ 102,1x127/ London, GAL/ Inv.#/ IT/ R3062. 226.

1742 PAZZI, Antonio: Venere della vita marina (aft CAMPIGLIA, Domenico) *(Frontespizio inciso 'Index Musei Nocolai Gualtieri')*/IL/ Roma, BAL/ Antetomaso 2004, / R3473.227.
c1750 (att) DIZIANI, Gaspare : Venus mit ihrem Gefolge und Triton auf dem Meer (Venus with attendants and Triton on the sea)/ DR/ d/ 13,6 x 38,2/ Berlin, BAS 30.11.07/ Sl. 090-6419/ R11000.228.
c1750 FONTEBASSO, Francesco: La fontaine de Vénus/ DR/ d/ 26,5x24/ Paris, PIA 22.3.'07/ Sl.-38/ IT/ R8960.229.
1770 LAPIS, Gaetano: Nascita di Venere (*Venus-child presented to Jupiter*)/ FR// ?/ Roma, PaBo/ Inv. E42220iccd/ IT/ R8913.230.
Also PA/ oc/ ?/ Roma, GNB/ Inv. 2402/ exh/ R355V.231.
c1775 CERACCHI, Giuseppe: Vénus sortant de l'onde (Venus leaving the waves)/ SC/ m/86x86/ Paris, DRO 5.12.'89/Sl. #/ Drouot 1990,p.203/ R5100.232.
c1800 FOLO, Giovanni: Il riposo di Venere (Venus sur les eaux) (eng aft NOCCHI, Bernardino)/ PR/ e/ 46.5x58/ UN/ Inv. #/ IT/ R9671.233.
c1800 GIANI, Felice : Birth of Venus/ PA/ ?/ ?/ UN/ Inv.#/ IT/ R2749.234.
c1830 PELAGI, Pelagio: Venere che nasce dal mare/ PA/ oc/ 85x73/ Venezia, CaR/ Inv.273 Col. Martini/ exh/ Martini 2002, p.220-221, n°178/ R967.235.
1839 MARINI, A./ Nascita di Venere/ FR/ t/ ?/ Firenze, UN/ Inv.#/ IT/ R8598V.236.
c1850 PODESTI, Francesco : The birth of Venus/ PA/?/?/ London, SOT 1.1.'95/ Sl. PL0067-92/ IT/ R4672.237.
c1900 BAZZANI, A.: Venus in a scallop shell/ SC/ m/ 56/ NY, CHR/ Sl. 1818-0126/ IT/ R8949.238.
c1900 TITO, Ettore: The birth of Venus/ PA/ ?/ ?/ Venezia, GAM/ Inv.#/ IT artresource/ R8516.239.
1909 BOZZACHI, Louis : Birth of Venus/ SC/ s/ 40/ London, CHR 23.2.'06/Sl. 7212-177/ IT/ R5778.240.
1923 CARRA, Carlo: Nascita di Venere/ PR/ e/ 31x20,5/ Milano, SdC/ Inv.#/ Pontiggia 2004,p.30,n°10/ R3520.241.
1923 DREI, Ercole: Figura femminile con delfino/ SC/ p/ ?/ UN/ Inv.#/ Di Genova 1994, p.684, n°893/ R8639. 242. *Although the name of Venus does not appear in the title, the attribute 'dolphin' as well as the attitude of the figure as an 'Anadyomene' make the reference to Venus obvious.*
1925-26 SAVINIO, Alberto: La naissance de Vénus/ 2DR/ du/ 14,8x11,1, 27,5x22,3/ Roma, PrC/ Inv.1925-26 n°4,5/ Vivarelli 1996, p.232/ R8686, R8687.243.
1933 GAJONI, Antonio Luigi: La nascita di Venere/ PA/ oc/ 120x90/ Paris, PrC/ Inv.#/ Di Genova 1995, p.1389, n°1846/ R8695.244.
1947 MIOZZO, Franco: Nascita di Venere versiliese/ PA/ oc/ 240x160/ PrC/ Inv. #/ IT/ R10339V.245.
1949 SAVINIO, Alberto: Nascita di Venere/ PA/ tf/ 79x57,5/ Roma, PrC/ Inv.1949 n°2/ Vivarelli 1996, p.193/ R8683.246.
1950 SAVINIO, Alberto: Nascita di Venere/ 2PA/ tf/ 46x38, 70x58/ Roma, PrC/ Inv.1950 n°25,26/ Vivarelli 1996, p.215-16/ R8684, R8685.247.
1968 VOLTERRANI, Egi: Nascita di Afrodite dalle acque/ MM/ c/ 140x80/ UN/ Inv.#/ CELIT 1977 Vol 4, p.2889/ R8674.248.
1969 VON RIEGER, Federico: La Venere nascente/ MM/ w/ 40x28,5/ UN/ Inv.#/ CELIT 1974 Vol 1, p.705/ R8679.249.
1974 DE PAOLI, Elio: Venere acquatica e putti/ PA/ oc/ 70x50/ UN/ Inv.#/ CELIT 1974 Vol 1, p.241/ R8677. 250.
1977 BASTIANO DA MONTALBANO, Maurizio: Venere tra le conchiglie (Venus *crouching* among shells)/ PA/ o/ 70x50/ UN/ Inv.#/ CEDE 1996 Vol 15, p.10188/ R8654.251.
1977 PANDOLFINI, Emanuele : La nascita di Venere/ PA ?/ ?/ UN/ Inv.#/ Bolaffi 1979, p.262/ R8627.252.
1985 BRUNI, Bruno: La nascita della Venere I (The birth of Venus I)/ PR/ lr/ 87x67/ WEB, arsmundi/Inv. ?-200/ IT/ R6802.253.
1985 BRUNI, Bruno: La nascita della Venere II (The birth of Venus II)/ PR/ lr/ 103x80/ WEB, arsmundi/ Inv. ?-75/ IT/ R6803.254.

1992 FABRO, Luciano: La nascita di Venere (Birth of Venus)/ AS/ / 263x70x118/ Maastricht, BMu/ Inv. #/ Mai ed. 2001, p.209, note n° 21/ R9749.255.
1993 PANDOLFI, Emanuele : Nascita di Venere/ PA/ ac/ 110x100/ UN/ Inv.#/ CEDE 1996 Vol 15, p.10720/ R8657.256.
1998 VERSETTI, Giorgio: Come Venere, Manuella usci dell'acqua/ PA/ ow/ 135x65/ UN/ Inv.#/ CEDE 2001 Vol 16, p.11636/ R8653.257.
2005 BONINI, Fabio: La nascita di Aphrodite/ PA/ ow/ 150x70/ WEB, Artabus 8.7.07/ Inv. #/ IT/ R9843. 258.

5. Toilet/Bath of Venus/Venus crouching

c1500 PORTA, Fra Bartolommeo della : Two studies of Crouching Aphrodite/ DR/ d/ 19,9x28,4/ Cambridge (Boston), FAM/ Inv. 1932.141/ IT/ R4186.259.
c1509 RAIMONDI, Marcantonio: Vénus agenouillée se tournant vers l'amour debout derrière elle/ DR/ d/ 21,1x15,9/ Paris, MdL/ Inv. 10401/ Cordelier 1992, p.166,n°224/ R2806.260. *Copy in landscape with tree : PR/e/ 22,9x14,5/London,BMu/Inv.1973U22/ Faietti 1988, p.164-166,n°36/ R3537*; (aft FRANCIA, Francesco, PA)/ PR/ Cambridge, FWM/ Inv. P.5358-R.
c1515 RAFFAELLO, Sanzio : Toilette der Venus/ DR/ d/ 25,3x20,8/ London, BMu/ Inv. 9-15-630/ Oberhuber 1999, p.95,n°34/ R3688.261.
c1515 RAIMONDI, Marcantonio: Venere dopo il bagno (Vénus essuyant les pieds, au sortir du bain, auprès de l'Amour) (Vénus sorte du bain) (Venus drying her feet after bathing, with Cupid aside) (aft RAFFAELLO)/ PR/ e/ 17x14/ Roma, ING/ Inv. FC4078/ de Liedekerke 1995, p.291, n°161 / R875.262. *Also in: Cambridge, FWM/ Inv. P.5352-R; Paris, MdL/ Inv.#/ Cordelier 1992, p.168,n°225.*; *in A'dam, RPK/ Inv.#/ Mai ed., p.426, n°G4*; *SF, FAM/ Inv. 30.36318. Many copies in reverse or with different background.*
c1540 CARUCCI, Jacopo (PONTORMO): Venus getting out of the bath with Cupid gambolling by her side/ DR/ d/ 39x18/ Firenze, GdU/ Inv. 341F/ Berenson 1938,p.275,n°937-1963/ R3589.263.
1546 VICO, Enea: Venus at her toilet/ PR/ e/ 18,3x12,2/ SF, FAM/ Inv. 1963.30.3241/ Bartsch 30 (15,3) 1985, p.29/ R1358.264. *Also in London, BMu.*
c1550 ABATE, Nicolo dell' : Toilette de Vénus (détail)/ PA/ ?/ ?/ Paris, MdL/ Inv.#/ Duca, 1966, fig.729, p.497/ R5359.265.
c1550 LIGORIO, Pirro: Venus crouching at her bath with two amoretti *(MS XIII)*/ IL/ Napoli, BiN/ Inv. B.8.200/ Bober 1986, p.63-64,n°19/R8126V.266.
c1550 MARCO da FAENZA: Venere al bagno (?)/ FR/ tf/ 21x90/ Firenze, PaV/ Inv.#/ IT/ R8594.267.
c1550 ORSI, Lelio: Die Toilette der Venus/ DR/ d/ 21.1x32/ Braunschweig, HAU/ Inv. Z143/ IT/ R10082. 268.
c1550 (cir) SALVIATI, Francesco: Das Bad der Venus/ DR/ d/ 8.5x15/ NY, CHR 10.1.'96/ Sl. ?-13/ IT/ R10080.269.
c1550 SCHIAVONE, Andrea Meldolla, detto: Venus after her bath *(playing with Cupid)*/ PR/ e/ 15.3x10.9/ London, BMu/ Inv.#/ Bartsch 32(16,1) 1979, p.102,n°75(67)/ R4925.270.
c1550 SCHIAVONE, Andrea Meldolla, detto: Venere al bagno/ PA/ oc/ 177x149/ Venezia, CaR/ Inv. Col.Martini 25/ Martini 2002, p.272-273, n°223/ R958.271.
1556 VASARI Giogio & MARCO da FAENZA: Toletta di Venere e putti reggicartiglio/ FR/ ?/ 60x150/ Firenze, PaV/ Inv.#/ IT/ R8597.272.
c1560 GIAMBOLOGNA : Venere inginocchiata in atto di asciugarsi (Crouching Venus drying herself)/ SC/ q/ 101/ Firenze, MuH/ Inv. 101/ Avery 1999, p.36-37/ R6941.273. *Replica in Firenze, MNB.*
c1565 GIAMBOLOGNA: Venus nach dem Bade/ SC/ z/ 24,8/ Wien, KHM/ Inv.#/ Avery 1999,p 54 fig.1/ R4545.274.
Several copies exist: e.g. Cleveland, MuA/ Inv. 1993.230/ IT/ R11746.275.
c1565 VASARI, Giorgio: Toilette der Venus/ PA/ ow/ 154x124/ Stuttgart, SGa/ Inv. 2777/ Mai ed. 2001, p.69, n°1; p.248-49, n°11/ R1565.276.
c1567 ANDREASI, Ippolito : Venus crouching/ DR/?/?/ Düsseldorf, KuM/ Inv. KA (FP) 10879/ Bober & Rubinstein, 1986, p.62-63/ R8079V.277. *Representing the Lely's Venus, London, BMu.*
c1570 ALLORI, Alessandro : The toilet of Venus/ PA/ ?/?/ Stuttgart, SGa/ Inv.#/ Duboucher, 2001, fig.60/ R7644.278.
c1573 BAROZZI, Jacopo detto VIGNOLA et al.: Bagno di Venere/OT//Roma, PaBo/ Inv. C8928iccd/ IT/ R8921.279. *See engraving **1684** VENTURINI.*

c1575 ABONDIO, Antonio : The toilet of Venus/ RE/ j/ 9,5x7,2/ Kopenhagen, SMK/ Inv. KMS5018Ka/ IT/ R7579.280.

c1575 GIAMBOLOGNA : Crouching Venus / SC/ z/ 25,3/ Firenze, MNB/ Inv. 62/ Massinelli 1992, p.134/ R6008.281. *Replica : 23,5/ Frankfurt, LHM/ Inv.St.P.130/ Mai ed. 2001, p.488, n°B4. Many more replica or copies.*

c1575 LORENZI, Battista: Venere al bagno/ SC/? /?/ UN/ Inv. #/ IT/ 11575V.282.

c1575 (wor) TINTORETTO, Jacopo : Toilet of Venus (*with mirror)*/ PA/ oc/ 117x108/ NY, SOT 29.1.'05/ Sl. N01752-71A/ IT/ R5704.283. *Berenson 1958, p.183 refers to: Venere allo specchio/ LA, JPG.*

c1580 VERONESE, Paolo Caliari: Venus at her toilette (*with Cupid holding a mirror)*/ PA/ oc/ 165x125/ Omaha, JAM/ Inv.#/ Prater 2002, p.26/ R2088.284.

c1580 (att) VERONESE, Paolo Caliari: Toilet of Venus (detail) (aft TIZIANO's 'Venus Genetrix', lost work)/ PA//?/ London, CIA/ Inv.#/ Goffen 1997, p.141, fig.82/ R5545.285.

c1585 SCARSELLINO, Ippolito: Il bagno di Venere (Toilet of Venus)/ PA/ oc/ 45x57/ Roma, GaB/ Inv.219/ Berenson 1968, p.391; Moreno 2004, p.265, n°20/ R367.286.

1587 ABONDIO, Antonio: Toilette der Venus/ RE/ j oval/ 9x7.5/ Nürnberg, GNM/ Inv. Pl.O. 962/ IT/ R10095.287.

1598-99 CARRACCI, Annibale: Toeletta di Venere *(in a chariot)*/ PA/ oc/ 90x100/ Bologna, PiN/ Inv.6503/ IT; Mai ed. 2001, p.77, n°11 / R2688.288.

c1600 BOSCOLI, Andrea : Toilette de Vénus/ DR/ d/ 15,1x12,7/ Paris, MdL/Inv. 11690/ Viatte 1988, p.49-50,n°59/ R3831.289.

c1600 (wor) GIAMBOLOGNA: Venus nach dem Bade/ SC/ z/ 14.5/ Braunschweig, HAU/ Inv. #/ IT/ R10085.290.

c1600 GIAMBOLOGNA : Badende Venus/ SC/ z/ 13/ Köln, MAK/ Inv. H494/ IT/ R10103.291.

c1600 (wor) GIAMBOLOGNA: Kauernde Venus/ SC/ z/ 9.5/ Braunschweig, HAU/ Inv. #/ IT/ R10086. 292.

c1600 PALMA Il Giovane, Jacopo Negretti : Venus bei der Toilette mit Amor/ PA/ oc/ 162x113/ Kassel, SKS/ Inv. 499/ IT/ R10089.293.

c1600 PROCACCINI, Giulio Cesare : Crouching Venus/ DR/ d/ 20,1x13,3/ Milano, BiA/ Inv. F 255 inf. n. 1982/ IT/ R8731.294.

c1600 (att) SUSINI, Antonio: Vénus agenouillée (aft GIAMBOLOGNA)/ SC/ z/ 23,5/ UN, PrC/ Inv.#/ Avery 1999, p.36-37/ R6940.295.

c1610 (wor) SUSINI, Giovanni Francesco : Crouching Venus (aft GIAMBOLOGNA)/ SC/ z/ 9,9/ A'dam, CHR 27.6.'06/ Sl. 2709 -242/ IT/ R6704.296.

1616 ALBANI, Francesco: Acconciatura di Venere (Venus at her toilet *in a chariot with attendants*)/ PA/ oc/ §154/ Roma, GaB/ Inv. 40/ Zuffi 2001, p.197; Mai ed. 2001, p.77 n°12 ; Moreno 2004, p.297, n°1/ R363.297. *Replica of Paris, MdL/ Inv.9/ IT/ R540.298.*

1616-46 (att) SUSINI, Giovanni Francesco: Kauernde Venus (aft GIAMBOLOGNA)/ SC/ z/ 26.5/ Vaduz, LMu/ Inv. #/ IT/ 10105.298.

c1621-1633 ALBANI, Francesco: La Toilette de Vénus (The toilet of Venus *with attendants and cupids*)/ PA/ oc/ 202x252/ Paris, MdL/ Inv.9/ IT/ R540.299.

Replicas: Brescia, PTM/ Inv.223/ IT/ R8182.300.;

***1633 :** El tocador de Venus/ PA/ oc/ 114x171/ Madrid, MNP/Inv.P1/Enciclopedia 2006, Tomo II, p.340-341/R539.301.;*

***1616** Acconciatura di Venere/ PA/ oc/ ∅154/ Roma, GaB/Inv. 40/ Zuffi 2001, p.197 ; Moreno 2004, p.297, n°1/ R363.302. Copy: London, SOT05.07.'05/Sl.W05717-526/ R3882. Copies in reverse: Chambéry, MBA/ Inv.M1241/ IT/ R6985 ; London, BON04.07.'06/Sl.13590-193/R6846; many engravings.*

1622 RENI, Guido: The toilet of Venus/ PA/ oc/ 281,9x205,7/ London, NGa/ Inv. NG90/ Anonymous 1989, Vol.I, p.957/ R3089.303. *Reverse PR by Strange, Robert.*

c1623 GUERCINO, Giovane Francesco Barbieri: The Toilette of Venus (Venera che si specchia con molti puttini e due altre femmine…)/ PA oc/ 149,9x190,3/ London, SOT 10.7.'02/ Sl. L02111-62/ IT/ R5886. 304.

c1625 (att) CAROSELLI, Angelo: Venus at her toilet *(with two mirrors)*/ PA/ ow/ 49,2x34,3/ NY, SOT 24.1.'02/ Sl.N07759-186/ IT/ R5400.305.
1633 ALBANI, Francesco: Venus attended by nymphs and cupids/ PA/ oc/ 114x171/ Madrid, MNP/Inv.1/IT/R539.306. *Replica of Paris, MdL/ Inv.9/ IT/ R540.298.*
c1640 GENNARI, Benedetto I : Toilet of Venus/ PA/ oy/ ?/ Milano, BiA/ Inv. 717/ IT/ R11551V.307.
c1640 (wor) GUERCINO, Giovane Francesco : Toilet of Venus/ DR/ d/ ?/ Windsor, RCo/ Inv. RL2896/ IT/ R11550V.308.
c1650 ALBANI, Francesco : Toilette der Venus/ FR/ / ?/ Bassano Romano, ViVG/ Inv. #/ IT/ R10102.309.
c1650 ALBANI, Francesco: La Toeletta di Venere (The toilet of Venus)/ PA/ oc/ 155x115/ Brescia, PTM/ Inv.223/ IT/ R8182.310. *Replica in reverse of Paris, MdL/ Inv.9/ IT/ R540.298.*
c1650 BOS(S)ELLI, Orfeo: Venus *(crouching, headless)*/ SC/ m/ ?/ Auckland, Aga /Inv. 1932.13/ IT/ R7227.311.
c1650 CITTADINI, Pier Francesco: L'abbigliamento di Venere/ PA/ ?/ ?/ Torino, GaS/ Inv.534/ IT/ R349. 312.
c1650 GARGIULO, Domenico : Toilette der Venus / DR/ d/ 8.6x17/ Berlin, KSK/ Inv. KdZ 24079/ IT/ R10111.313.
c1650 (cir) GIMIGNANI, Giacinto: Toilet of Venus/ PA/ oc/ 61,3x74,5/ London, SOT 30.10.'01/ Sl. W01403-237/ IT/ R4364.314.
c1675 LIBERI, Pietro : Toilette der Venus/ FR// ?/ München, BNM/ Inv. #/ IT/ R10114.315.
c1680 MEHUS, Livio: La toilette di Venere/ PA/ oc/ 140x92/ Firenze, PaP, Col.PrC/ Inv.#/ Casazza 2005, p.288,n°163/ R5126.316.
1684 VENTURINI, Givanni Francesco: Fontana detta 'Il bagno di Venere' *(Le fontane ne' palazzi e ne' giardini di Roma con li loro prospetti et ornamenti*/ IL/ e/?/ Roma, PaB/ Pocino 1996, p.156-157/ R10116.317.
c1750 POZZI, Stefano : Toletta di Venere/ FR// ?/ Roma, GDP/ Inv. E41317iccd/ IT/ R8939.318.
c1750 VANVITELLI, Luigi: Baths of Venus and statue of Venus/ SC/ s/ ?/ Caserta, PeP/ IT/ R2710.319.
c1775 LORENZI, Lorenzo: Toletta di Venere (aft VASARI, Giogio)/ PR/ e/ 38,5x30/ Firenze, GdU/Inv.#/ Mai ed. 2001, p.75, n°8/ R8470.320.
c1780 MULINARI, Stefano : Toeletta di Venere/ PR// 22x35,2/ Parma, BiP/ Inv. On22105/ Mussini 2003, p.216,n°463/ R3647.321.
1786 DAELLI, Filippo : Toilet of Venus ?/ DR/ d/ 14,6x19,4/ Milano, BiA/ Inv. F 283 inf. n. 89/ IT/ R8722.322.
1790-95 APPIANI, Andrea: La toeletta di Venere / PA/ / oc/ 81x112 oval/ Milano, PAB/ Inv. 586/ Baini 2006, p.356, Cat.586/ R3105.323.
c1795 ADEMOLLO, Luigi: Toletta di Venere/ PA/?/?/ UN, PrC/ Inv.#/ Sisi 2005, p.181, n°203/ R8682.324.
c1800 FAURO, ?: La toeletta di Venere/PA/oc/66x81/Roma, PadE 10-12.5.'91/ IT/ R5911.325.
c1825 BARTOLINI, Lorenzo: Vénus au bain, assise sur un rocher tenant un drapé (Venus at her bath, seated on a rock, holding a drapery)/ SC/ m/ 151/ WEB, Artprice 6.10.'04/ IT/ R6171V.326.
c1880 BARZANTI, Pietro : Crouching Venus/ SC/ s/ 72.5/ London, CHR 25.9.07/ Sl. 5193-0502/ IT/ R10529.327.
c1950 SANTINI, Amilcare : Aphrodite *(crouching, seated on a vase)*/ SC/ a/ 24,5x11,5x13/ Gent, PrC/ Inv.#/ exh/ R9352.328. *Copy of an antique in Vatican Museum.*
1997 GARNERO, Enzo: Venere *(crouching)*/ SC/ q/ 69x27x35/ UN/ Inv.#/ CEDE 2001 Vol 16, p.11261/ R8646.329.

6. Venus and Adonis

1499 COLONNA, Francesco: Monument of Adonis/ ILL/ e/ ?/ ?/ Godwin 2005, p.373/ R10401.330. *See **1527** G. ROMANO: 'Bath of Venus and Mars (or Adonis?)' and 'Adonis chased by Mars'/ FR/ Mantova, PdT/ Gombrich 1951,p.125, pl.24b.*
c1550 SCHIAVONE, Andrea Meldolla, detto: Venere e Adone/ PA/ ?/ ?/ Padova, MuC/ Inv. 150/ Berenson 1958, p.166/ R9625V.331.
c1550 SCHIAVONE, Andrea Meldolla, detto: Venere e Adone/ PA/ ?/ ?/ Venezia, PrC Conte Vittorio Cini/ Inv. #/ Berenson 1958, p.166/ R9627V.332.
c1550 VERONESE, Paolo Caliari, detto: Venere e Adone/ PA/ ?/ ?/ Darmstadt, HLM/ Inv. 96/ Berenson 1958, p.134/ R9621V.333.
c1550 VERONESE, Paolo Caliari, detto: Venere e Adone/ PA/ ?/ ?/ Edinburgh, NGS? or University?/ Inv. 125/ Berenson 1958, p.134/ R9622V.334.
c1575 TITO, Santi di: Venus and Adonis/ DR/ d/ ?/ London, BMu/ Inv. 1981,1003.00014/ IT/ R8437V. 335.
c1600 CARDI, Ludovico: Venus and Adonis/PA/?/?/Dallas, MMu/ Inv.#/ IT/ R4001V.336.
c1640 (wor) FANELLI, Francesco: Venus and Adonis/ 2SC/ z/ 15/ London, VAM: Inv. A.118-1910 and A.58-1956/ exh/ R10376V+10377V.337. *Two identical SC with minor differences.*
c1670 GIORDANO, Luca : Festmahl der Götter mit Adonis (Banquet of the gods with Adonis)/ PA/ oc/ 180x280/ Napoli, PrC/ Inv.#/ IT/ R2613.338.
1700 ROCCA, Michele : Venus and Adonis/ PA/ oc/ 50x37/ UN, LO/ Inv. 4356/ IT www.lootedart.com/ R10152V.339.
c1715 GARZI, Luigi : Venere e Adone/ PA/ ?/ ?/ Roma, PaDC/ Inv.#/ IT/ 8373V.340.
c1760 GIAQUINTO, Corrado : Venus y Adonis/ PA/ ?/ ?/ Madrid, PaR/ Inv.#/ IT/ R11027V.341.
c1800 CELEBRANO, Francesco: Vénus et Adonis/ PR/ e/ ?/ Caen, MBA/ Inv.#/ IT/ R825. 342.
1903 DE CAROLIS, Adolfo: Venere e Adone/ PA/ ob/ 69,5x102,5/ Roma, GCAMC/ Inv. AM1148/ Virno 2004, p.230-31, n°451/ R8643.343. *Preparatory for PA/ oc/ Perugia, PrC.*

o Adonis meeting Venus

c1712 DARDARONE, Giuseppe: Venus y Adonis/ FR// ?/ Palma: PaCV/ Inv. <Alcoba, n°4>/ Navarrete 2005, p.164, fig.287/ R11048.344.
c1712 DARDARONE, Giuseppe: Venus y Adonis/ FR// ?/ Palma: PaCV/ Inv. <Alcoba, n°5>/ Navarrete 2005, p.164, fig.288/ R11049.345.

▪ with Cupid

c1588 CARRACCI, Annibale: Venus, Adonis y Cupido/ PA/ oc/ 212x268/ Madrid, MNP/ Inv. P2631/ Boccardo ed. 2004,p.440-41, n°114; Enciclopedia 2006, Tomo II, p.646-647, Tomo VI, p.2160-62/ R006.346.
Preparatory drawing: Venere e Adone/ DR/ d/ 18x28,4/ Madrid, ASF / Inv.304 (or 2256?)/ Perez Sancho 1977, 26,n°16; Loisel 2004, p.32,n°III.35/ R3791.347.; other DR in Firenze, GdU/Inv. 12202F.
Replica: Venus and Adonis/ PA/ oc/ 217x246/ Wien, KHM/ Inv.#/ IT/ R7143.348.; copy c1650 'after' PA/ oc/ 79x101/ A'dam, SOT 22.3.'05/Sl. AM0956-34/ IT/ R2994.
c1617 ALBANI, Francesco:Venus y Adonis *(right arm upwards, with Cupid)*/ PA/ oy/ 45,5x60,5/ Palermo, GRS/ Inv.#/ Ubeda de los Cobos 2005, p.37 fig.14/ R7332. 349.
c1619 GUERCINO, Giovane Francesco Barbieri: Venus, Adonis and Cupid/ DR/ d/ 18,8x25,1/ Oxford, AMu/ Col Denis Mahon/ IT/ R7162.350.

1620 PASQUALINI, Giovanni Battista: Venus and Adonis with Cupid (aft GUERCINO)/ PR/ e/ 17,3x25,4/ SF, FAM/ Inv. 1995.124.2/ IT/ R868.351.
c1634 TASSI, Agostino: Adonis and Venus/ FR// ?/ Roma, PaDP/ Inv. #/ Cresti & Rendina 1998, p.342-343/ R9833.352.
1653 BRANDI, Giacinto: Venere e Adone/ FR// ?/ Roma, PDP/ Inv. E45881iccd/ IT/ R8916.353. *Also (att) CAMASSEI, Andrea.*
1713-15 (cir) RICCI, Sebastiano: Venere e Adone/ PA/ ?/ ?/ Milano, FiA/ Inv.#/ Scarpa 2006, p.267, fig.424/ R10444.354.
1717 LUTI, Benedetto: Venus und Adonis/ PA/ oc/ 146x185/ Pommersfelden, ScW/ Inv.334/ IT/ R8967. 355.
1781 VITALI, Pietro, Marco: Venus and Adonis (pl.VI of XII) (aft Anton von Maron) <aft FR LO in ancient roman home near Villa Peretti-Negroni (Stazione Termini), Roma>/ PR/ ?/ ?/ London, BMu/ Inv.#/ Joyce 1986, p.433, fig.13/ R11144.356.
c1800 FONTANA, Pietro: Vénus et Adonis (aft Giovanni ROMANELLI)/ PR/ e/ ?/ Christchurch, AGTPW/ Inv. 73-116/ IT/ R10494.357.

• with cupids

c1575 TINTORETTO, Jacopo : Venus and Adonis/ PA/ ?/ ?/ Firenze, GdU/ Inv.#/ Berenson 1958, p.178; IT artresource/ R8520.358.
c1610 ALBANI, Francesco: Venus, Adonis and Mars (*in the air*)/ PA/ oc/§154/ Roma GaB/ Inv.44/ Mai ed. 2001, p.25,n°9 ; Moreno 2004, p.297, n°13/ R8469.359.
c1621-1633 ALBANI, Francesco: Adonis conduit près de Vénus par les Amours (Adonis *-left arm downwards-* lead to Venus by Cupids *with cupids in the air*)/ PA/ oc/ 203x252/ Paris,MdL/ Inv.12/ IT/ R538.360.
Replica : Berlin,SSP/ Inv.4(7723) ; reverse PR in Frankfurt a/M, SKI/ Inv.Kat.A5/ Städelsches Kunstinsitut 1982, p.15/ R 3438.361.; Kassel,SKS/ Inv.L953 ; München, APk. Copies : Blois,MCh/ Inv.Louvre32 ; reverse: Adonis' right arm downwards, no cupids in the air, chariot/ Bordeaux,MBA/ Inv.M5882/ R2661; Braunschweig,HAU/ Inv.484 ; Cambridge,FWM ; reverse: Adonis' right arm downwards, cupids in the air/ SF, BON16.05.'06/ Sl.13786-3014/ R6426. Many engravings.
c1635 ALBANI,Francesco:Vénus et Adonis (*right arm upwards*)/ PA/ oc/ 45x60/ Paris, MdL/ Inv.20/ IT/ R2496.362.
c1650 ALBANI, Francesco: Venus, Amor und Adonis (*right arm downwards, 4 cupids around)*/ PA/ oc/ 195x285/ Pommersfelden, ScW/ Inv.5/ IT/ R4513.363.
c1650 GUERCINO, Giovane Francesco Barbieri : Venere e Adone/ DR/ u/ ?/ Roma, GaP/ Inv. E38416iccd/ IT/ R8902.364.
c1650 MOLA ? Pier Francesco : Venus and Cupid camping beneath a tree with Adonis hunting a stag in the distance/ DR/ d/ 22.2x19/ London, VAM/ Inv. Dyce 309/ Ward-Jackson 1979,Vol.II, p.70-71, n°772/ R11131. 365.
1736-40 AMIGONI, Jacopo: Venus and Adonis/ PA/ oc/ 142x173/ München, APk/ Inv.2857/ Mai ed. 2001, p.318-19 n°43/ R1280.366.

o Adonis loving Venus

c1600 ALBANI, Francesco: Adonis saca una astilla del talon de Venus/ PA/ oc?/ 126x174/ Barcelona, LL/ Inv. <salas de la Real Academia de Bellas Artes de San Jorge>/ Navarrete 2005, p.252/ R11084V.367.

▪ alone with Venus

c1350 SEMINTENDI da PRATO, Arrigo : Ven Adonis (*aut Ovidio, Metamorfosi)/* IM/ f/ ?/ Firenze, BNC/ Inv. 63(cat.n.187)/ Casazza 2005, p.31 Fig 2/ R8823.368.

1516-17 (wor) RAFFAELLO, Sanzio : Vénus et Adonis (in 'La stufetta del Cardinale Bibbiena)/ FR/ / ?/ Roma, MuV/ Inv.#/ Porcheron-Felsing 1983, p.24, 33, 61, 351, fig.10/ R8264.369.
*Also: **c1516** ROMANO, Giulio/ DR/ ?/ ?/ Wien, ALB/ Inv. 17632/ Massari 1993, p.37-38, fig.27; R3548.370.; a detail of the head of Venus in the hands of Adonis/ DR/ d/ 38x28,6/ Wien, ALB/ Inv. 17633/ Oberhuber 1999, p.100,n°39/ R3690.371.; a copy aft ROMANO/ DR/ d/ 20,3x17,2/ London, CHR 12.6.'05/ Sl. 5614-97/ IT/ R3622.*
c1516 RAIMONDI, Marcantonio: Venere e Adone (aft Giulio ROMANO, reverse of DR)/ PR/ e/ 26,4x17,3/ Roma, ING/ Inv. FC4991/ Massari 1989, p.30-31,n°8; Oberhuber 1999, p.102,n°41/ R3485.372. *Also in Wien, ALB/ Inv. 1971-436.*
c1520 VENEZIANO, Agostino: Venus und Adonis *(in landscape with housing)/ PR/ e/ 26x19,1/ Wien, ALB/ Inv. 346/* Oberhuber 1999, p.101,n°40/ R3689.373.
c1550 BONASONE, Giulio: Adonis seated next to Venus (From the Loves of the Gods)/ PR/ e/16,5x11/ Wien, ALB/ Inv.#/ Bartsch 29 (15,2) 1982,p.18,n°154-II(151)/ R4843.374.
c1575 PASSAROTTI, Bartolomeo: Vénus et Adonis (?)/ DR/ d/ 38.5x24.3/ Paris, MdL/ Inv. 8475, rec/ IT/ R10030.375.
c1625 VAROTARI, Alessandro : Venere e Adone/ PA/ oc/ 94x120/ Modena Mercato 20-28.2.'99/ Sl.#/ IT/ R5921.376.
c1700 MOLINARI, Antonio: Vénus et Adonis (?)/ DR/ d/ 20.2x20.9/ Paris, MdL/ Inv. 17402, rec/ IT/ R10024.377.
1784 APPIANI, Andrea: Venere e Adone/ PA/ ?/ ?/ S.Gregorio da Sassola, CaB/ Inv.#/ IT/ R3112.378.
c1789 CANOVA, Antonio: Venus and Adonis/ SC/ m/ 185x80x60/ Genève, VLG/ Inv.#/ Stefani 2003, p.60, n°54,55; Pinelli in Bonfait 2004, p.80/ R7164.379.
Replica: SC/ p/ 163x60x87/ Possagno, CdC/Inv. #/ Munoz 1957, Tav.XV/ R488.380.
Preparatory: Studio per Venere e Adone / DR/ u/ 58x43.7/ Bassano, Muc/ Inv. E.1.870 /Stefani 2003, p.59, n°53/ R10158.381. A PR was made by Antonio Banzo.
1791 BARTOLOZZI, Francesco: Venus and Adonis (aft GUERCINO, Giovanni)/ PR/ e/ 29,4x41/ SF, FAM/ Inv.1988.1.260/ IT/R720.382.

- **with animal(s) and Cupid(s)**

c1550 VERONESE, Paolo Caliari : Venus and Adonis/ PA/ oc/ 68x52/ Wien, KHM/ Inv.1527/ Berenson 1958, p.140, pl.1096/ R2724.383.
c1556 GHISI, Giorgio : Venere e Adone (aft GHISI, Teodoro)/ PR/ e/ 31,8x22,3/ Roma, ING/ Inv. FN1208/ Massari 1989, p.306-308,n°114; Bellini 1998, p.143-146,n°31/R1643.384. *Also in: Auckland, AGa/ Inv 1981/50/55; Dresden, SKS/Inv.#/Mai ed. 2001, p.428-29, n°G8; Glasgow, HMAG/ inv. 248.London, BMu/ Bartsch 31 (15,4) 1986, p.104,105n°42-II,III(402); NY, MMA/ Inv. 1953 (53.522.28); .Philadelphia, MuA/ Inv. 1975-28-2; SF, FAM/ Inv. 1963.30.3281 F; Paris, CHR 17.10.07/ Sl. 5477-0002/ IT*
b1580 (wor) VERONESE, Paolo Caliari: Venus and Adonis/ PA/ oc/ 224.4 x 168.3/ Seattle, AMu/ Inv. 61.174/ Berenson 1958, p.140/ R2707.385.
1580 VERONESE, Paolo Caliari: Venus and Adonis (*sleeping*)/ PA/ oc/ 162x191/ Madrid, MNP/ Inv. P482/ Mai ed. 2001, p.298 n°1 ; Enciclopedia 2006, Tomo VI, p.2163-66/ R1110.386.
c1595 CARRACCI, Annibale: Venus and Adonis/ PA/ oc/ 217x246/ Wien, KHM/ Inv.#/ Relouge 1958,p.150/ R453.387.
c1600 FARINATI, Paolo : Vénus et Adonis (aft VERONESE)/ DR/ d/ 26x31.7/ Paris, MdL/ Inv. 4717, rect/ IT/ R10019.388.
c1600 FARINATI, Paolo: Vénus et Adonis/ DR/ d/ 41,2x27,4/ Paris, MdL/ Inv. 4853/ IT/ R2824.389.
c1630 CARACCIOLO, Battistello: Venere e Adone/ PA/ oc/ 204x145/ Napôli, MdC/ Inv. #/ IT/ R10323. 390.
c1632 FANELLI, Francesco: Venus and Adonis/ SC/ jz/ 15,5/ London, BMu/ Inv. M&MESL 168/ IT/ R481.391.

c1640 TESTA, Pietro: Venus und Adonis/ PA/ oc/ 97,5x133/ Wien, ABK/ Inv.215/ Hutter 1980, p.37-38,53, n°31; Fleischer 2005, p.98/ R3755.392.
Preparatory: Venus und Adonis, umgeben von Putten/ DR/ d/ 19.6x26.8/ Berlin, KSK/ Inv. KdZ 4521/ IT/ R10109.393.;
also in Firenze, GdU/ Inv. 1717Esp/ Massari 1989, p.514, fig.59/ R3599.394.
Reverse PR/ e/ 36,2x45,7/ Roma, ING/ Inv. FC124430/ Bartsch 45 (20,2) 1982, p.147,n°25(222); Bartsch 45 C (20,) 1990, p.152-153,n°4506.025; Massari 1989, p.514-15,n°211/ R2594.395. Also in Lyon, BiM; Wien, ALB.
Hutter refers to a copy "aft" in Wien, ABK/ Inv.#/ R3756.
c1650 DIAMANTINI, Giuseppe: Venus and Adonis/ PR/ e/ 20,1x15,8/ Bassano, MuC/ Inv.#/ Bartsch 47 (21,2) 1983, p.401,n°17(276)/ R5000.396.
c1650 LEONE, Andrea di : Vénus et Adonis/ PA/ oc/ 116x153/ Web, Artprice 1.3.'07/ Inv. #220466/ IT/ R8861.397.
1655 SCARAMUCCIA, Luigi: Venus, Adonis y Cupido (aft CARRACCI, Annibale)/ PR/ e/ 24,1x29,1/ London, BMu/ Inv.#/ Bartsch 42 (19,2) 1981, p.173,n°4-I(192); Ubeda de los Cobos 2005, p.27 fig.6/ R7331.398.
1803 PELLEGRINI, Domenico: Venere e Adone/ PA/ oc/ 30x55/ Lisboa, MNAC/ Inv. #/ Stefani 2004, p.46, nr.52/ R10180.399.

- **with Cupid(s)**

c1508 (wor) GIORGIONE, Giorgio Barbarelli: Venus and Adonis/ PA/ ?/ ?/ London, NGA/ Inv. 1123/ Berenson 1958, p.89 ; Rochelle 1991, p.6/ R7400.400.
c1525 BORDONE, Paris : Venus and Adonis/ PA/ oc/ 136x121/ Dubrovnik, PiK/ Inv.#/ Baker & Henry 2001, p.52/ R11652.401. *Replicas ?* UN, pre.Col.Crespi/ Inv. #/ Berenson 1958, p.49/ R9608V.401.;
Wien, KHM/ Inv. 253#/ Berenson 1958, p.51/ R9610V.402.
c1534-37 PRIMATICCIO, Francesco: Le mariage de Vénus et d'Adonis, d'après un dessin de ROMANO, Giulio/ FR/ / ?/ Fontainebleau, MNC/ Inv. #/ IT/ R3404.403.
1548 PRIMATICCIO, Francesco: L'Amour endormi entre Vénus et Adonis (?)/ DR/ d/ 17,2x29,1/ Paris, MdL/ Inv. 8541/ IT/ R2816.404.
c1565 CAMBIASO, Luca: Venere e Adone/ PA/ oc/ 188x105/ Lugano, PrC/ Inv.#/ Damian 2005, p.32-37/R246.405. *Damian refers to a smaller replica in Padova, Museo Civico and to a copy (att) Ottavio SEMINO (ca. 1520-1604, brother of Andrea) in New York, PrC; a copy was at TEFAF Maastricht Auction 2004.*
1570-72 ZANGUIDI, Jacopo, detto BERTOJA: Venus and Adonis/ DR/ d/ 18x12/ Chatsworth, DCo/ Inv. 368#/ Jaffé 1993, p.30-31, Cat.20/ R10388.406.
c1570-75 CAMBIASO, Luca: Adonis in den Armen von Venus ruhend (Adonis resting in the arms of Venus)/ DR/ d/ 31x21,6/ Frankfurt, GAL/ Inv.#/ IT/ R4506.407.
c1575 CAMBIASO, Luca: Vénus et Adonis/ DR/ d/ 36.2x25/ Paris, MdL/ Inv. 9334, rect/ IT/ R10007.408.
b1583 CAMBIASO, Luca: Venere e Adone/ PA/ oc/ 141x98/ Roma, GaB/ Inv. 317/ Mai ed. 2001, p.304-05 n°36/ R7401.409.
c1625 VAROTARI, Alessandro: Venere e Adone/ PA/ oc/ 225x155/ Vicenza, PaT/ Inv. 80323/ IT/ R11485.410.
c1650 (att) PODESTA, Giovanni Andrea: Venus, Adonis, putti/ PR// 42,6x23,5/ London, BMu/ Inv.#/ Bartsch 45 C (20,2) 1990, p.84-85,n°4503.009/ R4985.411.
c1665 GIORDANO, Luca : Venus and Adonis *(with Cupid and dove)*/ PA/ oc/ 194x129/ Budapest, MFA/ Inv. 534/ Mai ed. 2001, p.314-15 n°41/ R8473.412.
c1700 (att) CIGNANI, Carlo: Venus and Adonis/ PA/ oc/ 126x188/ London, WMu/ Inv. 1612-1948/ Anonymous 1989, Vol.I, p.161; Canal 1989, Vol.131, p.111/ R10892.413.

1789 CANOVA, Antonio: Adone inghirlandato da Venere (Adonis crowned by Venus)/ SC/ p/ 145x185x104/ Possagno, CdC/ Inv.#/ Munoz 1957, Tav.XIII; Stefani 2003, p.58-59, n°52/ R489.414.
*Preparatory **c1787:** Studio per Adone coronato da Venere / DR/ d/ ?/ Bassano, MuC/ Inv.#/ Stefani 2003, p.51, n°42/ R10162.415.*

• with others or animals

c1500 TOMMASO (? GIOVANNI di TOMMASO): Venus asks Cupid to wound Adonis with the arrow of Love/ PA/ ow (cassone)/ ?/ Edenbridge, PrC/ Inv. #/ Berenson 1963, p.207, pl.1181/ R9949.416. *A companion cassone panel "Death of Adonis" in Longniddry (Scotland), PrC.*
c1525 (att) ROMANO, Giulio Pippi, detto: Pan, Hyménée et les amours président à l'union de Vénus et d'Adonis/ DR/ d/ 15.8x23/ Paris, MdL/ Inv. 3485, rec/ IT/ R10031.417.
1555 GHERARDI, Cristofano: Venere e Adone/ FR//254x183/ Firenze, PaV/ Inv. 530/ IT/ R8584.418.
c1600 FARINATI, Paolo : Vénus et Adonis enlacés/ DR/ d/ 42.4x27.7/ Paris, MdL/ Inv. 4855, rect/ IT/ R10020.419.
c1600 TEMPESTA, Antonio: Perditè a Venere adamatur Adonis (Venus and Adonis embracing) (pl. 96 from the series *Ovid's Metamorphoses, pub Wilhelmus Jansonnius)*/ PR/ e/ 10,2x11,6/ LA, CMA/ Inv. 65.37.179/ Bartsch 36(17,3) 1983, p.57,n°733(151)/ R1476.420. *Also in Glasgow, HMAG/ Inv. 13901;London, BMu.*
c1600 VALESIO, Giovanni Luigi: Venus writing a letter to Adonis, Cupid with an inkwell, and Mercury instructed to bear the letter (*from 'The Heroic Epistles' aut Antonio Bruni*)/ PR/ e/ 11,3x6,3/ Wien, ALB/ Inv.#/ Bartsch 40 (18,2) 1982, p.32,n°32(220) ; Bartsch 40 C 1(18,2) 1987, p.94,n°4002.097/ R4967.421.
c1622 ALBANI, Francesco: Venus and Adonis (Venus, reclining under a rustic canopy, with Adonis fastening her sandal)/ DR/ d/ 19,2x16,5/ Chatsworth, DCo/ Inv.7/ Jaffé 1993, p.22, Cat.6; Mai ed. 2001, p.414, n°T22/ R8480.422.
c1670 GIORDANO, Luca: Venere e Adone/ DR/ d/ 29x26,3/ Napoli, MSM/ Inv. 20363/ IT/ R6316.423.
c1700 FRANCESCHINI, Marcantonio: Venus enamoured of Adonis/ PA/ oc/ 395x291/ Wien, LMu/ Inv. 21/ Miller 1991, p.xi, pl.XI, p.81, Cat.n°15/ R9815.424.
Preparatory: study for the upper body and legs of Venus/ DR/ ?/ ?/ Wien, LMu/ Inv. 4881/ Miller 1991, p.xiii, pl.49, p.81, Cat.n°15/ R9819.425.;
compositional study/ DR/ d/ 27.4x33.8/ Newcastle, LAG/ Inv. #/ Miller 1991, p.xiv, pl.51, p.81-82, Cat.n°15/ R9820.426.
c1700 FRANCESCHINI, Marcantonio: Venus and Adonis hunting (Caccia di Adone)/ PA/ oc/ 481x255/ Vaduz, LMu/ Inv. 77/ Miller 1991, p.xi, pl.XIII, p.82-83, Cat.n°16/ R4424.427.
Preparatory: study for the right shoulder, head, and extended arm of Venus/ DR/ ?/ ?/ Genova, PaRo/ Inv. 4897/ Miller 1991, p.xiv, pl.56, p.83, Cat.n°16 /R9821.428.
1733-1771 LORENZINI, Giovanni Antonio (eng): Venere e Adone (aft F.Wouters or P.P. Rubens)/ PR/ e/ 62.2x108/ Roma, BNCR/ Inv. ALD281/ IT/ R10217V.429. *Engraving of PA/ Firenze, GdU/ Inv.1131.*

o Adonis leaving Venus

c1600 CAMBIASO, Luca: Venus hält Adonis zurück/ DR/ d/ 26x18/ eBay 27.8.06/ IT/ R7430.430. *Original or copy?*
c1600 FARINATI, Paolo : Vénus tente de dissuader Adonis de partir à la chasse / DR/ d/ 41.3x28.2/ Paris, MdL/ Inv. 4854, rect/ IT/ R10021.431.
1650 GIMIGNANI, Giacinto: Venere tenta di trattenere Adone dall'andare a caccia (Venus tries to keep Adonis from the hunt)/ PA/ oc/ 116x141/ Pistoia, MCR/ Inv.#/ IT/ R8588V.432.
c1700 CRETI, Donato: Venus and Adonis I & II/ 2DR/ d/ 14,6x19,7 & 14,3x18,7/ Cambridge (Boston), FAM/ Inv. 2002.95.62 & 2002.95.63/ IT/ R4199 & R4200.433.

c1700 GALEOTTI, Sebastiano*:* Venus et Adonis assis sur les nuages soutenues par des angelots/ DR/ d/ 27x20.5/ Paris, MdL/ Inv. 18199, rect/ IT/ R10022.434.
c1700 GAULLI (BACICCIO), Giovanni Battista: Venus dissuading Adonis from the hunt/ PA/ oc/ 180.3x148.6/ Burghley House, PrC/ Inv. #/ R10417V.435.
Preparatory DR/ d/ 23.1x16.8/ Windsor, RCo/ Inv. 6761?-155/ Blunt 1971, p.86/ R10399V.436.
c1712 DARDARONE, Giuseppe: Venus y Adonis/ FR// ?/ Palma: PaCV/ Inv. <Sala de Neptune y Anfitrite>/ Navarrete 2005, p.160, fig.282/ R11046.437.; *another FR of same subject is much deteriorated.*
c1850 GALLI, Antonio: Adonis forlader Venus (Adonis leaving Venus)/ SC/ p/ 23x43/ Kopenhagen, NCG/ Inv. 1045 a/ IT/ R7596V.438.

- ## Venus reclining

c1580 CAMBIASO, Luca: Venere e Adone/ PA/ oc/ 159x117/ Napoli, MdC/ Inv. Q 777/ Zuffi 2001,p.285/ R4510.439.
c1625 VAROTARI, Alessandro : Venus versucht, Adonis von der Jagd abzuhalten (Venus trying to hold Adonis back)/ PA/ oc/ 170x145/ Braunschweig, HAU/ Inv.693/ IT/ R4431.440.
c1625 VAROTARI, Alessandro : Venere e Adone/ PA/ oc/ ?/ PaMO/ Inv. E65790iccd/ IT/ R8938.441.
c1650 CANTARINI, Simone : Venere, Amore e Adone/ PR/ e/ 11,7x17,4/ Bologna, PNa/ Inv.#/ Bartsch 42 (19,2) 1981,p.108,n°33(143)/ R3592.442. *Also in Cambridge, FWM/ Inv. 24.I.2-47 ; Glasgow, HMAG/ Inv. 15394; S.F., FAM/ Inv. 1963.30.36524.*
c1650 ROMANELLI, Giovanni Francesco: Vénus avec Adonis partant à la chasse/ PA/ oc/ 182x136/ Paris, MdL/ Inv. MI 882/ IT/ R2442.443.
Also in SF, FAM.
1705-06 RICCI, Sebastiano : Venus and Adonis/ PA/ oc/ 70x40/ Orléans, MBA/ Inv.#/ IT/ R1507.444.

- ## Venus seated

c1550 CAMBIASO, Luca: Venus und Adonis / DR/ d/ 24,3x19,1/ Göttingen, KSU/ Inv. H 325/ IT/ R4502. 445.
c1550 CAMBIASO, Luca: Venus and Adonis/ DR/ ?/ ?/ Cincinnati, ULPC/ Inv. #/ Damian 2005, p.37, fig.7/ R10227.446.
c1550 CAMBIASO, Luca: Venere e Adone *(with Cupid)*/ PA/ oc/ ?/ Genova, GPB/ Inv. #/ Damian 2005, p36/ R354.447.
Replicas: Roma, GNB/ Inv.810/ IT; *Damian refers to another replica, PrC; (wor)/ 154.9 x 101.6/ S.F./NY, BON 7.11.07/ Sl. 15410-4/ IT/ R11076.448.*
1553 TIZIANO, Vecellio: Venus and Adonis /PA/ oc/ 186x207/ Madrid, MNP/ Inv. P422/ Berenson 1958, p.193; Mai ed. 2001, p.299 n°2/ R011.449. *More than thirty painted and engraved versions.*
*Replicas: **c1555** (wor ?)/ PA/ oc/ 160x196.5/ LA, JPG/ Inv. 92.PA.42/ Boccardo ed. 2004 p.312-313, n°71/ R297 ;**1559**/ PA/ / 160x197/ CH, PrC/ Inv.#/ Goffen 1997,p.251, n°148/ R5546.450. ;*
***c1560** (quite different) / PA/ oc/ 107x136/ Washington, NGA/ Inv. 1942.9.84/* Berenson 1958, p.198/ *R818.451.*
***c1570**/ PA/ oc/ 106,7x133,4/ NY, MMA/ Inv. 49.7.16/* Berenson 1958, p.195, pl.997:/ *R3596.451.;*
***c1555** (wor)/ PA/ oc/ 177.1 x 187.2/ London, NGa/ Inv. NG34/ Berenson 1958, p.192; Gould 1975, p.297-298 ; Anonymous 1989, Vol.I, p.956;Goffen 1997,p.252, n°149/ R5547.452.*
c1555 TIZIANO, Vecellio: Venere e Adone con capello rosso (with the red hunter's cap)/ PA/ oc/ 187x134/ Roma, GNB/ Inv. 922/ Mochi Onori 2001, p.54-55, n°34 / R352.453.
*Replica (or copy?):**c1555** (wor) (without Cupid in the picture) /PA/ oc/ 150x200/ London, SOT 10.7.'03/ Sl. L03031-4/ IT/ R5881.454.*
c1555 CARAGLIO, Giovanni J.: Venere e Adone (aft TIZIANO)/2PR/ e/ 40.8x32.2+41.8x33.2/ Roma, ING/ Inv. FC71096+97 (reverse)/ Catelli Isola 1976, p.34-35, nr.12+13/ R10479.455.

c1555 ROTA, Martino: Vénus tâchant de retenir Adonis (aft TIZIANO)/ PR// 24,1x17,5/ Wien, ALB/ Inv.#/ Catelli Isola 1976, p.53, nr.80 ; Bartsch 33 (16,2) 1979, p.117,n°108(282)/ R4930.456. *Also in Cambridge, FWM/ Inv. 22.I.9-33; Roma, ING with text at the bottom.*
c1555 ZELOTTI, Battista: Venere e Adone (aft TIZIANO)/ PA/ ?/ ?/ Dresden, SKS/ Inv. 182/ Berenson 1958, p.210/ R9629V.457.
1559 SANUTO, Giulio: Venus and Adonis (aft TIZIANO)/ PR/ e/ 53,5x41,1/ SF, FAM/ Inv. 1963.30.36160/ IT/ R887.458.
c1561 VERONESE, Paolo Caliari: Venere che tenta di dissuadere Adone dalla caccia/ PA/ oc/ 122x178/ Augsburg, SGK/ Inv.#/ Mai ed., 2001, p.300-01 n°34/ R1621.459.
1570-72 MACCHIETTI, Girolamo: Venere e Adone/ PA/ ow/ Ø17/ Firenze: PaP/ Inv. 6266/ Sframeli 2003,p.76,n°5; Casazza 2005, p.178 n°55/ R4018.460.
c1575 NELLI, Nicolo: Venere e Adone (aft TIZIANO)/ PR/ e/ 23.9x17.4/ Venezia, MuC/ Inv. 3010+11/ Chiari 1982, p.67, nr.30/ R10403.461.
c1585 PEROLI, G.B.&F.: Venus y Adonis/ FR// ?/ El Viso, PaM/ Inv. Conserjeria/ Navarrete 2005, p.50, fig.80/ R11018.462.
c1625 ROSA detto PACECCO, Francesco: Venus and Adonis/ PA/ ?/ ?/ Besançon, MBA/ Inv. #/ Labrot 1992, p.37,781, fig.11,Col. Carafa 1648-49/ R10002.463.
1640 FANELLI, Francesco: Venus and Adonis/ SC/ z/ 15/ London, GAL/ Inv.#/ IT/ R9238.464.
c1650 DI LIONE, Andrea: Venere e Adone/ PA/ oc/ ?/ Milano, POR 26.5.04/ Sl.?-42/ IT/ R10278.465.
c1650 (att) LAURI, Filippo: Vénus voulant détourner Adonis de la chasse : il tient une lance et un chien/ DR/ d/ 14.9x20.9/ Paris, MdL/ Inv. 3290, rect/ IT/ R10023.466.
c1700 CALANDRUCCI, Giacinto: Adonis partant à la chasse/ DR/ d/ 28x21/ Paris, MdL/ Inv. 15313, rec/ IT/ R10006.467.
c1700 CHIARI, Giuseppe: Venus and Adonis/ PA/ ?/ ?/ Stamford, BH/ Inv.#/ Kerber 1968, fig.8/ R11102. 468.
c1700 LUTI, Benedetto: Adonis takes his leave from Venus/ DR/ d/ 18.4x23.3/ Chatsworth, DCo/ Inv. 629/ Jaffé 1993, p.83-84, Cat.88/ R10390.469.
1707-08 RICCI, Sebastiano: Commiato di Venere da Adone (The parting of Venus from Adonis)/ FR// ?/ Firenze, PaP/ Inv. #/ IT/ R8996.470. *Preliminary DR exists.*
c1715 TREVISANI, Francesco: Venere e Adone/ PA/ oc/ 194x170/ Roma, GNB/ Inv. P C8330/ Anonymous 1998, p.242-243,n°119/ R4491.471.
c1725 (wor) FRANCESCHINI, Marcantonio : Venere ed Adone/ PA/ oc/ 246x207/ Venezia, SEM 4.7.04/ Sl. ?-53/ IT/ R11690.472.
c1750 AMIGONI, Jacopo: Venus and Adonis/ PA/ oc/ 45x75/ Venezia, GdA/ Inv.#/ Romanelli 1997, p.665 ; Calabrese, 2003, p.309/ R1279.473.
1750 SCACCIATI, Andrea: Venus and Adonis (aft TROTTI, Giovanni Battista) (from the series *Disegni originali d'eccelenti pittori...*)/ PR/ e/ 37,7x49,6/ SF, FAM/ Inv. 1963.30.36164/ IT/ R888.474.
c1780 GIANI, Felice: Venere e Adone (Adonis is being restrained by his lover)/ PA/ oc/ 43x30/ UN, PrC/ Inv.#/ IT/ R2079.475.
1787 GREGORI, Fernando: Venere e Adone (aft TIZIANO)/ PR/ eu/ 20.4x24.8/ Venezia, MuC/ Inv. 4439/ Chiari 1982, p.157, nr.180/ R10405.476.

o Adonis dying

c1425 PISANELLO, Antonio Pisano, detto: Vénus d'un sarcophage d'Adonis/ DR/ d/ 19.5x27.5/ Paris, MdL/ Inv. 2397, verso/ IT/ R10035.477.

c1510 ASPERTINI, Amico: Adonis relief /DR Roman sarcophagus Morte di Adone, Mantova, PaD/ ?/ ?/ Baden-Würtemberg, ScW/ Inv.ff.34v-35 / Bober & Rubinstein 1986, p.64-65, fig.21a-i/ R4593.478. *Bober & Rubinstein r(1986) refer to more drawing-representations: GENTILE da FEBRIANO/ Paris,MdL/ Inv.2397; 1358 PISANELLO/ Berlin, KSK; ANONYMOUS/ Milano,BiA/ Inv.F265,inf.91; FRANCO, Battista/ Torino, BiR/ Inv.cart.33 n°34;Cod.PIGHIANUS/?/ Inv.f258.*

1546 ALCIATO, Andrea : Amuletum Veneris (The amulet of Venus: Venus covered lifeless Adonis with leaves of lettuce) (*Emblematum libellus/ pub Mantius, Venezia)*/ IL/ LXXVII/ IT/ R6045.479.

c1560 BEZZI, Giovanni Francesco: La mort d'Adonis/ DR/ d/ 25.8x40.5/ Paris, MdL/ Inv. RF 52605r/ IT/ R10005V.480.

c1585 TINTORETTO, Domenico: Venus lamenting the death of Adonis/ PA/ oc/ 109x143/ Tucson, UAM/ Inv. 61.13.18/ IT/ R11445V.481.

c1650 DANEDI-MONTALTO, Giovanni Stefano: Morte di Adone/ PA/ ?/ ?/ Milano, CaS/ Inv.#/ Zuffi 2001,p.287/ R4512.

1650 GIMIGNANI, Giacinto: Venere piange la morte di Adone/ PA/ oc/ 116x141/ Pistoia, MCR/ Inv.#/ IT/ R8587V.482.

c1650 PALUMBO, Onofrio: Venus and Adonis/ PA/ ?/ 205x264/ Aix-e/P, MuG/ Inv. #/ Habert 1989, 131:59/ R11015.483.

c1750 VELLANI, Francesco: Venus *(leaving her chariot drawn by swans)* and Adonis/ PA/ oc/ ?/ Modena, GaE/ Inv.#/ IT/ R8993.484.

1787 CANOVA, Antonio **:** Morte di Adone (Venere e Adone)/ SC/ q/ 14x24x15/ Possagno, CdC/ Inv.#/ Stefani 2003, p.52, nr.44/ R10160.485.

1787 CANOVA, Antonio: Venere e Adone/ SC/ q/ 27.5x26/Possagno, CdC/ Inv.#/ Stefani 2003, p.52, n°45/ R3868.486.

*Replica **c1789** SC/ q/ 145?x104?x183?/Possagno, CdC/ Inv.#/ Stefani 2003, p.55, n°49/ R2564.487.*

• with animal(s)

c1600 PALMA Il Giovane, Jacopo Negretti: Venus und Adonis/ DR/ d/ 23,2 x 36,5/ Wien, DOR 24.4.'07/ Sl.-315/ IT/ R9399.488.

c1600 TEMPESTA, Antonio: Death of Adonis (from the series Landscapes with Mythological Subjects)/ PR/ e/ 13,7x19,1/ A'dam, RPK/ Inv. #/ Bartsch 36(17,3) 1983, p.114,n°616(153)/ R4960.489.

c1600 TEMPESTA, Antonio: Death of Adonis (from the series *Ovid's Metamorphoses)/* PR/ e/ 9,7x11,5/ London, BMu/ Inv. #/ Bartsch 36(17,3) 1983, p.58,n°735(151)/ R4958.490.

1637 RIBERA, Jusepe de : Venere scopre il corpo di Adone (Venus discovers the body of Adonis)/ PA/ oc/ 197x265/ Roma, GCi/ Inv.#/ exh/ R009.491.

1644 DELLA BELLA, Stefano: Venus *(arriving in chariot)* et Adonis *(Jeu des Fables: n°525)*/ IL/ e/ 8,3x5,1/ De Vesme 1971, Vol.I:105-107; Vol.II:108-113/ R8274.492.

c1700 FOGGINI, Giovanni Battista: Venus betrauert Adonis (Venus weeping Adonis)/ SC/ z/ 41,5/ München, BNM/ Inv. R3237/ Mai ed. 2001, p.498, n°B15/ R1576.493. *Replica : **c1690** /SC/ p/ ?/ München, BNM/ Inv. 35.*

c1700 PELLEGRINI, Giovanni Antonio : Adone e Venere piangente (Adonis and weeping Venus)/ PA/ oc/ 116x128/ Venezia, CaR/ Inv.124-col.Martini/ Martini, 2002, p.224,227, n°183/ R965.494.

c1750 (cir) CARLONE, Carlo Innocenzo : Death of Adonis/ PA/ oxc/ 24x41/ London, SOT 7.12.'88/ Sl.?/ IT/ R6256.495.

1778 CAMPANELLA, Angelo: Venus and wounded Adonis pl.II (aft Anton Raphael Mengs)/ PR/ er/ 50.5x64.1/ Wien, ALB/ Inv. 46122/ Joyce 1983; Roettgen 2001, p.248-251, fig.80b <aft FR LO in roman home near Villa Peretti-Negroni (Stazione Termini), Roma>/ R11011.*496.*

Plate II of XII; at auction among a set of seven/ London, CHR 9.3.06/ Sl. 7198-220/ IT/ R5924.497.; copy Leo von Klenze/ PA/ u g/ ?/ München, Stadtmuseum.

• with animal(s) and Cupid(s)

c1577 ZUCCHI, Jacopo: Morte di Adone/ PA/ ow/ 50x39/ Arezzo, MCV/ Inv.#/ Sframeli 2003,p.78/ R4017. 498.

c1600 (cir) CESARI, Giuseppe: Vénus et Adonis/ PA/ oc/ 54x71/ Dijon, MuM/ Inv. 1980 E 8/ IT/ R2445. 499.

c1600 MORO, Giulio del: La mort d'Adonis/ DR/ d/ 27.2x21/ Paris, MdL/ Inv. 12095, rec/ IT/ R10025. 500.

c1600 PALMA Il GIOVANE, Jacopo: Venus and Adonis/ PA/ oc/ 168,9x120,3/ NY, CHR 6.4.'06/ Sl. 1620/65/ IT/ R6081.501.

1603-1604 DOMENICHINO, Domenico: Morte di Adone/ FR// 174x330/ Roma, PaFa/ Inv. E29092iccd/ ITiccd/ R1531.502.

*Preparatory DR/ d/ ?/ Windsor, RCo/ Inv. 2094verso/ Blunt 1971, p.81, Cat.162/ R10397V.*503.

Replica: PA?//?/Genova, PDP/ Inv.#/ IT/ R4425.504.

c1625 TESTA, Pietro: Vénus pleurant la mort d'Adonis/ DR/ d/ 32.1x21.1/ Paris, MdL/ Inv. 13856, rec/ IT/ R10037.505.

c1625 TURCHI, Alessandro: Venus mit dem toten Adonis/ PA/ of/ 27,5x34/ Dresden, SKS/ Inv. 521/ Duca 1966, fig.115, p.94/ R5339.506.

Replica? Venus und Adonis/ PA/ ow/ ?/ Kassel, SKS/ Inv. #/ IT/ R10101.507.; copy 'aft': PA/ oc/ 46x58/ London, SOT 10.12.'01/ Sl. W01408-371/ IT/ R5321.

c1639 SAVONANZI, Emilio : Morte di Adone/ PA/ oc/ 146x185/ Roma, MuC/ Inv. 315/ IT/ R3741.508.

c1650 RIBERA, Jusepe de : Death of Adonis/ PA/ oc/ 185,4x238,8/ Cleveland, MuA/ Inv. 1965.19/ IT/ R7409.509.

c1675 (att) BERRETONI, Niccolo: Venus lamenting the dead of Adonis/ DR/ d/ oval 24.5x33.9/ London, VAM/ Inv. Dyce 208/ Ward-Jackson 1979,Vol.II, p.24-25, n°634/ R11127.510.

c1740 COSTANZI, Placido: Adone morente (Adonis dying – *Venus watching in the sky*)/ PA/?/? / Firenze, PrC/ Inv.#/ Anonymous, 2004, p.126-128,n°43a/ R4490.511.

1780 CADES, Giuseppe: Venus che piange Adone (Venus weeping over the body of Adonis)/ DR/d/20,5x40/London, CHR 5.7.'05/Sl.7066-122/IT/R3664.512.

• with attendant(s) and Cupid(s)

c1511 PIOMBO, Sebastiano del: Morte di Adone/ PA/ oc/ 189x285/ Firenze, GdU/ Inv.916/ Berenson 1958, p.168, pl.704 ; Berti, 1979, p.105/ R428.513.

c1515 ROMANO, Giulio : La mort d'Adonis/ DR/ d/ 30.5x62.1/ Paris, MdL/ Inv. 3490, rec/ IT/ R10034. 514. *Copy (aft) DR/ du/ 32.2x57.5/ Paris, MdL/ Inv.3660/ Massari 1993, p.XXXII, Tav.21 Tav.20/ R3545.*

1534-36 ROSSO FIORENTINO, Giovanni Battista: Mort d'Adonis (Galerie François 1°)/ FR// ?/ Fontainebleau, MNC/ Inv.#/ Berenson 1963, p.195 ; Porcheron-Felsing 1983, p.297,368 fig.102/ R4148.515.

c1542 (att) FANTUZZI, Antonio: Death of Adonis (aft ROSSO)/ PR/ /29,1x42,2/ London, BMu/ Inv.#/ Bartsch 33 (16,2) 1979, p.344,n°69(402)/ R4943.516.

c1550 BORDONE, Paris: Morte di Adone/ PA/ ?/ ?/ UN/ Inv.#/ Berenson 1958, p.51, pl.1127/ R9611.517.

c1550 PORTA, Guglielmo della: Venere e Adone/ RE/ z/ 13.5x14 octagonal/ Wien, KHM/ Inv. 7770/ Casazza 2005, p.178-79, fig 53/ R8831.518.

c1550 PUPINI, Biagio, dalle Lame, detto: La mort d'Adonis/ DR/ d/ 19.1x30/ Paris, MdL/ Inv. 8871, rec/ IT/ R10036.519.

c1570 CAMBIASO, Luca: Death of Adonis *(without cupids)*/ DR/ d/ 27,8x37,5/ London, CIA/Inv. D.1952.RW.607/ IT/ R4508.520.

*(att or wor but with cupids) : Lamenting the death of Adonis/ PR/ e/ 25,4x29,5/ NY, MMA/Inv. 17.37.33/ IT/ R1642.521.; **1576?** Venus und die drei Grazien beweinen den Tod des Adonis/ PR/ e/ 25x29.4/ Zürich, ETH/ Inv. D888/ Matile 2003, p.98-99, n°40; probably related to a PA/ LO in Col. Gian Vicenzo Imeriale, Genova.*

c1570 (att-wor) CAMBIASO, Luca: Venus betrauert Adonis (Venus lamenting Adonis)/ DR/ d/ 24,5x31,8/ Frankfurt, GAL/ Inv.#/ IT/ R4507.522.

c1575 CAMBIASO, Luca : Venere e Adone/ PA/ ?/ ?/ Genova, PaRo/ Inv.#/exh, IT/ R8890.523.
c1575 MAZZONI, Giulio: Morte di Adone/ FR/ op/ ?/ Roma, PaS/ Inv. E32269iccd/ IT/ R8942.524.
c1600 SCARSELLINO: Ippolito: Venere ed Adone/ PA/ oc/ 98x118/ Roma, GaB/ Inv. 212/ Berenson 1968, p.391; Bentini 2003, p.273, fig.199/ R366.525.
c1625 FURINI, Francesco: Venere e Adone/ PA/ ?/ ?/ Budapest, MFA/ Inv.#/ IT/ R11710.526.
c1650 CERVELLI, Federico : Venus crying over the death of Adonis/ PA/ ?/ ?/ Venezia, FQS/ Inv.#/ IT artresource/ R8536.527.
c1650 GUERCINO, Giovane Francesco Barbieri: Vénus et Adonis (?)/ DR/ d/ 26,3x39,5/ Bayonne, MuB/ Inv. NI 1589/ IT/ R7167.528.
c1684 GIORDANO, Luca: Death of Adonis/ FR//?/ Firenze, PMR/ Inv.#/ IT/ R6309.529.
c1700 FRANCESCHINI, Marcantonio: Venus discovers the body of Adonis/ PA/ oc/ 480x289/ Wien, LMu/ Inv. 5/ Miller 1991, p.xi, pl.XIV, p.84-85, Cat.n°17/ R9816.530.
Preparatory: compositional study/ DR/ d/ 48.5x28.1/ Windsor, RCo./ Inv. 3759/ Miller 1991, p.xiv, pl.60, p.84, Cat.n°17/ R9822.531.
c1700 FRANCESCHINI, Marcantonio: Ablutions over the body of Adonis/ PA/ oc/ 176x210/ Wien, LMu/ Inv. 4/ Miller 1991, p.xi, pl.XV, p.87, Cat.n°18/ R9817.532.
c1700 RICCI, Sebastiano: Venere accorre da Adone morente/ PA/ oc/ 130x153/ Venezia, MuC/ Inv. #/ IT/ R10303.533.
1721 MEUCCI, Vincenzo: Venere e Adone/ PA/ oc/ 268x178/ Firenze, PrC/ Inv.#/ Vezzosi 2003/ R4138. 534.
1790-95 APPIANI, Andrea: Morte di Adone/ PA/ oc/ 81x112 oval/ Milano, PAB/ Inv. 589, Sala: XXXVII/ Baini 2006, p.356, Cat.589/ R3107.535.
Preparatory DR/ d/ 13,7x15,8/ Milano, BiA/ Inv. F 284 inf. n. 14/ IT/ R3110.536.

- **with Cupid**

c1510 SESTO, Cesare da: Adonis dying in the arms of Venus/ DR/ ?/ ?/ NY, PML/ Inv. 50/ Bober & Rubinstein,1986, p.65,#22b/ R4595.537.
c1525 (att) PERINO DEL VAGA, Pietro Bonnacorsi detto: Venere trova Adone morte/ PA/ ow/ ∅75/ Firenze, GdU/ Inv. S.M&C 118/ Gli Uffizi-Catalogo Generale 1979,p.405, P.1154/ R.10155.538.
c1526 CARAGLIO, Iacopo: Venere e Adone morte (aft PERINO DEL VAGA)/ PR/ e/ 17,7x13,2/ Roma, ING/ Inv.FC5933/ Massari 1989,p.166-7,n°67;Bartsch 28 C (15,1) 1995,p.203-4,n°2802.066/ R3495.539. *Also in Bologna, PNa with text: 'Parla Venere sopra Adoni morte'; Berlin, BAS 29.11.07/ Sl. 090-5543/ IT.*
1536 PERINO DEL VAGA, Pietro: Venere e Cupido piangono Adone morente/ PA/ oc/ 120,5x159/ Firenze, MdC/ Inv. 1881 IV 353 1890 7620/ IT/ R8578V.540.
c1550 CAMBIASO, Luca: Venus and Adonis/ DR/ d/ 38,1x28,4/ SF, FAM/ Inv. 1963.24.189/ IT/ R728. 541.
1565-69 CAMBIASO, Luca: Venere e Adone (Morte di Adone)/ PA/ oc/ 130x94/ St.Petersburg, HMu/ Inv.#/IT/R3091.542.
1570-75 CAMBIASO, Luca: Vénus pleurant Adonis/ DR/ d/ 34x24.3/ Paris, MdL/ Inv. 9326, rect/ IT/ R10008.543.
Replica: (att) Tod des Adonis (Death of Adonis)/ DR/ d/ 33x24/ Frankfurt, GAL/Inv.#/IT/R4505.544.
c1575 CAMBIASO, Luca: Vénus pleurant Adonis (Venus left)/ DR/ d/ 35.2x24.1/ Paris, MdL/ Inv. 9327, rect/ IT/ R10009.545. *Several replicas: 27.8x20.7/ Paris, MdL/ Inv. 9328, rect/ IT/ R10010.545.;*
(Venus right)/33.2x22.5/ Paris, MdL/ Inv. 9330, rect/ IT/ R10016.546.;
(Venus right)/38.1x25.6/ Paris, MdL/ Inv. 9331, rect/ IT/ R10017.547.
c1580 CAMBIASO, Luca: Morte di Adone/ PA/ oc/ ?/ Moscow, PrC/ Inv.#/ Zuffi 2001,p.285/ R4511.548.
Consignment (?) from Roma, GNB/ Inv. E32610iccd.
c1625 BIANCHI, Isidoro: La morte di Adone/ PA/ ?/ ?/ Torino, PrC/ Griseri 1994,p.195,n°6/ R4296.549.
c1630 ALGARDI, Alessandro: Adonis dying in the arms of Venus/ SC/ z/ 47/ Paris, MAD/ Inv. Gr.121/ Mai ed. 2001, p.495-96, n°B13/ R8486.550.
c1640 CANTARINI, Simone : Vénus déplorant la mort d'Adonis/ DR/ d/ 38x26.1/ Paris, MdL/ Inv. 8937, rect/ IT/ R10018.551.

c1700 FRANCESCHINI, Marcantonio: Morte di Adone/ PA/ oc/ 31,6x45/ Roma, GNB/ Inv. E61959iccd/ Cicinelli A & Vasco Rocca S (1978), Vol.I, p.163/ R8903.552.
c1760 TIEPOLO, Giambattista: Venus and Adonis/ DR/ d/ 40,8x28,5/ NY, PrC/ Inv.#/ IT/ R7160.553.
c1775 GANDOLFI, Gaetano: Venere e Adone/ DR// 38,6x31/Bologna, PNa/ Inv. 3695/ Faietti 1998, p.316-7/ R3482.554.
c1806 MONTI, Gaetano: Venere e Amore piangono l'estinto Adone/ SC/ p/ 67x131x8/ Milano, VBB/ Inv. GAM 278/ IT/ R11716V.555.

- **with cupids**

1560-66 ZANGUIDI, Jacopo : Vénus conduite par l'Amour auprès d'Adonis mort/ PA/ oc/ 120x92/ Paris, MdL/ Inv. R.F.1995-8/ IT/ R551.556.
c1575 PENNI, Lorenzo: Morte di Adone/ PR/ e/ 49,1x37,1/ Roma, ING/ Inv. FC71099/ Massari 1989, p.320-321,n°118/ R3504.557.
c1575 VERONESE, Paolo Caliari: Venus mourning Adonis/ PA/ oc/ 145 x 173.5/ Stockholm, NMK/ Inv. NM 4414/ Berenson 1958, p.140/ R5806.558.
c1650 ALBANI, Francesco: Death of Venus/ DR/ d/ 18.9x26.5/ London, BMu/ Inv. JRC256/ Royalton-Kisch et al. 1996, p.96-97, Cat.46/ R10383.559. *Possibly a preparatory DR for a LO PA.*
c1650 (cir) ALBANI, Francesco: Venus and Adonis *(Venus standing on chariot with swans, many cupids around)*/ PA/ oc/ 132.7x93.3/ London, CHR 26.04.'06/ Sl.5013-174/ IT/ R6280.560.
c1650 RUSCHI, Francesco: Venere piange la morte di Adone I/ PA/ oc/ ?/ Milano, POR 26.5.04/ Sl.?-41/ IT/ R10280.561.
Replica: PA/ oc/ 118x147/ Venezia, SMCA 9.7.06/ Sl.?-45/ IT/ R10789.562.
1683-85 GAULLI (BACICCIO), Giovanni Battista: Death of Adonis I/ PA/ oc/ 153x122.5/ Oberlin, AMAM/ Inv. 1966.2/ Enggass 1964, p.133, fig.43 / R10287.563.
Preparatory DR/ d/ 23.9x16.8/ London, BMu/ Inv. 5211-71/ R10416V.564.
c1685 GAULLI (BACICCIO), Giovanni Battista: Death of Adonis II/ PA/ oc/ 147.3x116.2/ Puerto Rico, MAP/ Inv. #/ R10418V.565.
c1700 VACCARO, Nicola : Venere ed Adone/ PA/ oc/ 51.5x64.5/ Milano, POR 23.11.06/ Sl. ? -322a/ IT/ R10275.566.
c1715-16 SOLDANI-Benzi, Massimiliano : Venus and Adonis/ SC/ z/ 46,4x49x34,2/ LA, JPG/ Inv. 93.SB.4/ Holtman 1997, p.262/ R315.567.
Replica in Baltimore, WAG/ Inv. 54.677/ IT/ R8888.568.
c1722 AGRICOLA, Gioacchino : Venere e Adone (*dying*)/ FR// ?/ Roma, PaBo/ Inv. E42219iccd/ IT/ R8912.569.
1773 ROSSI, Mariano : Vénus et Adonis mort/ PA/ oc/ 37,5x49/ Paris, CHR 26.11.'05/ Sl. 5422 –282/ IT/ R5240.570.
1780-1800 GANDOLFI, Gaetano: Vénus découvrant le corps d'Adonis/ DR/ d/ 19,4x14,6/ Ottawa, MBA/ Inv. 30048/ IT/ R7020.571.

7. Venus and Anchises, Aeneas
(see also 15. Venus and Vulcan)

Anchises

c1550 BORDONE, Paris : Vénus et Anchise (?) (Représentation d'un couple mythologique)/ PA/ ?/ 130x124/ Paris, MdL/ Inv.125/ IT/ R554.572.
c1580 CARRACCI, Agostino: Anchises and Venus/ DR/ d/ 37x25,5/ Oxford, CrC/ Inv.930/ Pignatti 1977,n°57; Grafton 2003,n°14/ R4281.573. *Preparatory drawings for FR by CARRACCI Annibale.*
1597-1601 CARRACCI, Annibale: Venus et Anchise, genus unde latinum/ FR/ / ?/ Roma, PaFa/ Damisch 1997, p .220/ R1586.574.
c1650 GARGIULO, Domenico: Venus mit Amor und einer männlichen Figur (aft Ag.CARRACCI)/ DR/ e/ 19.5x21.7/ Berlin, KSK/ Inv. KdZ 24095 / IT/ R10110.575.
1657 CESIO, Carlo: Venus and Anchises (The Lovers Venus and Anchises, pl. I from the series The Farnese Gallery, 1657 by Annibale CARRACCI) / PR/ e/ 23,3x21,6/ NY, MMA/ Inv.#/ Bartsch 47 (21,1) 1983, p.53,n°21(109); Bartsch 47 C,Part 1 (21,1) 1987p.80-81,#4705.021 S3/ R739.576. *In many places*

Aeneas

o Aeneas wounded and nursed by Venus

c1640 TESTA, Pietro: Venere guarisce le ferite di Enea (Venus heals the wounds of Aeneas)/ PR/ e/ 37,1x34,9/ Madrid, ASF/ Inv. 225/ Perez Sancho 1977, n°38 Coll.Filippo V/ R3758.577.
1646-47 ROMANELLI, Giovanni Francesco: Vénus versant le dictame sur la blessure d'Enée/ PA/ oc/ 160x217/ Paris, MdL/ Inv. 579/ IT/ R616.578.
c1670 GIORDANO, Luca: Enea curato da Venere (Aeneas nursed by Venus)/ PA/ oc/ 171x132/ Novara, BPN/ Inv.#/ IT/ R2609.579.

o Aeneas escaping from Troy

1663 MITELLI, Giuseppe Maria : Venus leading Aeneas out of the Flames, plate 4 of L'Enea Vagante Pitture dei Caracci (Wanderings of Aeneas painted by the Carracci), from of a set of twenty prints after the paintings (frescos) by Ludovico, Annibale, and Agostino Carracci in the Palazzo Fava, Bologna/ PR/ e/ 24,8x42,6/ Bologna, CdR/ Inv.#/ Bartsch 42 (19,2) 1981, p.325,n°50(290)/ R1389.580. *Also: Glasgow, HMAG, Inv. 10748; Paris, ENSBA/ Inv Est.9197; SF, FAM/Inv. 1993.63.63.5.*
c1730 (cir) CONCA, Sebastiano: Venus appearing to Aeneas urging him to escape from burning Troy/ PA/ oc/ 97,5x137/ London, SOT 11.12.'03/Sl. L03033-25/IT/R5480.581.

o Aeneas getting arms from Venus (see also Venus and Vulcan)

b1626 GATTI, Oliviero: Venus delivering arms to Aeneas (from the *'Emblemata' of Paolo Maccio.LXII*)/ PR // 10,6x8,6/ Inv.#/ Bartsch 41 (19,1) 1981, p.226,n°106(65) / R4975.582.
1626 (att) ABBIATI, Filippo: Venus arms Aeneas/ DR// ?/ Milano, BiA/ Inv. F 254 inf. n. 1626/ IT/ R8721.
c1640 TESTA, Pietro: Venere consegna le armi ad Enea (Venus gives arms to Aeneas)/ PR/ e/ 39,1x41,1/ Roma, ING/ Inv. FC122431/ Bartsch 45 (20,2) 1982, p.146,n°24(221) ; Bartsch 45 C (20,) 1990, p.152,n°4506.024; Massari 1989, p.520-21,n°213/ R2592.583. *In many other places; ; Berlin, BAS 29.11.07/ Sl. 090-5826. Reverse PR/ d/ 13,9x18/ Pescia, MuC; also: Lyon, BiM; Frankfurt, SKI.*

1648-1653 GEMIGNANI, Giacinto: Venere indica sopra le armi ad Enea/ FR// ?/ Roma, PDP/ Inv. E45829iccd/ IT/ R8899.584.
c1675 GAULLI (BACICCIO), Giovanni Battista: Venus presenting arms to Aeneas/ DR/ d/ 23.1x37.7/ PrC/ Inv. Cat.n°45/ IT, exh Washington, NGA/ R11693.585.
c1680-82 GIORDANO, Luca : Venus giving arms to Aeneas/ PA/ oc/ 227,3x199,4/ Boston, MFA/ Inv. 1984.409/ IT/ R2016.586.
1744 RUSCA, Bartolomeo: Venus entraja las armas a Eneas/ FR// ?/ Segovia, GSI/ Inv. Sala 1/ Navarrete 2005, p.113, fig.200/ R11025.587.
1748 BATONI, Pompeo: Venus zeigt Aeneas die Waffen des Vulcans (Venus presenting Aeneas with armour forged by Vulcan)/ PA/ oc/ 99x74/ Wien, LMu/ Inv.G163/ IT/ R3141.588.
c1750 GIAQUINTO, Corrado : Venus presenting arms to Aeneas/ PA/ oc/ 153x115/ Durham, TBM/ Inv. B.M.568/ IT/ R8547.589.
c1775 GANDOLFI, Gaetano : Venus receiving the arms of Aeneas from Vulcan/ PA/ oc/ 61,6x80/ London, CHR 6.7.'06/ Sl. 7253-43/ IT/ R6966.590. *Replicas: Detroit, DIA; Stuttgart, SGa.*
c1785 AGRICOLA, Luigi: Venus giving arms to Aeneas/ PA /oc/ 46 x 25.7/ Cambridge,FWM/ Inv.PD.36-1992/ IT/ R4002.591.

o Venus appearing to Aeneas

c1450 GIOVANNI di TOMMASO, Apollonio di: Aeneas & Achates guided by Venus/ ILL/ Vergil-Codex/ ?/ Firenze, BiR/ Inv. 492 fol97r/ IT/ R11599V.592.
c1460 GIOVANNI di TOMMASO, Apollonio di: Neptun brings the sea to rest and Aeneas and Achates arrive in North Africa, Venus watching in the sky/ PA/ cassone/ ?/ New Haven, YUG/ Inv. #/ IT/ R11602V.593.
c1500 BRESCIA, Giovanni da: Aeneas and Achates meeting Venus disguised as a huntress, beneath a sky with a flight of swans. Illustrations to the Aeneid, (aft RAIMONDI)/ PR/ e/ 24,3x17,8/ London, BMu/ Inv.#/ Bartsch 25 C (13,2) 1984, p.348-9,n°2511.025/ R4803.594.
1508 RAIMONDI, Marcantonio: Venus appearing to Aeneas/ PR/ e/ ?/ Washington, NGA/ Inv. 1941.1.64/ IT/ R2748.595. *Also in Cambridge, FWM/ Inv. P.5346-R.*
c1574 CIRCIGNANI, Niccolo & PANDOLFI, Giannantonio : Vénus en chasseresse apparaît à Énée et Achate (Venus disguised as a huntress appearing…) / FR// ?/ Castiglione, PdC/ Inv.#/ IT/ R2576.596.
c1650 CORTONA, Pietro da: Vénus en chasseresse apparaît à Enée (Venus disguised as a huntress appearing…)/ PA/ oc/ 127x176/ Paris, MdL/ Inv. 112/ IT/ R705.597.
c1650 GIMIGNANI, Giacinto: Venus appearing to Aeneas and Achates/ PA/ oc/ 121,7x170,3/ London, SOT 9.12.'04/ Sl. L04034-182/ IT/ R5784.598.
1653 ALLEGRINI, Francesco: Venere e Giunone decidono e concordano sul matrimonio di Enea e Dido (Venus and Juno decide and agree about the marriage of Aeneas and Dido)/ FR// ?/ Roma, PDP/ Inv. E45827iccd/ IT/ R8911.599.
1656 GIMIGNANI, Giacinto: Venere appare ad Enea e Acate sotto le sembianze di Diana (Venus appearing to Aeneas and Achates under the disguise of Diana)/ PA/ oc/ 73x97/ Milano, PrC/ Inv.#/ IT/ R2587.600.
c1664 MARATTA, Carlo: Dido and Aeneas…. in the sky Juno, Venus and Hymen/ PA/ oc/ 152.9x224/ London, NGa/ Inv. NG95/ Anonymous 1989, Vol.I, p.236/ R6545.601. *The figures and the dogs are by Carlo Maratta, and the landscape by Gaspar Dughet.*
c1700 MATTEIS, Paolo di: Vénus apparaissant à Enée/ DR/ d/ 36,3x28/ Bayonne, MuB/ Inv.#/ IT/ R2625. 602.
b1713 BALESTRA, Antonio: Venere che appare a Enea e Acate (Venus appearing to Aeneas and Acatus/ PA/ oc/ 52,5x32/ Venezia, CaR/ Inv.267 Col.Martini/ IT/ R2633.603.
Preparatory DR/ d/ 23,3x16,2/ Washington, NGA/ Inv.1982.17.2/ IT/ R2636.604. Other DR/ d/ 47,2x33,7/ Windsor/ RCo/ Inv.3744/ Blunt 1971, p.49, Cat.23 <study for PA in Pa Bonnacorsi at Macerata>.
1725 ROTARI, Pietro: Venus appearing to Achilles *(obviously an error)*(aft Antonio BALESTRA)/ PR/ e/ ?/ Washington, NGA/ Inv. 1982.17.3/ IT/ R8440V.605.

1743-44 GIAQUINTO, Corrado: Venere appare a Enea/ PA/ ?/ ?/ Roma, PaQ/ Inv.#/ IT/ R11685.606.
1757 TIEPOLO, Giambattista: L'adio di Venere a Enea (Venus appears to Aeneas on the shores of Carthage)/ FR// 230 x 180/ Vicenza, ViV/ Inv.#/ Rizzoli 1968, p.123,n°240p ; Pedrocco 2002, p.293-94, cat.236.15 / R1554.607.
Preparatory DR/ d/ 31,2x19,4/ NY, PML/ Inv. 1983.59/ IT/ R8883V.608.
c1775 (cir) GANDOLFI, Gaetano: Venus and Aeneas/ PA/ oxc/ 40x32,5/ NY, SOT 27.1.'07/ Sl. N08285-526/ IT/ R8780.609.
1938-39 SAVINIO, Alberto: Venere indica a Enea il suo destino (Venus shows Aeneas his destiny)/ 3DR/ du/ 20,8x15,5, 38x29, 66x48/ Roma, PrC/ Inv.1938-39 n°2,3,4/ Vivarelli 1996, p.287-288/ R8690, R8691, R8692.610.
With the same topic : 2 works of unknown type, sizes and location/ Inv. 1938-39, n°1, 5/ Vivarelli 1996, p.287-288/ R8689, R8693.611.

o Aeneas immortalized

c1600 TEMPESTA, Antonio: Immortalization of Aeneas (from the series *Ovid's Metamorphoses)/* PR/ e/ 9,7x11,5/ London, BMu/ Inv. #/ Bartsch 36(17,3) 1983, p.80,n°778(151)/ R4959.612.
c1650 CARPIONI, Giulio: La deification d'Enée (Immortalization of Aeneas)/ PA/ ?/ 63,5x82/ Milano, GAL/ Inv#/ IT/ R2585.613.
1651-1655 CORTONA, Pietro da: Assembly of the gods (Apotheosis of Aeneas with Jupiter looking towards Venus…)/ FR/ /?/ Roma, PaDP/ Inv.#/ IT/ R8552.614.
Preparatory DR/ d/ ?/ London, BMu/ Inv.#/ IT/ R6873.615.
c1670 GIORDANO, Luca: Aeneas immortalized/ PA/ oc/ 258x314/ Vicenza, MuC/ Inv.#/ IT/ R2616.616.
Replica 55,5x74/ Salzburg, BMu/ Inv.0014/ IT/ R2618.617.
c1761 TIEPOLO, Giambattista: Apotheosis of Aeneas (sketch for ceiling painting in the Hall of the Royal Guard in the Royal Palace, Madrid)/ PA/ oc/ 67,3x51,1/ Boston, MFA/ Inv. 27.861/ Rizzoli 1968, p;132; IT/ R2750.618.
*Replica: **c1765** /PA/ oc/ 72,2x51,1/ Cambridge-Boston, FAM/ Inv. 1949.76/ Rizzoli 1968, p;132; IT/ R8544. 619.*
1766 TIEPOLO, Giambattista: Apoteosis de Eneas, or 'Venus encargando a Vulcano las armas para Eneas', or 'Eneas conducido al templo de la immortalidad' (Apotheosis of Aeneas, or 'Venus charging Vulcan to forge the arms of Aeneas' or 'Aeneas brought to the temple of immortality')/ FR// 2300x1600/ Madrid, PaR, Salon de Alabarderos/ Inv.#/ Rizzoli 1968, p;132, n°279E ; Navarrete 2005, p.137, fig.256/ R8543.620.

8. Venus and Anteros/Cupid

Anteros

c1560 VERONESE, Paolo Caliari: Venus and Mercury present Anteros to Giove/ PA/ oc/ 150x243/ Firenze, GdU/ Inv. 9942/ / Berenson 1958, p.135/ R931.621.
c1570 CAVALLERIS, Gianbattista de : Venus seated with Eros and Antheros *(Antiquarum Statuorum Urbis Romae,pl.51*)/PR/e/?/ Bober 1986,p.62,n°17c/ R4588.622.
1657 GALESTRUZZI, Giovanni Battista: Venere con Cupido e Anteros (from 'The Antique Figural Gems' Roma/ PR// 10,7x8,5/Milano, BiA/Inv.#/ Bartsch 46 (21,1) 1982, p.234,n°293(80); Bartsch 46 C 1985, p.254,n°4606.293/ R4992.623.
c1675 LIBERI, Marco : Venere, Cupido e Anteros/ PA/ oc/ 76,5x59/ Wien, DOR/ 14.4.'05/ Sl.73/ IT/ R8353.624.

Cupid

c1500 PERUZZI, Baldassare : Venus and Cupid/ FR/ from the Villa Stati-Mattei, Roma, transferred to canvas/ 35.2x68.3/ NY, MMA/ Inv. 48.17.13/ IT/ R11278V.625.
c1500 (wor) PINTURICCHIO, Bernardino : Venus and Cupid/ FR/ ceiling from the Palace of Pandolfo Petrucci, Siena/ ?/ NY, MMA/ Inv. 14.114.22/ IT/ R11413V.626.
c1525 ROMANINO, Girolamo di Romano, detto : Venus and Cupid/ FR/ / ?/ Trento, CaB/ Berenson 1968, p.369/ R9996V.627. *Berenson refers to two FRs of the same topic/ one as a lunette, one as a window embrasure.*
c1525 VERONESE, Bonifazio de'Pitati, detto : Uomo con guanti nella destra Venere e Cupido nello sfondo/ PA/ ?/ ?/ Padova, MuC/ Inv. 460/ Berenson 1958, p.45/ R9606V.628.
c1550 ABATE, Nicolo dell' : Vénus et l'Amour (Venus and Cupid) (after PRIMATICCI0/ DR)/ FR/ ?/ Fontainebleau, MNC/ Inv. PM 46/ IT/ R8033V.629.
1563 VASARI, Giorgio & LORENZI, Domenico di Benedetto: Venere e Cupido/ SC/ s/ ?/ Firenze, PaV/ Inv.#/ IT/ R8591.630.
c1575 ABONDIO, Antonio: Venus en Amor ?/ SC/ z/ 9.2x7.2/ A'dam, RMu/ Inv. BK-NM-1135/ IT/ R11277V.631.
c1575 CESARI del PALAGIO, Carlo di: Venus withholding a heart from Cupid/ SC/ z/ ?/ NY, MMA/ Inv.#/ IT/ R11616V.632.
c1575 VERONESE, Paolo Caliari: Studies of Venus with Cupid/ DR/ d/ ?/ London, BMu/ Inv. 1951, 1110. 00079/ IT/ R8438V.633.
1575-90 (att)CALIARI, Benedetto: Venus en Amor/ Pa/ oc/ 97x71/ A'dam : RMu/ Inv. SK-A-3010/ IT/ R3955.634.
c1590 NIGRONE, Giovanni Antonio: Wandbrunnen mit Venus und Amor/ ILL/ tx/ ?/ Napoli, BiN/ Inv. Ms. XII. G. 59-60/ IT/ R10097V.635.
c1600 PALMA Il Giovane, Jacopo Negretti: Venere e Amore/ DR/ d/ 146x119/ Venezia, FGC/ Inv. 29/ IT/ R10237V.636.
c1607 CARLONE, Giovanni Andrea: Venus with Cupid/ PA/ ?/ ?/ UN/ Inv. #/ IT/ R11408V.637.
c1650 ALBANI, Francesco: Venus and child (*Cupid?)*/ DR/ d/ 49.5x18.4/ Hanover, HMA/ Inv. D.947.25/ IT/ R11385V.638.
c1650 FRANCESCHINI, Baldassare: Amor and Venus/ PA/ ow/ 64x45/ Firenze, PaP/ IT/ R10108.639.

c1650 GUERCINO, Giovane Francesco: Venus and Cupid/ PA/ oc/ 77x102/ SF? FAM/ Inv. 42120/ IT/ R11358V.640.
c1675 (att) FERRI, Ciro: Venere e Amorino/ PA/ oc/ ?/ UN/ IT asta giudiziana/ R10344V.641.
c1675 LIBERI, Marco : Venus and Cupid/ PA/ ?/ ?/ Wien, ABK/ Inv.#/ Encyclopédie De L'Art 2005, p.585/ R8382V.642.
c1700 PELLEGRINI, Giovanni Antonio: Venere e Amorino/ PA/ oc/ 82x65/ Vicenza, PaT/ Inv. #/ IT/ R11484.643.
c1708 RUSCONI, Camillo: Venus and Cupid/ RE/m/ 32x47,5/ Kopenhagen, SMK/ Inv. KMS7695/ IT/ R7574V.644.
1711-24 PIAMONTINI, Giuseppe : Venus and Cupid/ SC/ z/ 37x25,4x22/ : Washington, NGA/ Inv. 1974.18.2/ IT/ R8442V.645.
Pre.?SC/ q/ ?/ Berlin, GSM/ Inv. 359/ IT/ R11613V.646.
c1750 BATONI, Pompeo: Vénus qui caresse l'Amour, dédié à son Excellence Monsieur le Prince de Voussoupoff.../PR/e/ ?/Haarlem, TMu/Inv.#/exh/R3138.647.
c1750 (att) BATTONI, Pompeo : Venus and Cupid/ PA/ oc/ 54x69/ Dublin, NGI/ Inv. 704/ IT/ R11310V. 648.
1800 MONTI, Niccolo : Venere e amorino/ PR/ l/ 47,8x31,4/ Firenze, UN/ Inv.#/ IT/ R8599V.649.
c1800 GIANI, Felice: Venus and Amor/ DR/ d/ 30.5x20.5/ Monte Carlo, GAL/ Inv.#/ IT/ R11692V.650.
c1800 SERANGELI, Gioacchino Giuseppe: Venere e Amore/ PA/ ?/18x13/ Lucerne, FIS 1996/ Inv.#/ IT/ R8317V.651.
c1880 DE ALBERTIS, Sebastiano: Venere e Cupido/ PA/ oc/ 19x26/ Milano, VBB/ Inv. GAM 2199/ IT/ R11712V.652.

o birth of Cupid / Cupid blindfolded

c1565 TIZIANO, Vecellio: Venere che benda Amore (Education of Cupid)/ PA/ oc/ 116x184/ Roma, GaB/ Inv. 170/ Berenson 1958, p.196; Panofsky 1969, fig.119, pl.LXV; Moreno 2004, p.403, n°13/ R357.653.
*Many copies; **c1660** false att VAROTARI, Dario (also false att Pietro del PO): Venus blindfolding Cupid/ PR reverse/ e/ 17,3x25/ Brescia, MuR/ Inv.#/ Bartsch 47 C 1987, p.286, n°4705.021/ R4999.654.*
c1575 BASSANO, il VECCHIO, Jacopo: The Birth of Love (The Nursing of an Infant God (?))*(Venus and Cupid)*/ PA/ oc/ 22.9x27.9/ Detroit, DIA/ Inv. 28.134/ IT/ R11307V.655.
c1575 MASTER of FLORA: Birth of Cupid/ PA/ ow/ 108x130,5/ NY, MMA/ Inv. 1941 (41.48)/ IT; Mai ed. 2001, p.98 n°8/ R4555.656.
1617 FIALETTI, Odoardo: Venus seated, blindfolding Amor (from the series 'Scherzi d'Amore'-The Sport of Love)/ PR/ e/ 15x9,5/ Roma, ING/ Inv. FC72775/ Bartsch 38 (17,5) 1983, p.214,n°16(269); Massari 1989, p.476,n°188/ R765.657. *Without text*; *with text also in Cambridge, FWM/ Inv. AD.1.18-143; London, BMu; Paris, BNF/ Inv.#/ Dunand & Lemarchand, s.d., III, p.951, fig.1478 à 1489/ R11151; SF, FAM.*
c1825 MARCHETTI, Domenico: Venere che benda Amore (aft TIZIANO)/ PR/ e/ 41.5x47.4/ Roma, ING/ Inv. FC49654/ Catelli Isola 1976, p.78, nr.334/ R10489.658.

o Cupid chastised

c1516 BRIOSCO, Andrea: Venere flagillifera o Venere che punisce Amore (Venus chastising Cupid)/ SC/ z/ 19/ Wien, KNB/ Inv.#/ Planischig 1925/ R3591.659.
c1525 BRIOSCO, Andrea: Venus chastising Cupid/ SC/ z/ 8,1x10,7/ Washington, NGA/ Inv. 1957.14.257/ IT/ R 8238V.660.
c1526 CALDARA da CARAVAGGIO, Polidoro: Venus threathening to clip Cupid's wings/ DR/ d/ 14x18.9/ London, VAM/ Inv. CAI.571/ Ward-Jackson 1979,Vol.I, p.45-46, n°64/ R11123.661.
c1575 CAMBIASO, Luca: Venus punishes Amor/ PA/ ?/ 120x95/ Genova, PaRo/ Inv.#/ IT/ R8889V.662.

1575-1599 CAMPAGNA, Girolamo: Venere castiga Amore/ SC/ z/ ?/ Roma, PaV/ Inv. D6601iccd/ IT/ R8906.663. *Also (att) SUSINI, Giovanni Francesco.*

c1590 CARRACCI, Agostino: Venus punishing Profane Love (from the Lascivie)/ PR/ e/ 15,3x10,7/ Roma, ING/ Inv. FC39422/ Massari 1989, p.334-5,n°123; Bartsch 39 (18,1) 1980, p.177,n°135(109);Bartsch 39 C Part 1 (18,1) 1995,p.340-341,n°3901.209/R734.664.

Original DR/ d/ 49,3x34,8/ Windsor, RCol./ Inv. 2014/ Wittkower 1952, p.116, Cat.117. PRs also in many other places; copies reverse: Venus chastising Cupid / Parma, BiP/Inv. 33878/ Bartsch 39 Commentary, Part 1(18, 1p.342, n°3901.209 C6)/R4964.665.; Venere che punisce Amore/ PR/ e/ 15,1x11,8/ Bologna, PNa/ Inv. PN15193/ Casazza 2005, p.185-186, n°62/ R8360; also in Cambridge, FWM/ Inv. 23.I.5-126; SF, FAM/ Inv. 1963.30.3182; Venus chatiant l'Amour/15,4x11/Paris, BNF/Inv.#/ Dunand & Lemarchand s.d., III p.758, fig.1217.

c1590 NIGRONE, Giovanni Antonio: Venus züchtigt Amor/ ILL/ tx/ ?/ Napoli, BiN/ Inv. Ms. XII. G. 59-60/ IT/ R10098V.666.

c1590 ROCCATAGLIATA,Niccolo: Venus chastising Cupid/ SC/ z/ 20,3/ NY, SOT 17.10.'00/ Sl. NY7516-33/ IT/ R4173.667.

c1600 VALESIO, Giovanni Luigi: Non si castiga Amor con lieue sdegno (Venus, *restrained by a satyr,* whipping Cupid with roses) (Venus chatiant l'Amour avec une gerbe de roses)/ PR/ e/ 20,2x13,4/ NY, MMA/ Inv. 1917 (17.50.16[188])/ Bartsch 40 C 1(18,2) 1987, p.143,n°4002.165/ R1645.668. *Also: SF, FAM/ Inv. 1963.30.36766 and in other places.*

c1605-10 MANFREDI, Bartolomeo: Cupid chastised *(by Mars, Venus restraining him)*/ PA/ oc/ 175x131/ Chicago, AIC/ Inv. 1947.585/ IT/ R3070.669.

1617 FIALETTI, Odoardo: Venere punisce Amore sculacciandolo (Venus chastizing Cupid on his back) (from the series 'Scherzi d'Amore' The Sport of Love)/ PR/ e/ 17,8x9,3/ Roma, ING/ Inv. FC89209/ Bartsch 38 (17,5) 1983, p.213,n°15(268); Massari 1989, p.475,n°187/ R3514.670. *Also in Cambridge, FWM/ Inv. AD.1.18-152; London, BMu; Paris, BNF/ Inv.#/ Dunand & Lemarchand, s.d., III, p.951, fig.1478 à 1489/ R11151*

1639 SUSINI, Giovanni Francesco : Vénus châtiant l'Amour/ SC/ z/ 74/ Paris, MdL/ Inv. OA 8276/ IT/ R673.671.

c1650 (cir) MONTELATICI, Francesco, detto CECCO BRAVO: The punishment of Cupid/ PA/ oc/ 39.7x52.1/ NY, CHR 4.10.07/ Sl. 1886-0129/ IT/ R10538.672.

1706-07 RICCI, Sebastiano : Punizione d'Amore (The Punishment of Cupid)/ PA/ oc/ ?/ Firenze, PMF/ Inv.#/ Zuffi 2001, p.118/ R1506.673.

c1750 AMIGONI, Jacopo : Cupido castigado/ FR// ?/ Madrid, PaRA/ Inv. <el tocador de Isabel II, planta principal>/ Navarrete 2005, p.125, fig.234/ R11042.674.

c1800 SANTI, Giuseppe : Venere e Cupido/ PA/ oc/ ?/ Milano, POR 9.11.05/ Sl. ?-347b/ IT/ R10322.675.

1850 PISANI, Louis: Venus straiking Love/ PA/ oc/ 57x44/ Melbourne, SOT 28.11.'05/ Sl. AU0696-231/ IT/ R5492.676.

o Cupid disarmed

1522-24 PALMA Il Vecchio, Jacopo: Venus disarming Cupid (Venus and Cupid in a landscape)/ PA/ oc/ 118x209/ Cambridge, Fmu/ Inv.109/ Berenson 1958, p.127, pl.926; Mai ed. 2001, p.63, n°9/ R522.677.

c1525 PARMIGIANINO : Vénus désarmant Cupidon/ DR/ d/ ?/ Rennes, MBA/ Inv.#/ IT/ R5722.678.

There are more than 6 sketches known of the same subject (Chicago, Los Angeles, Nürnberg, Washington, Wien) ; in London : 17.4 x 14/ London, CIA/ Inv. No. D.1978.PG.364/IT/ R10153V.679. ;

in Parma, GaN/ Inv. #/ exh/ R281.680.;

another one in reverse : 18.8x14.3/ Budapest, MFA/ Inv. 1890/ Zentai 2003, p.46-47, Cat.15/ R11001.681.

c1550 CAMBIASO, Luca: Venus entwaffnet Cupido (Venus disarming Cupid and satyr)/ PA/ oc/ 48,5x35/ Würzburg, MWM/ Inv.#/ IT/ R4503.682. *Maybe preparatory DR/ d/ 30.8x21.4/ Cambridge, FWM/ Inv. 2899/ IT. Copies "after" of different sizes were sold in London, CHR 2.11.'05 and London, SOT 20.4.'04.*

c1550 (cir) TIZIANO, Vecellio : Venus disarming Cupid/ PA/ oc/ 110x92/ Wien, DOR 29.9.'04/ Sl. ?-7/ IT/ R8354.683.

c1550 VERONESE, Paolo Caliari: Vénus enlevant son arc à l'Amour (Venus taking Cupid's bow)/ DR/ d/ 8x7,7/ Paris, MdL/ Inv.4675/ IT/ R2853.684.

Also : cir VERONESE/ PA/ ?/ ?oval/ Paris, MdL/ Inv.#/ Mai ed. 2001, p.168, fig.14/ R9720 .685.

c1550 VERONESE, Paolo Caliari: Venere che disarma Amore/ PA/ oc/ 225x157/ Roma, PrC/ Inv. #/ Safarik 1996, p.1036, fig.47, pre. Col.Colonna/ R10003.686.

Replicas or copies ?: Cupid disarmed by Venus/ PA/ oc/ 158,3 x 139/ NY, CHR 10.1.'90/ Sl. ?-230 / IT/ R8040.687. ;

Venus entwaffnet Amor/ PA/ ?/ 105x87/ Berlin, Leo Spik 17.3.05/ Sl. 612-279/ IT/ R10930V.688.

c1553 SEMINO, Andrea : Venere disarma Amore/ PA/ oc/ 174x123/ Genova, GPB/ Inv.PR320/ Boccardo ed. 2004 p.306-307, n°68/ R849.689. *Boccardo presents a photograph (p. 306, fig.1 where Venus is covered) before the restauration in 1960/ R10264.*

c1625 PONZONI, Matteo: Venus disarming Cupid (reverse aft CARUCCI aft MICHELANGELO)/ PR/e/ 27,1x41,6/ LA, CMA/ Inv. 54.70.25/ IT/ R1469.690.

c1625 RENI, Guido : Vénus désarmant l'amour/ DR/ d/ ?/ UN/ Inv. #/ IT/ R10554.691.

c1630 TURCHI, Alessandro : Venus and Cupid/ PA/ oc/ 115.8 x 158.8/ Chicago, AIC/ Inv. 1964.65/ IT/ R3067.692.

c1715-20 SOLDANI-BENZI, Massimiliano : Vénus arrachant les ailes de Cupidon (Venus taking Cupid's wings)/ SC/ z/ 41x29,5x22,1/ Ottawa, MBA/ Inv. 17107/ IT/ R7018.693.

c1735 AMIGONI, Jacopo: Venus disarming Cupid/ PA/ oc/ 76x63,7/ Chapell Hill, AAM/ Inv.86.47/ IT/ R3063.694.

c1760 BOSSI, Benigno: Venere che disarma Cupido (aft PARMIGIANINO/ DR/ Parma, GaN)/ PR/ / 13,6x9,1/ Parma, BiP/ Inv. On22057/ Mussini 2003, p.171,n°346/ R3643.695.

1795 VEDOVATO, Pietro : Venere chiding Cupid (aft Joshua Reynolds)/ PR/ e/ 25,7x19/ Napoli, IOB/ Inv. 1435/ Penta 2002, p.322/ R3525.696.

c1800 ROSASPINA, Francesco: Venere che disarma Cupido/ DR//17,1x17,1/ Parma, BiP/ Inv. On22144/ Mussini 2003, p.179,n°369/ R3645.697.

c1801 TODESCHINI, Tommaso: Venere che disarma Amore (aft VERONESE)/ PR/ e/ 24x19,6/ Napoli, IOB/ Inv. 9775/ Penta 2002, p.293/ R3524.698.

o Venus and Cupid in an arched niche/ in a landscape

c1500 GIROLAMO di BENVENUTO, Giovanni del Guasta: Venus and Cupid in a landscape/ PA/ ?/ ?/ Firenze, MuH/ Inv. 33/ Berenson 1968, p.186; Reid 1993, p.114/ R9592V.699.

c1505 (cir) GIORGIONE, Giorgio Barbarelli: Venus and Cupid in a landscape/ PA/ ow/ 11x20/ Washington, NGA/ Inv. 1939.1.142/ IT/ R808.700.

c1512 RAIMONDI, Marcantonio: Venere a Amore (aft RAFFAELLO)/ PR/ e/ 21,3x10,7/ Roma, ING/ Inv. FC5034/ Massari 1989, p.16-17,n°5/ R876.701.

Also copies in Firenze, GdU. SF, FAM. Reverse copy: PR/e/ 21,5x11,1/ Wien ALB/ Inv.#/ Bartsch 26 (14,1 1978, p.312,n°311A(234)/ R4815.702.

c1515 RAIMONDI, Marcantonio: Venus and Cupid in a niche (*right arm of Venus uphold, Cupid at left side)*/ PR/ E/ 19,7x11,2/ SF, FAM/ Inv. 30.36921/ IT/ R879.703.

c1524 DOSSI, Dosso : Venus and Cupid in a landscape/ PA/ oc/ 135x160/ Philadelphia, PrC/ Inv.#/ IT/ R7144.704.

1526 CARAGLIO, Iacopo : Venere (Cipria lascivi pulcherrima mater amoris)(*and Cupid in an arched niche)* (aft ROSSO, Fiorentino/ FR/ Roma, Castel S.Angelo)/ PR/ e/ 20,4x10,8/ Roma, ING/ Inv.FC5907/ Massari 1989,p.130,n°45; Bartsch 28 (15,1) 1985, p.110, n°33(78)/ R732.705. *Also in Glasgow, HMAG/ Inv.40023; SF,FAM /* Inv. 1963.30.37131/ R4842; *Paris, BNF ; reverse in Wien, ALB.*

c1651 GRIMALDI, Giovanni Francesco: Landscape with Venus and Cupid/ PA/ oc/ Ø69,9/ SF, FAM/ Inv. 1980.6/ IT/ R1399.706.

○ Cupid kissed/nursed by Venus

c1530 PARMIGIANINO : Vénus allaitant l'Amour (Venus nursing Cupid)/ DR/d/ ?/ Montpellier, UFM/ Inv.#/ IT/ R8001V.707.

1546-55 (att) RICCIARELLI, Daniele: Venus und Amor: PA/ oc/ 93x73/ Berlin, GSM/ Inv. #/ IT/ R11634V.708.

c1550 INDIA, Bernardino: Venus and Cupid embracing/ DR/ d/ 12,1x19,7/ NY, SOT 21.1.'04/ Sl. N07963-9/ IT/ R5478.709.

c1599 CARRACCI, Agostino: Venere e Amore (*Venus kissing Cupid*)/ DR/ d/ 26,1x43,8/ Budapest, MFA/ Inv.1947/ Czére 2002,p.36,n°6; Czére 2004, p.71-73, Cat.58/ R4516.710.

c1600 PAGGI, Giovanni Battista: Venere bacia Amore (Venus kissing Cupid)/ PA/ ?/ ?/ Genova, PrC/ Inv.#/ Boccardo ed. 2004,p.70/ R337.711. *Copy in reverse 'after'PA/ ow/ 65,5x51/ A'dam, SOT 1.11.'05/ Sl. A0966-1351/ IT/ R4913.*

1617 FIALETTI, Odoardo: Venus seated on a rock kissing Amor (from the series 'Scherzi d'Amore' (The Sport of Love)) / PR/ e/ 17,8x9,2/ Roma, ING/ Inv. FC89204/ (Bartsch 38 (17,5) 1983, p.207,n°9(268); Massari 1989, p.478,n°190/R1206.712. *Also in Glasgow, HMAG/ Inv. 6248&49; London, BMu; Paris, BNF/ Inv.#/ Dunand & Lemarchand, s.d., III, p.951, fig.1478 à 1489/ R11151; Washington, LoC.*

c1625 GUERCINO, Giovane Francesco Barbieri: Venere che allata Cupido (Venus nursing Cupid)/ PA/ ?/ ?/ Venezia, FGC/ Inv.#/ IT/ R2296V.713.

1627 SAN GIOVANNI, Giovanni da : Venere che pettina Amore o Le cure materne (Venus combing Cupid)/ PA/ oc/ 229x173/ Firenze, PaP/ Inv. 1890-2123/ Sframeli 2003, n°15,p.100/ R4012.714.

1636 FRANCESCHINI, Baldassarre detto Volterrano : Venere accudisce Cupido (Venus nursing Cupid)/ FR/ / 80x67/ Firenze, MuB/ Inv.866/ IT/ R8583V.715.

c1650 GENNARI, Lorenzo: Venera doji Amorja (Venus with suckling Cupid)/ PA/ ow/ 64x161/ Ljubljana, NGa/Inv. NG S 1929/ IT/ R4553.716.

c1650 GIMIGNANI, Giacinto: Venere che allata Amore/ PA/ oc/ ?/ Roma, GaP/ Inv. E29333iccd/ Cicinelli A & Vasco Rocca S (1978), Vol.I, p.50/ R8927.717.

c1750 CIPRIANI, Giovanni Battista: Venus reclining on a cloud, embracing Cupid/ PR/ e/ 23x30/ London, VAM/ Inv.#/ IT/ R3738.718.

c1808-10 PACETTI, Camillo: Amore bacia Venere/ SC/ q/ 30x14x14.5/ Milano, VBB/ Inv. GAM 307/12/ IT/ R11717V.719.

○ Cupid sleeping

c1510 MODENA, Nicoletto da: Venus (*standing*) and Eros (*sleeping*)/ PR/ / 14,6x10,3/ Wien, ALB/ Inv.#/ Bartsch 25 (13,2) 1980, p.119,n°47(280)/ R4792.720.

1534-36 ROSSO FIORENTINO, Giovanni Battista: Vénus frustrée ou tentant de réveiller l'Amour (Venus scolding Cupid) (Galerie François 1°)/ FR// ?/ Fontainebleau, MNC/ Inv.#/ Berenson 1963, p.195 ; Porcheron-Felsing 1983, p.131 fig.44 ; Beguin 1989, fig.31 ; Pérouse de Montclos 1998, p.70-71/ R3103.721.

1566 BOLDRINI, Nicolo: Venere e Cupido (Venere addormentata vicino ad Amore) (aft TIZIANO)/ PR/ e/ 31,1x23,4/ Bassano, MuC/ Inv.III-72-126/ Catelli Isola 1976, p.81, nr.31; Muraro 1976, p.134,137,n°78A/ R1081. 722. *Also in Auckland, AGa/ Inv.1957-31-2; Chapel Hill, AAM/ Inv. 58.1.175;LA,CMA/ Inv.M.88.91.252; Roma, ING/ Inv. FC69179; Venezia, MuC/ Inv. A15/35/ Chiari 1982, p.40-41, nr.10; Washington, NGA/ Inv. 1943.3.934; Wien, ALB; Zürich, ETH/ Inv. D36/ Matile 2003, p.65-66, n°19.*

1617 FIALETTI, Odoardo: Venus covering sleeping Amor (from the series 'Scherzi d'Amore'-The Sport of Love)/ PR/ e/ 18x9,3/ Roma, ING/ Inv. FC89202/ Bartsch 38 (17,5) 1983, p.206, n°8(267); Massari 1989, p.468,n°180/ R763.723. *Also in Glasgow, HMAG/ Inv. 6247; London, BMu; Paris, BNF/ Inv.#/ Dunand & Lemarchand, s.d., III, p.951, fig.1478 à 1489/ R11151*

c1641 BILIVERTI, Giovanni: Venere e Amore dormiente/ PA: oc/ 56.5x45.5/ Budapest, MFA/ Inv. 474/ Contini 1985, p.123-4, n°80b/ R9939.724.

c1650 DELLA BELLA, Stefano: Venus und Cupido/ DR/ d/ 5.5x25.5/ Berlin, KSK/ Inv. KdZ 15714/ IT/ R10107.725.

c1729 PEDRETTI, Giuseppe Carlo : Venere e Cupido(wor aft FRANCESCHINI)/ PA/ oc/ 31x47,4/ Budapest, MFA/ Inv. 842/ Miller 1991, p.95, Cat.n°36; Rozman 2005, p.242-49/ R8505.726. *Replica of FRANCESCHINI according to Miller.*
1751-58 (or 1851 ?) ANTESI, G. : Venere e Cupido (aft FRANCESCHINI)/ PR// ?/ UN/ Miller 1991, p.xv, pl.93, p.99-100, Cat.n°36<1851> Rozman 2005, p.242-49/ R8507.727. *FRANCESCHINI, M./ PA/oc/113x187/UN, Paris sale 1880, pre.Vaduz, LMu.*
c1800 BISON, Giuseppe Bernardino: Venere e Amore dormiente/ DR/ d/ ?/ Roma, ING/ Inv. FN 15235/ IT/ R10343.728.
c1825 POMPIGNOLI, Luigo: Venus and the sleeping Cupid/ PA/ oc/ 89,5x69,9/ SF, BON 15.11.'05/ Sl. 13309-48/ IT/ R6587.729.

o Cupid with arrow(s)

c1500 MELONE, Altobello: Venus and Cupid/ PA/ ?/ ?/ UN, PrC(pre.Stockholm, D.L. Telander)/ Inv.#/ Berenson 1968, p.4, n°1671/ R9962.730.
c1540 DOSSI, Battista : Venus and Cupid ('Rochdale' Venus in landscape)/ PA/ oc/ 158x128/ Philadelphia, MuA/ Inv. E1972-2-1/ Berenson 1968, p.112, pl.1760/ R2081.731. *Also att to his brother DOSSI, Dosso Giovanni.*
c1600 (att) FANELLI, Francesco: Petite Vénus et Cupidon (aft GIAMBOLOGNA)/ SC/ z/ 14,9/ London, CHR 1.7.'74/ Sl.#/ Avery 1999,p.43-45/ R6943.732.
1617 FIALETTI, Odoardo: Amore e Venere con freccia (Venus seated with an arrow in front of Amor) (from the series 'Scherzi d'Amore'-The Sport of Love)/ PR/ e/ 19,8x9,5/ Roma, ING/ Inv. FC89201/ Bartsch 38 (17,5) 1983, p.205,n°7(267); Massari 1989, p.467, n°179/ R3508.733. *Also in Glasgow, HMAG/ inv. 6246; London, BMu; Paris, BNF/ Inv.#/ Dunand & Lemarchand, s.d., III, p.951, fig.1478 à 1489/ R11151*
c1632 FANELLI, Francesco: Venus and Cupid (aft GIAMBOLOGNA)/ SC/ z/ 14x4,2x9/ London, SOT 10.12.'02 1.7.'74/ Sl. L02233-98/ Avery 1999,p.43-45/ R5781.734.
1639 SUSINI, Giovanni Francesco : Vénus brûlant les flèches de l'Amour (Venus burning Cupid's arrows)/ SC/ z/ 70/ Paris, MdL/ Inv. OA 8277/ IT/ R672.735.
c1650 LIBERI, Pietro: Venus and Cupid *(Venus takes an arrow from Cupid)*/ PA/ oc/ 90.2x69.8/ Wellesley, DMCC/ Inv. N 1956.35/ IT/ R11368.736.
c1650 LIBERI, Pietro: Venere toglie le frecce a Cupido/ PA/ oc/ 102x81.2/ Vicenza, PaT/ Inv. 73480/ IT/ R11483.737.
c1660 (cir) ALBANI, Francesco: Venus and Cupid/ PA/ oy/ 25.5xx34.8/ London, CHR20.04.'05/ Sl.5824-174/ IT/ R3447.738.
c1675 PIOLA, Domenico: Venus being given an arrow by Cupid (from an album originally containing 62 drawings)/ DR/ d/ ?/ London, BMu/ Inv. 1950,1111.00016. c/ IT/ R8435V.739.
c1676 GALLINARI, Giacomo: Venus (*seated*) and Cupid (*with arrow*)/ PR/ 28,1x20,4/ London, BMu/ Inv.#/ Bartsch 42 (19,2 1981, p.252,n°2(248)/ R4978.740. *Also in Cambridge, FWM/ Inv. 24.I.2-80; Glasgow, HMAG/ Inv. 6783*
c1700 GARZI, Luigi: Venere consegna la freccia ad Amore/ PA/ oc/ Ø23/ Roma, GaP/ Inv. E29328iccd/ Cicinelli, A. & Vasco Rocca, S. 1978 Vol.I, p.50/ R8898.741.
c1700 RICCI, Marco & Sebastiano: Venus und Armor/ PA/ ?/ ?/ London, CHo/ Inv.#/ IT/ R8985.742.
c1746-47 DIZIANI, Gaspare : Venus and Cupid/ DR/ d/ 19,7x25,4/ LA, CMA/ Inv. 54.12.12/ IT/ R1088. 743.

o Cupid with arrow(s) and bow

c1515 (wor) RAIMONDI, Marcantonio : Venus, *standing with arrow*, and Cupid/ PR// 30x21/ NY, MMA/ Inv.#/ Bartsch 28 (15,1) 1985, p.50,n°6-I(37); Bartsch 28 C (15,1) 1995, p.36-39,n°2801.042/ R4836.744. *Also in other places.*
1518-19 PERUZZI, Baldassare Tommaso: Venus and Cupid ('Sala delle Prospettive' -Hall of Prospective-detail of trompe l'oeil niche)/ FR// ?/ Roma, ViF/ IT/ R8997.745.

c1575 FARINATI, Paolo: Venus (*sitting on a cloud*) and Cupid/ PR/ /26,8x25/ London, BMu/ Inv.#/ Bartsch32(16,1) 1979,p.264,n°64(166)/ R4928.746.
1585 FONTANA, Lavinia: Venus and Cupid/ PA/ oc/ 215x134/ Venezia, PrC/ Inv.#/ Murphy 2003, p.102, n°89/ R.8680.747.
c1600 FIALETTI, Odoardo: Venus debout contre une butte et appuyée, se penchant d'un air de complaisance vers l'Amour/ PR/ e/ 16,8x11,7/ London, BMu/ Inv.#/ Bartsch 38 (17,5) 1983 p.224,n°30(273)/ R4961.748.
1617 FIALETTI, Odoardo: Venere e Amore che porta le frecce (Amor carrying a bundle of arrows to fill his quiver) (from the series 'Scherzi d'Amore' (The Sport of Love)) / PR/ e/ 17,8x9,6/ Roma, ING/ Inv. FC89205/ Bartsch 38 (17,5) 1983,p.210,n°12(268);Massari1989,p.469,n°181/ R3511.749. *Also in Glasgow, HMAG/ Inv. 6252; London, BMu; Paris, BNF/ Inv.#/ Dunand & Lemarchand, s.d., III, p.951, fig.1478 à 1489/ R11151*
1617 FIALETTI, Odoardo: Venere seduta si volge verso Amore che scocca una freccia (Venus regarding Amor who is discharging an arrow) (from the series 'Scherzi d'Amore'-The Sport of Love)/ PR/ e/ 17,8x9,3/ Roma, ING/ Inv. FC89212/ Bartsch 38 (17,5) 1983, p.217,n°19(268);Massari 1989, p.478,n°190/ R3516. 750. *Also in Glasgow, HMAG/ Inv. 6255; London, BMu; Paris, BNF/ Inv.#/ Dunand & Lemarchand, s.d., III, p.951, fig.1478 à 1489/ R11151*
c1650 DIAMANTINI, Giuseppe: Venus and Eros/ PR/ e/ 21,7x17,1/ Wien, ALB/ Inv.#/ Bartsch 47 (21,2) 1983 p.407,#23(279/ R5002.751.
c1650 LIBERI, Pietro : Venere e Cupido/PA/ ?/ ?/ Rovigo, PaR/ Inv.#/ IT/ R8383.752.
1664 SIRANI, Elisabetta: Venus och Cupido/ PA/ oc/ 105x82/ Stockholm, BUK 29.5.07/ Sl.?-434/ IT/ R11595.753.
c1678-79 FRANCESCHINI, Marcantonio: Venus with Cupid dipping his arrows/ PA/ oc/ 119,3x90,2/ NY, SOT 28.1.'05/ Sl. N08059-566/ IT/ R5694.754.
c1700 FRANCESCHINI, Marcantonio: Venere e Cupido/ PA/ oc/ ?/ Milano, POR 26.5.04/ Sl.?-31/ IT/ R10283.755.
1729-1739 AMIGONI, Jacopo: Venus and Cupid/ PA/ oc/ 39,4x52/ London, SOT 11.07.02/ Sl. L02112-231/ IT/ R5782.756.
c1740 DIZIANI, Gaspare : Venere con amorino/ PA/ oc/ 88x145/ Venezia, CaR/ Inv. Col. Martini inv. 165/ Martini 2002, p.118-119, n°87/ R966.757.
1785 BATONI, Pompeo: Venus and Cupid/ PA/ oc/ ?/ Moscow, ACM/ Inv.#/ IT/ R7456.758.
1806 CAMPANELLA, Angelo: Venus a Cupido vulnerata (aft RAFFAELLO)/ PR/ e/ ?/ Roma, BiH/ Inv. #/ IT/ R10121.759.

o Cupid with arrow(s) and bow, doves or swans

b1570 ALLORI, Alessandro: Venere e Cupido (Venus and Cupid)/ PA/ ow/ 29x38,5/ Firenze, GdU/ Inv.1890-1512/ Lecchini Giovannoni 1991, p.225-226, n.24, fig.51; Falletti & Nelson, 2002, Cat.43, p.226; Sframeli, 2003, p.74-75, fig.4/ R2235.760. *Sometimes considered as a smaller replica of PA/ Montpellier, MuF.*
c1570 ALLORI, Alessandro: Vénus et l'Amour/ PA/ ow/ 140x223 / Montpellier,MuF / Inv.#/ Lecchini Giovannoni 1991, p.245-246, n°60, fig.126/ R2376.761.
Replicas of different sizes: Venus disarming Cupid/ PA/ ow/ 140x226/ L.A.,CMA/ Inv.35.1/ Lecchini Giovannoni 1991, p.244, n°61 /R1068.762.;
Venere e Amore/ PA/ ow/ 154x221.6/ London, HC/ Inv.#/ Lecchini Giovannoni 1991, p.244, n°62, fig.127 /R9631. 763.;
Vénus et l'Amour/ PA/ oc/ 131x213/ Auxerre, MAH /Inv.#/ Lecchini Giovannoni 1991, p.244, n°63, fig.128/R7450. 764.;
PA/ ?/ 38x55/ Bucharesti, MNA/ Inv.#/ Duboucher 1992,n°92/ R7648.765.
c1625 RENI, Guido: Venus and Cupid (Venus punishing Cupid)/ PA/ oc/ 228,3x157/ Toledo (Ohio), MuA/ Inv.72.86/ IT/ R7161.766.
A replica?: Venus und Amor/ PA/ oc/ 222x151/ LO, pre.Berlin, GMS/ Inv.377/ IT/ R11621.767.
c1765 ZUGNO, Francesco: Venere e Amore/FR//Padova, PaM/ Inv.#/ IT/ R8322.768.

c1775 GANDOLFI, Gaetano: Venus and Cupid/DR/d/31,1x20/NY, SOT 10.1.'95 /Sl. 6651-102/ Cat.p.48-49/R4169.769.
c1812(?) CARATTONI(?): Venus and Cupid (aft ALLORI)/ PR/ e/ ?/ UN/ Duboucher 1992,n°33/ R7640.770.

○ Cupid with bow

1552-55 GUALTIERO: Venus and Cupid/ FR/// Vicenza, VGM/ Inv.#/ Wundram 1988,p.16/ R5896.771.
c1591 CARRACCI, Annibale: Venere e Cupido *(with apple in right hand of Venus, bow and doves)*/ PA/ oc/ 110x130/ Modena, GaE / Inv..333/ Casazza 2005, p.184-185, n°61/ R8359.772. ***1678** Dauphin, Olivier/ reverse PR/ e/ 19,4x23,2/ Firenze, GdA/ Inv.#/ IT/ R8581.*
c1600 VALESIO, Giovanni Luigi: Non fugge Amor, di Venere, à gli sdegni (Cupid escaping from Venus)/ PR/ e/ 16,1x22,2/ Wien, ALB/ Inv.#/ Bartsch 40 C 1(18,2) 1987, p.143-144, n°4002.166 S1 / R4972.773.
1617 FIALETTI, Odoardo: Venere (Venus - seen from the back - with Cupid (from the series 'Divinità Mitologiche' – 'Four Divinities' aft PORDENONE, Licinio da) / PR/ e/ 15x21,7/ Roma, ING/ Inv. FC89213/ Bartsch 38 (17,5) 1983, p.219,n°21 (271); Massari 1989, p.477,n°189/ R762.774. *Also in London, BMu; SF, FAM/ Inv. 1993.63.194.*
1617 FIALETTI, Odoardo: Venus regarding Cupid, who is cutting a bow (from the series 'Scherzi d'Amore'-The Sport of Love)/ PR/ e/ 15,2x9,5/ Roma, ING/ Inv. FC89211/ Bartsch 38 (17,5) 1983, p.216,n°18(269); Massari 1989, p.474,n°186/ R764.775. *Also in London, BMu; SF, FAM/ Inv.1987.1.165; Paris, BNF/ Inv.#/ Dunand & Lemarchand, s.d., III, p.951, fig.1478 à 1489/ R11151*
1617 FIALETTI, Odoardo: Venere gioca con l'arco di Amore (Amor demanding the bow from Venus) (from the series 'Scherzi d'Amore'-The Sport of Love)/ PR /e/ 18x9,2/ Roma, ING/ Inv. FC89207/ Bartsch 38 (17,5) 1983, ,p.211,n°13(268); Massari 1989, p.473, n°185/ R3512.776. *Also in Cambridge, FWM/ Inv. AD.1.18-150; Glasgow, HMAG/ Inv. 6253; London, BMu; Paris, BNF/ Inv.#/ Dunand & Lemarchand, s.d., III, p.951, fig.1478 à 1489/ R11151*
1617 FIALETTI, Odoardo: Venere spezza l'arco di Amore (Venus with Cupid whittling his bow, from the series 'Scherzi d'Amore' (The Sport of Love)) / PR/ e/ 17,8x9,3/ Roma, ING/ Inv. FC89210/ Bartsch 38 (17,5) 1983, p.213,n°17(268); Massari 1989, p.477, n°189/ R3515.777. *Also in London, BMu; Washington, NGA/ Inv. 1997.49.1; Paris, BNF/ Inv.#/ Dunand & Lemarchand, s.d., III, p.951, fig.1478 à 1489/ R11151*
1628-30 GUERCINO, Giovane Francesco: Venus and Cupid/ PA/ oc/ 113x85oval/ London, WMu/ Inv. WM.1511-1948/ Anonymous 1989, Vol.I, p.956/ R8526.778.
1641-43 GUERCINO, Giovane Francesco: Venus and Cupid/ DR/ d/ ?/ Haarlem, TMu/ Inv. #/ IT/ R11549V.779.
c1704 ALBANI, Francesco: Venus *and Cupid (seventh plate in Picturae Francisci Albani in aede Verospia[Rome?]*/ PR/ e/ 36,7x28,4/ S.F.,FAM/ Inv.#/ IT/ R1371.780.
1755 ANSALDI, Innocenzo Andrea : Venere e Cupido *(with apple in right hand of Venus, bow and doves)*/ DR/ d/ 23,5x28,8/ Pescia: MuC/ Inv. 1334/ IT/ R8573.781. *Reverse copy of CARRACCI's PA or copy of Dauphin's PR..*
c1800 DIANO, Giacinto: Venus stealing Cupid's bow/ PA/ oc/ 135,5x134,5/ London, SOT 1.11.'05/ Sl. W05718-140/ IT/ R5243.782.

○ Cupid with others

c1510 MASTER of the DIE: The power of Cupid/ PR, e/ ?/ NY, MMA/ Inv. 49.97.328/ Campbell 2006, p.99 fig.51/ R8804.783.
c1546 BONASONE, Giulio: Venere e Amore ricevono ghirlande (Venus and Amor receive laurels)/ PR/ e/ 32,7x42,7/ Roma, ING/ Inv.FN1126/ (Massari 1993,p.64-66)/ R3550.784.
c1550 BRONZINO, Agnolo: Vénus, Cupid and Jealousy *(with Cupid and two cupids)*/ PA/ ow/ 192x142/ Budapest, MFA/ Inv.163/ Berenson 1963, p.41, pl.1453; Mai ed. 2001, p.279, n°2/ R381.785.

c1575 (att) MICHELI, Parrasio: A Man, Venus and Cupid/ DR/ D/ 21,1x29,5/ Milano, BiA/ Inv. F 281 inf. n. 13 recto/ IT/ R8733.786.
1583 ALLORI, Alessandro : Ritorno di Venere ed Amore sull'Olimpo (Venere trionfante torna sul suo carro in cielo; The return of Venus and Cupid on the Olympus) *(after the Judgement of Paris)*/ DR/ d/ 39,2x55,5/ Roma, ING/ Inv.FC124149/ Lecchini Giovannoni 1991, p.261-262, n°95, fig.212; Antetomaso & Mariani, 2004, p.316-317/ R3476.787. *DR for a tapestry in Parma, GaN.*
c1600 PALMA Il Giovane, Jacopo Negretti: Kompositionsskizze mit Venus *(with Cupid and two other figures)*/ DR/ d/ 18.8x25.7/ Berlin, KSK/ Inv. KdZ 5551r/ IT/ R10090.788.
c1609 ALBANI, Francesco: Venus and Cupid (detail of the Grande Galleria: The Fall of Phaeton and the council of the gods to discuss its consequences)/ FR// ?/ Bassano Romano, ViVG/ Inv. #/ Czére 2004, p.17-18, Cat.1-b/ R10916.789.
c1700 PICCINI, Jacopo: Eros e Afrodite *(with mirror and others)* (aft FR LO)/ PR// ?/ Roma, MuV/ Inv. Cappon 285/ Borea 2000, Tomo II, fig. 4/ R1772.790.
c1700 RICCI, Sebastiano: Venus and Cupid with other figures before an altar/ DR/ d/ 22x16,5/ NY, PML/ Inv. 1950.5/ IT/ R8884V.791.
1809 PINELLI, Bartolomeo: Venere consegna Amore alla dea Calipso/ DR/ d/ 25x36,5/ Roma, PaBr/ Inv. MR 1846/ IT/ R3762.792.
c1810 PINELLI, Bartolomeo: Venus presents Cupid to Calypso/ DR/ d/ 46.4x58.8/ Chicago, AIC/ Inv. 1963.560/ IT/ R10257.793.
c1810 PINELLI, Bartolomeo: Venus watches Telemachus with Cupid seated on his knee, while Mentor observes in disgust/ DR/ d/ 47.2x59/ Chicago, AIC/ Inv. 1963.563/ IT/ R10252.794.
1972 TOMMASI FERRONI, Riccardo: Venere e Amore/ PA/ oc/ 200x140/ UN/ Inv.#/ CEDE 2001 Vol 16, p.11597/ R8652.795.

○ Cupid with Venus reclining

c1450 (att) SCHIAVO, Paolo: Reclining Venus with Cupid/ PA/ tw/ 52x170/ UN, pre.b1972 LA, JPG/ Inv. 72.PB.9 |a/ IT/ R11377V.796.
c1600 LUTI, Benedetto: Venus reclining with Cupid *(and her doves)*/ PA/ oc/ 112.1x161/ Sarasota, RMA/ Inv. SN164/ IT/ R11371V.797.
c1888-90 DURINI, Alessandro: Amore adorna con ghirlande e fiori Venere giacente/ PA/ oc/ 22x16/ Milano, VBB/ Inv. GAM 6361/ IT/ R11713V.798.

▪ Venus to the left

c1470 ZOPPO, Marco: Venus und Amor in einer Landschaft/ DR/ d/ 18.5x13.1/ Berlin, KSK/ Inv. KdZ 26274r/ IT/ R10056.799.
c1500 CREDI, Lorenzo di : Venus reclining and Cupid/ DR/ d/ 15x26,5/ Firenze,GdU/ Inv.212G/ Berenson 1938, vol.2, p.71; vol 3:n° 141-674A/ R3587.800. *Also **c1475** (att) VERROCCHIO, Andrea del ?*
1515-20 GIROLAMO di BENVENUTO, Giovanni del Guasta: Venus and Cupid/ PA/ tw/ 81x100/ Firenze, MuH/ Inv. 33/ Calabrese 2003,p.236; Casazza 2005,p.180,n°56/ R2228.801.
c1540 CARUCCI, Jacopo (PONTORMO): Venere e Cupido/ DR/ d/ 13x20,6/ Firenze, GdU/ Inv. 15644Frect/ Falletti 2002,p.219,n°40/ R4319.802.
c1550 MARCO da FAENZA: Venere e Cupido/ PA/ tf/ ?x?/ Firenze, PaV/ Inv.#/ IT/ R8596.803.
c1575 (att) ORSI, Lelio: Vénus et l'Amour/ DR/ d/ 14,7x38/ Paris, CHR 24.3.'05/ Sl. 5400-581/ IT/ R3026. 804.
c1639 RENI, Guido: Reclining Venus with Cupid/ PA/ oc/ 136x174,5/ Dresden, SKS/ Inv.324/ Mai ed. 2001, p.238-39, n°7/ R537.805.
c1643 LIBERI, Pietro : Venere e un amorino fra le nubi/ PA/ ?/ 112x140/ Venezia, CaR/ Inv. 286/ Martini 2002, p.179,181, n°141/ R963.806.
c1650 (cir) LIBERI, Pietro : Venus (*showing her back)* and Cupid/ PA/ oc/ 61,3x80,3/ London, CHR 20.4.'05/ Sl. 5824-167/ IT/ R3448.807.

c1700 BELLUCCI, Antonio: Venus und Amor/ PA/ ?/ ?/ München, APk/ Inv. #/ Weichardt s.d., pl.30/ R10412.808.
c1700 PELLEGRINI, Giovanni Antonio : Venere *(with Cupid)*/ DR/ d/ 9,2x9/ NY, PrC/ Inv.#/ Bettagno 1959, Racolta Moscardo.n°36/ R3797.809.
1710-15 BARATTA, Giovanni: Venus and Cupid/ SC/ m/ 98x48x40/ Milano, SOT 10.7.'07/ Sl. MI0279-252/ IT/ R9795.810.
c1725 PELLEGRINI, Giovanni Antonio : Venus and Cupid/ PA/ ?/ 103x126/ London, CHR 5.7.'91/ Sl. ?-7/ IT/ R2752.811.
1744-47 TIEPOLO, Giambattista: Vénus et l'Amour/ FR, pre. Palazzo Valle Marchesini, Vincenza / c/ 305x135/ UN, pre. Roma, PrC Simonetti/ Inv.#/ Pedrocco 2002, p.263-264, cat.180.6/ R11149.812.
1792 PELLEGRINI, Domenico: Venus and Cupid *(in a landscape)*/ PA/ oc/ 103x144/ London, SOT 23.11.'06/ Sl. L06122-69/ IT/ R7899.813.
c1798 CANOVA, Antonio: Venere con Amore/ PA/ oc/ 85x73/ Possagno, CdC/ Inv. 44/ Stefani 2004, p.38,165, nr.41 & 42/ R10179.814. *Replica of same dimension Inv.46.*
1820-1850 COCHETTI, Luigi : Venere e Amore e cinque caricature/ DR/ ?/ 41,5x46,9/ Roma, PaBr/ Inv. MR 41837/ IT/ R3748.815.
c1850 USSI, Stefano: Vénus et Cupidon/ PA/ ?/ ?/ UN/ Inv. #/ IT/ R9872.816.

▪ Venus to the right

c1470 ZOPPO, Marco: Venus und Amor/ DR/ d/ 18.5x13.1/ Berlin, KSK/ Inv. KdZ 26274v/ IT/ R10057. 817.
c1500 GIROLAMO di BENVENUTO, Giovanni del Guasta: Venus and Cupid/ PA/ ow/ 51.1x50.8/ Denver, DAM/ Inv. E-IT-18-XV-943 (pre. K222)/ IT/ R8260.818.
c1511 PIOMBO, Sebastiono del: Venus and a reclining Child/ DR/ d/ 27,5x42,5/ Milano, BiA/ Inv. F 290 inf. n. 22 verso/ IT/ R8735.819.
c1526 CARAGLIO, Iacopo : Venere e Amore (aft PERINO DEL VAGA)/ PR/ e/ 21,6x13,5/ Roma, ING/ Inv.Marucelliana IX.22/ Massari 1989,p.186-187n°77a; Bartsch 28 (15,1) 1985,p.98,n°21(76); Bartsch 28 C (15,1) 1995,p.112-14,n°2802.021/ R3497.820. *Also in A'dam, Paris*; *copies in reverse.*
c1526 (1540?) LOTTO, Lorenzo: Venus and Cupid/ PA/ oc/ 92,4x111/ NY, MMA/ Inv. 1986.138/ Zuffi 2001, p.188; Mai ed. 2001, p.61, n°7/ R414.821.
c1527 PERINO DEL VAGA, Pietro: Venere e Amore/ DR/ d/ 15,9x13,8/ Firenze, GdU/ Inv. 13552F/ Massari 1989, p.148,187,fig.33/ R3499.822.
c1550 (cir) PRIMATICCIO, Francesco: Venus and Cupid/ PA/ oc/ 131x154/ NY, SOT 27.1.'05/ Sl. N08061-127/ IT/ R5685.823.
c1565 CAMBIASO, Luca: Venus playing with Cupid under a tree/ DR/ d/ 27x21.5/ Chatsworth, DCo/ Inv. 386/ Jaffé 1993, p.31-32, Cat.22/ R10389.824.
c1570 ALLORI, Alessandro: Studio per una Venere e Cupido (Study for a Venus and Cupid)/ DR/ d/ 25,5x20,6/ Firenze, GdU/ Inv.1432S/ Lecchini Giovannoni 1991, p.226, n°25, fig.52; Falletti & Nelson, 2002, Cat.44, p.227/ R4320.825.
c1600 PAGGI, Giovanni Battista: Venus et Cupidon/ PA/ ?/ ?/ Genova, PrC/ Inv.#/ IT/ R2283.826.
c1600 SCARSELLINO, Ippolito: Amor and Venus/ PA/ ow/ 21x34/ Parma, GaN/ Inv.998/ Berenson 1968, p.390; Bentini 2003, p.272, fig.198/ R8894.827.
b1607 (att) CESARI, Giuseppe: Venere incoronata di Amore (Venus crowned by Amor *with two doves)*/ PA/ oc/ 82x112/ Roma, GaB/ Inv.138/ Cicinelli 1978, Vol.I, p26, 73; Mai ed. 2001, p.232-33, n°4; Calabrese Omar 2003,p.297/ R2225.828. *Also (att) BAGLIONE, Giovanni.*
1628 VAROTARI, Alessandro : Vénus et l'Amour/ PA/ oc/ 120x175/ Paris, MdL/ Inv.730/ Calabrese 2003, p.145/ R2233.829.
Replica (or original, but later altered?): Venere con un amorino (Venus fully clothed)/ PA/ oc/ 116,5 x 151/ Venezia, CaR/ Inv. 294 Col. Martini/ Martini 2002, p.212-213, n°171/ R961.830.

c1700 FRANCESCHINI, Marcantonio: Cupid departs from Venus after he has accidentaly wounded her with his arrow (*prelude to her love for Adonis*)/ DR/ d/ 9,8x27,5/ Princeton, UAM/ Inv.76-61c/ Miller 1991, p.xiv, pl.64, p.88, Cat.n°20/ R9823.831. *Compositional study of PA/oc/86x254/UN, Paris sale 1880, pre.Vaduz, LMu.*
c1700 RICCI, Sebastiano: Venere con un putto/ PA/ ?/ ?/ PrC (pre. Monaco-Montecarlo, Maison d'Art/ Inv.#/ Scarpa 2006, p.250, cat.300, fig.17/ R10434.832.
c1707 FRANCESCHINI, Marcantonio: Cupid extracting a thorn from Venus' foot)/ DR/ d/ 12.5x22.3/ NY, CHM/ Inv.?/ Miller 1991, p.xv, pl.106, p.105-106, Cat.n°41/ R9826.833.; *compositional study of PA/ oc/ 113x187/UN, Paris sale 1880, pre.Vaduz, LMu.*
Preparatory: Study for Venus/ DR/?/?/ Genova, PaRo/ Inv. #/ Miller 1991, p.xv, pl.107, p.105-6, Cat.n°41/ R9897.834.
c1710 MELONI, Francesco Antonio: Venus (*reclining*) and Cupid (*with arrow)* (Cupid departs from Venus after he has accidentaly wounded her with his arrow (*prelude to her love for Adonis*) (aft Marcantonio FRANCESCHINI)/ PR// 16,4x50,9/ Wien, ALB/ Inv.#/ Bartsch 43 (19,3) 1982, p.463,n°11(448); Miller 1991, p.xiv, pl.64, p.88, Cat.n°20/ R4981.835. *Print of PA/ oc/ 86x254/ UN, Paris sale 1880, for Vaduz, LMu.*
c1725 (att) AMIGONI, Jacopo: Venere e Cupido/ PA/ oc/ 96,5x130/ Firenze, PrC/ Inv.#/ Casazza 2005, p.188, n°64/ R5125.836.
c1775 NOVELLI, Pietro Antonio: Venus and Cupid in the clouds/ DR/ d/ 22.5x32.2/ Monte Carlo, GAL/ Inv.#/ IT/ R11691.837.
1822 TENERANI, Pietro: Venere e Amore/ SC/ m/ 16x29/ Roma, PaBr/ Inv. MR 43160/ IT/ R3767.838. *Several replicas.*

▪ Venus to the right (aft) MICHELANGELO

c1520 MICHELANGELO,Buonarroti:Venere e Amore/ DR// ?/ London, BMu/ Inv.#/ Negro 2001, p.15, fig.8/ R4304.839.
1532 MICHELANGELO, Buonarroti: Venere e Cupido/ DR/ d/ 8,5x12,1/ London, BMu/ Inv. 6-25553/ Falletti 2002, p.199, Cat.29/ R4314.840.
1532-34 CARUCCI, Jacopo (PONTORMO): Venere e Amore (aft LO cartoon by MICHELANGELO)/ PA/ ow/ 128x193/ Firenze, GdU/ Inv. 1890.1570/ Gli Uffizi-Catalogo Generale 1979, p.431, P.1258; Berenson 1963, p.147, pl.1224; Falletti 2002 ,p.189 ,n°23; Sframeli 2003,p.49; Casazza 2005, p.128-129, n°2/ R2229.*841.*
*Replica ?**c1550:** Venus und Amor (without mask at left)/ PA/ ?/ ?/ Brühl Köln, ScAB/ Inv.#/ IT/ R10069. 842.*
Preparatory DR/ ?/?/ Firenze, GdU/ Inv.#/ Duboucher, 2001,fig.102/ R7651.843. Many other painters have made copies, also details of the painting.
c1550 GHIRLANDAIO, Michele : Venere e Amore (aft MICHELANGELO or CARUCCI (PONTORMO))/ PA/ ow/ 134x193/ Roma, GaC/ Inv.117/ Berenson 1963, p.150; Negro 2001, p.11, 28/ R3299. 844. and R4303 before restauration.
Replica PA/ ow/ 135x193/ Dublin, NGI/ Inv. 77/ Negro 2001, p.18, fig.19/ R4306.845.;
(wor) PA/ ow/48x66/ Genève: MAH/ Inv. CR 354/ Negro 2001, p.16, fig.9 / R4305.846.
c1550 VASARI, Giogio : Venus and Cupid (after Jacopo PONTORMO CARUCCI)/ PA/ ow/ 128x193/ London/ RCo/ Inv.RC433/ Joannides 1996, p.27, fig.23; Falletti 2002, p.135/ R3563.847.
Replica: c1575 (cir) Venere e Cupido/ PA/ ow/ 134x194/ Firenze, GdU/ Inv. 1890-5658/ Falletti 2002, p.204/ R4315.848.
c1570 ALLORI, Alessandro: Vénus et l'Amour (aft MICHELANGELO)/ DR/ d/ 30,1x42,1/ Paris,MdL/ Inv.24/ Viatte,1988/ R2822.849.
Replica: DR/ d/ 28,2x40,9/ Paris, MdL/ Inv.12598 or 1029recto/ Viatte,1988/ R3829.850.

o with Venus seated

▪ Cupid in her arms

c1560 (att) DANTI, Vincenzo : Reclining Venus with Cupid/ SC/ z/ 19,1x22,9x12,7/ Boston, MFA/ Inv. 63.1250/ IT/ R8356.851.

c1570 CAMBIASO, Luca : Venus and Cupid/ DR/ d/ 34x23,5/ Cambridge,FAM/ Inv.1988.418/ IT/ R4197. 852.

1570-75 CAMBIASO, Luca: Venus and Cupido *(with doves)*/ PA/ oc/ 107.7x95.9/ Chicago, AIC/ Inv. 42.290/ IT/ R4451.853.

▪ Venus to the left

1510-15 (att) TIZIANO, Vecellio: Venus and Cupid/ PA/ oc/ 110,5x138,4/ London, WaC/ Inv. P19/ Anonymous 1989, Vol.I, p.956/ R648.854.

1525 PALMA Il Vecchio, Jacopo: Venus and Cupid/ PA/ oc/ 134x142/ Kopenhagen, SMK/ Inv. KMSst288/ IT/ R7560.855.

1531 ALCIATO, Andrea : Amor *(collecting honey, stung by a bee)* runs to Venus (*Emblematum liber)*/ IL/ CXIII/ IT/ R6048.856.

c1540 PRIMATICCIO, Francesco: Vénus (et l'Amour)/ DR/ d/ 20,7x15,8/ Paris, MdL/ Inv. 8557r/ IT/ R3433.857.

c1550 MANNOZZI, Giovanni: Venus and Cupid/ PA/?/?/WEB, Corbis/ Inv.#/ IT/ R2717.858.

c1550 MARCO da FAENZA: Venere colpita accidentalmente dalla freccia di Cupido/ FR/ tf/ 61x48/ Firenze, PaV/ Inv.#/ IT/ R8593.859.

1592 FONTANA, Lavinia: Vénus et Cupidon (Isabelle Ruini as Venus ; Venus Casta ; Diane de Poitiers)/ PA/ oc/ 75x60/ Rouen, MBA/ Inv. D 874.15/ Murphy 2003, p.102, n°88/ R8681.860.

c1600 (att) ALBANI, Francesco : Venus and Cupid/ PA/ oc/ 38.2x40.5/ UN, LO/ Inv. 13314/ IT www.lootedart.com/ R10151.861.

c1600 BILIVERTI, Giovanni: Vénus enchainée par l'Amour (Venus chained by Amor)/ PA/ oc/ 108x81/ Paris, MdL/ Inv.20225/ IT/ R2489.862.

c1600 (cir) TINTORETTO, Domenico: Venus and Cupid/ DR/ d/ 19x14/ NY, BON 27.1.'06/ Sl. 13698-158/ IT/ 6517.863.

c1620 PROCACCINI, Guido Cesare: Venus and Cupid/ DR/ d/ 20.2x17.7/ Milano, BiA/ Inv. 2155/ IT/ R11553V.864.

c1625 SAN GIOVANNI, Giovanni da : Venus and Cupid/ PA/ ?/ ?/ UN, Corbis/ IT/ R2717.865.

c1650 GUERCINO, Giovane Francesco Barbieri: Venere con un amorino (?)/ DR/ d/ 26,2x23,7/ Madrid, ASF/ Inv.205/ Perez Sancho 1977, n°28 Coll.Filippo V/ R3757.866.

c1787 CANOVA, Antonio: Venere e Amore/ DR/ d/ 15.6x16/ Bassano, MuC/ Inv. 1081/ Stefani 2003, p.51, n°43; Stefani 2004, p.34, 165, nr.35/R10161.867.

1789 CANOVA, Antonio: Venere con Amore in fasce/ PA/ oc/ 132x82/ Possagno, CdC/ Inv. 43/ Stefani 2004, p.35,165, nr.37/R10176.868.

Preparatory DR/ d/ 20.8x13.1/ Bassano, MuC/ Inv. 1241/ Stefani 2004, p.34,165, nr.36/ R10175.869.

c1789 CANOVA, Antonio : Venere e Amore/ SC/ p/ 26.5x24x11/ Possagno, CdC/ Inv.98/ Stefani 2003, p.52-53, nr.46/ R10159.870.

c1830 (cir) BIGATTI, Tommaso : Venus coronando al Amor/ PA/ gi/ 15.6x12/ Madrid, MLG/ Inv. 7478/ IT/ R6355.871.

▪ Venus to the right

1516-17 (wor) RAFFAELLO, Sanzio : Venus wounded by Cupid's arrow (in 'La stufetta del Cardinale Bibbiena) (att ROMANO, Giulio)/ FR// ?/ Roma, MuV/ Inv.#/ Porcheron-Felsing 1983, p.24,291,351, fig.10 ; Bober 1986, p.62, n°17 ; Massari 1989, p.44-46,n°12b;fig.8, p.46; Clayton 1999, p.118-20, fig.55 / R3527.872.

Several att ROMANO, Giulio/DR/ d/ 21,1x17,2/ Windsor,RCo/Inv.RL12757/ R3526.873. Copy in Wien, ALB/ Inv.215/ R3487. Copies by other artists.

c1516 RAIMONDI, Marcantonio : Venus and Eros *(in a landscape)* (after RAFAELLO)/PR/e/ 18,2x13,1/ Wien, ALB/ Inv.#/ Bartsch 26 (14,1) 1978, p.271,n°286-II(218)/ R4809.874.
'in an interior': PR//16,1x12/ Wien, ALB/ Inv.#/ Bartsch 26 (14,1) 1978, p.273,n°286-A(218)/ R4810.875.
1516 VENEZIANO, Agostino: Venere ferita da Cupido (aft ROMANO, Giulio) (*pub Antonio Salamanca)*/ PR (with initials AV upper left)/ e/ 17,6x13,3/ Roma, ING/ Inv. FN355/ Massari 1989, p.44-46,n°12b/ R3486. 876. *Copies in Cambridge, FWM, Philadelphia, SF, Washington and Wien.*
c1525-32 UDINE, Giovanni da : Venere e Amore (Il bagno di Clemente VII)/ FR/?/ Roma,CSA/ Inv. E51496iccd/ IT iccd ; Porcheron-Felsing 1983, p.38,63, fig.22/ R8267.877.
1540 BORDONE, Paris : Venere e Cupido/ PA/ oc/ 107x93/ Firenze, PaV/ Inv. 1890, n. 9940/ IT/ R8579. 878.
c1550 FRANCO, Giovanni Battista: Venus and Cupid/ DR/ d/ 24,3x16,3/ London, BMu/ Inv. 1946-7-13-341/ ?/ R6950.879.
c1550 PRIMATICCIO, Francesco: Vénus et l'Amour/ DR/ d/ 38,5x24,8/ Fontainebleau,MNC/ Inv. 1986.2.11/ IT/ R2821.880. *Replica : DR/ d/ 15,7x22,2/ Haarlem, TMu/ Inv. A*60/ Mai ed. 2001, p.408,n°T14.*
1617 FIALETTI, Odoardo: Venere pettina Amore (Venus combing Amor's hair) (from the series 'Scherzi d'Amore' (The Sport of Love))/ PR/ e/ 18x9,3/ Roma, ING/ Inv. FC89203/ Bartsch 38 (17,5) 1983, p.208,n°10(268); Massari 1989, p.470,n°182/ R3509.881. *Also in Glasgow, HMAG/ Inv. 6250; London, BMu; Paris, BNF/ Inv.#/ Dunand & Lemarchand, s.d., III, p.951, fig.1478 à 1489/ R11151*
1617 FIALETTI, Odoardo: Venere rimprovera Amore che piange (Venus reproaching Amor) (from the series 'Scherzi d'Amore' -The Sport of Love/ PR/ e/ 14,8x9,2/ Roma, ING/ Inv. FC89208/ Bartsch 38 (17,5) 1983, p.212, n°14(269) ; Massari 1989, p.474,n°186 / R3513.882. *Also in Cambridge, FWM/ Inv. AD.1.18-151; Glasgow, HMAG/ Inv. 6254; London, BMu; Paris, BNF/ Inv.#/ Dunand & Lemarchand, s.d., III, p.951, fig.1478 à 1489/ R11151*
c1625 VAROTARI, Alessandro : Venere che riposa con un amorino/ PA/ oc/ 156x109/ Venezia, CaR/ Inv.40 Col.Martini/ Martini 2002, p.211-212, n°169/ R960.883.
c1650 GUERCINO, Barbieri Giovane Francesco, detto: Venere e Amore/ PA(FR)// ?/ Roma, GASL/ Inv. E21289iccd/ Cicinelli A & Vasco Rocca S (1978), Vol. I, p. 34/ R8901.884.
c1700 BELLUCCI, Antonio: Venus und Amor (*with dove)*/ PA/ ?/ ?/ Dresden, SKS/ Inv. #/ Weichardt s.d., pl.31/ R10413.885.
c1800-10 APPIANI, Andrea: Venere e Amore/ DR/ d/ 11.1x13.6/ Milano, VBB/ Inv. GAM1197/ IT/ R9066.886.
c1830 (cir) BIGATTI, Tommaso : Venus y el Amor/ PA/ gi/ 15.5x12/ Madrid, MLG/ Inv. 7479/ IT/ R8282. 887.

o with Venus standing

▪ Venus in the centre

c1500 (att) PARENTINO, Bernardo: Venus and Cupid trampling on a serpent beside an altar/ DR: df/ 24.2x17.1/ London, VAM/ Inv. Dyce 1../ Ward-Jackson 1979, Vol.I, p.19-20, n°14/ R11121.888.
c1550 FRANCIA, Jacopo : Venus holding a draftsman's square and Cupid at her side/ PR/ e/ 22,8x14,9/ London, BMu/ Inv.#/ Bartsch 31 (15,4) 1986, p.295,n°6(459)/ R4922.889.
c1550 (att) TORELLI, Lodovico: Venus and Cupid/ DR/ d/ 10,9x10,3 oval/ Milano, BiA/ Inv. F 281 inf. n. 19/ IT/ R8732.890.
c1575 CAMBIOASO, Luca : Vénus debout sur le globe du monde, avec l'Amour à ses pieds/ DR/ d/ 34.8x21.5/ Paris, MdL/ Inv. 9335, rect/ IT/ R10197.891.
c1878 FRANCHI, Pietro: Vénus et l'Amour (aft C.-A.Fraikin)/ SC/ m/ 89/ London, SOT 16.11.'06/ Sl. L06232-4/ IT/ R7922.892.

▪ Venus to the left

c1525 GRANACCI, Francesco: Venus and Amor ? (standing nude woman with putto)/ DR/ d/ 26.5x11.2/ Stockholm, NMK/ Inv. NMAnck471/ Bjurström 2001, Cat.1087/ R11007.893. *Closely related to DR/ Firenze, GdU/ Berenson 1938, n°922, fig.382.*

c1539 SALVIATI, Francesco : Venere e Cupido (aft MICHELANGELO)/ DR/ d/ 35,5x24,3/Firenze,GdU/Inv. 14673F/ Falletti 2002, Cat.9, p.158/ R4311.894.

c1550 BONASONE, Giulio: Venus and Cupid (aft RAFFAELLO, Sanzio?)/ PR/ e/ 16,8x8,5/ Wien, ALB/ Inv.HB XXXV/ Bartsch 28 (15,1) 1985, p.351, n°145 (149/ R4841.895.

c1550 (att) CATTANEO, Danese: Venus and Cupid/ SC/ z/ 42/ A'dam, SOT 18.5.'99/ Sl.-309/ IT/ R8272. 896.

c1550 (cir) SANSOVINO, Jacopo: Venus and Cupid/ SC/ z/ 87,5x35x14,5/ LA, JPG/ Inv.87.SB.50/ IT/ R296.897.

1564-75 AMMANNATI, Bartolomeo & BIGIO, Nanni di B.: grotesque of Venus and Cupid (The 'Studiolo' of Francesco de'Medici (1541-87))/ FR// ?/ Roma, ViM/ Inv.#/ IT/ R8999.898.

c1577 ZUCCHI, Jacopo : Vénus *(and Cupid)*/ FR// Roma, ViM/ Inv.#/ Porcheron-Fersing1983p.67,70, n°37 / R8268.899.

1590 ASPETTI, Tiziano : Venere e Cupido/ SC/ z/ 41x15/ Firenze, PaD/ Inv. 61/ IT/ R8575.900.

c1590 CAMPAGNA, Girolamo: Venere e Amore/ SC/ z/ ?/ Roma, PaV/ Inv. F14967iccd/ IT/ R8930.901.

c1630 GUIDI, Giovanni Citosibio: Venus e Cupido (aft SC? by Bloemaert, Cornelis)/ PR/ e/ 55x37/ Lisboa, BNP/ Inv. E. 468 A/ IT/ R10215.902.

1657 GALESTRUZZI, Giovanni Battista: Venere e Amore (with poppies; from 'The Antique Figural Gems' Roma/ PR// 9,7x7,8/Milano, BiA/Inv.#/ Bartsch 46 (21,1) 1982, p.175,n°176(73); Bartsch 46 C 1985, p.214, n°4606.176 /R4990.903.

c1810 MAESTRI, Michelangelo : Venus und Cupido Venus über dem Erdkreis schwebend (Venus and Cupid hovering above the earth)/ PA/ gb/ 57x39/ München, HAM 15.12.07/ Sl. ?-304/ IT/ R11597.904.

1972 MAROTTA, Gino: Venere/ PR/ lj/ 190x80/ UN/ Inv.#/ Bolaffi 1979, p.215/ R8626.905.

▪ Venus to the right

c1510 ALBERTINELLI, Mariotto di Biagio di Bindo: Venus mit Amor/ DR/ d/ 21.3x26.8/ Berlin, KSK/ Inv. KdZ 2309/ IT/ R10059.906.

c1510 SERBALDI da PESCIA, Pier Maria: Venus and Cupid/ SC/ s/ 25,6/ Firenze, PaP/ Inv. 1067/ Sframeli 2003, n°3,p.72/ R6007.907.

c1515 (wor) RAFFAELLO, Sanzio: Venus and Cupid (in 'Stufetta' of Cardinal Bibbiena)/ FR//?/ Roma, MuV/ Inv. #/ Redig de Campos 1981, p.124, fig.94/ R10790.908.

c1525 PARMIGIANINO (MAZZOLA), Girolamo Francesco: Venus and Cupid/ DR/ d/ 13.7x6.9/ Chicago, AIC/ Inv. 1922.2688/ IT/ R10255.909.

c1529 PERINO DEL VAGA, Pietro Bonaccorsi, detto: Venus and Amor/ FR/ / ?/ Genova, PDP/ Inv. #/ IT/ R10083.910.

c1550 ALBERTI, Cherubino: Venus (*showing her back)* and Cupid (aft CALDARA da CARAVAGGIO, Polidoro)/ PR/ e/ 17,7x12,1/ London, BMu/ Inv.#/ Bartsch 34(17,1) 1982 p.214,#93(81) / R4953.911.

c1550 ALBERTI, Cherubino: Venus (*running)* triumphant and Amor (copy in reverse from *Mythological Subjects* aft CALDARA da CARAVAGGIO, Polidoro)/ PR/ e/ 16,2x13,9/ London, BMu/ Inv.#/ Bartsch 34(17,1), 1982 p.204,n°84(79) / R713.912. *Also in Glasgow, HMAG/ Inv. 10444; S.F.,FAM/ Inv. 30.36822.*

c1550 (cir) CAMPI, Bernardino : Venus (?) and Cupid/ DR/ d/ 22.7x13.9/ Chicago, AIC/ Inv. 1922.1037/ IT/ R10253.913.

c1550 (att) PRIMATICCIO, Francesco: Vénus et l'Amour/ PA/ ow/ ?/ Ecouen, MuR/ Inv. ECL819/ / R7630 Quignard 1982,p.68/ R7630.914.

1561 VICO, Enea : Venere e Cupido/ PR/e/ 41,8x28,3/ Roma, PaBr/ Inv. MR 15545/ Bartsch 30 (15,3) 1985, p.34, n°24-II(293)/ R3769.915.

c1600 BOSCOLI, Andrea : Venere e Amore/ FR// ?/ Corliano, VAS/ Inv.#/ IT/ R4154.916.
Preparatory DR/ d/ 13,1x6,7/ Milano, BiA/ Inv. F253inf.n.933/ IT/ R8715.917.

8. VENUS STANDING AND CUPID

c1850 ROMANELLI, Pasquale: Venus y Cupido/ SC/ s/ 98 x 38 x 31/ Madrid, MLG/ Inv. 5558/ IT/ R6352.918.
Replica (?) ***c1850*** *SC/ m/ 139.7/ NY, SOT 22.11.'05/ Sl. N08128-195/ IT/ R5155.919.*

9. Venus and Cupids

c1485 FERRUCCI, Francesco di Simone: Skizzen zweier Venusfiguren und Putti / DR/ d/ 27.9x19.8/ Berlin, KSK/ Inv. KdZ 1360r/ IT/ R10058.920. *Also (att) VERROCCHIO?*
c1590 NIGRONE, Giovanni Antonio: Wandbrunnen mit Venus und Amoretten/ ILL/ tx/ ?/ Napoli, BiN/ Inv. Ms. XII. G. 59-60/ IT/ R10100V.921.
1740 (att) PINTUCCI, Niccolo: Venere e putti/ FR//?/ Firenze, UN/ Inv.#/ IT/ R8602V.922.

○ with other people

c1550 GHISI, Giorgio: Venere con due dee e due putti (aft PRIMATICCIO)/ PR/ e/ 18x23,8/ Paris, BNF/ Inv. Eb14a/ Bartsch 31 (15,4) 1986, p.115,n°49(404); Bellini 1998, p.194-195,n°43/ R3656.923. *Also in Glasgow, HMAG/Inv.6328.*
c1621-33 ALBANI, Francesco: Les Amours désarmés (The Cupids disarmed *by Diana, Venus watching in the sky*)/ PA/?/ 202x250/ Paris, MdL/ Inv. 11/ IT/ R542.924.
c1752 VANVITELLI, Luigi: Venus with cherubs and hand maidens/ FR//?/ Caserta, PeP/ Inv.#/ IT/ R2754. 925.

○ with Venus reclining

▪ Venus in the centre

c1700 BELLUCCI, Antonio: Venus und Amor (with cupids around)/ FR//?/Wien, LMu/ Inv. #/ IT/ R10305.926.
c1776 BRENNA, Vicenzo: Grotesken mit liegender Venus (Tafel 10: Domus Aurea, Saal 85) (*eng CARLONI, Marco)*/ PR/ ?/ ?/ Roma, BiH/ Inv. 1997.04#/ IT/ R10127.927. *DR by BRENNA, Vicenzo.*

▪ Venus to the left

c1500 BOTTICELLI, Sandro : Vénus et trois putti (Venus and three putti)/ PA/ ow/ 85x219/ Paris, MdL/ Inv. MI 546/ Reid 1993, p.114/ R510.928.
Also (att) SELLAIO, Jacopo del/ Berenson 1963, p.198-99; similar (fol or school) BOTTICELLI (prev. att SELLAIO): Venus with three putti (Clothed, reclining Venus in landscape with three cupids - an allegory)/ PA/ ow/ 92.1x173/ London, NGa/ Inv. NG916/ R10273.929.
c1525 BRESCIANINO, Andrea: Reclining Venus with cupids/ PA/ ow/ 68x149/ London, PrC/ Inv.#/ Berenson 1968, p.66; Falletti 2002, p.162,n°11/ R4312.930.
1548 PRIMATICCIO, Francesco: Une femme nue approchée par des enfants portant des fruits, Vénus ? (*Venus reclining like Venus of Urbino)*/ DR/ d/ 21,5x29,1/ Paris, MdL/ Inv. 8522/ IT/ R3403.931.
c1550 RICCIARELLI da Volterra: Lagernde Venus mit zwei Putten/ DR/ d/ 9.8x13.1/ Berlin, KSK/ Inv. KdZ5585/ IT/ R10079.932.
c1625 ALBANI, Francesco: Venere e Cupido/ PA/ ?/ ?/ Roma, GaB/ Inv.#/ IT fototeca/ R8500.933.
c1650 ALBANI, Francesco: Venus och amoriner i ett landskap (Landscape with Venus and Cupids)/ PA/ oy/ 31x42/ Stockholm, NMK/ Inv.NM 2/ IT/ R5812.934.
c1650 (wor) ALBANI, Francesco: Venus and Cupid*(s)*/ PA/ cy/ 29,7x39,6/ London, WaC/ Inv. P642/ Anonymous 1989, Vol.I, p.957/ R647.935.
c1650 DIAMANTINI, Giuseppe: Venus and many putti/ PR/e/25,2x19,3/London, BMu/ Inv.#/ Bartsch 47 (21,2) 1983 p.412,#28(282) / R5004.936.
c1650 (cir) ROMANELLI, Giovanni Francesco: Venere *(with cupids)*/ FR// ?/ Roma, PaLR/ Inv. #iccd/ IT/ R8936.937.
c1660 MARATTA, Carlo: Venere con tre amorini/ FR// ?/ Roma, GNB/ Inv. E28915iccd/ IT/ R8914.938.

c1660 (att) SIRANI, Elisabetta: Venus und amoretti in Landschaft/ PA/ oc/ 75x99/ München, HAM/ Sl.?-272/ IT/ R11596.939.

1690 RICCI, Sebastiano: Venere con due putti/ PA/ oc/ 119x169,5/ Wien, DOR 4.10.'06/ Sl. 105/ Calabrese 2003, p.307; IT/ R2222.940.

1694 FRANCHI, Antonio: Venere e amorini/ PA/ oc/ 104x143/ Firenze, PaP/ Inv.4905/ Sframeli 2003, p.114, °22/ R4005.941.

c1700 CHIARI, Giuseppe Bartolomeo : Venere e amore in un paesaggio/ PA/ oc/ 70 x 88/ WIEN, DOR 24.4.'07/ Sl. –47/ IT/ R9398.942.

c1700 RICCI, Sebastiano: Venere con amorini/ PA/ oc/ 119x169,5/ Vicenza, PaT/ Inv. #/ Scarpa 2006, p.266, cat.352, fig.235 (Paris, PrC: replica?)/ R10438.943.

c1705 VIANI, Domenici Maria: Venus mit zwei Amoretten (Venus with two cupids)/ PA/ oy/ 28,5x36,5/ Dresden, SKS/ Inv.404/ Mai ed. 2001, p.236-37, n°6/ R2223.944.

c1725 BONECCHI, Matteo: Venus and Cupid with putti/ PA/ oc/ 42,2x62/ London, CHR 2.11.'05/ Sl.5827-117/ IT/ R4881.945.

1777 BARTOLOZZI, Francesco: Venere circondata da putti (For the benefit of Mr.Giardini) (aft CIPRIANI, Giovanni Battista)/ PR/ e/ 9,2x11,5/ Roma, ING/ Inv.FC67602/ Jatta 1995 p.136, fig.45/ R3749. 946.

1783 BARTOLOZZI, Francesco: Venere e Cupido (Venus and Cupid *and other cupid)* (aft Reynolds, Joshua)/ PR/ e/ 57,4x29,4/ Roma, ING/ Inv.FC70027/ Jatta 1995 p.154-155, fig.79/ R3752.947.

▪ Venus to the right

c1515 ROMANO, Giulio Pippi, detto: Venus with the Erotes of Philostratus/ DR/ d/ 35.3x37.8/ Chatsworth, DCo/ Inv. #/ Jaffé 1995, Cat.25/ R10386. *Preparatory DR for FR?/ Roma, ViM/ Inv. #/ R10078V. 948.*

c1525 (att) DOSSI, Battista: Venus und Amoretten/ PA/ ow/ 65x47/ Berlin, GSM/ Inv. 350/ IT/ R10070. 949.

c1545 BONASONE, Giulio: Venere con amorini (Venus on a cloud ... a river god below)/ PR/ e/ 16,5x11,3/ Roma, ING/ Inv.FN1169/ Bartsch 29 (15,2) 1982,p.27n°163-II(152); Massari 1989, p.202-203,n°82a/ R3500.950. *Also in NY, MMA.*

c1625 VAROTARI, Alessandro : Venere con amorini/ PA/ ?/ 62x101/ Venezia, PaG 6-22.10.'84/ Sl.#/IT/ R5914.951.

c1650 ALBANI, Francesco: Venus resting *(with Cupids around)/* PA/ oy/ 37x51/ Firenze, GdU/ Inv.#/ IT/ R4515.952.

c1650 GIMIGNANI, Giacinto: Venus awakened by Cupid(s)/ PA/ oc oval/ 49,6x64,1/ NY, CHR 6.4.'06/ Sl. 1776-248/ IT/ R6056.953. *Pre. (att) ROMANELLI, G. F.*

c1725 LORENZINI, Fra Antonio: Reclining Venus and cupids (aft Carlo CIGNANI, aft M. FRANCESCHINI)/ PR/ ?/ ?/ Forli, PrC?/ Inv. #/ Miller 1991, p.99-100, Cat.n°36, pl.94/ R9825.954.

1755 ANSALDI, Innocenzo Andrea : Venere e putti/ DR/ d/ 39,5x58/ Pescia: MuC/ Inv. 1366/ IT/ R8574. 955.

1779 BARTOLOZZI, Francesco: Venere con amorini (Biglietto per il concerto di Felice Giardini) (aft CIPRIANI, Giovanni Battista)/ PR/ e/ 15,4x17,5/ Roma,ING/ Inv.FC67617/ Jatta 1995 p.139, fig.52/ R3772. 956. *Also in London, RAA/Inv.03-743.*

○ with Venus seated

c1500 ROBETTA, Christofano: Venus surrounded by cupids/ PR/ e/ 24,7x18/ Wien, ALB/ Inv.#/ Bartsch 25 (13,2) 1980, p.292,n°18(403)/ R4796.957.

c1525 ROMANINO, Girolamo di Romano: Sitzende Venus (?) mit Putten/ DR/ d/ ?/ Berlin, KSK/ Inv. KdZ 25174/ IT/ R9991.958.

c1527 (att) PARMIGIANINO (MAZZOLA), Girolamo Francesco: Venus with Cupid and putto/ DR/ d/ 28.8x20.9/ Chicago, AIC/ Inv. 1960.359/ IT/ R10251.959.

a1552 MASTER of FLORA: Venus and Cupid/ PA/ oc/ 96x70/ SF, FAM Inv. 1973-4/ Mai ed. 2001, p.376-77, n°68/ R8476.960.

c1575 MONTEMEZZANO, Francesco: Venus and cherubs/ PA/ ?/ ?/ Venezia, GdA/ Inv.520/ Berenson 1958, p.124/ R9000.961.
c1620 GUERCINO, Giovane Francesco Barbieri: Venus scolding Cupid *(with second cupid around)*/ DR/ d/ 18,2x26,2/ Chattsworth, DCo/ Inv. 514/ IT/ R7163.962.
c1650 CARPIONI, Giulio: Venus surrounded by cupids/ PR/e/30,5x17/ Wien, ALB/ Inv.#/ Bartsch 45 (20,2) 1982,p.81,n°8(186); Bartsch 45 C (20,2) 1990,p.102,n°4504.014/ R4984.963. *Also in Berlin.*
c1650 GIMIGNANI, Giacinto: Venus und Amor/ PA/ oc/ 44.5x31/ Wien, DOR 16.10.07/ Sl. ?-36/ IT/ R11093.964.
c1750 CIPRIANI, Giovanni Battista: Venus binding her hair with a garland, attended by cupids/ PR/ e/ ?/ London, VAM/ Inv.#/ IT/ R8990.965.

o with Venus standing

c1510 RAIMONDI, Marcantonio : Venus *(with torch)* attended by two cupids (aft RAFFAELLO?)/ PR/ e/ 7,9x4,7/ Wien, ALB/ Inv.#/ Bartsch 26 (14,1) 1978, p.236,n°239(192)/R4808.966.
c1520 BRESCIANINO, Andrea: Venere tra due amorini (Venus between two cupids in a niche)/ PA/ oc/ 150x66/ Roma, GaB/ Inv.324/ Berenson 1968, p.66, pl.1574; Porcheron-Felsing 1983, p.242,n°48; Staccioli 1985,p.75; Moreno 2004, p.238, n°4/ R003.967.
c1525 PARMIGIANINO, Girolamo: Venus *(holding arrow)* and Amor *(holding bow and cupids around)*/ DR/ d/ 24,3x15,9/ Wien, ALB/ Inv. 2663/ Mai ed. 2001, p.405,n°T10/ R8477.968.
1636 PODESTI, Giovanni Andrea: Statue of Venus with Numerous Putti (reverse aft TIZIANO R469)/ PR/ e/ 31,4x38,9/ SF, FAM/ Inv. 1993.63.4/ IT/ R8557.969.
c1705 RICCI, Sebastiano: Venus und Cupido (*with cupids*)/ FR/ pre.ceiling of Pa Mocenigo-Robilant/ 223x84/ Berlin, GSM/ Inv. 02554583,T,003/ Scarpa 2006, p.156, cat.39, fig.172/ R10436.970. *Part of 9 frescoes.*
1778 CAMPANELLA, Angelo: Venus with putti pl.I (aft Anton Raphael Mengs)/ PR/ er/ 48.6x60.5/ Wien, ALB/ Inv. 46123/ Joyce 1983; Roettgen 2001, p.248-251, fig.80a <aft FR LO in ancient roman home near Villa Peretti-Negroni (Stazione Termini), Roma>/ R11010.971.
Plate I of XII; at auction among a set of seven/ London, CHR 9.3.06/ Sl. 7198-220/ IT/ R5924.972. A wall decoration exists in the Pompeian Room, Ickworth Rotunda, Bury St.Edmunds

10. Venus and the Judgement of Paris/ Venus with Helen and Paris

c1530 PERINO DEL VAGA, Pietro: Studies of figures, including a Judgement of Paris/ DR verso/ d/ ?/ London, BMu/ Inv. 1948,0710.00006/ IT/ R8439V.973.
1543 FANTUZZI, Antonio: Jupiter decides for the judgement of Paris/ PR/ e/ 34,7x50/ München, SGS/ Inv.#/ Mai ed. 2001, p.436, n°G13/ R8483.974.
c1550 SCHIAVONE, Andrea Meldolla, detto: Giudizio di Paride/ PA/ ?/ ?/ Torino, GaS/ Inv. 562/ Berenson 1958, p.166/ R9626V.975. *DR (preparatory?) in London, BMu/ Inv. fol.72/ Healy 1997, p.169, note nr.118.*
c1550 UDINE, Giovanni da : Judgement of Paris (representation of Roman sarcophagus, Vatican Loggia)/ Roma, MuV/ Inv.#/ Bober 1986, p.149-150,n°119/ R8136V.976.
c1600 ALBANI, Francesco: Paris awarding the apple to Venus/ DR/ d/ 24,6x25,3/ Washington, NGA/ Inv. 1972.59.1/ IT/ R8444V.977.
c1600 PARIGI, Giulio: Il guidizio di Paride/ PR/ e/ 19.5x27.5/ Venezia, FGC/ Inv. N.10/ IT/ R11500V. 978. *Scenograph eng by Remigio Cantagallina.*
c1600 PROCACCINI, Camillo: Jugement de Pâris/ DR/ d/ 17.1x13.8/ Rennes, MBA/ Inv. 794.1.3168/ IT/ R10629V.979.
c1700 FREZZA, Giovanni Girolamo: The judgment of Paris/ PR/ e/ 39 x 46.3/ Cambridge, FAM/ Inv. R2892/ IT/ R9952V.980.
b1741 (att) LOCATELLI, Andrea: Jugement de Pâris/ PA/ oc/ 48x68/ Troyes, MBA/ Inv. 892.1.3/ IT/ R10610V.981.

○ alone with the goddesses

c1515 (cir) RAFFAELLO, Sanzio:Judgement of Paris (beneath Parnassus lunette, Stanza della Segnatura/ FR// ?/ Roma, MuV/ Inv.#/ Healy, 1997, p.163, note nr.12/ R10781V.982.
c1636 COCCAPANI, Sigismondo: Parisapfel and Palla Medicea (wedding allegory)/ PA/ ?/ ?/ Stuttgart, SGa/ Inv. #/ Healy 1997, p.168, note nr.100/ R10786V.983.
c1700 MARINALI, Orazio: Giudizio di Paride: Venere, Paride, Minerva, Giunone/ SC/ s/ ?/ Vicenza, PaT/ Inv.#/ IT/ R11486.984.

▪ Paris in the centre

c1505 FRANCIA, Francesco : Giudizio di Paride/ DR/ d/ 31x25,9/ Wien, ALB/ Inv. 4859/ Faietti 1988, p.262, XXIV,n°67; Healy 1997, fig.15, p.165, note nr.55/ R3538.985.
c1650 SAN GIOVANNI, Giovanni da: Judgment of Paris (and) Paris awarding Golden Appel to Venus/ RE//?/ Firenze, PaP/ Campbell 1994, fig.5-6, p.267/ R4297.986.
c1950 BARBARO, Achille: Giudizio di Paride/ SC/ p/ 270x140/ Crema, MCC/ Inv.#/ IT/ R8514.987.

▪ Paris to the left

c1420-1461 (att) DOMENICO VENEZIANO: Judgement of Paris/ PA/ tw cassone/ 39,7x49,8/ Glasgow, GAGM/ Inv. 35-634, pre. PrC Burell/ Berenson 1963, p.61; Healy 1997, fig.6, p.164, note nr.26/ R10269.988. *Also (att) MAESTRO del GIUDIZIO di PARIDE or PARIS MASTER. According to Berenson, a companion panel 'June, Venus and Minerva approaching Paris' was in Wien, Col. Lanckoronski.*
c1500 BIAGIO di Antonio: Judgement of Paris/ PA/ cassone/ 44.5x39/ London, PrC/ Inv. #/ Healy 1997, fig.10, p.164, note nr.31./ R10495.989. *Also (att) UTILE da FAENZA.*

c1500 MASTER IO.FF: Jugement de Paris/ RE/ z/ ∅5.6/ Ecouen, MuR/ Inv. E.Cl.20058/ Schwartz & Garcia 2004, p.144/ R10609.990. *Also in Cleveland, MuA/ Inv. 1984.54; Hanover, HMu/ Inv. EL.S.993.19.20.*
c1500 (att) MASTER of PARIS: The sleep of Paris/ PA/ cassone/ ?/ UN, pre. Wien, Lanckoronski Col/ Inv. #/ Healy 1997, fig.11, p.164,165, notes nr.30, 37./ R10496.991.
c1500 MODENA, Nicoletto da: Judgment of Paris (upper part of ornamental panel)/ PR// 25,9x12,6/ Wien, ALB/ Inv.#/ Bartsch 25 (13,2) 1984, p.126-,n°54(284)/ R4793.992. *Also in Cleveland, MuA/ Inv. 1963.460.*
c1505 (att) GIORGIONE, Giorgio Barbarelli: Judgement of Paris/ PA/ oc/ 52x67/ Dresden, SKS, LO 2nd World War/ Inv.187/ *Berenson 1958, p.88; Healy 1997, fig.23, p.20-21,168, note nr.102-104*/R6295.993. Original or *copy ? Copy: **c1575** Anonimo giorgionesco: Giudizio di Paride (with Mercury in the sky)/ PA/ oc/ 60x74: Chiavari, PrC Lanfranchi Col./ Inv.#/ Healy 1997, 23, 168-169, note nrs.103,117/ R10787.*
c1520 (cir) RAFFAELLO, Sanzio : Jugement de Pâris/ DR/ d/ 19.4x26.4/ Paris, MdL/ Inv. 4300r/ Cordelier & Py 1992, p.163-164,n°219/ R3834.994.
c1550 ABATE, Nicolo dell' : Le jugement de Pâris/ DR/ d/ 2,20x18,6/ Paris, MdL/ Inv. 5862,recto / IT/ R8030.995.
1634 SAN GIOVANNI, Giovanni da: Giudizio di Paride/ FR//Ó62/ Firenze, GdU/ Inv. 5416/ Casazza 2005, p.208, n°83/ R8361.996.
1644 DELLA BELLA, Stefano: Jugement de Paris *(Jeu des Fables: n°526)*/ IL/ e/ 8,3x5,1/De Vesme 1971, Vol.I:105-107; Vol.II:108-113/R8275.997.
c1760 GUARDI, Francesco: Il giudizio di Paride/ PA/ oc/ 41x55/ Venezia, CaR/ Inv.#/ Romanelli 1998,p.4 ; Llorens 1997, p.156-157, Cat.33/ R951.998.
1880 QUADRONE, Giovan Battista : Il giudizio di Paride/ PA/ oc/ 40x58/ UN/ Inv.#/ CELIT 1981 Vol 7, p.4901/ R8671.999.

▪ Paris to the right

c1475 GIORGIO MARTINI, Francesco di: Judgment of Paris/ RE/ z/ 13,7x13,2/ Washington, NGA/ Inv. 1957.14.140/ Berenson 1968, p.142/ R8244.1000. *Berenson 1968, p.140 refers to a "cassone"(?) in Boston, Edward Wheelwright.*
1495 (wor) BOTTICELLI, Sandro : Il giudizio di Paride (Judgement of Paris)/ PA/ tw/ 81x187/ Venezia, FGC/ Inv.#/ Healy 1997, fig.8, p.164, note nr.28/ R3733.1001.
c1500 COLONNA, Francesco: Le jugement de Pâris *(Hypnerotomachia Poliphili fol.k7r)*/ IL/ e/ ?/ Damisch 1997, p.151; Healy 1997, fig.12/ R7977.1002.
1504-05 RAIMONDI, Marcantonio: Paris dom/ PR/ e/ 18,2x22,1/ Stockholm, NMK/ Inv. NMG B 1011/ Bartsch 27 (14,2) 1978, p.34,n°339(254); Faietti 1988, p.117-119, n°14; Healy 1997, fig.16, p.166, note nr.62/ R3533.1003. *Also in Berlin, London.*
c1525 VENDRI, Antonio da: Het oordeel van Paris/ PA/ oc/ 71x77/ A'dam, RMu/ Inv. SK-A-1296/ IT/ R10597.1004.
b1626 GATTI, Oliviero: Judgment of Paris (from the *'Emblemata' of Paolo Maccio*.XXXII)/ PR //10,9x9,1/ Inv.#/ Bartsch 41 (19,1) 1981, p.90,n°80(27)/ R4973.1005.
c1695-1700 SOLDANI-Benzi, Massimiliano : The judgement of Paris/ SC/ z/ 38/ Wien, LMu/ Inv. SK911/ exh/ R6914.1006.
c1750 FONTEBASSO, Francesco: Judgment of Paris/ FR/ /?/ Venezia, PaB/ Inv.#/ IT artresource/ R8537.1007.
1860-63 CARNOVALI, Giovanni : Giudizio di Paride/ DR/ d/ 10,8x17,7/ Cremona, MAP/ Inv.#/ IT/ R8513.1008.
c1926 MONTANARI, Giuseppe: Il pomo (*a man offering the apple to one of three women)*/ PA/ o/ ?/ UN/ Inv.#/ Di Genova 1994, p.839, n°1106/ R8640.1009. *Although nor the name of Paris nor the name of Venus appear in the title, the attribute 'apple' and the three women make the reference to the Judgement of Paris obvious.*
1971 PETAZZI, Elio : Il giudizio di Paride/ PA/ oc/ 100x120/ UN/ Inv.#/ CELIT 1985 Vol 10, p.7034/ R8668.1010.
1986 MANIGLIO, Carlo: Il giudizio di Paride/ PA/ oc/ 60x80/ UN/ Inv.#/ CELIT 1988 Vol 12, p.8293/ R8664.1011.

1987 BRAGHIERI, Giancarlo : Giudizio di Paride/ PA/ oc/ 50x60/ Piacenza, PrC/ Inv.867/ IT/ R7035. 1012.

○ Cupid(s) around

▪ Paris in the centre

c1670 GIORDANO, Luca: Das Parisurteil/ PA/ oc/ 232x182/ Wien, ABK/ Inv.291/ Fleischer 2005,p.99/ R7861.1013.

▪ Paris to the left

c1500 GIROLAMO di BENVENUTO, Giovanni del Guasta: Jugement de Paris/ PA/ ow/ Ø71/ Paris, MdL/ Inv. MI 587/ Berenson 1968, p.187; Healy 1997, fig.7, p.164, note nr.27/ R4151.1014.

c1550 CAMPAGNOLA, Domenico: Jugement de Pâris/ DR/ d/ 24.8x20/ Paris, MdL/ Inv. 5519, rect/ Healy 1997, fig.25, p.23, 169, note nr.119/ R10500.1015.

c1550 (att) SCHIAVONE, Andrea Meldolla, detto: Il giudizio di Paride/ PA/ ow/ 19x34/ Wien, DOR 14.4.05/ Sl. ?-320/ IT/ R11104.1016.

c1550 (att) ZUCCARO, Taddeo: Judgement of Paris/ DR/ d/ 26,8x33/ Milano, BiA/ Inv. F 269 inf. n. 10 recto/ IT/ R8736.1017.

c1600 SCARSELLINO: Ippolito Scarsella, detto Lo: Judgement of Paris/ PA/ ow/ 50x72/ Firenze, GdU/ Inv.1382/ Berenson 1968, p.389; Berti, 1979, p.87; Healy 1997, p.20-21, 168, note nr.106-107/ R4540.1018.

1620-30 ALBANI, Francesco: El juicio de Paris(Judgment of Paris)/ PA/ oc/ 113 x 171/Madrid, MNP/ Inv. 2-671/ Healy 1997, p.200-201, fig. 146; Enciclopedia 2006, Tomo II, p.340-341/ R4514.1019.

c1645 ROSA, Francesco: Das Urteil des Paris/ PA/ ow/ 34x53/ Wien, ABK/ Inv. 696/ IT/ R6916.1020.

c1670 GIORDANO, Luca: Das Urteil des Paris/ PA/ oc/ 244x326/ LO, pre.Berlin, GSM/ Inv. 441/ IT/ R6314.1021.

Replica in Wien, ScR/Inv.#/ IT/ R6915.1022.

c1670 GIORDANO, Luca: Giudizio di Paride/ PA/ oc/ 179x252/ Vicenza, MuC/ Inv.A321/ Fleischer 2005,p.212-213, n°87/ R8363.1023.

c1691 CIGNANI, Carlo : El Juicio de Paris/ oc/ 130,5 x 160/ Madrid, GALAlcole/ Inv.#/ IT/ R10658. 1024.

c1700 PELLEGRINI, Giovanni Antonio : Giudizio di Paride/ DR/ du/ 25x19/ Venezia, MuC/ Inv. 5508/ R3798.1025.

c1788 BARTOLOZZI, Francesco : Judgement of Paris (aft A.Kaufmann)/ PR/ e/ 43.9x50.2/ SF, FAM/ Inv. 1963.30.36203/ IT/ R10717.1026. *Other copies of different sizes on the market :24.5x30.5 oval/ London, BON 5.12.06/ Sl. 14201-520/ IT/ R6169.1026.*

▪ Paris to the right

c1525 BELLI, Valerio : Jugement de Pâris/ RE/ z/ 5.7x4.6/ Ecouen, MuR/ Inv. E.Cl.18274/ IT/ 10605.

c1570 ZANGUIDI, Jacopo, detto BERTOJA : Le jugement de Pâris/ PA/ oc/ ?/ Tours, MBA/ Inv. #/ Healy 1997, fig.22, p.168, note nrs.98-99./ R10498.1027. *Replica ? (att) NY, SOT 4.6.80/Sl.?-183.*

c1574 (att) CIRCIGNANI, Niccolo: Il giudizio di Paride/ FR/ ceiling/ ?/ Castiglione del Lago, PdC/ Inv.#/ Healy 1997, fig.21, fig.21, p.168, note nr.96/ R8346.1028. *Other artists proposed: Giovanni Antonio PANOLFI, Salvio SAVINI,Federico ZUCHARI.*

c1595 CALIARI, Carletto: Judgement of Paris/ PA/ oc/ 101.6x116.6/ Washington, NGA, on loan to Bucknell University, Lewisburg, PA/ Inv. K1078X and BL-K8/ Healy 1997, fig.26, p.23, 169, note nr.120/ R10501.1029.

Preparatory (?) DR/ d/ 39.2x51.1/ Cleveland, MuA/ Inv. 1946.216/ IT/ R11759V.1030.

c1621 CRESCENZI, Francesco: Judgement of Paris/ PA/ ow/ 123x92/ Roma, GaB/ Inv. 24/ Mai ed. 2001, p.368-69, n°65/ R8475.1031.

c1670 GIORDANO, Luca: Paris' dom (Judgement of Paris)/ PA/ oc/ 189X231/ Kopenhagen, SMK/ Inv.4932/ IT/ R6313.1032.

1685-86 GIORDANO, Luca: Giudizio di Paride/ PA/ oc/ 188 x 215/ Roma, GaP/ Inv. E29344iccd/ Cicinelli A & Vasco Rocca S (1978), Vol.I, p.50/ R8944.1033.

c1775 BARDELLINO, Pietro: Il giudizio di Paride/ PA/ oc/ 75x101,5/ Milano, FiA 2.12.'02/ Sl.137/ R6023.1034.
c1800 GUARANA, Jacopo : Paris' dom (Judgement of Paris)/ PR/ e/ 38x48/ Stockholm, NMK/ Inv. NMG 175-1868/ IT/ R5852.1035.
c1800 PEDRO, Francesco del: Giudizio di Paride (aft Kauffmann, Angelica)/ PR/e/ 34x30,5/ Venezia, FQS/ Inv. XII-25/ Succi 1983, p.275,n°339/ R3662.1036.

o goddesses alone

c1500 MODENA, Nicoletto da: Judgment of Paris (*four naked women*) (aft Dürer, Albrecht: The four witches)/ PR//?/ Wien, ALB/ Inv.#/ Bartsch 25 (13,2) 1984, p.135,n°62(289); Healy 1997, p.165-166, note nr.58/ R4794.1037.
c1590 NIGRONE, Giovanni Antonio: Brunnen mit Juno, Minerva und Venus in Begleitung Amors/ ILL/ tx/ ?/ Napoli, BiN/ Inv. Ms. XII. G. 59-60/ IT/ R10099V.1038.
1952 DELPRETE, Giovanni: Juicio de Paris/ PA/ oc/ 159x102/ Buenos Aires, MBA/ Inv.#/ exh/ R6192. 1039.

o many around

c1460-99 GIORGIO MARTINI, Francesco di: Story of Paris/ PA/ ?/ ?/ L.A., JPG/ Inv. #/ IT/ R9989.1040.
c1500 ASPERTINI, Amico: Judgement of Paris/ DR reconstruction sarcophagus Medici// ?/London, BMu/ Inv. 1898-23-3-f.37/ Healy 1997, p.164, note nr.19 / R10782V.1041.
c1500 BIAGIO di ANTONIO TUCCI: Judgement of Paris/ PA/ tc from w/ 65.1x111/ Cambridge, FAM/ Inv. 1928.169/ Berenson 1963, p.210-211/ R9950.1042. *Companion cassone panel in London, PrC pre. W.H. Woodward. In Cambridge FAM: (att)MASTER of the ARGONAUT Panels/ Healy 1997, fig.9, p.164, note nr.29.*
c1501 ASPERTINI, Amico : Judgement of Paris/DR Roman sarcophagus, Jupiter with eagle/ ?/ ?/ London, BMu/ Inv.Skb I,ff38v-39/ Bober 1986 p.149-150, n°119/ R8138V.1043.
c1525 LUINI, Bernardino: Jugement de Pâris/ DR/ d/ 16.5x13.6/ Paris, MdL/ Inv. 6358,verso/ IT/ R10622. 1044.
c1525 PERUZZI, Baldassare Tommasi: Judgement of Paris/ FR/ ceiling/ ?/ Siena, CaB/ Berenson 1968, p.333, pl.1840; Healy 1997, fig.20, p.167, note nr.95/ R9963.1045.
c1550 (att) CARPI, Girolamo da: Judgement of Paris (representation of sarcophagi)/ DR/ ?/ ?/ London, BMu/Inv.f.137v/ Bober 1986,p.149-50,n°119,120/ R8146V.1046.
Other (aft) or (wor) DR in BMu/Inv. f137v n°154 and 5226-138/ R8140V and R8141V.1047.
c1550 FRANCO, Giovanni Battista: Judgment of Paris (Roman (2nd c. AD) sarcophagus representation, right half with godesses returning to Olympus)/ DR/ d/ ?/ Köln, WRM/ Inv. Z-1956/ Bober 1986, p.149-150,n°119/ R8139V.1048.
c1550 SCHIAVONE, Andrea Meldolla, detto: Judgement of Paris/ PR/ e/ 29.5x43.5/ Wien, ALB/ Inv.#/ Bartsch 32(16,1) 1979, p.107,n°80(69)/ R4926.1049.
c1550 VENEZIANO, Agostino: Judgement of Paris/ PR/ e/ ?/ UN/ Inv. #/ Bober 1986, p.150, n° 120/ R8150V. 1050.
c1570 ZANGUIDI, Jacopo, detto BERTOJA: Guidizio di Paride/ FR/ ?/ ∅89/ Parma, GaN/ Inv. 893/ Healy 1997, p.168, note nr99./ R10738.1051.
c1575 DOSIO, Giovanni Antonio: Judgement of Paris (representation of SC in Villa Doria Pamphili)/ DR/ / ?/ Berlin, KSK/ Inv. Skb.f.8/ Bober 1986, p.150,n°120/ R8152.1052.
c1575 LANDINI, Taddeo: Judgement of Paris/ DR/ d/ ?/ Wien, ALB/ Inv. 745/ Healy 1997, p.168, note nr. 97/ R10784V.1053.
c1700 AMIGONI, Jacopo: Giudizio di Paride (parte) (The judgement of Paris –detail)/ FR/?/?/ Stra, VNP/ Inv.#/ Impelluso 2003, p.276/ R4432.1054.
c1700 LOCATELLI, Pietro: Giudizio di Paride/ PA/ ow/ ?/ Roma, GaB/ Inv. F5305iccd/ Cicinelli A & Vasco Rocca S (1978), VOL.I, p..155/ R8943.1055.

c1725 CARLONE, Carlo Innocenzo: Hermes conduce a Juno, Venus y Minerva hacia el encuentro con Paris/ PA or FR?/ ?/ ?/ UN/ Inv.#/ Hermes conduce a Juno, Venus y Minerva hacia el encuentro con Paris/ Alamillo 2003/ R6300.1056. *A PA "after" was sold in London, SOT 7.12.'88.*

1931-32 SAVINIO, Alberto: Giudizio di Paride/ DR/ d/ 65x52/ UN, PrC/ Inv.1931-3249 n°2/ Vivarelli 1996, p.260/ R8688.1057.

▪ Paris in the center

c1837 BIGIOLI, Filippo: Giudizio di Paride (Judgement of Paris)/ PA/ tc/ Ǿ124/ Roma, PaBr/ Inv.MR45204/ exh/ R3660.1058.

▪ Paris to the left

1550-55 GHISI, Giorgio/ Judgement of Paris/ PR/ e/ 40,2x53,1/ Roma, ING/ Inv. FN1142/ Massari 1989, p.300-301, n°112; Bellini 1998, p.115-119,n°25; Healy 1997, fig.19, p.19, 167, note nr.89/ R3503.1059. *Also with other owners*: Bartsch 31 (15,4) 1986, p.128#60; Damisch 1997, p.243; Schwartz 2004, p.367; *in Dresden, KSK/Inv.#/* Mai ed. 2001, p.427, G7.

c1550 PENNI, Luca: Jugement de Paris/ DR/ d/ 31,5x44,5/ Paris, MdL/ Inv. 1395/ Healy 1997, p.18, 167, note nr.86 / R7948.1060. *aft RAFFAELLO according to Damisch 1997, p.87. Copy by Jean Mignon known..*

c1555 BERTANI, Giovanni Battista : Il giudizio di Paride (The judgement of Paris)/ DR/ d/ 38,8x52,4/ Pavia, MuC/ Inv. 28bis, Col. Malaspina/ Healy 1997, fig.19, p.19, 167, note nr.89; Bellini 1998, p.115-19,n°70/R3653. 1061. DR could be aft GHISI's eng

1737 BEAUMONT, Claudio Francesco: Il Giudizio di Paride/ FR// ?/ Torino, PaR/ Inv.#/ IT/ R11676. 1062.

c1875 ANGELIS, Domenico de: Il giudizio di Paride (The judgement of Paris)/ PA/ ?/?/ Roma, GaB/ Inv.#/ Staccioli 1985, p.15/ R8278.1063.

▪ Paris to the right

c1430 (att) CECCHINO da Verona: Judgement of Paris/ PA/ tw /Ǿ70/ Firenze, MNB/ Inv.2026/ Berenson 1968, p.177; Damisch 1997,p.244; Healy 1997, fig.5, p.164, note nr.25/ R1505.1064. *Replica without Mercury-Paris in right upper corner. Also att MAESTRO del GIUDIZIO di PARIDE or Giovanni di PAOLO (Berenson).*

c1513 RAIMONDI, Marcantonio: Giudizio di Paride (aft RAFFAELLO)/ PR/ e/ 29,5x44/ Roma, ING/ Inv. FC4975/ Massari 1989, p.22-27,n°7a; Healy 1997, fig.2; Oberhuber 1999, p.94,n°33; Antetomaso 2004, p.198-200/ R3474. 1065. *Also: Berlin, KSK/Inv.#/ Mai ed. 2001, p.424, n°G3;* Paris, *ENSBA/ Inv. Est9107/ Schwartz & Garcia 2003, p.363, Cat.n°37; in many other places. Reverse copy* ***c1650*** */ PR/ e/ 28,9x42,6/ Paris, MdL/ Inv.4190/ Cordelier 1992, p.164-165,n°221/ R3833.*

c1550 BONASONE, Giulio: Giudizio di Paride (Judgement of Paris)/ PR/ e/ 30,2x46,2/ Roma, ING/ Inv.FC5488/ Massari 1989 p.216-17,n°87; Bartsch 28 C (15,1) 1995 p.318,n°2803.112; Healy 1997, fig.18, p.18, 167, note nr.87/ R3501.1066. *Also with many other owners.*

○ Mercury around

c1500 PINTURICCHIO, Bernardino di Betto, detto: Judgement of Paris/ FR/ ceiling→c/ ?/ NY, MMA/ Inv. 14.114.15/ Healy 1997, fig.17, p.166, note nr.67/ R10497.1067. *From Siena, Pa Reale.*

c1520 BUSTI, Agostino, detto Il BAMBAIA: Frauenfiguren all'antica in der Konfiguration eines Parisurteils/ DR/ d/ 21.1x14.6/ Berlin, KSK/ Inv. KdZ 1516/ IT/ R10064.1068.

c1520 BUSTI, Agostino, detto Il BAMBAIA: Abwandlung eines Parisurteils/ DR/ d/ 15.3x18.6/ Berlin, KSK/ Inv. KdZ 4431/ IT/ R10065.1069.

c1520 ROMANO, Giulio: Il giudizio di Paride (Camera di Ovidio o delle metamorfosi)/ FR// ?/Mantova, PdT/ Inv.#/ Damisch 1997, p.246/ R7254.1070.

c1536 (wor) ROMANO, Giulio: Il giudizio di Paride (Sala di Troia)/ FR/ / ?/ Mantova, PaD/ Inv.#/ Damisch 1997, p.269/ R7991.1071.

c1550 BONASONE, Giulio: Judgement of Paris (From the Loves, Rages and Jealousies of Juno)/ PR/ e/ 13,5x10,3/ NY, PuL/ Inv.#/ (Bartsch 28 (15,1) 1985,p.340,n°134(147);Bartsch 28 C (15,1) 1995 p.337,n°2803.134)/R4840.1072. *Also with many other owners.*

c1580 ALLORI, Alessandro: Judgement of Paris (Le tre dee si spogliano davanti a Paride)/ DR/ d/ 36,6x47,4/ NY, MMA/ Inv. 63-96/ Lecchini Giovannoni 1991, p.261-262, n°95, fig.210 ; Mai ed. 2001, p.409-10, n°T16/ R8479.1073. *Preparatory design for a tapestry LO.*

c1600 (att) CARRACCI, Annibale: The judgment of Paris/ DR/ d/ 39.5x46/ Cambridge, FAM/ Inv. 1932.333/ IT/ R9951.1074.

c1600 FARINATI, Paolo: Judgement of Paris/ DR/d/40,7x27,9/NY,SOT 10.1.'95/ Sl.6651-44/ Cat.p.16/ R4168.1075.

c1600 PALMA Il Giovane, Jacopo Negretti: The judgement of Paris/ PA/ oc/ 160x253/ UN, PrC/ Inv. 13310/ IT www.lootedart.com/ R10154.1076.

c1619 CARRACCI, Ludovico: Jugement de Pâris/ DR/ d/ 15.5x22.9/ Paris, MdL/ Inv. 7719, rect/ IT/ R10613.1077. *Preparatory DR for PA/ London, RCo.*

c1650 DIAMANTINI, Giuseppe: Judgement of Paris/ DR/ d/ 34,4x24,1/ St.Petersburg, HMu/ Inv.#/IT/ R1175.1078.

c1650 (cir) GHISOLFI, Giovanni : Giudizio di Paride/ PA/ oc/ 95x131/ Venezia, SEM 4.7.04/ Sl. ?-14/ IT/ 11687.1079.

c1650 MAZZONI, Sebastiano : Il giudizio di Paride/ PA/ ?/ ?/ PrC/ Inv. #/ Scarpa 2006, p.12/ R10432.1080.

c1670 GIORDANO, Luca : Das Urteil des Paris/ PA/ ?/ ?/ UN, PrC/ IT/ R2612.1081.

c1690 BOTTI, Francesco: Giudizio di Paride/ PA/oc/74x100/ Firenze, PrC/Inv.#/ (Casazza 2005, p.210, n°85)/R8362.1082.

c1690 DAVID, Ludovico: The judgement of Paris/ PA/ oc/ 172.7x245.1/ Sarasota, RMA/ Inv. SN11033/ IT/ R7544.1083.

c1700 GARZI, Luigi : Judgement of Paris/ DR/ d/ 31,3x46,2?/ Stockholm, NMK/ Inv. NM613-863/ Bjurström 1995, p.222, n°174/R1940.1084.

c1706 FRANCESCHINI, Marcantonio : Mercury bringing the golden apple for the judgement of Paris/ FR// ?/ Bologna, PaM/ Inv. #/ Miller 1991, p.xi, pl.86, p.95, Cat.n°29/ R9824.1085.

Preparatory: Mercury summoning the goddesses to the judgement of Paris/ DR/ d/ ?/ Windsor, RCo/ Inv. 3587/ Blunt 1971, p.84/ R10398V.1086.

c1712 DARDARONE, Giuseppe: El juicio de Paris/ FR// ?/ Palma: PaCV/ Inv. <Alcoba, n°2>/ Navarrete 2005, p.163, fig.286/ R11047.1087.

b1727-30 CARLONI, Carlo Innocenzo : Der Aufbruch der Göttinnen Juno, Venus und Minerva, geleitet von Merkur, zum Parisurteil/ PA/ oc/ 64.5x85.5/ Berlin, GSM/ Inv. 2003/ IT/ R11609.1088. *Preparatory PA for FR in Prague, library Palace Clam-Gallas ; a preparatory DR in St.Louis, AMu.*

c1836-37 PODESTI, Francesco : Giudizio di Paride/ DR/ ?/18x31/ Roma, PaBr/ Inv. MR 16989/ IT/ R3764.1089.

1946 DE CHIRICO, Giorgio: Il giudizio di Paride/ PA/ oc/ 140x100/Milano, PrC/ Inv.#/ IT/ R7033.1090.

Venus and Helen/Paris

c1650 FERRARI, Luca: Venus preventing Aeneas from killing Helen (Alexander prevented from killing Roxana; Menelaus prevented from killing Helen [by Pity])/ PA/ oy/ 26x31,4/ Bloomington, IUAM/ Inv. 66.77/ IT/ R8553.1091.

1776 HAMILTON, Gavin: Venere presenta Elena a Paride (Venus offers Helena to Paris)/ PA /oc/ 306x259/ Roma, PaBr/ Inv. MR 3796/ ITiccd/ R3761.1092.

1793 PIROLI, Tommaso: Aphrodite conduit Hélène auprès de Pâris (Venus disguised inviting Helen) (aft Flaxman, John; *from The Iliad of Homer*)/ PR/ e/ 46.5x27.8/ Hanover, HMA/ Inv. PR.996.27.36/ Damisch 1997, p.102/ R7949.1093.

1793 PIROLI, Tommaso: Venus presenting Helen to Paris (aft Flaxman, John; *from The Iliad of Homer*)/ PR/ e/ 46.5x27.8/ Hanover, HMA/ Inv. PR.996.27.37/ IT/ R11381V.1094.

11. Venus and Mars
(see also Venus and Vulcan)

c1525 GAROFALO, Benvenuto Tisi, detto: Mars, Venus and Cupid/ PA/ ?/ ?/ Krakow, WRC/ Inv.#/ Berenson 1968, p.158/ R10223V.1095. *Prev. Wien, Lanckoronski Col.*
c1550 ABATE, Nicolo dell' : Vénus parée des armes de Mars (Venus decorated with the arms of Mars) (aft PRIMATICCIO/ FR/ ?/ Fontainebleau, MNC/ Inv. PM 45/ IT/ R8034V.1096.
c1550 BORDONE, Paris: Venere, Marte e Cupido (?)/ PA/ ?/ ?/ Surrey, HCP/ Inv. 1086(124)/ Berenson 1958, p.48/ R9607V.1097.
c1575 CAMBIASO, Luca: Mars et Vénus/ DR/ d/ 27.5x17/ Marseille, MGL/ Inv. 1924#/ IT/ R10195V. 1098.
c1600 ZUCCARO, Federico: Mars surprenant Venus en compagnie d'Adonis sous la tonnelle de Venus/ DR/ d/ 20.9x13.8/ Rennes, MBA/ Inv. 794.1.3057/ IT/ R10038V.1099.
c1625 GUERCINO, Barbieri detto, Giovanni Francesco: Mars and Venus/ PA/ oc/ 95x70/ UN, LO/ Inv. 17478/ IT www.lootedart.com/ R10150V.1100.
c1650 (wor) CORTONA (BERRETTINI), Pietro da: Marte e Venere/ DR/ d/ 40x25/ Venezia, SEM 4.7.04/ Sl. ?-3/ IT/ R11688V.1101.
c1725 PIAZZETTA, Giambattista: Venere e Marte/ PA/ oc/ 33x42/ Roma, PaV/ Inv.#/ exh; IT/ R5922V. 1102.
1784 APPIANI, Andrea: Venere e Marte (Venus and Mars)/ PA/?/?/ S.Gregorio da Sassola, CaB/ Inv.#/ IT/ R8052V.1103.
1793 PIROLI, Tommaso: Venus wounded in the hand, conducted by Iris to Mars (aft Flaxman, John; *from The Iliad of Homer*)/ PR/ e/ 46.5x27.8/ Hanover, HMA/ Inv. PR.996.27.39/ IT/ R11382V.1104.

o Mars alone with Venus
c1525 PORDENONE, Giovanni Antonio: Mars(?) and Venus (*in chariot with doves)*/ DR/ d/ 7,5x6,9/ Milano, BiA/ Inv. F 268 inf. n. 151/ IT/ R8727.1105.
c1650 (cir) BALASSI, Mario : Venus crowning a sleeping Mars with a wreath/ PA/ oc/ 116,7x174/ SF,BON16.05.'06/ Sl. 13786-3015/ IT/ R6427.1106.
c1740 TIEPOLO, Giambattista: Venere e Marte/ DR/ d/ 28,5x37,5/ Firenze, MuH/ Inv. 6335/ Casazza 2005, p.168-169, n°42/ R8358.1107.
1783 BRENNA, Vicenzo: Venus und Mars; Groteskenrahmung/ PR/ e/ ?/ München, BSBi/ Inv. #/ IT/ R10122.1108.
c1790 CANOVA, Antonio: Scene della storia di Venere e Marte/ DR/ d/ ?/ Bassano, MuC/ Inv. 1125/ Stefani 2004, p.32,165, nr.31/R10173.1109.
1820 CANOVA Antonio: Mars and Venus/ SC/ m/ ?/ London, BPa/ Inv.#/ Stefani 2003, p.125-127, n°146/ R781.1110.
*Replica **1816** La pace e la guerra/ SC/ p/ ?/ Possagno, CDC/ Inv. #/ Munoz 1957, Tav.L; Preparatory: **c1816** Studio per Venere e Marte/ DR/ d/ 20.1x15.6/ Bassano, MuC/ Inv.#/ Stefani 2003, p.125-127, n°147/ R10156. 1111.*
1973 PAOLINI, Giulio: Venere e Marte/ CL//?/ UN, Artist Col/ Inv.#/ IT/ R8235.1112.

o Mars bathing with Venus

1527-30 ROMANO, Giulio: Marte e Venere al bagno (Sala di Psiche)/ FR// ?/ Mantova, PdT/ Inv.#/ Cavicchioli 2002, p.124,n°78/R1628.1113. *Maybe Adonis and not Mars/ Gombrich 1951,p.125, pl.24a.*

c1543 (att) FANTUZZI, Antonio : Mars et Vénus au bain, deux amours et deux servantes (aft PRIMATICCIO, Francesco)/ DR/ d/ 22,2x38,7/ Paris, MdL/ Inv. 8527, Rect/ IT ; Mai ed. 2001, p.97 n°6/ R8450.1114.

Also :PR/e/21,8x44,8/Paris, BNF/Inv. bd19,t.2/ Zerner 1969,n°AF59 ; Bartsch 33 (16,2) 1979, p.339,n°19(344) ; Mai ed. 2001, p.97 n°6, p.435, n°G12 ; *Primatice, 2004, p.203, Cat.80/ R3434.1115.*

c1550 FRANCO, Giovanni Battista : The bath of Mars and Venus (aft ROMANO, Giulio)/ DR/ d/ 40,9x57/London, BMu/Inv. 1946-7-13-1282/IT/R6951.1116.

Reverse PR/ e / 41x55,2/ London, BMu/ Inv.#/ Bartsch 32(16,1) 1979, p.202,n°47(135)/ R4927.1117.; also in Paris, BNF.

1790-95 APPIANI, Andrea: Gli svaghi di Venere e Marte (Venere e Adone al bagno -Venus and Adonis bathing)/ PA/ oc/ 81x112 oval?/ Milano, PAB/ Inv. 587, Sala: XXXVII/Baini 2006, p.356, Cat.587/ R3104. 1118.

o Cupid around

▪ Venus in the center

b1524 PARMIGIANINO, Girolamo Francesco: Mars and Venus with Cupid (on a relief left in "Portrait of a man)/ PA/ ow/ 89.5 x 63.8/ London, NGa/ Inv. NG6441/ Gould 1994, pl.31/ R10272.1119. *Copies in Firenze, GdU; Minneapolis.*

c1543-44 GAROFALO, Benvenuto: Die vor Troja verwundete Venus bittet Mars um seinen Wagen (Mars und Venus vor Troja)/ PA/ oc/ 133,5x240/ Dresden, SKS/ Inv.135/ Berenson 1968, p.153/ R525.1120.

c1670 GIORDANO, Luca: Venere, Cupido e Marte/ PA/ oc/ 152x129/ Napoli, MdC/ Inv. Q1194/ IT/ R6308.1121.

c1775 OTTAVIANNI, Giovanni: Venus crowning Mars (aft GUERCINO)/ PR/e/ 30,9x59,1/ SF, FAM/ Inv. 1963.30.36391/ IT/ R866.1122.

c1800 (att) APPIANI, Andrea: Mars, Venus, and Cupid/ DR/ d/ 25,3x19/ Milano, BiA/ Inv. F 268 inf. n. 96/ IT/ R3111.1123.

▪ Venus to the left

c1520 PALMA Il Vecchio, Jacopo: Mars, Venus and Cupid/ PA/ oc/ 91,4x137/ Wales, NMG/ Inv. NMW A 238/ IT/ R523.1124.

c1550 BORDONE, Paris: Venere, Marte e Cupido/ PA/ oc/ 118x130,5/ Roma, GDP/ Inv. i15PC321/ Berenson 1958, p.50; Safarik 2002, p.22-23,n°10/ R002.1125. *(aft) BELLINI, Giovanni (?) /Cicinelli 1978, p.114.*

1560 BORDONE, Paris : Mars disarming Love between Venus and Flora (Mars restraining Cupid)/ PA/ oc/ 110x176/ Wien, KHM/ Inv. 69/ IT/ R9830.1126.

b1634 GUERCINO, Giovane Francesco : Venus, Mars and Cupid/ DR/ d/ 22x30,5/ Vaduz, LSK/ Inv. R822/ Mai ed. 2001, p.415-16, n°T24/ R8481.1127.

1653 BRANDI, Giacinto : Venere e Marte/ FR// ?/ Roma, PDB/ Inv. E45883iccd/ IT/ R8917.1128. *Also (att) CAMASSEI, Andrea.*

c1700 BOTTI, Francesco: Venus and Mars/ PA/ oc/ 116x96,5/ NY, CHR 6.4.'06/ Sl. 1776-296/ IT/ R6055. 1129.

a1706 RICCI, Sebastiano: Marte e Venere/ PA/ oc/ 180x120/ UN/ Inv. #/ Scarpa 2006, p.348, cat.571, fig.247/ R10441.1130.

c1720 PITTONI, Giambattista: Mars et Vénus/ PA/ oc/ ?/ Paris, MdL/ Inv.#/ IT/ R2076.1131. *Replica in Warsaw Museum of Fine Arts?*

1978 DODDIS, Alfredo: Venere e Marte/ PA/ oc/ 70x50/ UN/ Inv.#/ CELIT 1982 Vol 8, p.5299/ R8670.1132.

▪ Venus to the right

1508 RAIMONDI, Marcantonio: Marte, Venere e Amore (aft MANTEGNA? not according to Mai ed., 2001)/ PR/ e/ 29,4x21/ Roma, ING/ Inv. FC4966/ Bartsch 27 (14,2) 1978, p.41n°345-II(257); Massari 1989, p.6-9, n°2/ R1470.1133. *Also: A'dam, RPK/Inv.#/ Mai ed. 2001, p.423-24, n°G2; in many other places.*
*Reverse copy: **c1650** GALESTRUZZI, Giovanni Battista/ PR// 29,8x21,1/Brescia, MuR/ Inv.#/ Bartsch 46 C 1985; p.274,276n°4606.344/ R4995.1134. Also in London, BMu; Milano, BiA..*

c1509-10 (att) BARBARI, Jacopo de': Mars and Venus (standing, *with Cupid on left arm of Venus)*(aft? ROSSO, Fiorentino)/ PR/ e/ 26x17,5/ Chantilly, MuC/ Inv.Est Suppl 3/ Bartsch 13(7,4) 1981, p.274 n°20(525);Bartsch 24 C(Part 4) 1988,p.32,n°2410.020; Mallé 1968, p.203-204, n°69/ R2407.1135. *Also in Dresden, SKS/ Inv.#/* Mai ed. 2001, p.451, n°G30. *PRs in all major musea.*

c1750 TIEPOLO, Giambattista: Marte e Venere con Amore (stanza degli Dei dell Olimpo)/ FR// 200x185/ Vicenza, ViV/ Inv.#/ Rizzoli 1968, p.123/124 n°240 Y; Pedrocco 2002, p.293-94, cat.236.23/ R4440.1136.

1793 CARATTONI, Francesco or Girolamo: Mars, Venus and Cupid (pl.IX of XII) (aft Anton von Maron) <aft FR LO in ancient roman home near Villa Peretti-Negroni (Stazione Termini), Roma>/ PR/ ?/ London, BMu/ Inv.#/ Joyce 1986, p.433, fig.14/ R11145.1137. *A wall decoration exists in the Pompeian Room, Ickworth Rotunda, Bury St.Edmunds, UK.*

o Cupid(s) and others around

c1485 BOTTICELLI, Sandro : Venus and Mars/ PA/ tow/ 69,2x173,4/ London, NGa/ Inv. NG915/ Berenson 1963, p.36 ; Anonymous 1989, Vol.I, p.956 ; Dempsey 2001, p.107,145; Zuffi 2001,p.65; Mai ed. 2001, p.320, n°1/ R378. 1138.

1490 COSIMO, Piero di : Venus, Cupid and sleeping Mars/ PA/ ow/ 72x182/ Berlin, GSM/ Inv.107/ Berenson 1963, p.175; Bacci 1966, p.87; Bisschoff 1995, p.153, fig.2; Zuffi 2001,p.65/ R519.1139.

c1535 PARMIGIANINO (MAZZOLA), Girolamo Francesco: Venus and Mars with putti/ DR/ d/ 12.2x17.5/ Chicago, AIC/ Inv. 1922.2365r/ IT/ R10256.1140.

c1605 SARACENI, Carlo : Marte e Vênus, com uma Roda de Cupidos e Paisagem (Venus and Mars with cupids in a landscape)/ PA/ oy/ 40x50/ Sao Paulo, MASP/ Inv.#/ IT/ R4463.1141.

b1620 BADALOCCHIO, Sisto: Mars et Vénus/ PA/ oc/ 87x167/ Rouen, MBA/ Inv.803.20/ IT/R7080. 1142.

1625 MANNOZZI, Vincenzo: Marte e Venere/ PA/ oc/ 41x52/ Firenze, GaC/ Inv. 371-114/ IT/ R8592. 1143.

c1625 VAROTARI, Alessandro: Marte e due amorini con specchio/ PA/ ?/100x130/ Venezia, CaR/ Inv. 45/ Martini 2002, p.206,208 n°166/R959.1144.

c1630 GUERCINO, Giovane Francesco Barbieri: Mars, Venus and Cupid/ DR/ d/ 24,1x33,7/ NY, SOT 21.1.'03/ NY7870-51/ cat; Old Masters Drawings/ R5437.1145.

c1632 GUERCINO, Giovane Francesco Barbieri: Mars, Venus and Cupid/ DR/ d/ 20,7x34,3/ London, BMu/ Inv. 1910-2-12-4/ Mai ed. 2001, p.416-17, n°T25/ R1595.1146.

1633 GUERCINO, Giovane Francesco Barbieri: Venere, Marte e Cupido/ PA/ oc/ 139x161/ Modena, GaE/ Inv.40/ Mai ed. 2001, p.338-39, n°52/ R007.1147.

1635 CHIARI, Fabrizio : Mars and Venus (aft Nicolas POUSSIN)/ PR/ e/ 28,5x38,5/ SF,FAM/Inv. 1988.1.281/(Brugerolles 2001,p.101, Cat.[III,4] ; Verdi 1986, p.9,n°6)/ R2900.1148. *Also in London, BMu ; Paris, MdL.*

c1675 GIORDANO, Luca : Mars and Venus with a Cupid/ PA/ oc/ 110x156/ Sarasota, RMA/ Inv. SN160/ IT/ R11354V.1149.

c1706 FRANCESCHINI, Marcantonio: Mars, Venus and Cupid with Diana in the heavens/ PA/ ?/ ?/ Wien, LMu/ Inv. 4070/ Miller 1991, p.xi, pl.XX, p.96-95, Cat.n°29/ R9818.1150.

c1725 ROCCA, Michele: Venus and Mars with cupids/ PA/ oc/ 47,7x67,5/ UN, PrC/ Inv.#/ IT/ R5967. 1151. *Prev. att Coypel, A./pre. Den Haag, NKB/ Inv. NK3250.*

c1750 TIEPOLO, Giovanni Battista: Mars and Venus/ DR/ d/ 25x37/ London, CHR 3.7.'07/ Sl. 7409-0061/ IT/ R9554.1152.

c1801 APPIANI, Andrea; Marte e Venere/ PA/ ow/ 24.5x34.5/ Milano, GAM or VBB/ Inv. GAM 7139/ Precerutti-Garberi 1969, p.22, nr.4/ R9636.1153.

○ Mars loving Venus

▪ alone with Venus

1476-84 ROBERTI, Ercole de' : Mars and Venus (Allegory of the month September: Triumph of Vulcan)/ FR//216x320/ Ferrara, PaS/ Inv.#/ Fels 1968, p. 101,n°112; Malraux 2004, p.244/ R7242.1154.

c1550 GHISI, Giorgio: Venus and Mars on a bed/ PR/ e/ Ǿ 12,8/ London, BMu/ Inv. #/ Bartsch 31 (15,4) 1986, p.14,n°7(379)/ R4920.1155. ***c1555** Venus and Vulcan seated on a bed (after Perino del Vaga ?)PR/ e/ 28.2 x 20.1/ Ottawa, NGC/ Inv. 40412.*

c1550 PALMA Il Vecchio, Jacopo : Venere e Marte/ PA/ ?/ ?/ NY, BMu/ Inv. 37.529/ Berenson 1958, p.127, pl.912/ R9619.1156.

c1580-90 SONS, Giovanni : Bacco e Arianna(sic) *(Marte e Venere)*/ PA/ oc/ oval 61x39/ Napoli, MdC/ Inv. Q1349/ Spinosa 1994, p.94/ R8380.1157.

c1640 PELLEGRINI, Carlo : Venere, Marte o Adone (Venus, Mars or Adonis)/ PA/ oc/ ?/ Roma, GNB/ Inv. E62028iccd/ IT/ R8941.1158.

▪ Cupid(s) around, Venus to the left

1460-65 (att) POLLAJUOLO, Antonio : Venus and sleeping Mars / RE/ p/ ∅50.8/ London, VAM/ Inv. 5887-1859/ Pope-Hennessy 1964, Cat.129, pl.151 ; Bischoff 1995, p.153, fig.6 / R10379.1159.

c1515 RAIMONDI, Marcantonio: Mars and Venus (aft ROMANO, Giulio) *('Modi'-illustration in Aretino's Sonnetti Inssuriosi)/* IL/ Weddingen 1994, fig.13, p.108/ R4288.1160.

a1541-42 VICO, Enea: Marte e Venere (aft ANDREASI, Ippolito)/ PR/ e/ 28,3x20,5/ Roma, ING/ Inv. FC31024/ Bartsch 30 (15,3 1985, p.31; Massari 1989, p.257-59, n°98/ R1478.1161. *Also:PR/ e/ 30.32 x 20.64/ LA, CMA/ Inv. M.88.91.56 / IT ; aft PARMIGIANINO?/ SF, FAM/ Inv 1963.30.3243/IT; also in London, BMu ; **1539** eng SCULTORI, Givanni Battista; London, CHR 30.6.'94/ Sl. ?-53*

c1541 (att) ANDREASI, Ippolito : Marte e Venere (Mars and Venus)/ PR/ e/ 20,5x14,7/ Roma, ING/ Inv.FN1138/ Massari 1989, p.238,FIG.98c/ R3598.1162. *Reverse of SCULTORI/ R8482.1175.*

1548 PRIMATICCIO, Francesco: Mars, Vénus, l'Amour sur les nuées/ DR/ d/ 16,4x26,8/ Paris, MdL/ Inv. 8538 r/ IT/ R2846.1163.

c1550 BARBIERI, Domenico: Venus, Mars and Cupid/PR/e/6,7x10,9/London, BMu/ Inv.#/ Bartsch 33 (16,2) 1979, p.261,n°5(358)/ R4935.1164. *Also in Wien, ALB/ Inv.#/* Mai ed. 2001, p.441, n°G20.

c1575 CAMBIASO, Luca : Mars caressant Vénus/ DR/ d/ 23.7x23.5/ Paris, MdL/ Inv. 9325, rect/ IT/ R10196.1165.

c1575 FRANCO, Giacomo: Mars et Vénus /PR// ?/ Milano, PrC ?/ Inv.#/ Arasse 1997, p.96, ill.82/ R5601. 1166.

c1578 VERONESE, Paolo Caliari: Mars and Venus united by love *(with horse right)*/ PA/ oc/ 205,7 x 161/ NY, MMA/ Inv. 10.189/ Berenson 1958, p.138; Howard 1987, p.159/ R532.1167.

c1585 CINCINATO, Romulo : Venus, Cupido y Marte/ FR// ?/ Guadalajara, Pal/ Inv. Sala de los Dioses/ Navarrete 2005, p.86, fig.158/ R11019.1168.

1585-90 PALMA Il GIOVANE, Jacopo : Mars and Venus/ PA/ oc/ 130,9x165,6/ London, NGa/ Inv. NG1866/ Gould 1975, p.183-184 ; Anonymous 1989, Vol.I, p.957; Zuffi 2001, p.242/ R342.1169.

c1600 CARRACCI, Annibale: Mars and Venus in a landscape/ DR/ d/ 18,9x38,9/ Windsor, RCo/ Inv.1987/ Wittkower 1952, p.156, Cat.422; Benati 1999, p.232-233,n°72/ R3567.1170. *Also in Wien, ALB.*

c1650 PIGNONI, Simone: Venere, Marte e Amore/ PA/ oc/ ?/ Roma, PaMo/ Inv. E65734iccd/ IT/ R8926. 1171.

c1775 GIGOLA, Giambattista: Amori di Venere e Marte *(? or Adonis?)*/ PA/ ox/ 18,5x13,6/ Brescia, MAS/ Inv.#/ IT/ R8508.1172.

c1800 SANTI, Giuseppe: Marte e Venere/ PA/ oc/ ?/ Milano, POR 9.11.05/ Sl. ?-347a/ IT/ R10281.1173.

▪ Cupid(s) around, Venus to the right

c1526 CARAGLIO, Iacopo : Marte e Venere (aft PERINO DEL VAGA)/ PR/ e/ 21,2x13,6/ Roma, ING/Inv.FC5932/ Bartsch 28 (15,1) 1985,p.92,n°15(74); Massari 1989,p.164-65,n°66; Casazza 2005,p.172, n°46)/ R3493. 1174. *Also in A'dam, Paris. Copy in reverse.*

1539 SCULTORI, Giovan Battista : Mars and Venus *(on bed, with Cupid and doves)* (aft PARMIGIANINO?)/ PR: ey/ 28,1x20,2/ Berlin, KSK/ inv. #/ Mai ed. 2001, p.430, n°G10/ R8482.1175.
c1543 VERONESE, Paolo Caliari: Venus and Mars/ PA/ oc/ 165 x 126,4/ Edinburgh, NGS/ Inv. 339/ Berenson 1958, p.135/ R534.1176.
Replica : PA/ oc/ 167 x 128/ Frankfurt, SKI/ Inv. 893/ Panofsky 1969, p.163 ; IT/ R533.1177.
c1545 VERONESE, Paolo Caliari: Mars et Vénus/ PA/ oc/ 142x109/ Chantilly, MuC/ Inv. PE55/ Duca 1966, fig.620, p.433 / R5358.1178.
c1550 ANGELI, Marco d': Mars and Venus (*left standing. with Cupid right of Mars)*/ PR// 31,4x18,8/ London, BMu/ Inv.#/ Bartsch 32(16,1) p.316,#5(206)/ R4929.1179. *Also in Cambridge, FWM/ Inv. 22.I.5-205.*
c1550 BONASONE, Giulio: Mars embracing Venus (from 'The Loves of the Gods')/ PR/e/16,5x11/Wien,ALB/Inv.#/ (Bartsch 29 (15,2) 1982,p.28,n°164-II(152))/ R4846.1180.
c1550 GHISI, Giorgio: Venus and Mars with Cupid on a bed/ PR/ e/ 28,1x20,2/ London, BMu/ Inv. #/ Bartsch 31 (15,4) 1986, p.20,n°13(381) / R4921.1181. *Copy (?) of SCULTORI/ R8482.1175.*
c1550 SCULTORI, Giovan Battista : Gli amori di Marte e Venere/ PR/ e/ 20,6x32,5/ Paris, BnF/ Inv. H102867/ Massari 1993, p.111,n°103/ R3551.1182.
c1570 TIZIANO, Vecellio: Venus and Mars with Cupid/ PA/ oc/ 97x109/ Wien, KHM/ Inv.13/ Mai ed. 2001, p.322-23, n°44/ R1551.1183.
c1575 SEMINO, Andrea: Mars and Venus, beside Cupid/ DR/ d/ 14.9x12.7/ London, SOT 4.7.'07/ Sl. L07040-46/ IT/ R9782.1184.
c1575 VERONESE, Paolo Caliari: Venere e Marte con Cupido *(left with horse)*/ PA/ oc/ 47x47/ Torino, GaS/ Inv. 461/ Berenson 1958, p.140, pl.1092; Astrua 2000, p.78-79/ R343.1185.
c1606 SARACENI, Carlo : Venus and Mars (*on a bed, with cupids around)*/ PA/ oy/ 39,5x55/ Madrid, MTB/ Inv. #/ IT/ R1545.1186.
c1640 CANTARINI, Simone : Marte che spoglia Venere, e Amore (aft VERONESE)/reverse PR/ e/ 26,3x19,7/ Roma, ING/ Inv. FN2950/ Bartsch 42 (19,2) 1981,p. 107,n°32(142)/ R3507.1187.
1972 TOMMASI FERRONI, Riccardo: Venere, Marte e Amore/ PA/ oc/ 141x280/ UN/ Inv.#/ CEDE 2001 Vol 16, p.11596/ R8651.1188.

○ others around

c1497 MANTEGNA, Andrea: Mars et Vénus dit Le Parnasse/ PA/ tc/ 159x192/ Paris, MdL/ Inv. 370/ Berenson 1968, p.241 ; Zuffi 2001, p.69 / R518.1189.
c1525 PARMIGIANINO : Mars et Vénus assis, avec Cupidon porté en triomphe, les Trois Grâces/ DR/ d/ 15,8x21,3/ Paris, MdL/ Inv. 6409/ Mai ed. 2001, p.405,n°T11/ R2845.1190.
c1527 ROMANO, Giulio: Venus retains Mars of pursuing Adonis (Camera of Psyche : the story of Cupid and Psyche)/ FR// ?/ Mantova, PdT/ Inv.#/ Cavicchioli 2002, p.125, n°78/ R7252.1191. *Adonis chased by Mars (with Cupid pointing at the rose on the ground which is about to prick the foot of Venus)/ Gombrich 1951,p.125, pl.24c.*
c1529-1535 ROSSO FIORENTINO, Giovanni Battista: Mars et Vénus, servis par les Nymphes et les Amours/ DR/ d/ 43x34/ Paris, MdL/ Inv. 1575/ IT/ R2833.1192.
Also PR/ e/ ?/ Fontainebleau, MNC/ Inv.#/ Beguin 1989, fig.29 ; Bartsch 28 C (15,1) 1995, n°2802.051 p.339; Pérouse de Montclos 1998, p.20-21/ *R4298.1193. ; Anonymous/ PR/ ?/ ?/ Paris, BNF/ Inv.#/ Mai ed. 2001, p.95, fig.2. The PA was lost.*
c1550 CARAGLIO, Iacopo : Mars and Venus (aft ROSSO, Fiorentino)/ PR/ e/ 41,8x33,3/ Berlin, KSK/ Inv.#/ Bartsch 28 (15,1) 1985,p.190,n°51(87)/ R4919.1194. *Also reverse in SF, FAM.*
c1550 ZELOTTI, Battista : Venere fra Marte e Nettuno (Venus between Mars and Neptune)/ FR//?/ Venezia, PaD/ Inv.#/ Berenson 1958, p.210; Itartresource/ R8517.1195.
c1590-95 (att) TINTORETTO, Jacopo : Venere, Marte e le Tre Grazie in un paesaggio/ PA/ oc/ 106.5 x 142.8/ Chicago, AIC/ Inv. 1929.914/ Rizzoli 1970, p.134, n° E13/ R8379.1196.
c1605-09 PALMA Il GIOVANE, Jacopo : Venus and Mars/ PA/ oc/ 143x205/ LA, JPG/ Inv. 71.PA.50/ Boccardo ed. 2004 p.228-229, n°38/ R298.1197.

c1650 MONOGRAMMISTA CpP: Mars abducting Venus/ DR// 39,5x28,8/ Wien, ALB/ Inv.#/ Bartsch 42 (19,2) 1981, p.164,n°7(186)/ R4976.1198.
1653 ROMANELLI, Giovanni Francesco : Marte, Venere e Mercurio/ FR// ?/ Roma, PaLR/ Inv. E58424iccd/ IT/ R8934.1199.
1742-43 TIEPOLO, Giambattista : Marte e Venere (Venus welcomes Mars)/ FR// 450x800/ Venezia, PPM/ Inv.#/ Rizzoli 1968, p.107,n°143; *Romanelli 1997, p.616-617*/ R8527.1200. *In collaboration with Francesco ZANCHI.*
Replica : PA/ oc/ 41x72/ Paris, PrC/ Inv.#/ Rizzoli 1968, p.107,n°143a / R8528.1201.
c1780 MULINARI, Stefano: Mars and Venus/ PR/e/ ?/ SF, FAM/ Inv. 1963.30.36871/ IT/ R841.1202.
1790-95 APPIANI, Andrea: L'ira di Marte trattenuto da Venere (Adone trattenuto da Venere e Cupido - Adonis withheld by Venus and Cupid)/ PA/ oc/ 81x112 oval/ Milano, PAB/ Inv. 588, Sala: XXXVII/Baini 2006, p.356, Cat.588/ R3106.1203. *The title with Mars is probably the correct one, because in the background a man –Adonis- is fleeting.*

o Venus and Mars surprised by Apollo/Vulcan (see also Vulcan)

c1511 BAZZI, Giovanni, detto SODOMA: Mars and Venus trapped by Vulcan *(with Apollo telling Vulcan of his wife's infidelity on the left)*/ PA/ oc/ 30.5x68.7/ London, SOT 6.7.'94/ Sl. ?-35/ IT/ R8886.1204.
c1525 PARMIGIANINO (MAZZOLA), Girolamo Francesco: Venus, Mars and Vulcan/ PA/ ?/ ?/ Firenze, GdU/ Inv. P546/ Gould 1994, p.154/ R10735V.1205.
c1525 (att) PARMIGIANINO : Vulcan shows Mars and Venus to the gods/ PR/ e/ ?/ London, BMu/ Int.#/ Weddingen 1994, p.111, n°17/ R4291.1206.
c1545 BONASONE, Giulio: Venus and Mars discovered by Apollo (From the Loves of the Gods)/ PR/ e/16,5x11,0/Roma, ING/Inv.FC5527/ (Bartsch 29 (15,2) 1982, p.26, n°162-III(152); Weddingen 1994, p.106,n°10; Casazza 2005,p.172, n°47)/R4844.1207. *Also in NY, MMA.*
c1548 BORDONE, Paris: Mars und Venus, von Vulkan überrascht (Mars and Venus surprised by Vulcan)/ PA/ oc/ 168x198/ Berlin, GSM/ Inv.#/ IT/ R936.1208.
c1550 ALBERTI, Cherubino: Mars and Venus surprised by Vulcan (*Mythological Subjects* aft CALDARA da CARAVAGGIO, Polidoro)/ PR/ e/ 15,5x14,8/ London,BMu/ Inv.#/ Bartsch 34(17,1)1982 p.208,#88(70)/ R4952.1209.
c1550 CARAGLIO, Iacopo : Vulcan surprising Mars and Venus/ PR/ e/ 20,7x25/ Dresden, SKS/ Inv.#/ Bartsch 28 (15,1) 1985,p.191,n°52(88); Bartsch 28 C (15,1) 1995, p.184, n°2802.052; Lowenthal 1995, p.56, fig.39/ R4839. 1210. *Also in Paris.*
Reverse: Weddingen 1994, 109,n°14/ R4289.1211.
c1550 UDINE, Giovanni da : Venere, Marte, Vulcano (Il bagno di Clemente VII)/ FR/ ?/ Roma, CSA/ Inv. E51493iccd/ IT iccd ; Porcheron-Felsing 1983, p.38,49,61 fig.20/ R8266.1212.
c1551 TINTORETTO, Jacopo: Vulkan überrascht Venus und Mars/ PA/ oc/ 135x198/ München, Apk/ Inv. 9257/ Berenson 1958, p.181 ; Rizzoli 1970, p.95,n°89; Weddingen 1994 ; Lowenthal 1995, p.559, fig.41 ; Mai ed. 2001, p.324-25, n°45/ R443.1213.
Preparatory DR/ d/ 20,1x27,2/ Berlin, GSM/ Inv. KdZ 4193/ Mai ed. 2001, p.409, n°T15/ R531.1214.
c1553 PORTA, Guglielmo della: Vulcan capturing Mars and Venus/ RE/ z/ 14x14 octagonal/ Washington, NGA/ Inv. 1987.9.2/ IT/ R815.1215.
1555 GHERARDI, Cristofano: Marte e Venere sorpresi e intrappolati nella rete di Vulcano/ FR// 254x183/ Firenze, PaV/ Inv. 533/ IT/ R8586.1216.
c1600 BALDUCCI detto COSCI, Giovanni : Venus, Mars and Cupid with Vulcan entering by a door behind/ DR/ d/ 15.5x22.5/ London, VAM/ Inv. D123-1888/ Ward-Jackson 1979,Vol.I, p.30-31, n°26/ R11122. 1217.
c1600 TEMPESTA, Antonio: Martem Veneremqz adulterantes Vulcanus reti suo implicat (Vulcan entrapping Mars and Venus) (pl. 34 from the series Ovid*s Metamorphoses, *pub Wilhelmus Jansonnius)*/ PR/ e/ 10,5x11,8/ SF, FAM/ Inv. 1989.1.167/ Bartsch 36(17,3) 1983, p.26,n°671(151)/ R1390.1218. *Also in London, BMu.*

c1670 GIORDANO, Luca : Mars und Venus von Vulkan gefangen (Mars and Venus captured by Vulcan)/ PA/ oc/ 232x182/ Wien, ABK/ Inv.310/ Fleischer 2005, p.98/ R980.1219.
c1684 (att)CARLONE Giovanni Battista: Marte e Venere sorpresi da Vulcano (Mars and Venus surprised by Vulcan)/PA/oc/197x245/Savona, PcC/ Inv.# IT/ R4500.1220.
c1700 BELLUCCI, Antonio: Mars and Venus entrapped by Vulcan/ PA/ oc/ 84.4x231/ London, SOT 5.7.'07/ Sl. L07032-199/ IT/ R9792.1221.
c1700 CEDINI, Costantino : Venere e Marte sorpresi nella rete (Venus and Mars surprised in the net *of Vulcan*)/FR/?/?/Padova, PEC/Inv.#/ (Impelluso 2003,p.161) /R4429.1222.

12. Venus and other Gods, Deities or Heroes
(Apollo, Bacchus, Ceres, Diana, Diomedes, Europa, Flora, Graces/Nymphs, Hercules, Juno, Jupiter, Mercury, Minerva, Neptun, Pluto, Pygmalion, Saturn or Chronos orTime)

Apollo

c1540 MASTER of the DIE: Chariots of Venus and Apollo (aft RAFFAELLO)/ PR/ ?/ ?/London, BMu/ Inv.#/ Bartsch 29 (15,2) 1982, p.181 n°24(200)/ R4850.1223.
c1560 VERONESE, Paolo Caliari : Apollo, Venus and Cupid/ FR// ?/ Maser, ViB/ Inv.#/ Berenson 1963, p.92/ R2719.1224.
c1625 (att) SCORZA, Sinibaldo: Amour, Vénus et Apollon/ DR/ d/ 16,3x14/ Brussel, KMSK/ Inv. 4060 – 1907/ IT/ R6938.1225.
c1762 TIEPOLO, Giambattista: Venere e Apollo (Le char de l'Aurore)/ PA/ oc/ oval 88.5x70,7/ NY, PrC/ Inv.#/ Rizzoli 1968, p.133, n°282 ; Pedrocco 2002, p.302, cat.263/ R8540.1226.
c1800 APPIANI, Andrea : Apollo citaredo fra Venere con Amore e le tre Grazie/ DR/ d/ 65x138/ Milano, GAM/ Inv. 1618/ Precerutti-Garberi 1969, p.45, n°61/ R6940V.1227.

Bacchus

c1539 ROSSO FIORENTINO, Giovanni Battista: Bacchus, Vénus et l'Amour/ PA/ oc/ 210x162/ Luxembourg, MHA/ Inv.#/ Beguin 1989, fig.24,25,26 ; Mai ed. 2001, p.268-69, n°20/ R1618.1228.
1578 TINTORETTO, Jacopo : Ariadne, *(crowned by)* Venus and Bacchus/ PA/ oc/ 146x167/ Venezia, PaD/ Inv.#/ Nichols 1999, p.231, n°203/ R530.1229.
Replica? PA/ ?/ ?/ Strasbourg, ChR/ Inv.#/ Dunand & Lemarchand s.d., III p.807, fig.1277/ R10755.1230.;
PR reverse// ?/ Venezia, MuC/ Inv.#/ Dunand & Lemarchand s.d., III p.794, fig.1261/R10751.1231.
c1590 NIGRONE, Giovanni Antonio: Wandbrunnen mit Venus, Bacchus und Faunen/ ILL/ tx/ ?/ Napoli, BiN/ Inv. Ms. XII. G. 59-60/ IT/ R10096V.1232.
c1597 CARRACCI, Annibale: Triumph of Bacchus and Ariadne (with Cupid leaning on Venus in right bottom corner)/ FR//?/ Roma, PaFa/ Inv. #/ Czére 2004, p.86/ R10919.1233.
c1600 RENI, Guido: Venus with Cupid leaning on her shoulder (aft CARRACCI FR "Triumph of Bacchus and Ariadne")/ DR/ d/ 30.5x25/ Budapest, MFA/ Inv. K.67.193/ Czére 2004, p.90, Cat.78verso/ R10920.1234.
c1648 CAMASSEI, Andrea: Bacco presenta Arianna a Venere/ FR//?/ Roma, PDP/ Inv. E45867iccd/ IT/ R8910.1235.
c1650 AQUILA, Pietro: Cupid leaning on Venus (detail of 'Triumph of Bacchus and Ariadne' aft FR CARRACCI)/ PR/ e/ ?/ Budapest, MFA/ Inv. #/ Czére 2004, p.86, Cat.72-a/ R10917.1236.
c1653 VECCHIA, Pietro della: Venere e Bacco/ PA/ oc/ 91,5x120/ Venezia, CaR/ Inv. 73 Col.Martini/ Martini 2002, p.306-307, n°252/ R962.1237.

c1700 PARODI, Domenico: Bacco. Venere e Apollo/ FR//?/ Genova, PaRe/ Inv. #/ IT/ R10290V.1238.
c1750 CONCA, Sebastiano: Bacchus, Ariane et Vénus/ PA/ oc/ 73,5x99/ Marano di Castenaso, PrC/ Inv.#/ IT/ R2078.1239.
c1750 WAGNER, Giuseppe: Bacco e Venere/ PR/ e/ 30,9x45,7/ Gorizia, MuP/ Inv. 2176/ Succi 1983, p.437,n°592/ R3663.1240.
1770-71 ROBIGLIARD, Vincenzo: Triumph des Bacchus und der Ariadne *(Cupid leaning on Venus in right bottom corner)* (aft CARRACCI)/ FR// ?/ Wörlitz, ScG/ Inv. #/ IT Deutsche Fotothek/ R10918.1241.

Ceres and Bacchus, Ceres & Venus

c1550 GHISI, Giorgio: Cérès avec deux déesses (*Venus)* et deux putti (aft PRIMATICCIO)/ PR/ e/ 18x24/ Lyon, BiM/ Inv. GH003919/ Bellini 1998, p. 196-197, n°44/ R2604.1242. *Also : Venus, two Goddesses, and two putti /PR/ e/ ?/Cambridge, FWM/ Inv. 37.1-49.*
c1590 CARRACCI, Agostino: Sine Cerere et Baccho friget Venvs (Venus and Eros in a landscape)/ PR/ e/ 22x15,4/ London, BMu/ Inv.#/ Bartsch 39 (18,1) 1980, p.157, n°115(103); Bartsch 39 C Part 1 (18,1) 1995, p.366, n°3901.217/ R4962.1243. *Also in many other places.*
b1626 GATTI, Oliviero: Ceres, Venus and Bacchus (*the 'Emblemata' XLV aut Paolo Maccio*)/ PR // 10,6x8,6/ Inv.#/ Bartsch 41 (19,1) 1981, p.96,n°92(27) / R4974.1244.
c1650 DIAMANTINI, Giuseppe: Bacchus, Ceres and Venus/ PR/ e/ 24,2x17,4/ Wien, ALB/ Inv.#/ Bartsch 47 (21,2) 1983 p.411,#27(281)/ R5003.1245.
c1653 GIMIGNANI, Giacinto: Sine Baccho et Cerere friget Venus/ PA/ oc/ 42,7x32,2/ London, SOT 11.7.'02/ Sl. L02112-185/ IT/ R5874.1246.
1653 GIMIGNANI, Giacinto: Sine Baccho et Cerere friget Venus/ PA/ oc/ 230,5x342,5/ London, SOT 13.12.'01/Sl. L01124-51/ IT/ R5882.1247.
c1700 CHIARI, Giuseppe : Bacchus and Venus/ DR/d/ 28.7x29/ Chatsworth, DCo/ Inv.586/ Kerber 1968, fig.9/ R11103.1248.
c1700 PIOLA, Domenico : Sine Cerere et Bacco friget Venus/ PA/ oc/ 144x192,5/ Milano, SOT 28.11.'06/ Sl. MI0266-330/ IT/ R8090.1249.

Diana

c1500 MANTEGNA, Andrea: Mars, Venus (?) and Diana/ DR/ d r/ 36,4x31,7/ London, BMu/ Inv. 1861-8-10-2/ Popham & Pouncey 1950, Vol.I: p.94-95; Vol.II: pl.CXLVIII; Grafton 2003,n°2/ R4280.1250.
c1800 TRABALLESI, Giuliano : Diana and Venus?/ DR/ d/ 30,7x31,2/ Milano, BiA/ Inv. F 284 inf. n. 36/ IT/ R8729.1251.

Diomedes

c1790 GIANI, Felice: Venere ferita da Diomede (Venus wounded by Diomedes)/ PA/?/ 27,1x41,3/ Roma, PaBr/ Inv. MR 13505/ IT/ R3760.1252.

Europa

c1520 LUINI, Bernardino: Europa, Venus und Amor/ FR/ transferred to c/ 169x199/ Berlin, GSM/ Inv. 219A/ IT/ R11633.1253. *Part of a series of FRs from Casa Rabia La Pelucca, Monza.*

Flora

c1550 BORDONE, Paris : Venus, Flora, Mars and Cupid/ PA/ oc/ 108x129/ St.Petersburg, HMu/ Inv.1846/ Berenson 1958, p.48, pl.1134/ R2329.1254.

Graces/Nymphs

c1430 NARDO, Mariotto di : Venus hockt unter den Grazien auf einer blumigen Wiese (Venus with the Graces on a flower meadow) (Szenen aus der Teseida des Giovanni Boccaccio)/ PA/ tw/ ?/ Stuttgart, Sga/ Inv. #/ IT/ R10785.1255.
c1483 BOTTICELLI, Sandro : Vénus et les Trois Grâces offrant des présents à une jeune fille (Giovanna degli Albizzi) (Venus and the Three Graces giving presents to a young girl)/ FR/ c/ 211x283/ Paris, MdL/ Inv. RF 321/ Berenson 1963, p.37/ R509.1256.
1524-27 PARMIGIANINO, Girolamo Francesco: Bathing nymphs with Venus and Cupid/ DR/ d/ ?/ Firenze, GdU/ Inv.#/ Roberts 1986, p.54/ R11141V.1257.
1543 FANTUZZI, Antonio : Venus with nymphs bathing (aft PARMIGIANO)/ DR/ Firenze, GdU)/ PR/ / 25,6x19,1/ London, BMu/ Inv.#/ Zerner 1969,n°AF59/ R5082.1258.
c1550 BONASONE, Giulio : Venus attended by the Graces (aft RAFFAELLO, Sanzio?)/ PR/ e/ 21,6x15,7/SF,FAM/ Inv. 1963.30.2775/ Bartsch 29 (15,2) 1982,p.31, n°167(153))/ R4847.1259. *Also in Glasgow, HMAG/ Inv. 11986; London, BMu.*
c1600 PALMA Il Giovane, Jacopo Negretti : Venere e le tre Grazie/ PA/ oc/ ?/ Roma, PaMo/ Inv. E65561iccd/ IT iccd/ R8940.1260.
c1785 BARTOLOZZI, Francesco: Venus and the Three Graces (aft CIPRIANI, Giovanni Battista)/ PR/ e/ 10,3x14,6/ London, RAA/ Inv.03-768/ IT/ R8339.1261.
c1798 CANOVA, Antonio: Le Grazie e Venere danzano davanti a Marte (The Graces and Venus dance in front of Mars)/ PA/ tb/ 25x39/ Possagno, CdC/ Inv.98/ Stefani 2004, p.117, nr.158/ R487.1262.
Replica RE/ p/ ?/ Possagno, CdC/ Inv.99/ Stefani 2004, p.118, nr.160/ R10182.1263.; *DRs/ ?/ ?/Bassano, MuC/Inv. 955,1346 &1659.*
c1800 PEDRINI, Filippo : Vénus entourée d'anges/ DR/ ?/ ?/ Bologna, MDB/ Inv.381/ IT/ R8015V.1264.
c1836-37 PODESTI, Francesco : Venere con le ancelle/ DR// 18x31/ Roma, PaBr/ Inv. MR 16985/ IT/ R3765.1265.

▪ Cupid(s) around

c1460 (att) MANTEGNA, Andrea: Venus and the Graces (aft Master of the E-Series Tarocchi)/ PR/ ey/ 17,7x9,7/ SF, FAM/ Inv. 1998.201.15/ Seznec 1961, p.204, n°86; Trottein 1993, p.41, n°15/ R6034.1266.
c1509 PRIMATICCIO, Francesco: Les trois Graces dansent devant les dieux (*Vénus with bow*)/ FR/ /?/ Fontainebleau, MNC/ Inv. #/ IT/ R7285.1267.
1539-45 CATTANEO, Danese: Venus Cyprica *(with nymphs and Cupid)* RE/ m/ ?/ Venezia, Loggetta)/ Inv. #/ Pope-Hennessy 1964, p.530; Pope-Hennessy , Vol.III,1996, p.261, pl.243/ R10382.1268.
c1550 BONASONE, Giulio : Roman Venus *(and Cupid)* with the Graces and Greek Aphrodite *with the Charites* and Anteros (from *'Emblems of Bocchius'*)/ PR// 11x8/ London, BMu/ Bartsch 29 (15,2) 1982, p.82,n°257(163)/ R4848.1269.
c1575 MASTER of FLORA: Vénus, Cupidon et les Grâces/ PA/ ?/ ?/ UN, PrC/ Quignard 1982, p.44-45/ R7625.1270.
c1590 CARRACCI, Annibale: Venus adorned by the Graces (Toilet of Venus)/ PA/ owc/ 133x170,5/ Washington, NGA/ Inv. 1961.9.9/ Berenson 1967, fig.399; Mai ed. 2001, p.73, n°6 and p.256-57, n°15/ R806.1271.
1626 MALFATTI, Cesare : Venere, le tre Grazie e amorini('Immagini degli dei delli Antichi' *aut Vincenzo Catari, pub Pietro Paolo Tozzi)*/ PR/ e/ 22.6x16.3/ WEB, eBay 21.12.07/ R11669.1272.
c1650 LIBERI, Pietro: Vénus, les Graces et les amours/ PA/ oc/ 150x201/ Caen, MBA/ Inv. 30/ IT/ R11695.1273.
c1660 LIBERI, Pietro : Venere adornata dalle Grazie/ PA/oc/ 162x215/ Vicenza, MuC/ Inv. A306/ IT/ R8365.1274.
c1716 RICCI, Sebastiano: Vénus entourée de nymphes contemplant une ronde de Cupidons/ PA/ ow/ 49x86/ Paris, MdL/ Inv. MI 866/ IT/ R2077.1275.

1778 CAMPANELLA, Angelo: Venus and nymph with putti pl.III (aft Anton Raphael Mengs)/ PR/ er/ 48.8x61/ Wien, ALB/ Inv. 46121/ Joyce 1983; Roettgen 2001, p.248-251, fig.80c <aft FR LO in ancient roman home near Villa Peretti-Negroni (Stazione Termini), Roma>/ R11012.1276. *Plate III of XII; at auction among a set of seven/ London, CHR 9.3.06/ Sl. 7198-220/ IT/ R5924; copy Leo von Klenze/ PA/ u g/ ?/ München, Stadtmuseum.*

1782-84 BARTOLOZZI, Francesco: Venere e le Grazie (Venus attired by the Graces) (aft Kauffmann, Angelica)/ PR/ e/ 35,9x43,2/ Roma, ING/ Inv.FC70036/ Jatta 1995 p.153, fig.74/ R3751.1277. *Also: **1784** (pub S.Watts)/ Cambridge, FWM/ Inv. P.1-1951/IT;*
Toilet of Venus/ PR/ e/ 44x50/ SF,FAM/ Inv.1963.30.36202/ IT/ R722.1278.

1785 BARTOLOZZI, Francesco: Venere e le Grazie (Venus attired by the Graces) (aft CIPRIANI, Giovanni Battista)/ PR/ e/ 18,3x23,5/ Roma, ING/ Inv. FC70034/ Jatta 1995 p.165, fig.94/ R3754.1279.

c1799 CANOVA, Antonio : Le Grazie e due Amorini danzano davanti al simulacro di Venere/ DR/ ?/ ?/ Bassano, MuC/ / Inv. #/ Stefani 2004, p.125, nr.170/ R10183.1280.

c1800 SERANGELI, Gioacchino Giuseppe: Venere e Amore tra le tre Grazie/ PA/ ?/100x75/ UN 1991/ Inv.#/ IT/ R8318V.1281.

Hercules

c1500 ROBETTA, Christofano: The choice of Hercules/ PR/ e/ 25,6x18,9/ Wien, ALB/ Inv.#/ Bartsch 25 (13,2) 1980, p.294,n°?(404)/ R4797.1282.

c1670 GIORDANO, Luca: Venus, Hercules and Mercury (Allegory of divine wisdom)/ DR/ d/ 22x27,5/ Northwestern, BMu/ Inv. 1985.2.243/ IT/ R6310.1283.

c1700 PIOLA, Domenico: Hercule enfant entre Mars et Vénus/ PR/ e/ 34x21,5 (*eng Tasnière, Georges*)/ UN/ Inv.#/ IT/ R7637V.1284.

1748 BATONI, Pompeo: Hercules at the crossroads (*Venus at the feet of Hercules, on Hercules'right stands Pallas, cupids around)*/ PA/ oc/ 99x74/ Vaduz, LMu/ Inv.G161/ IT/ R3140.1285.

c1750 BATONI, Pompeo: Ercole al bivio (Pallas, Hercules and Venus; Athena invites Hercules to leave Venus)/ PA/ oc/97x75/ Firenze, GdU/ Inv.8547/ Berti 1979, p.128/ R3139.1286.

c1753 BATONI, Pompeo: Ercole al bivio tra la Virtù e la Volutta (Hercules at the crossroad between Virtue and Pleasure)/ PA/ oc/ 72x94/ Torino, GaS/ Inv.460, V.471/ Astrua 2000, p.73/ R4427.1287. *A popular presentation where Pleasure is associated with Venus.*

c1755 GANDOLFI, Ubaldo: Venere, Ercole e Athena/ PA/?/?/ Venezia, FGC/ Inv.#/ IT/ R2297V.1288.

c1770 MARCOLA, Marco: Venere unisce in matrimonio Ercole e Ebe/ DR/ d/ 32x40,8/ Verona, MdC/ Inv. 12994 2B 465/ Marinelli 1999, p.123, n°94/ R3564.1289.

c1800 BENVENUTI, Pietro: Athena, Hercules and Venus/ PA/?/?/ Firenze, PaP/ Inv.#/ IT/ R4528.1290.

Juno

1570 COSCIA, Francesc del: Giunone chiede a Venere la sua cintura/ PA/ oc/ 117x68/ Firenze, PaV/ Inv. n. 257 inventario 1890, n. 6344/ IT/ R8582.1291.

c1730 TIEPOLO, Giambattista: Junon, la Fortune et Vénus honorent les insignes des Archinto et des Borromée/ FR//900x700/ LO, pre. Milano, Pa Archinto/ Pedrocco 2002, p.219-20, cat.71.4/ R11148.1292.

1743 CIGNAROLI, Giambettino: Juno and Venus/ DR/ d/ 42,5x28,4/ Milano, BiA/ Inv. F 257 inf. n. 202/ IT/ R8724.1293.

c1800 APPIANI, Andrea: Venere che pone il cinto a Giunone (Venus fastening her gurdle to Juno)/ DR/ d/ 25.1x34.7/ Milano, CaS/ Inv. B52/ Precerutti-Garberi 1969, p.48-49, n°70/ R9641.1294.

Jupiter

c1525 PARMIGIANINO : Zeus (or Neptun ?), Mars and Venus/ DR/ d/ 20x19,2/ Parma, GaN/ Inv.510-18/ Weddingen 1994, p.110, n°16/ R4290.1295. *Entitled "Vulcan, Mars and Venus"/ Arasse 1997, p.93-105 ; reverse **c1760** BOSSI, Benigno: Marte e Venere sorpresi da Vulcano/ PR/ /139,1x21/ Parma, BiP/ Inv. On22040/ Mussini 2003, p.166,n°327/ R3641.1296..*

c1530 PERUZZI, Baldassare Tommaso : Power of Cupid (Jupiter disarmed)/ PR/ e/ 19x22/ NY, MMA/ Inv. 1949 (49.97.328)/ IT/ R1646.1297.
c1550 CARAGLIO, Iacopo : Der Götterrat (Venus und Amor vor Jupiter) (The council of gods: Venus and Cupid in front of Jupiter)/ PR/ y/ Wien, ALB/ Inv.HB,X.2/ Oberhuber 1999,p.132,n°73; Bartsch 28 C (15,1) 1995,p.187-191,n°2802.054/ R4146.1298. *Also in other places.*
b1570 VERONESE, Paolo Caliari: Jupiter and Venus (or Juno?)/ PA/ oc/ 27.1x101/ Boston, MFA/ Inv. 60.125 / Berenson 1958, p.134; Boccardo ed. 2004, p.372-373,n°94 a/ R968.1299.
1583 ALLORI, Alessandro : Venere offre a Giove il pomo delle Esperidi (Venus offering the apple of the Esperides to Jupiter)/ DR/ d/ 39x53,2/ Roma, ING/ Inv.FC124148/ Lecchini Giovannoni 1991, p.261-262, n°95, fig.213; Antetomaso & Mariani, 2004, p.316-317/ R3475.1300. *Preparatory for a tapestry, UN.*
1583 ALLORI, Alessandro : Ritorno di Venere ed Amore sull'Olimpo (The return of Venus and Cupid on the Olympus)/DR/d/39,2x55,5/Roma, ING/Inv.FC124149/ Antetomaso & Mariani, 2004, p.316-317/ R3476. 1301.
c1600 CASTELLO, Bernardo: Jupiter and Venus/ DR/ d/ ?/ London, BMu/ Inv. 1962,1208.00003/ IT/ R8434V.1302.
1644 DELLA BELLA, Stefano: Venus, fille de Jupiter *(Jeu des Fables: n°504)*/ IL/ e/ 8,3x5,1/De Vesme 1971, Vol.I:105-107; Vol.II:108-113/R3565.1303.
c1650 PIGNONI, Simone : A poet, presented to Jupiter by Hercules, is crowned by Glory, below Venus, Cupid and the poet/ PA/ oc/ 45x25/ Cambridge, FWM/ Inv. PD.20-1992/ IT/ R11348.1304.
c1800 APPIANI, Andrea : Giove accoglie Venere ferita/ FR/ f/ ?/ Milano, POR 18.5.05/ Sl. ?-152/ IT/ R10277.1305.
c1800 APPIANI, Andrea : Giove e Venere/ DR/ d/ 24.6x23.7/ Milano, CaS/ Inv. B34/2-571/12/ Precerutti-Garberi 1969, p.45, nr.59/ R9639.1306.
1809 PINELLI, Bartolomeo: Vénus comparaît devant son père Jupiter pour intercéder en faveur de son fils Énée (Venus intervenes in favour of her son Aeneas with her father Jupiter)/ DR/ d/ 44,3x59,9/ Ottawa, MBA/ Inv. 41261/ IT/ R7019.1307.
c1875 ANGELIS, Domenico de: Venere intercede per Enea presso Giove (Venus intervenes for Aeneas with Jupiter/ PA/?/?/ Roma, GaB/ Inv.#/ Staccioli 1985, p.15/ R8279V.1308.

Mercury

c1525 CORREGGIO, Antonio: Venus with Mercury and Cupid (The School of Love or Celestial Venus)/ PA/ oc/ 155,6x91,4/ London, Nga/ Inv. NG10/ Landon 1912; Berenson 1968, p.92; Gould 1975, p.57-61 ; Anonymous 1989, Vol.I, p.957; Mai ed. 2001, p.76, n°10/ R528.1309. *Many copies and engravings.*
c1550 (wor) TIZIANO, Vecellio: Education of Cupid by Venus and Mercury/ PA/ oc/ 182x117/ El Paso, MuA/ Inv. 1961-6.28/ IT/ R11446V.1310.
c1575 VERONESE, Paolo Caliari: Studies of Mercury, Venus, Cupid and Saturn and other figures/ DR/ d/ 30,3x20,3/ London, CHR 05.12.'06/ Sl. 7367-12/ IT/ R8062.1311.
c1650 CHIARI, Fabrizio: Venus and Mercury (aft Nicolas Poussin) /PR/ e/ ? / London, PrC R.Verdi/ Inv.#/ Verdi 1986,p.13,n°9/ R2899.1312.
1717 LUTI, Benedetto: Erziehung Amors durch Merkur and Venus (The education of Cupid by Mercury and Venus)/ PA/ oc/ 245x198/ Pommersfelden, ScW/ Inv.335/ Anonymous (2005) Encyclopédie de l'Art, p.605; IT/ R8966.1313.
a1717 DE NIGRIS, ?: Venere, Mercurio e Amore (aft LUTI, Benedetto)/ PA/ oc/ ?/ Roma, PaMO/ Inv. 624- E65774iccd/ IT/ R8923.1314.
c1725 BALESTRA, Antonio: Venus, Mercury and Cupid/ PA/ oc/ 122x94/ WEB, ArtPrice 8.7.'99/ Inv.#/ IT/ R8495V.1315.
c1750 (att) GRAZIANI, Ercole: Mercurio,Venere e Amore/ PA/ oc/ ?/ Roma, PaMo/ Inv. 698-E65715iccd/ IT/ R8924.1316.
c1800 BARTOLOZZI, Francesco: Venus and Mercury/ DR/ d/ 22x27.9/ NY, CHR 1.10.07/ Sl. 1883-0997/ IT/ R10516.1317.

Minerva

1502 MANTEGNA, Andrea: Minerve chassant (Vénus) les Vices du Jardin de la Vertu (Triumph of Wisdom over Vice ; Allegory of Vice and Virtue)/ PA/ tc/ 160x192/ Paris, MdL/ Inv. 371/ Seznec 1961, p.111, n°37; Berenson 1968, p.241, pl.707/ R6026.1318.
c1504 RAFFAELLO, Sanzio: Sogno del cavaliere (The dream of the knight *a choice between Minerva and Venus)*/ PA/ ow/ 17x17/ London, NGa/ Inv.#/ IT/ R1654.1319.
c1516 (att) DENTE, Marco: Venere, Amore e Pallade (Venus, Cupid and Pallas, central part of the 'Judgement of Paris' by RAIMONDI, M. aft RAFFAELLO, S.)/ PR/ e/22,7x13/ Roma, ING/ Inv. FC4974/ Massari 1989, p.22-27,n°7f/ R3484.1320.
1531 ALCIATO, Andrea : O Cyprian, why have you vanquished Pallas (*Emblematum liber)*/ IL/ CIX/ IT/ R6047.1321.
1555 BOCCHI, Achille : Minerva and Venus reconciled (and crowning the drunken Silenus) (*aut 'Symbolicae quaestiones')*/ IL/ X/ Wind 1980, p. 71, fig.56/R10426.1322.
c1575 (att) TINTORETTO, Jacopo : Venere e Minerva/ PA/ ?/ ?/ St.Louis, AMu/ Inv. 173.55/ Berenson 1958, p.183 ; Rizzoli 1970, p.134, n° E12/ R8378.1323.
c1590-1620 (cir) TIBALDI, Pellegrino: Venus and Minerva/ PA/ oy/ oval 28,5x22/ A'dam, RMu/ Inv. SK-A-3952/ IT/ R3954.1324.
c1633 CORTONA, Pietro da: Moral knowledge and Minerva foresaking the drunken Silenus and Venus/ DR/ d/ 27.8x41.9/ Ottawa, NGC/ Inv. 6134/ IT/ R10268.1325.
1641 CORTONA, Pietro da: Adolescentiam Pallas a Venere avellit (Pallas takes the youth from the arms of Venus)/ FR// ?/ Firenze, PaP/ Inv.#/ Czére 2002,p.245,n°3/ R701.1326.
Preparatory : Studi per la figura di Venere/ DR/ d/ 20,5x27/ Firenze, GdU/ Inv. 11725F/ Rodino 1997,p.154,n°8.11/ R3559.1327.;
Sketch for Venus/ DR/ d/ 7.2x7.6/ Budapest, MFA/ Inv. 2300/ Czére 2004, p.135, Cat.124/ R10921.1328.;
Schizzo di figure con Venere/ DR/ d/ 14,5x21/ Budapest, MFA/ Inv.2301/ Czére 2002,p.125,n°50; Czére 2004, p.134-135, Cat.123/ R4518.1329. Several drawings and prints "after": Fragonard/ Rosenberg 1987,p.129,n°47; reverse by eng Lambert Van Visscher/ PR/ e/ 42,5x65,2/ SF, FAM/ Inv.#/ IT/ R1382.
c1750 AMIGONI, Jacopo : Minerva y Venus/ FR// ?/ Madrid, PaRA/ Inv. < Sala de la planta baja>/ Navarrete 2005, p.124, fig.231/ R11041.1330.
1772 ANGELETTI, Pietro: Riconciliazione fra Venere e Minerva/ FR// ?/ Roma, PaBo/ Inv. E42223iccd/ IT/ R8945.1331.

Neptun

c1585 CINCINATO, Romulo : Venus, Cupido y Neptuno/ FR// ?/ Guadalajara, PaI/ Inv. Sala de Atalanta/ Navarrete 2005, p.87/ R11021V.1332.
1637 DELLA BELLA, Stefano : Seashore on Cyprus, with Neptune and Amphitrite enthroned, Venus on cloud, and tritons dancing a ballet (The Wedding of the Gods; Act III, Scene 2) (aft Alfonso Parigi II)/ PR/ e/ 20.2x29.2/ Hanover, HMA/ Inv. PR.979.66.4/ IT/ R11383.1333.
c1856-60 PODESTI, Francesco : Incontro di Venere e Galatea (Trionfo di Venere)/ PA/ ?/28x36/ Roma, PaBr/ Inv. MR 922/ Anonymous 1975, Vol.1/ R3763.1334.
1889 FERRARESI, Adriano: Studio di Tritone per "Venere e Nettuno premiano il vincitore di una corsa di cavalli marini"/ DR/ d/ 57,5x33/ Roma, GCAMC/ Inv. AM424-a-d/ Virno 2004, p.276-278, n°547/ R8644. 1335.

Pluto

c1526 PRIMATICCIO, Francesco: Vénus, Bacchus, Mars, Mercure… auprès de Pluto et Proserpine ?/ DR/ d/ 16x39,7/London, BMu/ Inv. 1946-7-13-44/ Primatice 2004, p.91, Cat.10/ R3432.1336. *Sometimes interpreted as part of the Psyche story.*

1548 PRIMATICCIO, Francesco: Vénus demande à l'Amour de frapper Pluton/ DR/ d/ 30x77,2/ Paris, MdL/ Inv. 3497/ IT ; Primatice 2004, p.87-89, Cat.9/ R3431.1337. *Erroneously interpreted as part of the Psyche story / Pérouse de Montclos 1998, p.23.*
c1600 TEMPESTA, Antonio: Venus with Cupid shooting at Pluto (*from Ovid's Metamorphoses)*/ PR/ e/ 9,7x11,5/ London, BMu/ Inv. #/ Bartsch 36(17,3) 1983, p.32,n°683(151)/ R4957.1338.

Pygmalion

1717-1724 RICCI, Sebastiano: Pigmalione e Galatea (with Venus in a cloud above Galatea)/ PA/ oc/ ?/ Ruvigliano, PrC/ Inv. #/ IT/ R10306.1339.

Saturn or Cronos or Time

1540-50 BRONZINO, Agnolo: Venus, Cupido and the Time (Venus, Cupid, Folly and Time; Allegory of Lust; The exposure of Luxury)/ PA/ ow/ 146x117/London, NGA/ Inv. NG651/ Berenson 1963, p.43 Panofsky 1969, fig.66, pl.XXXVIII; Gould 1975, p.41-44 ; Anonymous 1989, Vol.I, p.956; Mai ed. 2001, p.93, n°3/ R382.1340.
c1545 SALVIATI, Francesco : Allégorie du triomphe de Vénus (aft BRONZINO)/ DR/ d/ 11,4x9,8/ Ottawa, MBA/ Inv. 41430r/ IT/ R5728.1341.
c1550 GUERCINO, Barbieri detto, Giovane Francesco : Venere, Marte, Amore e il Tempo/ PA/ ?/ ?oval/ Altrincham, DM Col.Stamford/ Inv. #/ Morselli 1998, p.620, fig.25/ R10004.1342.
c1570 ALLORI, Alessandro : Le Temps, Vénus et l'Amour et deux autres figures (Time, Venus and Cupid and two other figures)/ DR/ d/ 25,7x19/ Paris, MdL/ Inv.20/ IT/ R5386.1343.
c1577 VERONESE, Paolo Caliari: Les Dieux de l'Olympe : Vénus, Saturne et Mercure/ FR/ c/ 310x226/ Paris, MdL/ Inv. RF 2183bis/ IT/ R2501.1344.
c1624-26 GUERCINO, Giovane Francesco Barbieri: An Allegory with Venus, Mars, Cupid and Time/ PA/ oc/ 127x175/ Cheshire, DMC/ Inv.#/ IT/ R1497.1345.
c1650 DIAMANTINI, Giuseppe: Saturn, Venus and Eros/ PR/ e/ 28,4x20,7/Berlin, KKa/Inv.#/ Bartsch 47 (21,2) 1983, p.421,n°37(286) / R5005.1346.
c1665 COLONNA, Angelo Michele : Studi per Venere inseguita dal Tempo/ DR// 22,3x31,5/ Bologna, Pna/ Inv.4291/ Faietti 1998,p.184-85,n°65/ R3480.1347.
1665-66 COLONNA, Angelo Michele & ALBORESI, Giacomo: Venere inseguita dal Tempo/ FR//? Bologna, VAT/ Inv.#/ Faietti 1998,p.184/ R3481.1348.
c1758 TIEPOLO, Giambattista: Allegory with Venus and Time (*Venus consigns Cupid to Father Time)*/ PA/ oc/ 292x190,4/ London, NaG/ Inv. NG6387/ Anonymous 1989, Vol.I, p.957; Zuffi 2001, p.119; Pedrocco 2002, p.298 cat.246..1; Calasso 2006, p.261, n°78/ R1502.1349. *A preparatory DR/ NY, MMA/ Inv.#/ Baker & Henry 2001, p.661; replica(?) or copy(?): London, CHR 27.6.'69.*
c1758 TIEPOLO, Giandomenico: Venus entrusting an infant to Time (aft Giambattista TIEPOLO)/ PR/ e/ 46,8x30,6/ NY, MMA/ Inv. 57.619.5/ IT/ R1637.1350.
c1767 TIEPOLO, Giambattista: Il Tempo affida Cupido a Venere-Venere affida Cupido al Tempo (Time consigns Cupid to Venus-or- Venus consigns Cupid to Time)/ PA/ oc/ 46x57/ pre. Lisboa, PrC/ Inv.#/ Rizzoli 1968, p.134-135, n°297; Pedrocco 2002, p.311, cat.284 ; Calasso 2006, p.260, n°77/ R8541.1351.

13. Venus and Psyche

1468 MASTER of the ARGONAUT Panels : Szenen aus dem antiken Märchen Amor und Psyche/ PA/ w (2 cassone)/ 40x130/ Berlin, GSM/ Inv. 1823-24/ Berenson 1963, p.210 ; Cavicchioli 2002, p.70-71, n°35/ R9281. 1352. *Berenson attributes to BIAGIO di ANTONIO.*
1493-1500 (wor) SELLAIO, Jacopo del : Story of Cupid and Psyche/ PA/ ow (principal panel of cassone)/ 43.8x152/ Boston, MFA/ Inv. 12.1049/ Berenson 1963, p.196 ; Cavicchioli 2002, p.73, n°38/ R9282.1353. *Replica : 42x158,5/ Riggisberg, AS/ Inv. 14.123.72. Another principal panel of cassone 58.4x179/ Cambridge, FWM/ Inv. M75/ Berenson 1963, p.196 ; Cavicchioli 2002, p.74-75, n°39/ R9283 and with a replica 59x179/ NY, PrC (pre. Amsterdam, Col. Ernst Proehl)/ Berenson 1963, p.196, pl.1105-1106 ; Cavicchioli 2002, p.68, n°34/ R9280.1354.*
1517 RAFFAELLO, Sanzio : Loggia di Psiche/ FR// ?/ Roma, ViF/ Inv.#/ Berenson 1968, p.353 ; Cordellier &Py 1992, p.362-370 ; Cavicchioli 2002, p.89,n°47/ R527.1355. *The individual frescoes of the Loggia are attributed to RAFFAELLO's workshop collaborators.*
1527-34 ROMANO, Giulio: Vénus et le triton (Camera of Psyche)/ FR// ?/ Mantova, PdT/ Inv.#/ Cavicchioli 2002, p.132, n°82/ R7150.1356.
1532 PRIMATICCIO, Francesco : Histoire de Psyché/ DR/ d/ ?/ Fontainebleau, MNC/ Inv. #/Pérouse de Montclos 1998, p.23/ R4299.1357. *Preparatory DR for a FR LO.*
c1540 MAESTRO B nel Dado: Venere su delfini con Oceano e Nereidi/ (aft Coxie, Michel)/ PR/ e/ 20,2x20/ Roma, ING/ Inv. FC586(34302)/ Massari 1989, p.90-91,n°26/ R3490.1358. *Also: MASTER of the DIE: White bird telling Venus of Cupid's illness (from the Fable of Psyche)/ PR/ e/ 19,4x22,8/ London, BMu/ Inv.#/ Bartsch 29 (15,2) 1982, p.210 n°54-II(218)/ R4851; also in Cambridge, FWM/ Inv. P.6036-R & P.6037-R.*
c1543 PERINO DEL VAGA, Pietro: Venere su delfini con Oceano e Nereidi (*Psyche story)*/ FR// ?/ Roma CSA/ Inv.#/ Massari 1989, p.84,90,fig.18/ R8387.1359.
1600 CASTELLO, Bernardo : Sala di Psiche/ FR/ / ?/ Bassano Romano, ViVG/ Inv. #/ IT/ R10091.1360.
1695-97 GIORDANO, Luca : Venus learns about Cupid's plight (*on the sea, with white bird*)/ PA/ oy/ 67.2x68.9/ Windsor, RCo/ Inv. RC406772/ exh/ R10536.1361. *x of xii PAs on Story of Psyche, painted for Spanish Court.*

○ Venus on her chariot, showing Psyche to Cupid

1516-17 (wor) RAFFAELLO, Sanzio : Venus in a chariot (La Loggia di Psiche)/ FR// ?/ Roma, ViF/ Inv.#/ Cavicchioli 2002, p.97,n°53/ R7138.1362. *DR 'aft' known : 42,6x31,8/ Paris, MdL/ Inv. 4197r/ Cordelier 1992/ R3841; 35,5x26,5/ Lille, BA/Inv.W.2355/ IT/ R2837.*
1516-17 (wor) RAFFAELLO, Sanzio : Venere indica ad Amore la rivale (Venus pointing out Psyche to Cupid)('La Loggia di Psiche)/ FR// ?/ Roma, ViF/ Inv.#/ Cavicchioli 2002, p.92-93,n°49/ R1253.1363. Also *'aft' **c1600**/ DR: d/ 96x24,6/ Paris, MdL/ Inv. 4196rr/ IT/ R3837; DR/ d/ 36x26,8/ Lille, MBA/ Inv. W.2358/ IT/ R2839; DR/ d/ 27.5x53/ Chicago, AIC: Inv. 1927.7689/ R10259V.*
1527-34 ROMANO, Giulio: Venus shows Psyche to Cupid (Camera of Psyche : the story of Cupid and Psyche)/ FR// ?/ Mantova, PdT/ Inv.#/ Cavicchioli 2002, p.125, n°78/ R7252.1364.
c1540 DADDI, Bernardo: The people rendering divine honors to Psyche (*Venus and Cupid in the sky*) (pl. 2 from the series the Fable of Psyche aft RAFFAELLO, Sanzio)/ PR/ e/ 19,6x22,9/ SF, FAM/ Inv. 1963.30.2882/ IT/ R10724.1365.
1695-97 GIORDANO, Luca : Psyche honoured by the people *(Venus watching in the sky and showing Psyche to Cupid)*/ PA/ oy/ 57.5x68.9/ Windsor, RCo/ Inv. RC461/ exh/ R10538.1366. *i of xii PA on Story of Psyche, painted for Spanish Court.*

c1700 PIETRI, Pietro di: Vénus sur son char/ DR/ d/ 21,3x31,9/ Paris, MdL/ Inv. 4199/ Cordelier 1992, p.386,n°598/ R3846.1367.
c1700 PIETRI, Pietro di: Vénus désignant Psyché à l'Amour/ DR/ d/ 20,7x31,4/ Paris, MdL/ Inv. 4202recto/ Cordelier 1992, p.362-390,n°601/ R3849.1368.

o Venus with Jupiter, with Ceres and Juno, with Mercury

1516-17 (wor) RAFFAELLO, Sanzio: Venus devant Jupiter (Loggia di Psiche)/ FR/ ?/ Roma, ViF/ Inv.#/ Cavicchioli 2002, p.98, n°54/ R8461.1369. *Also 'aft' DR/ d/ 50,2x39,7/ Paris, MdL/ Inv. 4194r/* Cordelier 1992, p.362-370,n°541/ R3843.
1516-17 (wor) RAFFAELLO, Sanzio : Concilio degli dei (Loggia di Psiche)/ FR/ ?/ Roma, ViF/ Inv.#/ Bardon 1960, pl.II; Cavicchioli 2002, p.91, n°48/ R7248.1370.
c1515 *preparatory DR(detail)/ d/ 22x24,3/ Paris, FoC/ Inv. JBS 117/ Oberhuber 1999, p.132-133,n°74/ R3691. 1371.*
1516-17 (wor) RAFFAELLO, Sanzio : Venere presso Giunone e Cerere (La Loggia di Psiche)/ FR// ?/ Roma, ViF/ Inv.#/ Cavicchioli 2002, p.96,n°52./ R2705.1372. *Other DR 'aft' known : c1600/ 22x19/ Paris, MdL/ Inv. 4015r/* Cordelier 1992, p.362-370,n°535/ *R3838;* ***c1516****: 'Trois femmes nues (Vénus, Cérès et Junon)/ 28,4x193/ Lille, MBA/ Inv. W.2150/ IT/ R2828 ; another detail 'Venus' :DR/ d/ 36,8x26,6/ Lille, MBA/ Inv. W.2361/ IT/ R2841.*
c1516 ROMANO, Giulio : Venus sucht Rat bei Juno und Ceres/ DR/ d/ 24,6x19,3/ Wien, ALB/ Inv. 271/ Oberhuber 1999, p.136-137,n°78/ R3692.1373.
c1516 DENTE, Marco: Venere si allontana da Giunone e Cerere (Venus leaving Juno and Ceres, episode of the Psyche story) (aft ROMANO, G. or RAFFAELLO, S.)/ PR/ e/ 26,6x20/ Roma, ING/ Inv. FN 524/ Massari 1993, p.39-40/ R3549.1374. *Also: 'Venus sucht Rat bei Juno und Ceres'/ PR/ e/ 26x19,9/ Wien, ALB/ Inv. It.,I.21/* Oberhuber 1999, p.138,n°79/ *R3693.*
1527-34 ROMANO, Giulio : Venere chiede a Giove l'aiuto di Mercurio per trovare la fuggiasca (Camera di Amore e Psiche)/ FR// ?/ Mantova, PdT/ Inv.#/ Cavicchioli 2002, p.126, n°79/ R7249.1375.
Preparatory : Study for Venus asking Jupiter for the services of Mercury as herald/ DR/ d/ 20.3x28.8/ Chicago, AIC/ Inv. 1922.732/ IT/ R10260.1376.
1527-34 ROMANO, Giulio : Cerere e Giunone intervengono in favore di Amore (Camera di Amore e Psiche)/ FR// ?/ Mantova, PdT/ Inv.#/ Cavicchioli 2002, p.128-29, n°80/ R7251.1377.
c1540 DADDI, Bernardo: Venus complains to Jupiter, pl. 18 from the series the Fable of Psyche (aft RAFFAELLO, Sanzio)/ PR/ e/ 19,2x22,7/ SF, FAM/ Inv. 1963.30.2898/ R752.1378. *Also: MASTER of the DIE (aft Michiel Coxcie) / PR/ e/ 20x23.5/ Chicago, AIC/ Inv. 2001.493.18/ Bartsch 29 (15,2) 1982, p.212 n°56-II(219)/ R4853; also in Cambridge, FWM/ Inv. P.6040-R ; London, BMu.*
c1540 DADDI, Bernardo: Venus and Cupid pleading their cause in the presence of Jupiter and the other gods, pl. 30 from the series the Fable of Psyche (aft RAFFAELLO, Sanzio)/ PR/ e/ 19,8x22,7/ SF, FAM/ Inv. 1963.30.2910/ R750.1379.. *Also: MASTER of the DIE (aft Michiel Coxcie) / PR/ e/ 20x23.5/ Chicago, AIC/ Inv. 2001.493.30/ Bartsch 29 (15,2) 1982 p.224 n°68-II(223)/ R4856; also in Cambridge, FWM/ Inv. P.6064-R ; London, BMu.*
c1543 PERINO DEL VAGA, Pietro: Venere si lamenta con Giunone e Cerere (detail)/ FR// ?/ Roma, CSA/ Inv.E50742iccd/ Cavicchioli 2002, p.21 n°6/ R8463.1380.
c1550 ALBERTI, Cherubino: Venus with Juno and Ceres; Venus ascending towards Mount Olympus; Venus and Jupiter (aft RAFFAELLO)/ PR/ e/ 31x60,8/ London, BMu/ Inv.#/ Bartsch34(17,1),1982 p.228,#106(84)/ R4955.1381.
c1700 PIETRI, Pietro di: Vénus implorant Jupiter/ DR/ d/ 20,8x32/ Paris, MdL/ Inv. 4200recto/ Cordelier 1992, p.362-3390,n°599/ R3847.1382.
c1700 PIETRI, Pietro di: Vénus, Ceres et Juno/ DR/ d/ 22x31/ Paris, MdL/ Inv. 4201recto/ Cordelier 1992, p.362-390,n°600/ R3848.1383.
1781 NOVELLI, Pietro Antonio: Venere chiede Mercurio di cercare Psiche/ FR//oval/ Roma, GaB/ Inv.#/ exh/ R015.1384.

o Venus chides Cupid and punishes Psyche

1516-17 (wor) RAFFAELLO, Sanzio : Psyche before Venus *offering the waters of the Styx* ('La Loggia di Psiche)/ FR// ?/ Roma, ViF/ Inv.#/ Cavicchioli 2002, p.99,n°57/ R7139.1385.
*Also DR/ d/ 26,4x19,7/ Paris, MdL/ Inv. 3875r/*Cordelier 1992, p.362-370,n°548/ *R904.1386.;also (aft): DR/ d/ 36,2x26,3/ Lille, MBA/ Inv. W.2359/ IT/ R2840 and DR/ d/ 23.7x17.6/ Chicago, AIC/ Inv. 1922.3678/ R10258V.*
1527-34 ROMANO, Giulio : Venera rimprovera e minaccia Amore ferito (Camera di Amore e Psiche)/ FR// ?/ Mantova, PdT/ Inv.#/ Cavicchioli 2002, p.129, n°86/ R7250.1387.
1527-34 ROMANO, Giulio: Psyche trainée devant Vénus/ FR// ?/ Mantova, PdT/ Inv.#/ Cavicchioli 2002, p.125, n°78/ R8488.1388.
c1540 DADDI, Bernardo: Venus reprimanding her son, pl. 17 from the series the Fable of Psyche (aft RAFFAELLO, Sanzio)/ PR/ e/ 19,3x22,9/ SF, FAM/ Inv. 1963.30.2897/ IT/ R753.1389.
Also MASTER of the DIE (aft Michiel Coxcie, aft RAFFAELLO)/ PR/ e/ 20x23.5/ Chicago, AIC/ Inv. 2001.493.17/ Bartsch 29 (15,2) 1982, p.211 n°55-II(218)/ R4852. Also in Cambridge, FWM/ Inv. P.6038-R ; London, BMu.
Also VENEZIANO, Agostino: Venus and Amor/ PR/ e/ ?/ R6044.1390.
c1540 DADDI, Bernardo: Venus ordering Psyche to seek water from a fountain guarded by dragons, from the series the Fable of Psyche (aft RAFFAELLO, Sanzio)/ PR/ e/ 19,4x22,7/ SF, FAM/ Inv. 1975.1.151/ IT/ R749.1391. *Replica without text PR/ e/ 18,3x22,4/ SF, FAM/ Inv. 1963.30.2912/ IT/ R754. Also: MASTER of the DIE/ PR/ e/ 19,4x22,8/ London, BMu/ Inv.#/ Bartsch 29 (15,2) 1982, p.227 n°71(224)/ R4857; also in Cambridge, FWM/ Inv. P.6161-R; Chicago, AIC/ Inv. 2001.493.33.*
c1540 DADDI, Bernardo: Venus ordering Psyche to sort a heap of grain, pl. 22 from the series the Fable of Psyche (aft RAFFAELLO, Sanzio) PR/ e/ 19,3x22,7/ SF, FAM/ Inv. 1963.30.2902/ R751.1392. *Also: MASTER of the DIE/ PR/ e/ 19,4x22,8/ London, BMu/ Inv.#/ Bartsch 29 (15,2) 1982, p.216 n°60-II(220)/ R4854; also in Cambridge, FWM/ Inv. P.6048-R ; Chicago, AIC/ Inv. 2001.493.22.*
c1540 MAESTRO B nel Dado: Psiche tormentata delle ancelle di Venere (aft Coxie, Michel)/ PR/ e/ 19,8x22,8/ Roma, ING/ Inv. FN591(34307)/ Massari 1989, p.92-93, n°27/ R3491.1393.
c1540 MASTER of the DIE: Venus ordering Psyche to seek the golden wool (sic) (*Golden Fleece*)/ PR/ e/ 19,4x22,8/ London, BMu/ Inv.#/ Bartsch 29 (15,2) 1982, p.217 n°61-II(220)/ R4855.1394. *Also: without text (aft* engr *MAESTRO B nel Dado, aft DR of Coxie, Michiel, aft RAFFAELLO) DR/ d/ 18x24/ Paris, MdL/ Inv. 4014/* Cordelier 1992, p.392, n°612/ *R3852.*
c1543 PERINO DEL VAGA, Pietro: Vénus réprimande Eros/ ; réunion avec Céres et Juno/FR// ?/ Roma CSA/ Inv.#/ Cavicchioli 2002, p.20-21 n°6 / R8367.1395.
c1543 PERINO DEL VAGA, Pietro: L'épreuve des grains (detail)/ FR// ?/ Roma, CSA/ Inv.#/ Cavicchioli 2002, p.23-24 n°7-8/ R8462.1396.
1545-46 PERINO DEL VAGA, Pietro: Psiche è percossa da affanno e transcinata da abitudine davanti a Venere/ FR// ?/ Roma CSA/ Inv. E50741iccd/ Massari 1989, p.84,92,fig.19; Cavicchioli 2002, p.22-23 n°7/ R8368. 1397.
1545-46 PERINO DEL VAGA, Pietro: Psiche riceve da Venere il vaso da riempire con l'unguento di Proserpina/ FR// ?/ Roma CSA/ Inv. E50740iccd / IT/ R8929.1398.
c1692-1702 GIORDANO, Luca: Venus punishing Psyche with a task (?)/ PA/ oy/ 58,1x68,9/ Windsor, RCo/ Inv.RC463/ exh/ R463.1399. *PA on Story of Psyche, painted for Spanish Court.*
1695-97 GIORDANO, Luca : Venus chides Cupid/ PA/ oy/ 57.2x70.2/ Windsor, RCo/ Inv. RC406773/ exh/ R10537.1400. *N° xi of xii PAs on Story of Psyche, painted for Spanish Court.*
c1700 GIANI, Felice : Venere ordina a Psiche di portare l'acqua dello Stige/ PA/ ?/ ?/ Roma, PaA/ Inv. #/ Stefani 2004, p.52, nr.58/ R10181.1401.
c1700 PIETRI, Pietro di: Psyché présentant à Vénus l'eau du Styx/ DR/ d/ 21,5x31,5/ Paris, MdL/ Inv. 4203/ Cordelier 1992, p.362-390,n°602/ R3850.1402.

o marriage of Psyche, feast of the gods

1516-17 (wor) RAFFAELLO, Sanzio : Banquet of the gods (*Venus dancing on the left side)* (Loggia di Psiche)/ FR/ ?/ Roma, ViF/ Inv.#/ Cavicchioli 2002, p.90, n°48/ R8460.1403. *Copy 'aft'/ DR/ d/ 14,2x49/ Paris, MdL/ Inv. 4018, Rect/ Cordelier 1992/ R8455.*

c1524 (att) CALDARA da CARAVAGGIO, Polidoro: Psyché reçue dans l'Olympe/ PA/ ow/ 104.5x160.5/ Paris, MdL/ Inv. 135/ IT/ R11631.1404. *Pre. decoration Palazzo Bernardino Rota, Napoli.*

1527-34 ROMANO, Giulio: Le banquet des dieux (*Vénus mène la danse*) (Camera of Psyche)/ FR// ?/ Mantova, PdT/ Inv.#/ Cavicchioli 2002, p.126, n°79/ R8490.1405. *Another scene is called : Il banchetto sull'isola di Citera/ Bardon 1960, pl.III/ R7253.*

c1540 MASTER of the DIE: Le festin des dieux/ PR/ ?/ ?/ Paris, BNF/ Inv.#/ Bardon 1960, pl.Iva/ R7259. 1406.

c1543 PERINO DEL VAGA, Pietro: Il convito degli dei (*Vénus with Cupid sitting on the right side)*/ FR// ?/ Roma, CSA/ Inv. E50739iccd/ Cavicchioli 2002, p.30-31 n°11/ R8464.1407.

c1575 SCULTORI, Diana: Il simposio degli dei ovvero i preparativi per il convito di Amore e Psiche/ PR/ e/ 38x112/ Roma, ING/ Inv. FC50749/ Massari 1993, p.160-164, n°155/ R3552.1408.

1756 BATONI, Pompeo: Die Vermählung Amors mit Psyche (Marriage of Cupid and Psyche)/ PA/ oc/ 85x119/ Berlin, GSM/ Inv.504/ Cavicchioli 2002, p.200-201, n°141; Greer 2003, p.81/ R2381.1409.

14. Venus and Satyrs

c1590 CARRACCI, Annibale: Venus y un satiro/ PA/ oc/ 21x31/ Madrid, MNP (en deposito en la Casa Museo de Colon, Las Palmas de Gran Canaria)/ Inv. P71/ Enciclopedia 2006, Tomo II, p.646-47/ R10731V.1410.
c1725 AMIGONI, Jacopo: Venus and Pan/ PA/ ?/ ?/ UN/ Inv.#/ IT/ R11404V.1411.

o alone with Venus

c1565 GIAMBOLOGNA : Schlafende Venus und Satyr; Venere dormiente (Venus sleeping and satyr)/ SC/ z/ 21x34x17,7/ Dresden, SKS/ Inv. IX34/ IT/ R6749.1412.
c1640 TURCHI, Alessandro : Venere e Pan/ DR/ d/ 20x23.8/ Venezia, FGC/ Inv. 61/ IT/ R10235V.1413.
c1650 MARATTA, Carlo: Venus and Pan (or satyr)/ PR//?/ UN/Inv.#/ Bartsch 47 C Part 1(21,2) 1987, p.42,n°4703.021/ R5006V.1414.
c1720 PELLEGRINI, Giovanni Antonio : Venus and satyr/ PA/ oc/ 120x160/ Zürich, KuH/ Inv. Koetser 59/ IT/ R8422.1415.
1790-98 CANOVA, Antonio : Venere con il Fauno/ PA/ oc/ 151x205/ Possagno, CdC/ Inv.8/. Munoz 1957, Tav. XLVIII; Duca 1966,p.413,n°584(detail); Stefani 2004, p.37, 165, nr.40/ R10178.1416.
*Copies eng: **c1792** VENZO, Gaetano: Venere sdraiata e satiro/ PR/ e/ 37,2x44,4/ Roma, PaBr/ Inv. MR 16312/ IT/ R3768.1417.*
***c1798** VITALI, Pietro Marco: Venere sdraiata (detail, without the satyr)/ PR/ e/ ?/ Roma, PaBr/ Inv. MR 16322/ IT/ R3747.1418.*

o Cupid(s) around

▪ Venus in the centre

c1550 BONASONE, Giulio: Venere con satiro e Amorino/ PR/ e/ 20,7x12,7/ Roma, ING/ Inv.71109vol.46H2/ Casazza 2005, p.235,237, n°112/ R8364.1419. *Also **c1550** GRECHI LUCCHESE, Michaeli/ PR/ e/ 20,3x12,3/ SF, FAM/ Inv. 30.36252/ IT/ R835.*
c1575 CAMBIASO, Luca: Vénus et l'Amour *(and satyr)/* DR/ d/ 36.5x25/ Paris, MdL/ Inv. 9333, rect/ IT/ R10199.1420.
c1625 DOMENICHINO, Domenico, detto ZAMPIERI: Venus von Faunen belauscht/ PA/ ?/ ?/ Braunschweig, HAU/ Inv. #/ Weichardt s.d. pl.32/ R10414.1421.
c1725 (att) DIZIANI, Gaspare : Venus with a satyr and putti/ DR/ d/ 30x20,5/ Milano BiA/Inv. BA Shelfmark F 253 inf. n. 1150/ IT/ R1810.1422.

▪ Venus to the left

c1540 TIZIANO, Vecellio: Pardo-Venus (La Venere del pardo) (pre.entitled 'Jupiter and Anthiope')/ PA/ oc/ 196x386/ Paris, MdL/ Inv. 1587/ Berenson 1958, p.195/ R470.1423.
c1550 BORDONE, Paris: Venere e satiro/ PA/ oc/ 122x148/ Roma, GaB/ Inv.119/ Berenson 1958, p.49/ R365.1424.
c1550 VERONESE, Paolo Caliari, detto: Venere, satiro e Cupido/ PA/ ?/ ?/ NY, SOT 11.1.96/ Sl.?-?/ Scarpa 2006, p.302-303, fig.428/ R10446.1425.
c1553 BRONZINO, Agnolo: Venere, Cupido e Satiro/ PA/ ow/ 135x231/ Roma, GaC/ Inv.32 (56)/ Berenson 1963, p.44; Falletti 2002 p.209,n°34/ R4316.1426.
1575 PETERZANO, Simone: Venere e Cupido con due satiri in un paesaggio/ PA/ oc/ 135x207/ Milano, PAB/ Inv. 7428/ Mai ed. 2001, p.64, n°12; Casazza 2005, p.238,n°115/ R3108.1427.
1592 CARRACCI, Agostino: Venere dormiente e satiro (Venus and satyr) / DR/ ?/ 15,6x22,7/ Wien, ALB/ Inv.2113/ Massari 1989, p.362-363, n°53; Bartsch 39 Commentary Part 2(18,1)1996, p.217-219,#3906.016/ R3506.1428.
c1600 (att) CARRACCI, Agostino: Venus lutinee par un satyre/ DR/ d/ 11,5x10/ UN/ Inv.#/ Dunand & Lemarchand s.d., III p.1009, fig.1570/ R10773.1429.

c1600 PALMA Il Giovane, Jacopo Negretti: Venus crowned by Cupid while satyrs and a nymph hand them fruits/ PA/ oc/ 141x201/ Zürich, GAL 23.3.'07 (pre. Pardo Col. Venezia)/ Sl.-3017/ Stefani 2004, p.31, nr.29 / R8962.1430.
c1630 BILIVERTI, Giovanni: Venere, Amore e Pan/ PA/ oc/ 191x165/ Dresden, SKS/ Inv. 386/ Contini 1985, p.102-103, nr.38, fig.50b/ R9603.1431.
A replica ***c1640***/ *PA/ oc/ 208x168/ Potsdam, Sanssouci LO/Inv. N7623/ Contini 1985, p.136, n°98c/ R9940. 1432.;*
preparatory DR/?/?/ Firenze, GdU/ Inv.9648F/ Contini 1985, p.102-3, n°50a/ R9604.1433.; other DRs at Paris, MdL/ Inv.563 and Edinburgh, NGA/ Inv. D1639.
1638 BILIVERTI, Giovanni: Venere addormentata con Cupido che l'incatena e Pan (Sleeping Venus)/ PA/ oc/ 79x64.5/ UN, pre. Dortmund, PrC (Joseph Cremer)/ Inv.#/ Contini 1985, p.120-1, nr.60, fig.74/ R9560.1434. *Replica : Modena, PrC/ Contini 1985, p.133, nr.76. Copy* ***c1700*** *aft: Vénus enchainée par l'Amour (without satyr)/ PA/ oc/ 108x81/ Paris, MdL/ Inv.20225/ Contini 1985, p.133, nr.76, fig.104d/ R2489; another copy (with satyr) of lager size: Firenze, SOT 18.6.'82/ Sl. ?-1161/ Contini 1985, p.133, nr.76, fig.104c/ R9936.*
c1650 GARGIULO, Domenico: Cupid held captive by a faun and scourged by Venus/ DR/ d/ 15.5x19.3/ London, VAM/ Inv. Dyce 341/ Ward-Jackson 1979,Vol.II, p.50, n°701/ R11129.1435.
c1650 GRIMALDI, Giovanni Francesco : Portrait of a Landscape with Venus, Pan and Cupids/ PA/ ?/ ?/ Roma, GDP/ Inv.#/ IT artresource/ R8534.1436.
c1663 GIORDANO, Luca : Venus sleeping, with Cupid and satyr/ PA/ oc/ 133x187,5/ UN, PrC/Inv.#/ IT/ R2611.1437.
c1675 LIBERI, Pietro : Venus und Satyr mit zwei Amoretten/ PA/ oc/ 237x140,5/ Berlin, GSM/ Inv. 95.1/ IT/ R10112.1438.
c1675 LIBERI, Pietro : Venus *(with satyr and cupids)*/ PA/ oc/ 153x195/ Wiesbaden, PrC/ Inv. #/ IT/ R10113.1439.
c1700 RICCI, Sebastiano: Venere, Cupido e satiro/ PA/ oc/ 85x135/ FR, PrC/ Inv. #/ Scarpa 2006, p.196, cat.154, fig.233/ R10437.1440.
c1700 RICCI, Sebastiano: Venere dormiente spiata da un satiro (sleeping Venus with spying satyr)/ PA/ oc/ 15.7x18.5/ Lille, MBA/ Inv.#/ Scarpa 2006, p.208, cat.185, fig.425/ R10443.1441.
c1700 RICCI, Sebastiano: Venere, satiro e Cupido (Giove e Antiope)/ PA/ oc/ 176.5x129/ Stamford, BH/ Inv. 295/ Scarpa 2006, p.302-303, cat.455, fig.427/ R10445.1442.
c1708 PELLEGRINI, Giovanni Antonio : Venus, Cupid and a faun *(and doves)*/ PA/ oc/ 127.5 x 102.2/ London, CHR 10.7.'98/ Sl. 5999-75/ IT/ R8421.1443.
c1713 RICCI, Sebastiano : Venere con satiro e Cupido/ PA/ oc/ 118x180/ Venezia, CaR/ Inv. 105, Col. Martini/ Martini 2002, p.257-58, n°211/ R964.1444.
c1720 RICCI, Sebastiano : Venus von einem Satyr überrascht/ PA/ oc/ 101,5x128/ Stuttgart, Sga/ Inv. 2754/ Mai ed. 2001, .p.242, n°9/ R1566.1445.
c1725 TIEPOLO, Giambattista : Vénus dormant et un satyre/ PA/ oc/ 40x48.5/ PrC/ Inv.#/ Pedrocco 2002, p.209, cat.54/ R11147.1446.
c1750 FONTEBASSO, Francesco : Venere, satiro e amorini/ PA/ ?/ ?/ London, PrC/ Inv. #/ Scarpa 2006, p.37/ R10433.1447.

- ## Venus to the right

c1525 CORREGGIO, Antonio: Vénus, Satyre et Cupidon (Le sommeil d'Antiope ou Jupiter et Antiope or Terrestrial Venus)/ PA/ oc/ 188x125/ Paris, MdL/ Inv.42/ Berenson 1968, p.92 ; Gould, s.d.p.8, pl.3/ R2497.1448. *Copy « after » PA/ oc/ 190x124,5/ London, SOT 19.5.'05/ Sl. W05716-112/ IT.*
c1588 CARRACCI, Annibale: Venere, satiro e amorini (Una bacchante) (Venus with a satyr and cupids)/ PA/ oc/ 112x142/ Firenze, GdU/ Inv.1890-1452/ Gli Uffizi 1979, P.372; Petrioli Tofani 1996,p.179; Casazza 2005,p.286, n°161 / R454.1449. *Replica Roma, CdD/ Inv.669/ IT ICCD;*
preparatory drawing: Inv. 766E/ Loisel 2004,p.31, n°III.34/ R3790.1450.
c1600 CARRACCI, Annibale : Venere dormiente e satiro (aft Agostino CARRACCI/ DR)/ PR/ e/ 15,7x22,6/ Roma, ING/ Inv. FC30495/ Massari 1989, p.362-63/ R3505.1451. *Also in Cambridge, FWM/ Inv. 23.I.4-83.*

c1650 MOLA, Pier Francesco: a putto protecting the sleeping Venus from a spying faun/ DR/ d/ 11,5x12,6/ London, SOT 5.7.'06/ Sl. L06040-36/ IT/ R6852.1452.
c1705 (cir) RICCI, Sebastiano: Venere con satiro e amorini/ PA/ ?/ ?/ UN/ Inv. #/ Scarpa 2006, p.266, fig.237/ R10440.1453.
c1713 RICCI, Sebastiano : Venere dormiente sorpresa da un satir/ PA/ oc/ 140x160/ Roma, PadE 10,26.5.'91/ Inv.#/ IT/ R5910.1454.
c1720 CHIARI, Giuseppe Bartolomeo: Eros revealing a sleeping Venus to a bashful Satyr/ PA/ oc/ 112.1 x 161/ Sarasota, RMA/ Inv. SN163/ IT/ R11319.1455.
c1720 RICCI, Sebastiano : Venus and satyr (Venere addormentata spiata da un satiro)/ PA/ oc/ 102x126/ Budapest, MFA/ Inv.58.43/ Scarpa 2006, p.168-169, Cat.69, fig.423/ R1508.1456.
1787 BARTOLOZZI, Francesco: Venus, Cupid und Satyr (aft GIORDANO, see Venus asleep)/ PR/ e/ 34x47/ Berlin, LS 22.3.07/ Sl. ?-418/ IT/ R10936V.1457.

○ with others

1663 GIORDANO, Luca : Venere dormiente con un satiro (Venus sleeping, with Cupid and satyr *and others in the background*)/ PA/ oc/ 137x190/ Napoli, MdC/ Inv.259-E65541iccd/ Calabrese Omar 2003,p.304-305/ R2224.1458.
c1700 RICCI, Sebastiano: Venus mit Nymphen und Satyrn (detail)/ FR//?/ Wien, ScS/ Inv. #/ IT/ R10304. 1459.
c1710 RICCI, Sebastiano: Venere, satiro e ninfe/ PA/ oc/ 180x140/ Ravenna, PrC/ Inv. #/ Scarpa 2006, p.288, cat.405, fig.409/ R10442.1460.

15. Venus and Vulcan

(see also Aeneas, Mars)

c1550 BORDONE, Paris : Venere e Vulcano/ PA/ ?/ ?/ New York, MMA/ Inv. K1112/ Berenson 1958, p.49/ R9609V.1461.
c1550 PRIMATICCIO, Francesco : Vulcain forgeant les flèches de Vénus/ DR/ d/ 12,8x9,2/ Paris, MdL/ Inv. RF50883,r/ IT/ R8449V.1462.
c1550 SCHIAVONE, Andrea: Venus and Vulcan/ PA/ of/ 15.5x12.9/ Canton, MuA/ Inv. 58.6/ IT/ R11425V.1463.
c1550 ZELOTTI, Battista : Vulcan and Venus (Sala di Sofonisba)/ FR//?/ Vicenza, ViC/ Inv.#/ ITartresource/ R8533.1464.
c1600 CARRACCI, Annibale: Venus and Vulcan (working at a distance)/ DR/ d/ 20.1x32.5/ Windsor, RCo/ Inv. 1872/ Wittkower 1952, p.158, Cat.438< aft classical statue in Napoli>/ R10420V.1465.

o at the forge (Venus requesting arms for Aeneas)

c1540 LUINI, Bernardino : Venere nella fucina di Vulcano/ FR/ ?/ ?/ Milano, PAB, Sala I/ Inv. 748/ Berenson 1968, p.233/ R3109.1466. *Detached fresco from Villa Pelucca near Monza.*
1543 VICO, Enea: Venere nella fucina di Vulcano (*Venus sleeping alone)* (aft PARMIGIANINO)/ PR/ e/ 20,6x37,6/ Parma, BiP/ Inv. On21829/ Bartsch 30 (15,3) 1985, p.40,n°27-II(294); Massari 1989, *p.264-65*; Lowenthal 1995, p.71, fig.48; Mussini 2003, p.136-137,n°245/ R3639.1467. *Also: Roma, ING/Inv.FC31025; SF, FAM/Inv 1963.30.3245/IT; London, BMu.*
c1550 ABATE, Nicolo dell' : Vulcain forgeant des armes demandées par Vénus pour l'Amour(sic) (Vulcan forging arms requested by Venus for *Aeneas) (*after PRIMATICCIO)/ FR/ ?/ Fontainebleau, MNC/ Inv. PM 11/ IT/ R8032V.1468.
c1575 BASSANO il Vecchio, Jacopo: La fragua de Vulcano *(Venus left, looking into the forge)*/ PA/ ?/ ?/ Madrid, MNP/ Inv. P5263/ Enciclopedia 2006, p.1088-1089/ R10473.1469.
c1590 BASSANO II, Francesco: Allegory of fire (Venus in the forge of Vulcan)/ PA/ oc/ 140x182/ Sarasota, RMA/ Inv. SN86/ IT/ R11308.1470.
c1600 BASSANO, Leandro da Ponte, detto: Venere nella fucina di Vulcano/ PA/ ?/ ?/ Wien, KHM/ Inv. 315/ Berenson 1958, p.26/ R9605V.1471.
c1610 VICENTINO, Andrea Michieli: Venus in the forge of the Cyclops *(of Vulcan)*/ FR// ?/ Venezia, PaD/ Inv.#/ IT/ R8556.1472.
c1775 COSTANTINI, Ermenegildo: Venere e Vulcano (*Venus sitting in her chariot)/* PA/ oc/ ?/ Roma, GASL/ Inv. E62130iccd/ Cicinelli A & Vasco Rocca S (1978), 1978, I, p.166/ R8904.1473.

▪ Cupid around

c1500 MAESTRO I.B. con la Colomba : Vulcano forgia le armi di Enea e Venere le consegna (Vulcan forges arms for Aeneas and Venus offers them to Aeneas?) PR/ e/ 30,3x21,9/ Pavia, MuC/ Inv. StMal1564/ Lomartire 2003, p.110,n°55/ R3651.1474. *Also : **c1505** PALUMBA, Giovanni Battista : Mars, Venus and Vulcan (Vulcan forging the arms for Achilles)/ PR/ e/ 29,8x21,3/ London, BMu/ Inv. 1854-11-13-167/ McDonald 2005, p.110-111, n°12/ R6740.*
c1610 PALMA Il GIOVANE, Jacopo : Venus und Amor in der Schmiede des Vulkan/ PA/ oc/ 114.8x167.3/ Kassel, SKS/ Inv.GK502/ Weddingen 1994, p.124, n°38/ R341.1475.

c1650 CESIO, Carlo: Venus requesting arms from Vulcan for her son (from 'The ceiling of the Doria Pamfili Palace' in Roma aft Pietro da CORTONA) / PR/ e/ 26,5x21,2/ NY, MMA/ Inv.#/ Bartsch 47 (21,1) 1983, p.103,n°75(117); Bartsch 47 C,Part 1 (21,1) 1987, p.101,n°4705.075 S2/ R4997.1476. *In many places.*

1651-1655 CORTONA, Pietro da: Venere chiede a Vulcano di forgiare le armi ad Enea (Venus asks Vulcan arms for Aeneas)/ FR//?/ Roma, PaDP/ Inv. E45926iccd / IT/ R7151.1477. *'Venus dans les forges de Vulcan'/ FR/ Roma, GDP(?)/* Bailey 1991,p.293,n°1.

1704 SOLIMENA, Francesco : Venus at the Forge of Vulcan/ PA/ oc/ 202x151/ LA, JPG/ Inv. 84.PA.64/ IT/ R318.1478.

Preparatory DR/ d/ 20,6x13,8/ LA, JPG/ Inv. 91.GG.72/ IT/ R305.1479. Another ***c1700*** *(att) : Venus in Vulcan's Forge/ DR/ d/ 37.9 x 24/ Ottawa, NGC/ Inv. 41346r.*

c1725 GIAQUINTO, Corrado : Vénus rend visite à Vulcain dans sa forge/ PA/ oc/ 48x74/ Rennes, MBA/Inv.#/ IT/ R8554.1480.

c1775 MULINARI, Stefano : Vulcan's forge *(Venus and Cupid at foreground, arms for Aeneas hanging above)* (aft DR of Gaspare CELIO)/ PR/ e/ 29x16/ Wien, GaBW/ Inv. 19448/ IT/ R9900.1481.

c1800 APPIANI, Andrea : Venere e Amore nella fucina di Vulcano/ DR/ d/ 102x87/ Milano GAM/ Inv. 575/ Precerutti-Garberi 1969, p.40, nr.29/ R9638.1482. *Preparatory for FR..*

c1800 MAESTRI, Michelangelo: Vénus demande à Vulcain des armes pour Énée/ PA/ g/ 28,7x36,2/ Paris, TAJ 20.6.'06/Sl.51/ IT/ R6824.1483.

- **cupids around**

1552-1563 SALVIATI, Francesco: Venere e amorini prendono in consegna le armi di Ranuccio il Vecchio forgiate da Vulcano/ FR// ?/ Roma, PaFa/ Inv. E64029iccd/ IT/ R8909.1484.

1616 ALBANI, Francesco: Venere nella fucina di Vulcano (Venus at the forge of Vulcan/ PA/ oc/ Ø154/ Roma, GaB/ Inv.35/ Moreno 2004, p.297, n°5/ R362.1485.

c1650 SCARAMUCCIA, Luigi: Venus with Vulcan forging the arms of Aeneas/ DR//?/ Milano, BiA/ Inv. 4794 BA Shelfmark F 254 inf. n 1582 / IT/ R2589.1486.

1712-14 GARZI, Luigi : Venere nella fucina di Vulcano/ PA/ ?/?/ Macerata, PaB/ Inv.#/ IT/ R2637.1487.

Preparatory DR/ ?/?/ Macerata, PaB/ Inv.#/ IT/ R2639.1488.

c1715 GARZI, Luigi : Venere nella fucina di Vulcano/ PA/ oc/ 50x64/ Roma, GNB/ Inv.# Col.Lemme/ Anonymous 1998, p.144-145 / R2638.1489.

c1720 (cir) GRASSI, Nicola Maria : Vénus demandant les armes à Vulcain/ PA/ oc/ 121x130/ Paris, DRO 27.6.'01/ l.31/ IT/ R4133.1490.

c1725 GIAQUINTO, Corrado : Vénus chez Vulcain offrant les armes à Enée/ PA/ ?/ ?/ München ScS/ Inv.#/ IT/ R8546.1491.

1744 RUSCA, Bartolomeo: Venus pide a Vulcano las armas para Eneas/ FR// ?/ Segovia, GSI/ Inv. Sala 2/ Navarrete 2005, p.110, fig.196/ R11024.1492.

c1750 CIGNAROLI, Giambettino : Vulcan presenting the arms of Aeneas to Venus/ DR/ d/ 44,2x59,6/ Milano, BiA/ Inv. F 257 inf. n. 174/ IT/ R8555.1493.

Replica with minor difference: DR/ d/ 44,4x61/ Milano, BiA/ Inv. F 256 inf. n. 78/ IT/ R8723.1494.

c1750 MARMORELLI, Liborio: Venere nella fucina di Vulcano/ FR// ?/ Roma, Gci/ Inv. E66858iccd/ IT/ R8908.1495.

c1755 GANDOLFI, Gaetano: Venere nella fucina di Vulcano/ PA/ ?/ 190x140/ Detroit, DIA/ Inv.#/ IT/ R4439.1496.

c1760 GIAQUINTO, Corrado: Venus recibe de Vulcano las armas de Eneas/ PA/ oc/ ?/ Madrid, PaR/ Inv.#/ IT/ R11026.1497. *Replica?:* ***c1739*** *Venere riceve da Vulcano le armi di Enea/ PA/ ?/ ?/ Molfetta, PrC/ IT Wikipedia.*

○ Venus at the forge of Vulcan with Mars

c1525 (att) PENNI, Giovanni Francesco: Venus, Cupid and Mars in Vulcan's Forge/ DR/ d/ 21x22.2/ NY, SOT 25.1.05/ Sl. ?-98/ Gnann 2007, p.229-235, fig.1<pre. att B.BANDINELLI, cir G.ROMANO, PERINO del VAGA>/ R10844.1498.

1543 VICO, Enea: Vulcan at his forge with Mars and Venus *(Venus and Mars in bed)* (aft PARMIGIANINO)/ PR/ e/ 23x32,7/ NY, MMA/ Inv. 1949 (49.97.351)/ Bartsch 30 (15,3) 1985, p.38, n°27-I(294); Lowenthal 1995, p.70, fig.47/ R1641.1499. *Also in Dresden, KSK/ Inv. A 1921-131; Wien, ALB.*
c1575 ORSI, Lelio: Vénus et les amours dans la forge de Vulcain et Mars apportant ses armes/ DR/ d/ 39,5x26,5/ Paris, MdL/ Inv. 19076/ IT/ R 2864V.1500.
1637 DELLA BELLA, Stefano : The forge of Vulcan on the Isle of Lemnos, with Jupiter and retinue in the clouds, choruses of Venus and Juno in the clouds, Mercury in flight, and the battle between Mars and Vulcan (The Wedding of the Gods; Le Nozze degli dei: Scena Grotta di Vulcano) (aft Alfonso Parigi II)/ PR/ e/ 20.6x28.2/ Hanover, HMA/ Inv. PR.979.66.5/ IT/ R11384.1501.
c1670 GIORDANO, Luca: Venus and Mars at the forge of Vulcan/ PA/ oc/ 105x103,5 octogonal/ UN, PrC/ Inv.#/ IT/ R2615.1502.
c1670 GIORDANO, Luca: Mars et Vénus dans le forge de Vulcain/ PA/ oc/ 63x77/ Paris, MdL/ Inv. 306/ IT/ R2498.1503. *Replica sold NY, SOT 22.1.'04/ Sl. N07965-77/ IT; reduced replica 45x55/ Firenze, PrC.*
c1670 GIORDANO, Luca: Venere, Marte e la fucina di Vulcano/ PA/ oc/ 131x158/ Roma, PaRu/ Inv.#/ IT/ R2610.1504.

o Venus with Vulcan and Cupid

c1504 RAIMONDI, Marcantonio: Venere, Amore e Vulcano/ PR/ e/ 25,5x20,4/ Wien, ALB/ Inv. 1971-338/ Bartsch 27 (14,2) 1978, p.20,n°326(247); Faietti 1988, p.119-121,n°15./ R3534.1505. *Also: PR/ey/24,9x20,5/Berlin, KSK/ Inv.#/* Mai ed. 2001, p.423, n°G1; *Boston, FA ;* ***c1506*** *Vulcan, Venus and Eros /PR/ e/ ?/Cambridge, FWM/ Inv. 1880.4.21-22 & P.5368-R.*
c1525 BRIOSCO, Andrea: Vulcan, Cupid and Venus/ SC/ z/ Ø7,6/ Washington, NGA/ Inv. 1957.14.259/ IT/ R 8240V.1506.
c1525 BRIOSCO, Andrea: Venus, Cupid and Vulcan/ SC/ z/ 10,8x7,8/ Washington, NGA/ Inv. 1957.14.260/ IT/ R 8239V.1507.
c1525 LEONBRUNO, Lorenzo: Venus, Vulcan and Cupid/ FR// ?/ Mantova, PaD/ Inv.#/ IT/ R9001.1508.
c1525 (att) PENNI, Giovanni Francesco: Venus, Cupid in Vulcan's Forge/ DR/ d/ 22.5x22/ Paris, MdL/ Inv. 618/ Gnann 2007, p.229-235, fig.4/ R10845.1509.
c1530 (att) BECCAFUMI, Domenico di Giacomo di Pace, detto MECARINO : Venus and Cupid with Vulcanus/ PA/ ow/ 128x96,5/ New Orleans, MuA/Inv.# /IT /R1549.1510.
c1540 ROMANO, Giulio: Venus and Cupid, Vulcanus/ DR/ d/ 24,9x20,5/ Windsor, RCo/ Inv. RL0302/ Clayton 1999, p.159-160,n°45/ R3528.1511.
c1550 CLOVIO, Giulio: Venus, Vulcan and Cupid (aft MICHELANGELO)/ DR/ d/ ?/ Windsor, RCo/ Inv.#/ IT/ R9561.1512.
1551 TINTORETTO, Jacopo: Venere, Vulcano e Amore/ PA/ oc/ 85x197/ Firenze, PaP/ Inv. 1912n°3/ Berenson 1958, p.178; Sframeli 2003, p.92-93,n°12; Calabrese 2003, p.294/ R2226.1513.
c1590 CARRACCI, Agostino: Venus, Cupid and Vulcan/ DR/ d/ 17.4x27.3/Windsor, RCo/ Inv. 2303/ Wittkower 1952, p.114, Cat.101, fig.14<almost identical DR in London, BMu, probably copy>; Massari 1989, p.496-97,n°58; Czére 2004, p.71-73, Cat.58-a/ R3518.1514. *Copy 'Venus sur sa couche en avant de la forge de Vulcain'/ Dunand & Lemarchand s.d., III p.798, fig.1266;* ***c1650*** *aft/ PR/ e/ 19.1x26.5/ Berlin, BAS/ Sl. 090-5678/ IT/ R10997; reverse: Pietro del PO.*
c1650 CARPIONI, Giulio: Venus at Vulcan's forge (Fire, from the series 'Allegories of Four Elements')/ PR/ e/ 10,9x15,6/ SF, FAM/ Inv.1987.1.163/ Bartsch 45 (20,2) 1982,p.85; Bartsch 45 C (20,2) 1990,p.103,n°4504.018/ R733.1515. *Several in other places.*
c1650 MOLA, Pier Francesco: The forge of Vulcan *(with Venus and Cupid at right side)*/ DR/ d/ 26x40.5/ Chatsworth, DCo/ Inv. #/ Jaffé 1995, Cat.66/ R10387.1516.
c1650 PO, Pietro del: Venere, Amore e Vulcano (aft CARRACCI, Agostino)/ PR/ e/ 18,8x28,9/ Roma, ING/ Inv. FC30939/ Bartsch 45 (20,2) 1982, p.228,n°32(256) ; Bartsch 45 C (20,2) 1990, p.246-247,n°4510.032 ; Massari 1989, p.496-97,n°203/ R3517.1517. *Also in Glasgow, HMAG/ Inv. 6887; London, BMu.*
Reverse copy of DR in Windsor, RCol/ R3518.1518.
c1675 (att) CARNEO, Antonio/ PA/ oc/ 103.5 x 139.4/ Durham, TBM/ Inv. B.M.3/ IT/ R8549.1519.

c1700 MAGNASCO, Alessandro: Venus at the Forge of Vulcan with Cupid blindfolded/ PA/ oc/ 118x170/ NY, CHR 19.4.'07/ Sl. 1822-0095/ IT/ R9108.1520.
c1705 RICCI, Sebastiano: Venere, Cupido e Vulcano/ PA/ ?/ 98.5x85.5/ UK, PrC/ Inv. #/ Scarpa 2006, p.201, cat.167, fig.99/ R10435.1521.
1705-06 RICCI, Sebastiano: Venus, Vulcan and Cupid/ PA/ oc/ 164.5x126.5/ St.Petersburg, HMu/ Inv.9517/ Scarpa 2006, p.190, Cat.435, fig.98 / R8984.1522.
1735 FALDONI, Giannantonio: Vulcano, Venere e Cupido/ PR/e/19,2x14,3/ Parma, BiP/ Inv. On21933/ Mussini 2003, p.162,n°317/R3640.1523. *Also Padova, MuC/Inv. R.I.G.2085.*
c1757 TIEPOLO, Giandomenico: Venere nella fucina di Vulcano/ FR/ v/ 110x170/ Vicenza, ViV/ Inv.#/ Rizzoli 1968, p.123, 124 n°281/ R8524.1524.

○ cupids around

c1500 (wor) RAFFAELLO, Sanzio: Vénus, l'Amour, Vulcain, cinq putti (*four cupids)*/ DR/ d/ 37,1x24,1/ Paris, MdL/ Inv. 3657/ Cordelier 1992, p.490,n°861/ R2818.1525.
*Also : **c1500** ROMANO, Giulio/ DR/ d/ ?/ Windsor, RCo/ Inv. 0303/ Massari 1993, p.18-20, n°8/ R3595.1526. and PA/ ow/ 37x24/ Paris, MdL/ Inv.424/ IT/ R665.1526.; cop Venus and Vulcan/ DR/ d/ 33x25.4/ London, VAM/ Inv. D.844-1886/ Ward-Jackson 1979, p.80, n°167. According to Ward-Jackson, there is also an anonymous cop PA in Roma, GaB.*
*Reverse copies: **c1515** RAIMONDI, Marcantonio/ PR/ e/ 38,5x26,2/ London, BMu/ Inv.#/ Bartsch 27 (14,2) 1978, p.46,n°349-I(261)/ R4835.1527.;*
***1530** VENEZIANO, Agostino: Venere e Vulcano tra amorini (aft ROMANO, Giulio)/ PR/ e/ 39x26,4/ Roma, ING/ Inv. F.C.30760/ Massari 1989, p.54-55, n°15/ R627.1528.. Also in Cambridge, FWM/ Inv. P.4122-R-190.*
c1516 DENTE, Marco: Vulcan, Venus and Three Cupids, from the series Ancient Bas-Reliefs/ PR/e/11,1x17,6/SF, FAM/Inv. 1963.30.3144/IT/R759.1529. *Also in Glasgow, HMAG/ Inv.#10240.*
c1527 PERINO DEL VAGA, Pietro: Vulcano e Venere/ PR/ ?/?/ Roma, PaBr/ Inv. MR 3885/ IT/ R3745. 1530.
c1527 PERINO DEL VAGA, Pietro: Venere, Vulcano e tre amorini (Venere e Vulcano sul letto)/ DR/ d/ 23,4x19,4/ Oxford, CCh/ Inv. 1214/ Massari 1989, p.297-98, fig.48; Bellini 1998, p.69-70,n°36/ R3502.1531.
c1535 PUPINI, Biagio: Vénus, l'Amour, Vulcain, cinq putti (aft RAFFAELLO/ROMANO) / DR/ d/ 35,1x37,6/ Paris, MdL/ Inv. 3478/ Cordelier 1992, p.492,n°862/ R2817.1532.
c1550 GHISI, Giorgio: Venere e Vulcano seduti su di un letto (Venus and Vulcan Seated on a Bed) (aft PERINO del VAGA)/ PR/e/ 30,5x22,2/ Roma, ING/ Inv. FN1210/ Bartsch 31 (15,4) 1986, p.89, n°35(399); Massari 1989, p.297,n°111, Bellini 1998, p.68-70,n°13/ R1094.1533. *Also in Cambridge, FWM/ Inv. 37.1-31 ; London, BMu; LA, CMA/ Inv. M.88.91.145; SF, FAM/ Inv. 1998.201.4; Dresden, KSK/Inv.#/ Mai ed. 2001, p.427, n°G6 ; Glasgow, HMAG /Inv.#11889; Hanover, HMu/ Inv. PR.986.27.*
c1550 GHISI, Giorgio: Venus and Vulcan at the Forge (aft PERINO del VAGA)/ PR/ e/ 19,0x30,8/ LA, CMA/ Inv. M88.91.189/ Bartsch 31 (15,4) 1986, p.119, n°54(405); Bellini 1998, p.65-67,n°12/ R1093.1534. *Also in Cambridge, FWM/ Inv. 37.1-74 ; London, BMu; SF, FAM/ Inv. 1963.30.36954.*
c1550 TINTORETTO, Jacopo: Venus, Vulkan und Eroten bewaffenen Amor (aft RAFFAELLO)/ PA/ oc/ ?/ Treviso, MuC/ Inv.#/ Weddingen 1994, fig.5, p.104/ R4285.1535.
1621 – 1633 ALBANI, Francesco: Le repos de Vénus et de Vulcain (The rest of Venus and Vulcan)/ PA/ oc/ 203x252/Paris, MdL/ Inv. 10/ IT/ R541.1536.
Replica in Roma, GaB/ Inv.35/ R362V.1537.; reverse copy : Le repos de Vénus et de Vulcain ou le Feu/ PA/ oc/ 63x79,5/ *Chambéry, MBA/ Inv. M1242/ R6986. Copies in Braunschweig, HAU/ Inv. 482 ; Fontainebleau, MCh/ Inv Louvre31. Many engravings.*
1640-50 (wor) ALBANI, Francesco: Venus and Vulcan/ PA/ oc/ 139x184/ Dresden, SKS/ Inv. 341/ Mai ed. 2001, p.348-49, n°56 / R8474.1538.
Replica of Paris, MdL/ Inv. 10/ R541.1539.
c1650 PERUZZINI, Domenico: Venus and Vulcan/ PR/ ?/13,3x13,4/ Berlin, KSK/ Inv. 238-21/ Bartsch 47 C (Part 1 (21,1) 1987, p.226-227,n°4710.027/ R4998.1540. *Also at many other places.*

c1700 BAMBINI, Nicolo: Vulkan reicht Venus einen von ihm geschmiedeten Pfeil; Vulcano presenta a Venere una freccia da lui battuta/ PA/ oc/ 151 x 110/ Wien, DOR 16.10.07/ Sl. ?-104/ IT/ R11095.1541.
c1700 GIORDANO, Luca: Venus at the forge of Vulcan/ PA/ ?/ ?/ UN, PrC/ Inv.#/ IT/ R9002.1542.
c1750 DIZIANI, Gaspare: Venus and Vulcan/ PA/ oc/ 62x74/ NY, SOT 26.1.'06/ Sl. N08163-143/ IT/ R5892.1543.

o many around

1530-35 BECCAFUMI, Domenico : Vulcan und der Philosoph (Theoria)...*(left Venus with dove)*/ PR/ e/ 17.7x12.1/ Zürich, ETH/ Inv. D219.2/ Matile 2003, p.90-93, n°33/ R11008.1544.
c1550 VASARI, Giogio: Vénus dans les forges de Vulcan/ DR/ d/ 13,6x24,6/ Wien, ALB/ Inv. 517.1545. *Copies : Firenze, GdU/ Inv. 760E ; Paris, MdL/ Inv. 2160 recto/ IT/ R7658.*
1555 VASARI, Giogio & Cristoforo GHERARDI detto il Doceno : The forge of Vulcan/ FR// ?/ Firenze, PaV/ Inv.#/ IT/ R8892.1546.
c1565-67 VASARI, Giogio: La Fucina di Vulcano/ PA/ oy/ 38x28/ Firenze, GdU/ Inv. 1890-1558/ Petrioli Tofani 1996, p.141/ R2575.1547.
Preparatory : Venus, Cupid and Vulcan/ DR/ d/ 14.3x12.1/ Plymouth, CM&AG/ Inv. CD234/ IT/ R11697.1548.; also in Paris, MdL ; reverse in Windsor, RCo.
c1700 PIOLA, Domenico: Venere nella fucina di Vulcano/ PA/ ?/ 200x154/ UN, PrC/ Inv. #/ Boccardo ed. 2004, p.79,81, fig.29/ R339.1549.
c1765 TIEPOLO, Giambattista: Venus and Vulcan (sketch for the ceiling of the Salón de Alabarderos, Palacio Real, Madrid) /PA/ oxc/ 69,2x87,3/ Philadelphia, PMA/ Inv. 287/ Mai ed. 2001, p.360-61, n°62; Pedrocco 2002, p.298 cat.247.1; Calasso 2006, p.81, n°19/ R1647.1550.

16. Venus asleep/ Venus of Urbino/ Venus with the Musician

Venus asleep

o alone

c1508-10 GIORGIONE, Giorgio Barbarell & TIZIANO, Vecellio: Schlummernde Venus (Sleeping Venus)/ PA/ oc/ 108,5x175/ Dresden, SKS/ Inv.185/ Berenson 1958, p.87; Clark 1969, T.I, p.188 ; Pleynet 1991 ; Zuffi 2001,p.81 ; Mai ed. 2001, p.57, n°1 / R464.1551. *Replica 'with Cupid' att TIZIANO/ Dresden, SKS/ Inv.#/ Gamba 1928/ R3590.1551.*

c1520 TREVISO, Girolamo : Venere dormiente/ PA/ oc/ 130x212/ Roma, GaB/ Inv. 30/ Berenson 1958, p.93, pl.896; Staccioli 1985, p.108/ R361.1552.

c1525 BOCCACCINO, Camillo : Sleeping Venus/ DR/ d/ 9,3x19,2/ Milano, BiA/ Inv. F 265 inf. n. 39bis/ IT/ R8719.1553.

c1525 SAVOLDO, Giovanni Gerolamo : Venere dormiente/ PA/ oc/ ?/ Roma, GaB/ Inv. E55662iccd/ IT/ R8937.1554.

c1600 CARRACCI, Agostino: Sleeping Venus/ DR/ d/ 57.8x30.7/ Cambridge, FWM/ Inv. PD.10-1959/ IT/ R11349V.1555.

1638 BILIVERTI, Giovanni: Sleeping Venus/ PA/ ?/ ?/ UN/ Inv. #/ IT/ R9560V.1556. *Painted for Don Lorenzo de' Medici in 1638, pre. Col. Joseph Cremer, Dortmund.*

c1675 LIBERI, Pietro : Vénus (*endormie*)/ PA/ ?/ ?/ Vercelli : MFB/ Inv.#/ Duca 1966, p.500, n°734/ R5360. 1557.

c1752 CIGNAROLI, Giambettino : Sleeping Venus/ DR/ d/ 30,8x30/ Milano, BiA/ Inv. F 258 inf. n. 310/ IT/ R8725.1558.

1752 CIGNAROLI, Giambettino : Sleeping Venus (*with doves)*/ DR/ d/ 14,2x19,2/ Milano, BiA/ Inv. F 258 inf. n. 312/ IT/ R8726.1559.

c1755 VALESI, Dionigi: Sleeping Venus (*with doves*) (aft CIGNAROLI, Giambettino)/ PR/ e/ 24,9x31/ Milano, BiA/ Inv. F 258 inf. n. 298/ IT/ R8720.1560.

o with Cupid(s)

1499 COLONNA, Francesco : Venus asleep *(with cupids and satyr) (Hypnerotomachia Poliphili)*/ IL/ e/ ?/ Himmel 2000 , p.290, Abb.27/ R4785.1561.

c1500 BUGIARDINI, Giuliano: Sleeping Venus (*with Cupid*)/ PA/ ?/ ?/ Venezia, CdO/ Inv.#/ Berenson 1963, p.46, pl.1257; Bacci 1966, p.130/ R8535.1562.

c1523 PARMIGIANINO, Girolamo Francesco: Sleeping Venus with two amorini/ DR/ d/ 11.8x7.8/ London, RoC/ Inv. RL0546/ Roberts 1986, p.54, n°33/ R11140.1563.

c1525 BOCCACCINO, Camillo : Studies of a Sleeping Venus and a Sleeping Cupid/ DR/ d/ 10,1x20,8/ Milano, BiA/ Inv. F 265 inf. n. 39/ IT/ R8718.1564.

1540 POLIDORO da LANCIANO: Venere dormiente/ PA/ oc/ 65,5x81,8/ Firenze, GdU/ Inv. 1890, n. 5050/ Gli Uffizi-Catalogo Generale 1979, p.422, P.1221/ R8603.1565.

c1550 BORDONE, Paris : Venere dormiente / PA/ oc/ 86x137/ Venezia, CdO / Inv.d.39/ Berenson 1958, p.50; Relouge 1958, p.120 ; Mai ed. 2001, p.62, n°8 / R1263.1566.

c1550 (wor) TIZIANO, Vecellio : Venus asleep with three cupids/ DR/ d/ 8,5x 24,5/ Chantilly, MuC/ Inv.#/ IT/ R8986.1567.
c1560 ABATE, Nicolo dell' : Le sommeil de Vénus (The Venus asleep of Venus) / PA/ ow/ 107x87/ Quimper, MBA/ Inv.#/ exh/ R374.1568.
c1592 CARRACCI, Annibale : Vénus endormie avec des amours (Venus sleeping, with cupids)/ PA/ oc/ 190x328/ Chantilly, MuC/ Inv.63/ Prater 2002,p.36-37 ; Bonfait 2004, p.35-36/ R2089.1569.
Preparatory drawings : 'Vénus endormie et entourée d'Amours dans un paysage'/ DR/ d/ 25,6x41,5/Paris, MdL/Inv. 7571 Recto/ Loisel 2004, p.344n°913/ R2362.1570.; *an ANONYMOUS 'after' also in Paris, MdL/ Inv.7572 ;*
drawings with only Cupid :' Venus and Cupid'/ DR/ d/ 13,4x18,9/ SF,FAM/ Inv. 1963.24.193/ IT/ R736. 1571.;
'Sleeping Venus'/ DR// 27,9x37,9/ Frankfurt, SKI/ Inv.#/ Benati 1999, p.262-264,n°84/ R3566.1572.; *a copy 'after' 'Venus and Cupid'/ DR/ d/ 23,6x37,5/Boston, MFA/Inv. 1978.77/ IT/ R4198.*
1617 FIALETTI, Odoardo: Venere e Amore dormienti (from the series 'Scherzi d'Amore' (The Sport of Love)) / PR/ e/ 17,6x9,1/ Roma, ING/ Inv. FC89204/ (Bartsch 38 (17,5) 1983, p.209,n°11(268); Massari 1989, p.471,n°183/R3510.1573. *Also in Glasgow, HMAG/ Inv. 6251; London, BMu; Paris, BNF/ Inv.#/ Dunand & Lemarchand, s.d., III, p.951, fig.1478 à 1489/ R11151*
c1625 VAROTARI, Alessandro: Rêverie de Vénus/ PA/ ?/ ?/ Grenoble, MdP/ Inv.#/ Mai ed. 2001, p.63, n°10/ R5361.1574.
c1625-30 GENTILESCI, Artemisia : Sleeping Venus (Venus and Cupid)/ PA/ oc/ 93,9x144/ Richmond, MFA/ Inv. 2001.225/ IT/ R5727.1575.
c1650 ALBANI, Francesco : Venere dormiente e amorini/ PA/ oc/ ?oval/ Roma, GNB/ Inv. E35180iccd/ Cicinelli A & Vasco Rocca S (1978), Vol. I, p. 81/R8900.1576.
c1650 CASTIGLIONE, Giovanni Benedetto : Venere dormiente e amori/ PA/ oc/ ?/ Roma, GNB/ Inv. E61964iccd/ Cicinelli A & Vasco Rocca S (1978), Vol.I, p.83/ R8928V.1577.
c1700 GIORDANO, Luca : Sleeping Venus attended by two cupids/ DR/ d/ 18x23.2/ London, VAM/ Inv. 8639.D/ Ward-Jackson 1979,Vol.II, p.54, n°709/ R11130.1578.
c1800 SERANGELI, Gioacchino Giuseppe: Venere dormiente e Amore/ PA/ ?/95x127/ Wien, DOR 1993/ Inv.#/ IT/ R8319V.1579.
c1825 (cir) POCK, Giovanni/ Venere dormiente e Amore/ PA/ oc/ 42 x 51/ Wien, DOR 24.4.'07/ SL ;-8/ IT/ R9397.1580.
1921 SOCRATE, Carlo : Venere dormente/ PA/ ?/ ?/ UN/ Inv.#/ Di Genova 1993, p.520-21, n°720/ R8631. 1581.
c1934 CERACCHINI, Gisberto : Venere dormiente/ PA/ oc/ 182,5x141,5/ UN/ Inv.#/ Di Genova 1994, p.752, n°995/ R8633.1582.

Venus of Urbino

1538 TIZIANO, Vecellio : Venere di Urbino/ PA/ oc/ 119x165/ Firenze, GdU/ Inv. 1890, n° 1437/ Berenson 1958, p.191, pl.981 ; Clark 1969, T.I, p.189 ; Mai ed. 2001, p.13,n°3 ; Calabrese 2003/ R444.1583. *Many copies.*
1821 BARTOLINI, Lorenzo : Venere giacente (Venus of Urbino)/ SC/ p/ 69x176/ Firenze, GdA/ Inv. 1313/ IT/ R8228.1584.
1972 SPRINGOLO, Nino: Venere moderna/ PA/ oc/ 95x118/ UN/ Inv.#/ Bolaffi 1979, p.338/ R8629.1585.
1978 CAVALO, Franco: La vergine col cagnolino (The virgin with dog)/ OT/ w/ 50x70/ UN, PrC/ Inv.#/ CELIT 1986 Vol 11, p.7374/ R8666.1586.
1980 BRUNI, Bruno : Venere di Urbino/ PR/ l/ 59x80/ WEB, Artprice/ Inv. 201918/ IT/ R8417.1587.
2003 LODOLA, Marco : M.lle Persiflage/ PA/ ?/ ?/ UN, Artist Col./ Inv.#/ Calabrese 2003,p. 331/ R2218. 1588.

Venus with the Musician

1548 TIZIANO, Vecellio: Venus and Cupid with an organ-player (Venus recree par la musique)/ PA/ oc/ 148x217/ Madrid, MNP/ Inv. 421/ Berenson 1958, p.193; Giorgi 1990, p.45; Dunand & Lemarchand s.d., III p.773, fig.1232/ R447.1589. *Berenson considers this PA as a replica of Berlin, GSM/ Inv.1849, however without dog.*

c1550 TIZIANO, Vecellio: Venus and a dog with an organ-player (Venere con cucciolo e giovane che suono l'organo)/ PA/ oc/ 136x220/ Madrid, MNP/ Inv. 420/ Berenson 1958, p.193; Giorgi 1990, p.15; Enciclopedia 2006, Tomo III,p.746/ R1330.1590. *Copy: (aft) Venus with an organist and a dog/ PA/ oc/ 157x213/ Den Haag, MaH/ Inv. 343/ Duca 1966, fig.570, p.406/ R5350.*

c1550 TIZIANO, Vecellio: Venus mit dem Orgelspieler (Venere, Cupido, l'organista e il cagnolino ; Venere distesa e Filippo II in figura d'organista)/ PA/oc/ 115x210/ Berlin, GSM/ Inv.1849/ Berenson 1958, p.189 ; Giorgi 1990, p.16/ R4000.1591.

a1555 TIZIANO, Vecellio: Venus, crowned by Cupid, and a lutist (Venere distesa e suonatore di luto)/ PA/ oc/ 150x197/ Cambridge, FWM/ Berenson 1958, p.190 ; Giorgi 1990, p.19/ R520.1592.

*Replica: **c1565** /PA/ oc/ 65.1 x 209.6/ NY, MMA/ Inv. 36.29/* Berenson 1958, p.195, pl.1095; *Giorgi 1990, p.26/ R3999.1593.;*

(wor) Venus, von Amor bekränzt, zu ihren Füßen ein Lautenspieler/ PA/ oc/ 142x208/ Dresden, SKS/ Inv. 177/ IT/ R10061.1594.

a1555 TIZIANO, Vecellio: Venere con Cupido e il cagnolino (Venere con civetta; Venere con un amorino, un cane e una pernice)/ PA/ oc/ 139x195/ Firenze, GdU/ Inv. 1890-1431/ Berenson 1958, p.191; Giorgi 1990, p.35/ R446.1595.

c1990 MANARA, Milo: La Venere di GIORGIONE / PR/ c/ 50x70/ WEB, MiloManara/ Inv.#/ IT/ R1312. 1596.

17. Venus statues
(armata, Callipyga, Capitolina/Knidos, Cesarini, Felix, Genetrix, Italica/Hope, Mazarin, Medici, Milo, pudica, Victrix)

armata

c1470 ZOPPO, Marco : Venus armata (Venus Victrix)/ DR/ ?/ ?/ London, BMu/ Inv. #/ Wind 1980, p.91,94, fig.73/ R10425.1597.
c1525 VENEZIANO, Agostino : Venus Victrix (Aphrodite as a war goddess)/ PR/ e/ ?/ London, BMu/ Inv. #/ Paraskos 2000, p.16/ R1245.1598.

Callipyga

1600-24 (att) SUSINI, Antonio: Venus Callipygos/ SC/ z/ 10/ London, VAM/ Inv. A.141-1910/ exh/ R10373V.1599.
c1725 PAN(N)INI, Giovanni Paolo: Venus Callipygian (A capriccio of classical ruins with the pyramid of Caius Cestius, an arch, a ruined temple with Ionic olumns and a statue of Venus, figures standing by a water-pool nearby)/ PA/ oc/ 123,2x172,9/ NY, SOT 24.1.'02/ Sl. N07759-41/ IT/ R5873.1600.
c1770 VALADIER, Luigi: Vénus Callipyge/ SC/ z/ 101/ Pais, MdL/ Inv. MR 3276/ exh/ R677.1601. *Replica c1775 (wor) VALADIER, Luigi: Callipygian Venus/ SC/ z/ 102/ London, SOT 9.12.'05/ Sl. L05234-130/ IT/ R5306.*
1783 PIRANESI, Francesco: Venere Callipyga in atto di guardarsi allo specchio/ PR/ y/ ?/ Stockholm, NMK/ Inv.#/ Säflund 1963, p.21, n°8/ R2987.1602.
1882 CLERICI, Leone : Callipygian Venus/ SC/m/ 88,5/ London, SOT 12.12.'03/ Sl. L03233-246/ IT/ R5786.1603.
1985 PARISI, Carlo: Gallipige/ PA/ ut/ 50x30/ UN/ Inv.#/ CEDE 2001 Vol 16, p.11415/ R8648.1604.

Capitolina/Knidos

1302-1310 PISANO, Giovanni: Strength and Chastity (Fortitude and Chastity; *Venus Capitolina)/* SC/ m/ ?/ Pisa, DUO/ Inv.#/ Panofsky 1969, fig.113, pl..LXI/ R8213.1605.
c1540 PRIMATICCIO, Francesco (& Jacopo Barozzi da Vignola): Vénus de Cnide / SC/ z/ 192/ Fontainebleau, MNC/ Inv.MR3293/ Primatice 2004, p.150,n°40/ R2427.1606.
c1875 BARZANTI, Pietro: Venus (Capitolina)/SC/m/81,5/NY, SOT 27.4.'06/ Sl.N08180-216/ IT/ R6272. 1607.
1886 CLERICI, Leone: Diane(sic) au bain *(Venus Capitolina)*/ SC/ m/ 97/ Paris, TAJ 8.11.'00/ Sl.35/ IT/ R8347.1608.
1999 PARMIGGIANI, Claudio : Venus of Montreal (Aphrodite of Knidos)/ SC/ p/ ?/ Montréal, MBA/ Inv. 2004.4.1-2/ IT/ R8808.1609.

Cesarini

1583 GIAMBOLOGNA : Venus Cesarini/ SC/ m/ 154/ Roma, PaMa/ Inv. #/ Avery 1999, p.55, n°2/ R6053. 1610. *Many replica or copies.*
c1600 SUSINI, Antonio: Vénus Cesarini (aft GIAMBOLOGNA)/ SC/ z/ 43,3/ UN, PrC/ Inv.#/ Avery 1999, p.52-55/ R6949.1611.

Felix

c1500 ANTICO, Pier Jacopo : Venus Felix/SC/z/29,8x-x2,4/Wien, KHM/ Inv.5726/ Bober & Rubinstein,1986 p.62,n°16; Pope-Hennessy 1996, Vol.II, p.294-97, pl.280 /R2698.1612.
c1510 ASPERTINI, Amico : Venus Felix/ DR representation statue Vaticani/ ?/?/ London, BMu/ Inv.Skb I,ff14v-15c/ Bober & Rubinstein, p.62, n°16/ R8070V.1613.
1518 COSTA, Lorenzo: Venere Felix/ PA/ ?/ ?/ Budapest, MFA/ Inv.#/ Clark 1969,T.II, p.170; Panofsky 1969, p.153; Faietti 1988, p.104-5/ R3532.1614.
c1550 CARPI, Girolamo da: Venus Felix (representation of statue Musei Vaticani)/ DR/ ?/ ?/ Bober 1986,p.62,n°16/ R8071V.1615.
c1575 DOSIO, Giovanni Antonio: Venus Felix (representation of SC in Vatican)/ DR/ ?/ ?/Berlin, KSK/ Inv. Skb.f.77a/ Bober 1986, p.62,n°16/ R8072.1616.

Genetrix (Genitrix)

c1510 ASPERTINI, Amico : Venus Genetrix/ DR representation of statue Mantova, PaD Inv.D677/?/?/ London, BMu/ Inv.Skb I,f12v/ Bober & Rubinstein, p.60, n°15/ R8068V.1617.
c1550 STRADA, Jacopo: Venus Genetrix/ ILL/ d/ ?/ Wien, NBi/ Codex Miniatus 21,2, f.145/ IT/ R10074V.1618.
c1600 TEMPESTA, Antonio: Iulius Caesar Veneris beneficio in Cometam mutatur (The murder of Julius Caesar) (*Venus immortalizes Julius Caesar*) (pl.150 from the series Ovid's Metamorphoses, *pub Wilhelmus Jansonnius)/* PR/ e/ 10,4x11,7/ SF, FAM/ Inv. 1989.1.277/ Bartsch 36(17,3) 1983, p.84,n°787(151)/ R1393.1619. *Also in London, BMu.*

Italica (Hope)

1788 CANOVA, Antonio: Venere Italica (*bust)*/ SC/ p/?/ Firenze, IAP/ Inv.#/ Calabrese Omar 2003,p.310/ R2220.1620.
c1800 CANOVA, Antonio: Studio per Venere Italica, da tergo/ DR/ d/ 22.4x19/ Bassano, MuC/ Inv#/ IT/ R11068.1621.
1804 CANOVA, Antonio: Testa di Venere (head of 'Venere Italica')/ SC/ m/ 56/ St.Petersburg, HMu/ Bettucchi 1991p.148/ R1256.1622. *Replica of bust of Firenze? of bust in plaster at Bassano, MuC? Many copies.*
1812 CANOVA, Antonio: Venere Italica (Venere del Canova)/ SC/ m/ 172x52x55/ Firenze, PaP/ Inv.#/ Stefani 2003, p.75, n°69,70,71; Pinelli in Bonfait 2004, p.86-88 / R385.1623.
*Replica: **1818-20** The Hope Venus/ SC/ m/ 178/ Leeds, CAG/ Stefani 2003, p.89, n°96/ R8989.1624.*
*.Preparatory: Studio per Venere Italica/ DR/ d/ 21.7x16.5/ Bassano, MuC/ Inv. #/ Stefani 2003, p.76, n°72/R10157.1625. Many copies: **c1850** Hope Venus/ SC/ z/ 134x39x40,5/ Berlin, NSM/ Inv.B II 76/ Mai ed. 2001, p.505, n°B23*
c1816 PISANI, Giovanni : Venus (Venere Italica)/ SC/ m/ ?/ Houston, MFA/ Inv. 95.201/ R8983.1626.
c1825 BARTOLINI, Lorenzo : Venus Italica (aft CANOVA, Antonio)/ SC/ m/ 100/ WEB, Artprice 30.4.'93/ IT/ R6172V.1627.
c1875 BARZANTI, Pietro: Venus Italica (aft CANOVA, Antonio)/ SC/ m/ 152/ NY, CHR 25.10.'05/ Sl.1567-391/ IT/ R4882.1628.
c1900 PUGI, G.?: Busto di Venere Italica/ SC/ m/ 48x27x14/ Como, GAL/ Inv.#/ IT/ R490.1629.

Mazarin

c1513 BRESCIA, Giovanni Antonio da: Venus Mazarin (*set in a landscape without dolphin)*/ Pr/ e/ ?/ UN/ Inv. #/ Bober 1986, p.61, n°15/ R8075V.1630.

c1516 RAIMONDI, Marcantonio : Venus at her bath (Mazarin Venus)/ DR/ ?/ ?/ Wien, ALB/ Inv.#/ Bober 1986, p.61,n°15a/ R4584.1631.
c1525 CIAMPOLINI, Giovanni : Venus at her bath (Mazarin Venus) /DR/ d/ ?/ Oxford, AMu/ Bober 1986,p.61,n°15b/ R4585.1632.

Medici

c1550 STRADA, Jacopo: Venus Medici/ ILL/ d/ ?/ Wien, NBi/ Codex Miniatus 21,2, f.155/ IT/ R10075V. 1633.
b1572 (att) PORTA, Guglielmo della : Venus Este/ SC/ m/ 192/ Wien, KHM/ Inv. 7520/ Leithe-Jasper 2002, p.136-163, fig.1,14/ R10850.1634.
c1635 DELLA BELLA, Stefano: Vénus Médicis/ DR/ d/ 27,1x12,2/ Paris, MdL /Inv.330-1/ Viatte 1974, p.191,n°300/ R3828.1635. *Many copies exist.*
c1680 MEHUS, Livio: Testa della Venere dei Medici/ DR/ d/ 41,2x20,4/ Roma, ING/ Inv. FC.125438/ Di Castro 1983, p.139-141, n°75/ R1944.1636.
c1699-1702 SOLDANI-Benzi, Massimiliano : Medici Venus/ SC/ z/ 158/ Wien, LMu/ Inv. SK537/ IT/ R6913.1637. *Replica: **1711**/ SC/ z/ ?/ Oxford, BPa/ Inv.#/ IT/ R1443; a copy aft "Venus in the garden" SC/ ?/ ?/ Oxford, Bpa/ Inv.#/ IT/ R1442.*
c1700 (wor) SOLDANI-Benzi, Massimiliano : Venus (Medici type) (*without dolphin)*/ SC/ z/ 40,6/ NY, MMA/ Inv.27.36.8/ IT/ R1459.1638.
*Replicas: Toronto, AGO/ Inv.85-7/ IT; **c1700** (wor) Venus de' Medici/ SC/ z/ 29,2/ London, CHR 6.7.'06/ Sl. 7252 –245/ IT/ R6791.1639.*
c1730 CAMPIGLIA, Giovanni Domenico: Venus with a dolphin (Medici Venus)/ DR/ d/ 53.7x37/ Edinburgh, NGS/ Inv. D 1988/ IT/ R9938.1640.
1784 SPINAZZI, Innocenzo: Venus Medici/ SC/ m/ 163/ Edinburgh, NGS/ Inv. #/ Llorens et al. 1997, p.52, fig.31/ R10848.1641.
1790 RIGHETTI, Francesco: Venus de' Medici/ SC/ z/ 32.4/ London, CHR 5.7.'07/ Sl. 7412-0051/ IT/ R9685.1642.
c1802 CANOVA Antonio: Study of the Medici Venus/ DR/ d/ 50,4x36,4/ Bassano, MuC/ Inv.#/ IT/ R7165.1643.
1917 MODIGLIANI, Amedeo: Vénus (nu debout, nu Médicis)/ PA/ oc/ 99,5x84,5/ NY, CHR 8.11.'06/ Sl. 1722-31/ IT/ R7874.1644.
1975 PAOLINI, Giulio: Mimesi/Mimesis nach der Venus Medici/ SC/ p/ 163x50x44/ Weimar, NMu/ Inv.#/ Bolaffi, 1979, p.262-263/ R8234.1645.
1982 PAOLINI, Giulio: Venus de Medicis/ CL// 50x70,5/ Milano, SOT 22.11.'05/ Sl. MI0248-225/ IT/ R5160.1646.

Milo

c1850 (wor) BOSCHETTI, Benedetto : Venus de Milo/ SC/ z/ 52,8/ London, CHR 6.7.'06 & 26.4.'07/ Sl. 7252-168 & 7391-0329/ IT/ R6796.1647.
c1875 BARZANTI, Pietro: Venus de Milo/ SC/ m/ 122/ London, SOT 25.9.'02/ Sl.B02942-422/ IT/ R5119.1648.
c1940 BOCCASILE, Gino : Affiche de propagande fasciste (*Venus of Milo in the arms of an American black soldier)*/ PR/?/?/ Salmon 2000/ R1862.1649.
1988 BEN: Projet pour Paolini (*Venus de Milo in a box)* /SC,AS/ p/ 85x30x30/ Paris,PrC/ Leydier 2003, p.52-53/R1814.1650.
2001 MONTELLA, Vincenzo : Venus/ PR / v/ 100x50/ WEB, abs/ Inv.#/ IT/ R3185.1651.
2001 MONTELLA, Vincenzo : Venus framed (*with Cupid)*/ PR / v/ 120x80/ WEB, abs/ Inv.#/ IT/ R8412. 1652.
2003 BEN : A chacun sa Vénus/ SC/ p/ ?/ Vez, Donjon/ exh 2003/ Leydier 2003, p.14-15/ R10352.1653.

pudica

c1500 RAFFAELLO, Sanzio: Nu féminin dans l'attitude d'une Vénus pudique (Psyché?)/ DR/ d/ 18,9x7,5/ Budapest, MFA/ Inv. 1934/ Cavicchioli 2002, p.110-111,fig.69/ R8366.1654.
(cir) 'Venus pudica of Cnidian type'/DR/?/?/ Oxford, AMu/ Inv. cat.628v/ Bober 1986, p.61/ R8066V.1655.
1550-1555 BRONZINO, Agnolo : Pierantonio Bandini (with statuette of Venus Pudica)/ PA/ ow/ 106.7 x 82.5/ Ottawa, NGC/ Inv. 3717/ Berenson 1963, p.43/ R10267.1656.
c1550 STRADA, Jacopo: Venus Pudica/ ILL/ d/ ?/ Wien, NBi/ Codex Miniatus 21,2, f.157/ IT/ R10076V. 1657.
1853 BARTOLINI, Lorenzo : Venus (*Venus Pudica*) (BARTOLINI faceva E.(?) Pasquale ROMANELLI termino)/ SC/ m/ 160/ Frankfurt, LHM/ Inv. St.P.202/ Beck 1985, p.67-71, Abb.49/ R7846.1658.
***1817** Figura femminile nuda nell'atteggiamento di Venere pudica/ SC/ p/ 158/ Firenze, GdA/ Inv.1212/ IT/ R8576V.1659.*

Victrix (Vincitrice)

c1550 ROMANO, Giu lio: Vénus Victrix/ DR/ d/ 25,9x33,3/ Paris, MdL/ Inv.3878/ IT/ R3853.1660.
c1625 ALBANI, Francesco : Stori' d'Amo–e - Venere Vincitrice (Allegory of summer: Venus in Vulcan's forge)/ PA/ ?/ ?/ Roma : GaB/ Inv.#/ IT fototeca, artresource/ R8499.1661.
1657 GALESTRUZZI, Giovanni Battista: Venere Vittrice (fr'm 'The Antique Figural G'ms' Roma/ PR/ / 9,7x7,8/ Milano, BiA/ Inv.#/ Bartsch 46 (21,1) 1982, p.176,n°177(73); Bartsch 46 C 1985; p.214,n°4606.176 / R4991. 1662.
1670-80 MARINARI, Onorio: Venere vincitrice (with apple in left hand)/ PA/ oc/ 116x85/ Firenze, GdU/ Inv. S.M&C 110/ Gli Uffizi-Catalogo Generale 1979, P.1000/ R9632.1663.
c1804 CANOVA, Antonio : Venere Vincitrice (Paolina Borghese)/ SC/ p/ 90x200x65/ Possagno, CdC/ IT/ R11069.1664.
1805 CANOVA, Antonio : Venere Vincitrice (Paolina Borghese)/ SC/ m /160x192/ Roma, GaB/ Inv.LIV/Munoz 1957, Tav.XXX; Staccioli 1985,p.28-29; Moreno 2004, p.75, n°15; Pinelli in Bonfait 2004, p.88-89/ R005. 1665.
*Preparatory drawings: **c1790**: Studio per Venere vincitrice/ DR/ d/ ?/ Bassano, MuC/ Inv. 952/ Stefani 2004, p.32, 165, nr.32/R10174.1666.;*
***c1807**: Venere vincitrice/ DR/ d/ ?/ Bassano, MuC/ Inv. 1509/ Stefani 2004, p.36, 165, nr.39/R10177.1667. Many copies.*
c1850 TADOLINI, Ad mo : Pauline Borghese as Venus (*Victrix)* (aft CANOVA)/ SC/ w/ ?/ London, GAC/ Inv. 16759/ IT/ R7070.1668.
c1880 BIGGI, Fausto: Venus Victrix (Venus *with apple*) (aft Thorvaldsen, Bertel)/ SC/ m/ 96/ London, SOT 12.6.'06/Sl.L06230-9/ IT/ R6598.1669. *There are several copies of Thorvaldsen's 'Venus with apple', but seldom called 'Venus Victrix'.*
1935 MARTINI, Arturo: Donna Nuda (Venus Victrix) (aft Pierre-Auguste Renoir)/ SC/ p/ 33.1x22.5/ Vicenza, PaT/ Inv. 14212/ IT/ R11487.1670.

18. Venus unaccompanied

1509 LOMBARDO, Antonio : Venere/ RE/ m/ 27x18/ Firenze, MNB/ Inv. 462/ IT/ R8590V.1671.
c1530 LUINI, Bernardino: "Mond" Venus/ PA/ ,/ ?/ Milano, PrC/ Inv. #/ Berenson 1968, p.233/ R10225V. 1672. *From Ludwig Mond Col., London.*
1534 GIOLITO DE FERRARA, Gabriele: Venus/ PR/ e/ ?/ Washington, NGA/ Inv. 1964.8.1041/ IT/ R8443V.1673.
c1540 CARIANI, Giovanni Busi: Venere/ PA/ ?/ ?/ Surrey, HCP/ Inv. 1103/ Berenson 1958, p.56/ R9613V. 1674.
c1540 DOSSI, Battista: Venus/ PA/ ?/ ?/ Hildesheim, Mu/ Inv. 350/ Berenson 1968, p.115/ R10222V.1675.
1570-72 DANTI, Vincenzo: Venere/ SC/ m/ ?/ Firenze, PaP/ Inv.#/ Pope-Hennessy 1964, Vol.I, p.458/ R11139V.1676.
c1585 CINCINATO, Romulo : Venus/ FR// ?/ Guadalajara, PaI/ Inv. Sala de Atalanta/ Navarrete 2005, p.87/ R11020V.1677.
c1600 (cir) CAMPAGNA, Girolamo: Andiron with figure of Venus/ SC/ z/ 103x56,3x40,2/ Washington, NGA/ Inv. 1961.9.101/ IT/ R8241V.1678.
c1625 DOMENICHINI, Domenico: Venus/ PA/ oc/ 121.9 x 168.9/York, AGa/ Inv.1785/ IT/ R1532V.
c1675 PARODI, Filippo: Venere/ SC/ m/?/ Genova, PaRe/ Inv.#/ IT/ R10302V.1679.
c1824 MARCHESI, Pompeo: Venere / SC/ p/ 113x140x66/ Milano, VBB/ Inv. GAM 1344/ IT/ R11714V. 1680.
1930 PRAMPOLINI, Enrico : Venere meccanizata (Polivalenza)/ MM// ?/UN/ Inv.#/ Di Genova 1994, p.1059, n°1461/ R8638.1681.
1945 DONATI, Enrico: Conception de Vénus/ PA/ oc/ 76,8x63,5/ NY, CHR 14.9.'06/ Sl. 1698-141/ IT/ R7339.1682.
1970 BERTINI, Gianni : Venus à l'hydrogene/ PA/ MM/ 55x50/ WEB, ArtPrice 14.2.'07/ Inv. 215719/ IT/ R8703.1683.
1970-80 ROBAZZA, Benedetto: Aphrodite (aka Brigitte Bardot)/ SC/ m/ ?/ UN/ Inv. #/ Mai ed.2001, p.220, note n° 71/ R9737V.1684.
1984 GULLO, Carmine : Le pietre di Venere/ DR/ dr/ 50x35/ UN/ Inv.#/ CELIT 1988 Vol 12, p.8256/ R8661. 1685.

o bust or head

c1500 OGGIONO, Marco d': Venus/ PA/ ?/ ?/ UN, pre.Wien Col.Lederer/ Inv. #/ Berenson 1967, p.181,187, fig.370/ R10393.1686.
c1600 (wor) GIAMBOLOGNA : Bust of Venus/ SC/ z/ 22/ London, SOT 7.7.'06/ Sl. L06231-74/ IT/ R6856.1687.
c1600 LUCA, Araldo de: Venus from the Salon of the Muses/ PA/ ?/ ?/ Firenze, VMP/ Inv.#/ IT/ R3730. 1688.
1692 MAZZA, Giovanni Giuseppe: Bust of Venus/ SC/ m/ ?/ Wien, LMu/ Inv.#/ exh/ R 7830V.1689.
1782 PECHEUX, Lorenzo: Venere/ PA/ oc/ 28,3x34,3/ Torino, GAM/ Inv. FD254/ Serra 1993, p.44/ R8641. 1690.
c1815 FOLO, Giovanni: Venere (aft Stefano TOFANELLI)/ PR/ e/ 32.4x22.4/ WEB, eBay 2.11.07/ R11036.1691.
c1850 BRUCCIANI, Domenico: Bust of Venus/ SC/ p/ 61/ London, CHR 7.7.'05/ Sl. 7053-506/ IT/ R3902.1692.

c1894 ORONZIO, Lelli: Busto di Venere/ SC/ p/ 40x40/ Firenze, Gip/ Inv.#/ IT/ R8589V.1693.
1933-35 RHO, Manlio: Venere - Figura in progressione/ 4SC/ p/ 40x43x21, 65x45x22, 77x45x22, 114x45x31/ UN/ Inv.#/ Di Genova 1996, p.211, n°296/ R8697.1694.
1971 BRUNI, Bruno: Frammenti toscani *(head of Botticelli's Venus)*/ PR/ lr/ 80,5x59,7/ UN/ Inv.#/ Flemming 1978, p.51/ R9199.1695.
1971 BRUNI, Bruno: Langweiliges Weekend der Venus in Florenz (Boring week-end in Florence) *(head of Botticelli's Venus)*/ PR/ lr/ 69,5x50/ UN/ Inv.#/ Flemming 1978, p.52/ R9200.1696.
1971 BRUNI, Bruno: Terra di Siena *(head of Botticelli's Venus)*/ PR/ lr/ 70,5x50/ UN/ Inv.#/ Flemming 1978, p.53/ R9201.1697.
1992 BRUNI, Bruno: Venus im Grünen (Venus in green) PR/ lr/ 74,5x63,5/ WEB, arsmundi/Sl. ?-1000/ IT/ R6809.1698.
1999 MARIANI, Carlo Maria: Venus/ PA/ oc/ 100x100/ UN/Inv.#/ IT/R6648.1699.
2003 PIGNATELLI, Luca: Afrodite/ PA/ of/ 43x31/ Milano, CHR 23.11.'05/ Sl. 2480-116/ IT/ R5302. 1700.
2007 GENTILI, Carlo: Pensieri di Venere/ 4xPA/ ?/ 34x24/ UN, exh/ IT/ R11097.1701.

o reclining

1800-1849 MARCHESI, Pompeo: Venere giacente/ SC/ p/ 60x58x40/ Milano, VBB/ Inv. GAM 4676/ IT/ R11715V.1702.
1969 BRUNI, Bruno: Reclining Venus *(on belly)*/SC/ z/ 78/ UN/ Inv. #/ Mai ed.2001, p.219, note n° 69/ R9736V.1703.
1978 PARISI, Carlo: Venere in meditazione/ PA/ u/ 60x90/ UN/ Inv.#/ CEDE 2001 Vol 16, p.11414/ R8647. 1704.
1982 VINCENZI, Mario: Venere al sole/ SC/ m/ 75x60x25/ UN/ Inv.#/ CEDE 1993 Vol 14, p.10073/ R8660. 1705.
1986 RIZZO, Vicenzo : La Venere di Trezza/ PA/ oc/ 70x100/ UN/ Inv.#/ CELIT 1988 Vol 12, p.8483/ R8665. 1706.

▪ to the left

1508-09 CAMPAGNOLA, Giulio: Venus reclining in a landscape/ PR/ e/ 12x18,1/ Cleveland, MuA/ Inv. 1931.205/ Bartsch 25 C (13,2) 1984,p.473,n° 2518.008/ R4805.1707. *Also with many other owners. Copy in reverse 11,2x15,9/ London, BMu/ R4806.*
c1525 (att) LICINIO, Bernardino : Venere giacente/ PA/ oc/ 80,5x154/ Firenze : PaV/ Inv. 1890, n. 9943/ IT; Lawner 1988, p.135/ R5744.1708.
c1540 CAMPAGNOLA, Domenico: Venus *(reclining)*/ PR/ e/ 9,7x13,3/ Wien, ALB/ Inv.#/ Bartsch 25 (13,2) 1980,p.262,n°7(382)/ R4795.1709.
c1630 (att) DOMENICHINI, Domenico: Liegende Venus/ PA/ oc/ 116,3 x 166/ Dessau, ScW/ IT/ R8370. 1710.
c1634 GUERCINO, Giovane Francesco : Nude (Venus?) holding a curtain/ DR/ d/ 20.3x24.3/ Liverpool, WAG/ Inv. WAG10849/ IT/ R11421.1711.
1785 BARTOLOZZI, Francesco: Venere sdraiata (Venus reclining) (aft CARRACCI, Annibale)/ PR/ e/ 29,4x34,7/ Roma, ING/ Inv.FC70030/ Jatta 1995 p.164, fig.94/ R3753.1712. *Also in Christchurch, AGTPW/ Inv.73-12 ; Gravelines, MDE (Vénus endormie).*
c1800 SCHIAVONI, Natale : Venere (*reclining, with doves*)/ PA/ oc/ 114x146,5/ Brescia, MAS/ Inv.#/ IT/ R8510.1713.
c1894-97 SEGANTINI, Giovanni: Dea dell'amore/ PA/ oc/ 210x133 oval/ Milano, GAM/ Inv. GAM 3634/ Anonymous 1975, Vol.2, 1975, n°967/ R11709.1714.
c1920 MODIGLIANI, Amadeo: Venus/ PA/ ?/ 48x69/ UN/ Inv. #/ IT AllPosters/ R9331.1715.
1934 CASORATI, Felice: Venere bionda/ PA/ o/ ?/ UN/ Inv.#/ Di Genova 1994, p.913-14, n°1216/ R8636.1716.
c2006 MEDICI, Adrian : Aphrodite/ PA/ ac/ 30x40/ WEB, trendart/ IT/ R8565.1717.

▪ to the right

c1425 PISANELLO, Antonio Pisano : Venus Luxuria/ DR/ d/ ?/ Wien, ALB/ Inv.#/ Clark 1969, T.II, p.108; Arscott 2000, p.28,fig.12/ R7294.1718.

c1525 DOSSI, Dosso : Réveil de Vénus (?)/ PA/ oc/ ?/ Roma, PaM/ Inv.#/ IT/ R3102.1719.

1500-40 CAPRIOLO, Domenico: Ruhende Venus/ PA/ ow/ 122x154/ Berlin, GSM/ Inv. 180/ IT/ R11576 1720. *Maybe unfinished and terminated c1535 by BORDONE, Paris*

c1600 CARRACCI, Annibale: Reclining Venus/ DR/ d/ 21.5x38.9/ Windsor, RCo/ Inv. 2091r/ Wittkower 1952, p.158, Cat.441, pl.56/ R10421.1721.

1855 MARCHESI, Pompeo: Venere/ SC/ m/ 110x140x70/ Milano, VBB/ Inv.ΓAM 8358/ IT/ R9067.1722.

c1975 FORMICA, Claudia : Venere della frutta/ SC/ m/ ?/ Roma, PrC/ Inv.#/ CELIT 1977 Vol 4, p.2530/ R8673.1723.

1997 BATACCHI, Franco: Venere e seppia/ MM/ w/ 64,7x21/ Vittorio Veneto, PrC/ Inv.#/ IT; Caramel 2001/ R2102.1724.

2007 MONTRONE, Vincenzo: La Venere pensatrice/ MM/ b/ 50x70/ WEB, eBay 3.12.07/ IT/ R11510. 1725.

▪ in a landscape

c1510 POMEDELLI, Giovanni Maria: Vénus éveillée/ PR/ e/ ?/ UN/ Inv.#/ Duboucher 1992, n°45/ R7642. 1726.

b1520 LOTTO, Lorenzo : Venere in un paese/ PA/ ?/ ?/ UN/ Inv.#/ Berenson 1958, p.108, pl.756/ R9617.1727.

c1520 PALMA Il Vecchio, Jacopo: Ruhende Venus (*Venus nude in a landscape)*/ PA/ oc/ 112x186/ Dresden, SKS/ Inv. 190/ Berenson 1958, p.127 ; Mai ed. 2001, p.228-29, n°2 ; Calabrese 2003, p.55/ R7085.1728.

c1520 PALMA Il Vecchio, Jacopo: Venus in a landscape (*Venus with drapery on lower part of the body)*/ PA/ oc/ 77,5x152,7/ London, CIA/ Inv. P.1978.PG.305/ IT/ R8998.1729.

Berenson (1958) refers to two more PA"Venus in a landscape" in London: 1° University Col. Lee of Fareham: =London, CIA? 2° PrC Count A. Seilern; replica ***c1515*** *'Venus (with drapery) and Cupid in a landscape' is in Passadena, NSAM/ R11336.1730.*

c1530 LUINI, Bernardino: Venus/ PA/ oc/ 107x136/ Washington, NGA/ Inv. 1939.1.120/ Berenson 1968, p.235./ R796.1731.

c1540 CAMPAGNOLA, Domenico: Venere distesa in un paesaggio (Venus reclining, *to the right,* in a landscape)/ DR/ d/ 12,2x17,4/ London, BMu/ Inv. 1896.6.2./ Tiziano 1995,p.212,282,n°51/ R5549.1732.

c1540 CAMPAGNOLA, Domenico: Paesaggio con Venere/ DR/ d/ 16.9x31.9/ Venezia, FGC/ Inv. 8/ IT/ R10236V.1733.

c1540 CAMPAGNOLA, Domenico: Venus reclining *to the left* in a landscape/ PA/ oc/ 121x175/ London, PrC/ Prater 2002,p.19/ R2086.1734.

c1550 BORDONE, Paris: Ruhende Venus/ PA/ ow/ Berlin, GSM/ Inv.180/ Berenson 1958, p.51/ R935.1735. *Copy aft?*

1936 BIANCHI BARRIVIERA, Lino: La rivelazione (La Venere di Viterbo)/ PA/ o/ 165x95/ Rho, PrC/ Inv.#/ Di Genova 1996, p.356, n°530/ R8698.1736.

c1970 ZETTI, Italo: Naked Aphrodite/ IL/ ex libris/ 6x11/WEB, eBay 13.8.'06/ IT/ R7308.1737.

1973 BIOLLA, Gerardo: Venere dei boschi/ PA/ oc/ 40x60/ UN, PrC/ Inv.#/ CELIT 1975 Vol 2, p.790/ R8675. 1738.

○ seated

c1510 RAFFAELLO, Sanzio: Venus seated on clouds pointing downwards *(with putti)*/ DR/ d/ 33x24.6/ Chatsworth, DCo/ Inv. #/ Jaffé 1995, Cat.9/ R10384.1739. *Preparatory for FR/ Roma, ViF.*

c1516 RAIMONDI, Marcantonio : Venus seated/ DR/ ?/ ?/ Wien, ALB/ Inv.#/ Bober 1986, p.62,n°17a/ R4587.1740.

c1525 PERUZZI, Baldassare Tommaso : Venere (Vénus au doigt agile)/ PA/ tw/ 97x75/ Roma, GaB/ Inv.92/ Duca 1966, p.304-305, n°408; Berenson 1968, p.334; Cicinelli 1978, Vol.IV, p.38/ R5341.1741.

c1540 CARUCCI, Jacopo (PONTORMO): Vénus (étude Loggia Careggi)/ DR/ / ?/ Firenze,GdU/ Inv. 6584 Fr./ Duboucher 1992,n°96/ R7649.1742.
c1545 PRIMATICCIO, Francesco: Vénus assise dans les nuées/ PR/ e/ 18,7x27/ Paris, MdL/ Inv. 8563bis/ IT/ R3435.1743.
c1550 GHERARDI, Cristofano detto il Doceno : Venus seated in the clouds (aft RAFFAELLO)/ FR// ?/ Borgo S.Sepolchro, ViB/ Inv. #/ Jaffé 1995, Cat.9/ R10385V.1744.
c1570 CAVALLERIS, Gianbattista : Aphrodite mit Hund unter dem Stuhl (Aphrodite with dog under the chair)/ PR//?/?/*<Kopien Torlonia, Verona, Uffizien...von Cavaleriis gezeichnet>*/Langlotz 1954,p.18,n°3/ R8218.1745.
c1571 GIAMBOLOGNA : Venus (?) (pre. called 'Bathseba')/ SC/ m/ 115/ LA, JPG/ Inv. 82.SA.37/ IT/ R5773.1746.
c1571 GIAMBOLOGNA : Venus « Fata Morgana »/ SC/ m/ 99/ London (Wrotham Park), SOT ?.9.'89/ Sl. ?- ?/ Bury 1990, p.96-100/ R10049.1747.
c1600 GIAMBOLOGNA: Venus as Architecture/ SC/ z/ ?/ Firenze : MNB/ Inv.#/ IT/ R1111.1748.
1854 MAGGESI, Dominique Fortuné: Vénus se coiffant/ SC/ p/ 35x19x19/ Bordeaux, MBA/ Inv. M 1111/ IT/ R2650.1749.
1927-28 SBISA, Carlo : La Venere della scaletta/ PA/ oc/ 100,5x90,5/ Trieste, CMR/ Inv.#/ Di Genova 1994, p.857, n°1132/ R8635.1750.
1928 FUNI, Achille: Venere innamorata (Enamoured Venus)/ PA/ ?/ ?/ Milano, GAM/ Inv.#/ Di Genova 1994, p.852; U. Reinhardt in Mai ed. 2001, p.214, Note n°45/ R8518.1751.
c1929 MARINI, Marino : Piccola Venere seduta/ SC/ ?/ ?/ Milano, MMM/ Inv.#/ IT/ R8048V.1752.
1932 MARTINI, Arturo : Venere dei porti/ SC/ q/ 115x91x74/ Treviso, MuC/ Inv.#/ DiGenova 1995, p.1512-13, n°2060/ R8559.1753.
2005 BRUNI, Bruno: Kleine Venus (Small Venus)/ SC/ z/ ?/ WEB, artbrokerage/ IT/ R3151.1754.

o standing

1923 SIRONI, Mario: Venere (Nudo con fruttiera)/ PA/ oc/ 100x75,5/ Torino, GAM/ Inv.P-1574/ Serra &Passoni 1993, p.211; Pinto 2002, p.58,n°27/ R8180.1755.
1965 CEROLI, Mario : Venere/ SC/ w/ c180/ NY, GAL Bonino/ Inv. #/ Kultermann 1967, p.22,n°24 ; Kahmen 1972, p.267, n°142/ R9154.1756.
1965 MARCHEGIANI, Elio : Venus/ MM/ v/ ?/ UN/ Inv. #/ Kultermann 1967, p.34,n°36, 37/ R9155.1757.
c1970 MAGNAVACCHI, Walter: Venere in attesa/ SC/ z/ 58/ UN/ Inv.#/ CELIT 1975 Vol 2, p.1111/ R8676. 1758.
1997 BATACCHI, Franco: Fluido di Venere/ MM/ w/ 64,7x21/ Vittorio Veneto, PrC/ Inv.#/IT; Caramel 2001/ R2101.1759.
1999 GRASSINI, Carlo: Venus, the goddess of Love/ DR/ du/ 112,5x80/ WEB, absolutearts/ IT/ R3181. 1760.
2001 BRUNI, Bruno: Venere assoluta/ SC/ z/ 40/ Wetzlar, GAL/ Inv.#/ IT/ R9219.1761.

▪ on left leg

c1486 BOTTICELLI, Sandro: Venus/ PA/ oC/ 158x68,5/ Berlin, GSM/ Inv.4118/ Mai ed. 2001, p.226-27, n°1/ R379.1762. *Replica in Torino, GaS/ Inv.172/ R346.1762.*
c1500 (att) ANTICO (Bonacolsi), Pier Jacopo Alari: Venus/ SC/ z/ 26.1/ Berlin, GSM/ Inv. 2395/ IT/ R10066.1763.
c1500 BRESCIA, Giovanni da : Venus (standing, half-draped)/ PR/ / 30,9x22,4/ Wien, ALB/ Inv.#/ Bartsch 25 C (13,2) 1984, p.344,n°2511.022/ R4801.1764.
c1500 RAFFAELLO, Sanzio: Venus/ DR/?/ ?/ Firenze, GdU/ Inv.#/ Clark 1969, T.I, p.218; Gombrich 1972, n°97/ R4601.1765.
c1500 RAIMONDI, Marcantonio: Antica statua di Venere/ DR/ d/ 21,5x10,5/ Cambridge, PrC/ Faietti 1988, p.84-85, fig.51/ R3531.1766.

1510 RAFFAELLO, Sanzio: Venere/ DR//23,8x10/ London, BMu/ Inv. 9-15-629/ Massari 1989, p.16, fig.3/ R3597.1767.
c1527 (att) MICHELANGELO, Buonarroti: Figura femminile stante (Venere?)/ DR/ d/ 27,9x13,3/ Firenze, GdU/ Inv. 251F/ Falletti 2002, p.157, Cat.8/ R4310.1768.
c1530-53 BANDINELLI, Baccio: Venere(Venus *of Medici type on inverted shell with dove in right hand)*/ SC/ z/ 37,8/ Firenze, MNB/ Inv.388/ Sframeli 2003, p.80, fig.7/ R4016.1769.
c1550 AMMANNATI, Bartolomeo : Venus/ SC/ z/ ?/ Firenze, PaV/ Inv. #/ R10081.1770.
c1550 CAMBIASO, Luca: Venus/ DR/ d/ ?/ Ottawa, MBA-NGC/ Inv. 5816/ IT/ R8891.1771.
1550-1599 VITTORIA, Alessandro : Venere/ SC/ z/ ?/ Roma, PaV/ Inv. F14815iccd/ IT/ R8907.1772.
1558-59 AMMANNATI, Bartolomeo: Venus/ SC/ z/ 180/ Madrid, MNP/ Inv. E171/ Enciclopedia 2006, p.377-378/ R10474.1773.
c1570 (cir) VITTORIA, Alessandro : Venus/ SC/ z/ 18,7/ London, CHR 7.12.'06/ Sl.#/ IT/ R8189.1774.
c1573 GIAMBOLOGNA : Venus Urania (Astronomie)/ SC/ z/ 38,8/ Wien, KHM/ Inv. KK5893/ IT/ R4546.1775.
c1585 BRAMBILLA the Younger, Francesco: Venus/ SC/ z/ 166x44x33,7/ Washington, NGA/ Inv. 1937.1.132/ IT/ R813.1776.
c1590 (cir) CAMPAGNA, Girolamo: Venus *(with drapery)*/ SC/ z/ 25.5/ London, CHR 5.7.07/ Sl. 7412-0021/ IT/ R9683.1777.
c1600 (att-wor) CAMPAGNA, Girolamo: Venus *(naked, with dolphin under right foot)*/ SC/ z/ 27,3/NY, SOT 17.10.'00/ Sl.?-37/ IT/ R4174.1778.
c1600 (att) CESARI, Giuseppe: Venus/ DR/ d/ 15,5x10,7/ SF, FAM/ Inv. 24.91 r-v/ IT/ R1366.1779.
c1600 VALESIO, Giovanni Luigi: Venere/ PR/e/ 37,5x23,5/ Roma, BiH/ Inv.#/ Bartsch 40 C 1(18,2) 1987, p.83,n°4002.067/ R4971.1780.
c1600 (att) VITTORIA, Alessandro: Venus/ z/ 30.3/ Braunschweig, HAU/ Inv. #/ IT/ R10084.1781.
1601-15 ROCCATAGLIATA, Nicolo: Venus/ SC/ z/ ?/ Berlin, GSM/ Inv. #/ IT/ 10104.1782.
c1650 PICCINI, Jacopo : Venere (aft TIZIANO)/ PR/ e/ 27,7x16,5/ Venezia, MuC/ Inv. P.D.1426/ Tiziano 1995, p.234,310,fig.127/ R5552.1783.
c1750 CAMPIGLIA, Giovanni Domenico: Two statuesque figures of Venus *(XXXIV on left leg, XXXV on right leg)*/ PR/ e/ 35,6x21,9/ WEB, aspireauctions 9.'04/ IT/ R7588.1784.
c1775 CAPELLANI, Antonio: Antique Venus/ PR/ e/ 21x12,5/ SF, FAM/ Inv. 1963.30.36526/ IT/ R730. 1785.
1862-1897 COSTA, Giovanni (Nino): Venere nel bosco (Alla fonte-La nimfa del bosco)/ PA/ oc/ 208x160/ Roma, GCAMC/ Inv. AM84/ Virno 2004, p.224-225, n°443/ R8642.1786.
1919 SIRONI, Mario: Venere dei porti/ CL/ tx/ 98x73,5/ Milano CRA/ Inv.#/ IT/ R8179.1787.
1929 FUNI, Achille: Venere Latina/ PA/ o/ ?/ UN/ Inv.#/ Di Genova 1994, p.853, n°1127/ R8634.1788.
1942 MARINI, Marino : Venere/ SC/ z/ ?/ Firenze, MMM/ Inv.#/ exh/ R8123.1789.
1948 SAVINIO, Alberto: Venere-Figurino/ DR/ d/ 33x24/ Milano, TaS/ Inv.1948 n°9/ Vivarelli 1996, p.375/ R8694.1790.
1970 SPINOCCIA, Pippo: La Venere di Palermo/ MM//140x100/ UN/ Inv.#/ Bolaffi 1979, p.337/ R8628. 1791.
1992 NEGRO, Roberto: La Venere giunomica delle spiagge romagnole/ PA/ oc/ 100x70/ UN/ Inv.#/ CEDE 1996 Vol 15, p.10692/ R8656.1792.

- **on right leg**

c1420-1430 PISANELLO, Antonio Pisano : Study for Venus –Luxuria (?)/ DR/ d/ 22,3x16,7/ Rotterdam, BBM/ Inv.#/ IT/ R6042.1793.
c1490 CREDI, Lorenzo di: Venere/ PA/ ow/ 160x76/ Firenze, GdU/ Inv.3094/ Berenson 1963, p.115, pl.198; Clark 1969, T.I,p.170; Sframeli 2003,p.70, n°2/ R930.1794.
c1490 FIORENTINO, Adriano: Venus/ SC/ z/41.6/ Philadelphia, MuA/ Inv. 1930-1-17/ IT/ R3375.1795.
c1500 MONTAGNA, Benedetto: Venus (standing nude)/ PR// 28,3x14,4/ London, BMu/ Inv.#/ Bartsch 25 C (13,2) 1984, p.414-6,n°2512.028/ R4804.1796.

c1510 (att) LOMBARDO, Tullio: Venus with a burning urn/ SC/ z/ 18.3/ Cleveland, MuA/ Inv. 1948.171/ IT/ R11745.1797.
c1520 MICHELANGELO, Buonarroti: Vénus dessinée (*probably inspired by the Capitoline Venus)*/ DR// ?/ Chantilly, MuC/ Inv.#/ De Tolnay 1967/ R2570.1798.
c1520 PERINO DEL VAGA, Pietro Bonnacorsi, detto : Venere/ FR// ?/ Genova, PDP/ Inv.#/ IT/ R10291. 1799.
1525-50 (att or wor) ANTICO (BONACOLSI), Pier Jacopo Alari : Venus/ SC/ z/ 30x12.2x8/ London, VAM/ Inv. A.96-1910/ exh/ R10368.1800.
c1540 ROMANO, Giulio: Vénus/ DR/ d/ 24,8x12,3/ Malmaison, MuC/ Inv. MDO 127/ IT/ R2805.1801.
1550-1570 AMMANNATI, Bartolomeo : Venere/ SC/ z/ ?/ Roma, PaV/ Inv. F14954iccd/ IT/ R8905.1802.
c1560 CATTANEO, Danese: Venus/ SC/ z/52.9/ Cleveland, MuA/ Inv. 1950.578/ IT/ R8273.1803.
c1560 GIAMBOLOGNA : Petite Vénus (Venus drying herself)/ SC/ z/ 14,3/ Braunschweig, HAU/ Inv. Bro.90/ Avery 1999, p.43,n°1/ R6944.1804. *Many replica or copies.*
c1565 GIAMBOLOGNA : Venerina in atto di asciugarsi (Venus drying her leg)/ SC/ z/ ?/ Firenze, MNB/ Inv. #/ Bober 1986, p.64, n°20; Avery 1999, p.48/ R6748.1805. *Many replica or copies*
c1570 GIAMBOLOGNA: Venere della Grotticella nella Grotta Grande del Buontalenti/ SC/ m/ 131/ Firenze : GiB/ Inv.#/ Avery 1999, p.49, fig.1/ R407.1806.
c1570 (wor) CAMPAGNA, Girolamo: Aphrodite/ SC/ z/ 72,4x15,2x19,7/ UN/ 1977.933/ IT/ R3072.1807.
c1575 ROCCATAGLIATA, Niccolo: Venus *(with apple in right hand)*/ SC/ z/ 14x5.4x5.4/ A'dam, RMu/ Inv. BK-16942/ IT/ R10596.1808.
c1600 GIAMBOLOGNA: Venus (standing on a pilar)/ SC/ z/ ?/ Firenze : MNB/ Inv.#/ IT/ R1111.1809.
c1600 CARRACCI, Agostino: Venus (*standing, showing her back)/* DR/ d/ 42,3x25,4/ SF, FAM/ Inv. 1963.24.164/ IT/ R737.1810.
c1600 (att) FONTANA, Lavinia: Standing Venus (or Andromeda)/ DR/ d/ 20,3x9,2/ London, SOT 10.7.'02/ Sl. L02121-123/ IT/ R5403.1811. *A PA exists in PrC/ Morena 2004, p.156, n°2.*
c1610 (cir) CAMPAGNA, Girolamo; Venus (with dolphin on left side)/ SC/ z/ 34/ Paris, CHR 27.6.'07/ Sl. 5493-0096/ IT/ R9581.1812.
c1650 VECCHIA, Pietro della: Titian with a statue of Venus beyond/ PA/ oc/ 113x91,2/ NY, SOT 28.1.'05/ Sl. 8059-543/ IT/ R6228.1813.
c1750 CAMPIGLIA, Giovanni Domenico: Pair of engravings depict two statuesque figures of Venus/ PR/ e/ 35,6x21,9/ WEB, aspireauctions 9.'04/ Inv.112/ IT/ R7588.1814.
1819 ANDERLONI, Pietro: Frammento greco rappresentante Venere (Greek fragment representing Venus)/ PR/e/23x14,5/Milano,CRB/Inv. Cat.75/Anonymous, 1996, p.97,280/ R3530.1815.
1836 PAMPALONI, Luigi: Venere/ SC/ p/ 170/ Firenze, UN/ Inv.#/ IT/ R8601.1816.
1844 BIENAIME, Luigi: Venere/ SC/ m/ ?/ Roma, GAM/ Inv.#/ exh/ R9586.1817.
1877 AMENDOLA, Giovan Battista : Venere nostra/ SC/ z/ 84.5x26.5x26/ UN, Esposizione Nazionale del 1877/ Inv. #/ IT/ R9873.1818.
1947 CARRA, Carlo: Venere/ PR/ / l/23x16,5/ Milano, SdC/ Inv.#/ Pontiggia 2004,p.77,n°82/ R3521.1819.
1965 PISTOLETTO, Michelangelo : Venere degli stracci (Venus in Rags)/ AS/ pv/ 150x280x100/ Rivoli, CMA/ Inv. n° 99.24/ Calabrese 2003, p.330/ R1049.1820.
1976 BRUNI, Bruno: La Venere annoiata/ SC/ z/ 56/ Wetzlar, GAL/ Inv.#/ Flemming 1978, p.154/ R9202. 1821.
1978 SFICO, Alfredo : Venere/ SC/ p/ 120/UN/ Inv.#/ CEDE 2001 Vol 16, p.11548/ R8649.1822.
1992 BRUNI, Bruno: Zopf der Aphrodite (*blue* Braid of Aphrodite)/ SC/ z/ 67,5x10/ Palm Desert, GAL/ IT; Mai ed. 2001, p.207 n°2/ R6814.1823.
Replica with golden braid: R9218.1824.

o **torso**

1512 CAPRIOLI, Domenico: Ritratto do giovane con statua di Venere e chiese nello sfondo/ PA/ ?/ ?/ London, PrC Duke of Grafton/ Inv.#/ Berenson 1958, p.54, pl.904/ R9612.1825.

c1520 MICHELANGELO, Buonarroti: Studi di antica statue di Venere/ DR/ d/ 20x14,7/ Firenze, CaB/ Inv. 41F-16F/ Falletti 2002, p.151, Cat.2,3/ R4308.1826.

c1520 MICHELANGELO, Buonarroti: Study of an antique statue of Venus/ DR/ d/ 25,6x18/ London, BMu/ Inv. 6-25570/ Falletti 2002, p.151, Cat.4/ R4309.1827.

c1550 (att) TIZIANO, Vecellio: Venus *(torso, with left hand before bossom)*/ PA/ oc/ 72.5x58/ Bonn, PrC/ Inv. #/ IT/ R10060.1828.

1924 GALANTE, Nicola: Natura morta-Torso di Venere allo specchio/ PA/ o/ ?/ UN/ Inv.#/ Di Genova 1994, p.922, n°1227/ R8637.1829.

1934 DREI, Ercole: Venere moderna/ SC/ m/ 147x48x40/ UN/ Inv.#/ Di Genova 1995, p.1494, n°2023/ R8696. 1830.

1970 DE LUCIA, Giuseppe: Venere/ RE/ z/ 29,5/ UN/ Inv.#/ Bononi 1973,p.122/ R9585.1831.

1975 BIZZO, Ardicia Pamela: Venere/ SC/ m/ 80x33x25/ UN/ Inv.#/ CEDE 1993 Vol 14, p.9464/ R8659.1832.

1976 PAGANO, Luisa : Venere con collana/ PA/ o/ 80x60/ UN/ Inv.#/ CELIT 1978 Vol 5, p.3389/ R8672. 1833.

1977GIULIANO, Anna: Natura morte con Venere/ PA/ ob/ 65x50/ UN/ Inv.#/ CELIT 1983 Vol 9, p.6134/ R8669.1834.

1983 VITTON, Daniele: Venere/ MM/c/ ?/ UN/ Inv.#/ CELIT 1986 Vol 11, p.7923/ R8667.1835.

1984 GULLO, Carmine : Venere di Atlante/ DR/ dr/ 70x50/ UN/ Inv.#/ CELIT 1988 Vol 12, p.8256/ R8662. 1836.

1988 FRASCOLLA, Giuseppe: Venere nera in azzurro/ PA/ oc/ 70x50/ UN/ Inv.#/ CEDE 1996 Vol 15, p.10460/ R8655.1837.

1995 RASOLA, Maria: Venere/ PA/oc/ 120x100/ UN/ Inv.#/ CEDE 1996 Vol 15, p.10793/ R8658.1838.

1997 COUTANDIN, Massimo: Venere/ PA/ oc/ 35x45/ UN/ Inv.#/ CEDE 2001 Vol 16, p.11155/ R8645.1839.

2006 BORGHI, Erica: Venus/ SC/ MM/ ?/ Bologna, AFAF/ IT/ R9230.1840.

Index of Artists

The following information is given in sequence: **SURNAME, given NAME** (other names)/dates and places (a<YEAR>=after; b<YEAR>=before; c<YEAR>=circa; b.=born; d.=dead; f.=first mentioned; l.=last mentioned; a.=active) and residences/ # of works/ topics identified in the catalogue/*comments.*

A

ABATE, Nicolo dell' / b.Modena c1509/1516 – Bologna 1530- Fontainebleau 1552- d.Fontainebleau(?) c1571/ 7/ chariot, Cupid, Mars, Paris, sleeping, toilet, Venus, Vulcan.
ABBIATI, Filippo/b. ?-c1625-d. ?/1/Aeneas.
ABONDIO, Antonio/b.Riva di Trento 1538 – d.1591/3/Cupid, toilet, Venus.
ADEMOLLO, Luigi/b. Milano 1764-d. Firenze 1849/1/Cupid.
AGRICOLA, Gioacchino/b. 1758-d.1785/1/Adonis.
AGRICOLA, Luigi/b. Roma 1759-d. 1821/2/Aeneas, Hymen.
Alari-Bonacolsi→ANTICO
ALBANI, Francesco/b.Bologna 1578-Roma 1601-d.1660/42/Adonis, birth, chariot, Cupid, cupids, Paris, toilet, Victrix, Vulcan/ *Many replicas, copies and engravings.*
ALBERTI, Cherubino/b. Borgo Sansepolcro 1533-Roma 1571-d. Roma 1615/5/
Cupid, Mars, Psyche, Venus.
ALBERTINELLI, Mariotto di Biagio di Bindo/b.1474-d.1515/1/Cupid.
Alboresi, Giacomo→COLONNA, Angelo Michele
ALCIATO, Andrea/b.Milano 1492-Bologna, Avignon, Paris-d.1550/8/Adonis, attributes, Cupid, Minerva, tortoise
ALGARDI, Alessandro/b.Bologna 1595-d.Roma 1654/2/Adonis, chariot.
Allegri, Antonio→CORREGGIO
ALLEGRINI, Francesco/b. Roma 1615,20-d.1663/1/Aeneas.
Allori, Agnolo→BRONZINO
ALLORI, Alessandro/b.Firenze1535-d.1607/14/Cupid, Jupiter, Olympus, Paris, Saturn.
AMENDOLA, Giovan Battista/ b. Episcopo di Sarno 1848-d. Napoli 1887/1/Venus.
AMIGONI, Jacopo/b.Napoli 1682-London 1730-Madrid 1747- d. 1752/ 10/ Adonis, Anadyomene, Cupid, Minerva, Paris, satyr.
AMMANNATI, Bartolomeo/b. 1511-d.1592/ 4/Cupid, Venus.
ANCILOTTI, Claudia/b. ?- a.2007-/1/attributes.
ANDERLONI, Pietro /b. S.Eufemia della Fonte 1785-d.Cabiate 1849/1/Venus.
ANDREASI, Ippolito/b. Mantova 1548-d. 1608/2/crouching, Mars.
ANGELETTI, Pietro/b.1758-d.1786/1/Minerva.
ANGELI, Marco d'(MORO dell' ANGOLO, Marco)/b. Verona 1536-d.a1586/1/Mars.
ANGELIS, Domenico de/b.1852-d.1904/2/Jupiter, Paris.
ANSALDI, Innocenzo Andrea/b.Pescia 1734 -Roma 1774-d.Pescia 1816/ 2/ Cupid, cupids.
ANTESI, G./b.?-c1750 or 1850 ?-d. ?/1/Cupid. *Engr for FRANCESCHINI.*
ANTICO, Pier Jacopo Alari Bonacolsi/ b.Mantova c1460-1528/3/ Felix, Venus.
APPIANI, Andrea/b.Milano 1754-d.1817/16/Adonis, Apollo, Hymen, Jupiter, Mars, Juno, toilet, triumph, Vulcan.
AQUILA, Pietro/b. ?-d.1692/1/Bacchus.
ARPINO, Giuseppe Cesari, detto il Cavaliere/b. Roma c1560-d.1640/1/birth.
ASPERTINI, Amico/b.Bologna 1474-Roma 1500, 1503-d.1552/5/Adonis, Felix, Genetrix, Paris, Venus.
ASPETTI, Tiziano/b.Padova 1565-d.1607/3/Cupid, Marina.
AVIBUS (OSELLA/OSELLO), Gaspar ab/b.1530-d.1583/2/rose

B

Baciccio→GAULLI, Giovanni Battista
BADALOCCHIO, Sisto/b.Parma 1585-d.Bologna 1647?/1/Mars.
BAGLIONE, Giovanni/b.Roma 1573-d.1644/*Possibly: 1/Cupid.*
BALASSI, Mario /b.1604-d.1667/1/Mars.
BALDINI, Baccio/b. c1436(?)-d. 1487/2/Planet.
BALDUCCI, detto COSCI, Giovanni/ b.?-d.1603/1/Mars.
BALESTRA, Antonio/b.Verona 1666-d.1740/3/Aeneas, Mercury.
BAMBINI, Nicolo/b.Venezia 1651-d.1738/1/Vulcan.
BANDINELLI, Baccio (Bartolommeo di Michelangelo de'Brandini/
(b.Firenze 1493-Roma 1514- d. Firenze 1560)/2/allegories, Venus.
BARATTA, Giovanni/b. Firenze 1670-d.1747/1/Cupid.
Barbarelli→GIORGIONE da Castelfranco, Giorgio
BARBARI, Jacopo de'(WALCH, Jakob; Master of the Caduceus)/b.Venezia? c1445-Nuremberg 1500-Netherlands 1505-d.c1515)/1/Mars.
BARBARO, Achille/b. 1910-d.1959/1/Paris.
BARBARO, Marcantonio/b.Venezia 1518-d.1598/1/Cupid.
BARBIERI, Domenico de, detto FIORENTINO/b.Firenze c1506-Fontainebleau 1537-d.Paris 1565/1/Mars.
Barbieri, Giovane Francesco→GUERCINO
BARDELLINO, Pietro/b.Napoli 1728-d.1806/1/Paris.
BAROZZI, Jacopo detto VIGNOLA/b.1507-d.1573/1/bath. *With many others.*
BARTOLI, Francesco /b.Roma 1670-d.c1730/1/Marina
BARTOLI, Pietro Santi/b.1635-d.1700/1/Hymen.
BARTOLINI, Lorenzo/b.Prato 1777-Paris 1799-d.Firenze 1850/6/bath, Italica, Pudica, Urbino.
BARTOLO, Francesco di/b.Catania 1826 -d.1913/1/allegories.
BARTOLOZZI, Francesco/b.Firenze c1727-Lisboa 1802-d.Lisboa 1815/10/Adonis, Cupid, cupids, Graces, Mercury, satyr, Venus.
BARZANTI, Pietro/b.1842-d.1881/4/Capitolina, crouching, Italica, Milo.
BASSANO il Vecchio, Jacopo/b.c1510-d.1592/2/Cupid, Vulcan.
BASSANO II, Francesco/b.1549-d.1592/1/Vulcan.
BASSANO, Leandro da Ponte, detto/ b.1557 Bassano del Grappa-d.1622 Venezia/1/Vulcan.
BASTIANO DA MONTALBANO, Maurizio/b. Montalbano Jonico 1955-/1/crouching.
BATACCHI, Franco/b.Treviso 1944-Venezia/2/Venus.
BATONI, Pompeo Girolamo/b.Lucca 1708-Roma 1728-d.Roma 1787/8/Cupid, Hercules, Psyche.
BATTISTA, Carlone Giovanni/b. ?-1684-d. ?)/1/Mars.
BAZZANI, A./b. ?-Carrara c1900-d.?/1/sea.
BAZZI, Giovanni Antonio, detto SODOMA /b.Vercelli 1477-Roma 1508-d.Sienna 1549/ 2/ allegories, Mars.
BEAUMONT, Claudio Francesco/b.Torino 1694-d.1766/3/Paris, triumph.
BECCAFUMI, Domenico di Giacomo di Pace, detto MECARINO/b.Montaperti 1482,86-Roma c1517-d.Siena 1551/2/Vulcan.
BELLI, Valerio/b.c1468-d.1546/1/Paris.
BELLINI, Giovanni/b.Venezia c1432-d.1516/1/attributes.
BELLUCCI, Antonio/ b.1654-d.1726/4/Cupid, cupids, Mars.
BEN/b.Napoli 1935-/2/Milo.
BENVENUTI, Pietro/b.Arezzo 1769-Roma 1782-d.Firenze 1844/1/Hercules.
BERRETONI, Niccolo/b.1637-d.1682/1/Adonis.
Berrettini →CORTONA, Pietro da

BERTANI, Giovanni Battista/ b.Mantova 1516-d.1576/1/Paris.
BERTINI, Gianni/b.1922-/1/Venus.
Bertoja, Jacopo→ZANGUIDI
BEZZI, Giovanni Francesco/ b. ?-a.c1549-d.1571/1/Adonis.
BIAGIO di ANTONIO TUCCI (da FIRENZE)/b.1446-d.1516/3/Paris, Psyche. *Also confused with Andrea Utili, Giovanni Battista Utili, Benedetto Ghirlandaio or Bertucci. In Berlin, GSM and Cambridge, FAM : (att) MASTER of the ARGONAUT Panels.*
BIANCHI, Isidoro/b.Mantova 1581-d.1662/1/Adonis.
BIANCHI BARRIVIERA, Lino/b. Montebelluna 1906-d.Acilia 1985/1/Venus.
BIENAIME, Luigi/b.1795 Carrara-d.1878 Roma/1/Venus.
BIGATTI, Tommaso/b. ?-a.1830-d. ?/3/Cupid, temple.
BIGGI, Fausto/b.?-c1880-d.?/1/Victrix.
BIGIO, Nanni di B./ b. ?-d.1568/1/Cupid.
BIGIOLI, Filippo/b.San Severino Marche 1798-d.Roma 1878/1Paris.
BILIVERTI, Giovanni/b.Firenze 1576-d.1644/6/Cupid ; satyr, Venus asleep.
BIOLLA, Gerardo/b. Torino 1939-/1/Venus.
BISI, Michele/b.Genova 1788-d.Milano 1874/1/Cupid.
BISON, Giuseppe Bernardino/ b. Palmanova, Udine 1762 - d. Milano 1844/1/Cupid.
BIZZO, Ardicia Pamela/b.Padova ?-c1975-/1/Venus.
BOCCACCINO, Camillo/b. Cremona 1504-d.1546/2/Venus asleep.
BOCCASILE, Gino /b.Bari 1901-d.Milano 1952/1/Milo.
BOCCHI, Achille/b. Bologna 1488 – d. 1562/1/Minerva.
BOLDRINI, Nicolo/b.Venezia c1510-d.c1566/1/Cupid.
Bonaccorsi→PERINO DEL VAGA
BONASONE, Giulio /b.Bologna 1488-Roma-d.c1574?)/11/Adonis, Cupid, cupids, Graces, Mars, Paris, satyr.
BONATO, Pietro/ b.1765-d.1820/1/allegory.
BONECCHI, Matteo/b.Firenze c1669-1672-d.Firenze 1756/1/Venus.
BONINI, Fabio/ b. 1965 Brescello-/1/birth.
BORDON(E), Paris/b.Treviso 1500-d.Venezia 1571/15/Adonis, Anchise, Cupid, Flora, Hymen, Mars, satyr, Venus asleep, Venus, Vulcan.
BORGHI, Erica/b. ?-a.2006-/1/Venus.
Borgnis, Pietro Maria→ZUCCHI, A.R.A.
BOSCHETTI, Benedetto/b.?-a.1850-d.?/1/Milo.
BOSCOLI, Andre/b. Firenze ? c1560-d.Roma 1608/3/birth, Cupid, toilet.
BOS(S)ELLI (BUSELLO), Orfeo/b. Roma c1600-d.Roma 1667/1/crouching.
BOSSI, Benigno/b.Arcisate 1727-d.Parma 1792)/3/Cupid, Mars.
BOTTANI, Giuseppe/b.Cremona 1717 – d.Mantova 1784/1/triumph.
BOTTI, Francesco/b.Firenze 1645-d.1711/2/Mars, Paris.
BOTTICELLI, Sandro (Alessandro di Mariano Filipepi, detto)/b.Firenze 1445-Roma 1481-d.1510/ 8/allegories, birth, cupids, Flora, Graces, Mars, Paris, Venus.
BOZZACHI, Louis/b.Milan ?-a.1902, 1909-d. ?/1/birth.
BRAGHIERI, Giancarlo/b. ?-1987-/1/Paris.
BRAMBILLA the Younger, Francesco/b.Milano 1530-d.1599/1/Venus.
BRANDI, Giacinto/b.1621-a.Roma-d.1691/2/Adonis, Mars.
BRENNA, Vicenzo/b. 1745-d.1820/2/cupids, Mars.
BRESCIA, Giovanni Antonio (Giovanantonio) da/b.?-Roma c1500-d.a1525/3/Aeneas, chariot, Venus.
BRESCIANINO, Andrea Piccinelli, detto/b.Brecia c1485-d.Firenze c1545/ 2/ cupids.
BRIOSCO, Andrea, detto RICCIO/b.Padova c1470-d.1532/4/Cupid, Vulcan.
BRONZINO, Agnolo Tori (di Cosimo Allori), detto/b.Firenze 1503-d.1572/6/Cupid, Hymen, Pudica, satyr, Saturn.

BRUCCIANI, Domenico/b.?-c1850-d.?/1/Venus.
BRUNI, Bruno/b.Granada (Pesaro) 1935-a. Germany/12/birth, Urbino, Venus.
BUGIARDINI, Giuliano di Piero/b.Firenze 1475-d.1554/1/Venus asleep.
Buonarroti→ MICHELANGELO
BUSTI, Agostino, detto Il BAMBAIA/ b.Busto Arsizio 1483-d.Milano 1548/2/Paris.

C

CADES, Giuseppe/b.Roma 1750-d.1799/1/Adonis.
CALANDRUCCI, Giacinto/b. 1646-d.1707/1/Adonis.
CALDARA da CARAVAGGIO, Polidoro/b. c1497-d.c1543/2/Cupid, Psyche. *See also ALBERTI, Cherubino, eng.*
CALIARI, Benedetto/b.Verona c1535-d.Venezia 1598/1/Cupid.
CALIARI, Carletto/b.1570-d.1596/2/Paris.
Caliari, Paolo→VERONESE
CAMASSEI, Andrea/b.Roma 1602-d.1649/1/Bacchus.
CAMBIASO, Luca (Luchetto da Genova (Cangiaso)/b.Genova 1527-d.Madrid 1585/ 36/Adonis, Cupid, dolphin, Mars, satyr, triumph, Venus.
CAMPAGNA, Girolamo/b.Verona c.1549-Venezia.c1625/8/Cupid, Venus.
CAMPAGNOLA, Domenico/b.Venezia ? 1500-d.Padova 1564/5/Paris, Venus.
CAMPAGNOLA, Giulio/b.Padova c1482-d.c1515/1/Venus.
CAMPANELLA, Angelo/b. 1746-d.1811/4/Adonis, Cupid, cupids, Graces.
CAMPI, Bernardino/b. 1521-d.1591/1/Cupid.
CAMPIGLIA, Giovanni Domenico/b.Lucca 1692-d.1768/3/Anadyomene, Medici, Venus.
CANOVA, Antonio/b.Possagno 1757-Roma c1780-d.Venezia 1822/23/Adonis, attributes, Cupid, Graces, Italica, Mars, Medici, mirror, satyr, Venus, Victrix.
CANTARINI, Simone/b.Pesaro 1612-Bologna-Roma c1639-Mantova c1642-d.Verona 1648/3/Adonis, Mars.
CAPELLAN(I), Antonio/b.Verona or Venezia b1740-d.Roma 1793/1/Venus.
CAPITELLI, Bernardino/b.1590-d.1637/1/Hymen.
CAPRIOLI/CAPRIOLO, Domenico/ b.1494-d.1528 Treviso/2/Venus.
CARACCIOLO, Battistello (Giovanni Battista)/ b.1578-d.1635/1/Adonis.
CARAGLIO, Giovanni Iacopo (Gian Giacomo)/b.Parma or Verona c1505-Roma 1520-Krakow 1527-d.Krakow or Parma 1565)/10/Adonis, Cupid, Jupiter, Mars. *Many copies known.*
CARATTONI, Francesco (or Girolamo?)/ b.Riva di Trento 1758-d.Verona c1806 (or b.Riva di Trento 1749 or c1757-d.Roma c1809)/2/Cupid, Mars.
Caravaggio, Polidoro da→CALDARA da CARRAVAGGIO
CARDI, Ludovico (detto CIGOLI)/b.Firenze 1559-d.Roma 1613/2/Adonis.
CARIANI, Giovanni Busi/ b.Venezia c1480-d.Venezia 1548/1/Venus.
CARLONE (CARLONI), Carlo Innocenzo/b.Scaria 1686-Wien 1710-Ludwigsburg-Praha-Italia 1737-d.1775/5/Adonis, Paris.
CARLONE, Giovanni Andrea/b.Genova 1584-a.Roma-d.1630/1/Cupid.
CARLONE, Giovanni Battista/b.Genova 1603-d.Torino 1677/1/Mars.
CARLONI, Marco /b.?-a.1776-d.?/1/Hymen.
CARNEO, Antonio/b. 1637-d.1692/1/Vulcan.
CARNOVALI, Giovanni, detto PICCIO/b.1804-d.1873/1/Paris.
CAROSELLI, Angelo/b.Roma 1585-d.1652/1/toilet.
CARPI, Girolamo (Sellari) da /b.Ferrara 1501-d.Ferrara 1556 or 1569/4/Anadyomene, Felix, Paris, swans.
CARPIONI, Giulio/b.Venezia 1613-d.Vicenza 1679/4/Aeneas, cupids, triumph, Vulcan.
CARRA, Carlo/b.Alexandria 1881-d.Milano 1966/2/birth, Venus.

Carraccetto→LAPIS, Gaetano
CARRACCI, Agostino/b.Bologna 1557-Roma 1594-d.Parma 1602/12/Anchises, Ceres, Cupid, dolphins, satyr, Venus, Venus asleep, Vulcan.
CARRACCI, Annibale/b.Bologna 1560-Venezia 1588-Roma 1594-d.Roma 1609/ 18/Adonis, allegories, Anchises, Bacchus, birth, Cupid, cupids, Graces, Mars, Paris, satyr, sea, toilet, Venus, Venus asleep, Vulcan.
CARRACCI, Ludovico/b.Bologna 1555-d.1619/1/Paris.
CARRIERA, Rosalba/b.Venezia 1675-Paris 1720-Modena 1723-Wien 1730-d.Venezia 1757/1/cupid.
CARUCCI, Jacopo (detto PONTORMO)/b.Empoli 1494-d.Firenze 1556/ 6/ Cupid, Venus, zodiac.
CASORATI, Felice/b. Novara 1883-d. Torino 1963/1/Venus.
CASSIOLI, Amos/b.1832-d.1891/1/sacrifice.
CASTELLO, Bernardo/ b.Genova 1557-d.1629/ 2/ Jupiter, Psyche.
CASTIGLIONE, Giovanni Benedetto, detto GRECHETTO/b. Genova c1610-d.Mantova 1665/1/Venus asleep.
CATTANEO, Danese/b.Carrara c1509-d.Padova 1572/3/Cupid, Venus.
CAVALLERI(I)S, Gianbattista (CAVALIERI)/b.Trento c1525-Roma c.1570-d.1601/3/crouching, Cupid, Venus.
CAVALO, Franco/b. Vittoria 1948-Asti-/1/Urbino.
CECCHINO da Verona/b.Verona ? c1406-Sienna 1432-Verona 1447-d.c1464/1/Paris. *Identified with Maestro del Giudizio di Paride.*
CEDINI, Costantino/b.1741-d.1811/1/Mars.
CELEBRANO, Francesco/b.Napoli 1729-d.1814/1/Adonis.
CELIO, Gaspare/ b.1571-d.1640/1/Vulcan. *Eng by MULINARI*
CERACCHI, Giuseppe/b.Roma 1751-d.Paris 1802/1/birth.
CERACCHINI, Gisberto/b. Foiano della Chiana 1889-d. Petrignano del Lago 1982/1/Venus asleep.
CEROLI, Mario/ b.1938 Castelfrentano-a.Roma-/1/Venus.
CERVELLI, Federico/b.1625-d.1700/1/Adonis.
CESARI, Giuseppe (detto Il Cavaliere d'Arpino)/b.Roma 1568-d.Roma 1640/ 3/ Adonis, Cupid, Venus.
CESARI del PALAGIO, Carlo di/b.1540-d.c1598/1/Cupid.
CESIO, Carlo (CESIUS)/b.Antrodoco c1625-Roma-d.Rieti 1686/2/Anchises, Vulcan.
CHIARI, Fabrizio/b.Roma 1621-d.1695/2/Mars, Mercury.
CHIARI, Giuseppe Bartolomeo/b. c1654 – d.1727 Roma/5/Adonis, Bacchus, cupids, rose, satyr.
CIAMPOLINI, Giovanni/b. ?-c.1550-d. ?/1/Mazarin.
Cianfanini, Giovanni→TOMMASO
CIGNANI, Carlo/b.Bologna 1628-d.Forli 1719/4/Adonis, Cupid, Paris, triumph.
CIGNAROLI, Giambettino/b.Verona 1706-d.1770/5/Olympian goddesses, Veus asleep, Vulcan.
Cigoli→CARDI, Ludovico
CINCINATO, Romulo/b.? Firenze-a.1585 Spain-d.?/3/Mars, sea, Venus.
CIPRIANI, Giovanni Battista/b.Firenze 1727-London-d.1785/3/chariot, Cupid, cupids. S*ee also engravings by BARTOLOZZI, Francesco.*
CIRCIGNANI, Niccolo, detto Il Pomarancio/ b.Pomarance, Volterra, c1517-1524 –d.1596)/2/Aeneas, Paris. *With PANDOLFI, Giannantonio*
CITTADINI, Pier Francesco/b.Milano 1616-d.Bologna 1681/1/toilet.
CLERICI, Leone/b. ?-Roma c1882-d. ?/2/bath, Callipyga.
CLOVIO, Giulio/b.1498 Grisone-d.1578/1/Vulcan.
COCCAPANI, Sigismondo/b.1583-d.1642/1/Paris.
COCHETTI, Luigi/b.Roma 1802-d.Roma 1884/1/Cupid.
CODAZZI, Viviano/ b.Bergamo 1604-Roma 1620-Napoli 1634-d.Roma 1670/1/sacrifice.
COLONNA, Angelo Michele/b.Rovenna,Como 1604-d.Bologna 1687/2/Saturn. *Collaborated with ALBORESI, Giacomo.*

COLONNA, Francesco/b. ?-Venezia c1500-d. ?/4/Paris, sacrifice, temple, Venus asleep. *The engravings are maybe not his work.*
CONCA, Sebastiano/b.Gaete 1680-d.Napoli 1764/2/Aeneas, Bacchus.
CORREGGIO, Antonio Allegri, detto/b.Modena c1489-Roma c1513-d.Modena 1534/3/birth, Mercury, satyr.
CORTONA, Pietro da, detto BERRETTINI /b.Cortona 1596- Roma 1612-Firenze 1637- d.Roma 1669/13/Aeneas, chariot, cupids, Hymen, Mars, Minerva.
COSCIA, Francesco di Lorenzo del/b. Rovezzano?-f1563-l1572-d.?/1/Juno.
COSIMO, Piero di, detto LORENZO/b.Firenze 1462-d.1521/2/Mars, Venus asleep.
COSSA, Francesco /b.Ferrara c1435-d.Bologna c1477/1/triumph.
COSTA, Giovanni (Nino)/b.Roma 1826-d. Marina di Pisa 1903/1/Venus.
COSTA, Lorenzo /b.Ferrara c1460-Bologna 1483- d.Mantova 1535/1/Felix.
COSTANTINI, Ermenegildo/b.?-a.1764,1791-d. ?/1/Vulcan.
COSTANZI, Placido /b.1702-d.1759/1/Adonis.
COTTAFAVI, Gaetano/b.?-f1837-l1864-d.?/1/temple.
COUTANDIN, Massimo/b.Pinerolo 1974-Torino-/1/Venus.
CREDI, Lorenzo di /b.c1459-Firenze-d.1537/2/Cupid, Venus.
CRESCENZI, Francesco/b. 1585-d.1648/1/Paris.
CRETI, Donato /b.Cremona 1671-d.Bologna 1749/3/Adonis, Planet.
CUNEGO, Domenico/b.Verona 1727-d.Roma 1779/1/temple.

D

DADDI, Bernardo/b.1512-Roma 1532-1550-d.1570/6/Psyche, rose. *Engraver, suggested identification with MASTER of the DIE.*
DAELLI, Filippo/b.?-c1785-d. ?/1/toilet.
DANEDI-MONTALTO, Giovanni Stefano /b.Treviglio 1612-d.Milano 1690/ 1/ Adonis.
DANTI, Vincenzo /b.Perugia 1530-d.1575/3/Anadyomene, Cupid, Venus.
DARDARONE, Giuseppe/b.? Milano- a.b1720 Palma de Mallorca-d.?/4/Adonis, Paris.
DAVID, Ludovico/b.1648-d.1728 ?/1/Paris. *Swiss but active in Roma and Venezia.*
DE ALBERTIS, Sebastiano/b. Milano1828 – d.1897/1/Cupid.
DE CAROLIS, Adolfo/b.Montefiore dell'Aso 1874-d.Roma 1928/1/Adonis.
DE CHIRICO, Giorgio/b.Volos(GR) 1888-d.Roma 1978/1/Paris.
DELEVI, Giuseppe/b. ?-c1650-d. ?/1/Marina.
DELLA BELLA, Stefano/ b. Firenze 1610-Roma 1633- Paris 1639- A'dam 1647-d.Firenze1664/8/Adonis, Cupid, garden, Jupiter, Medicis, Neptun, Paris, Vulcan.
DELPRETE, Giovanni/b.1897-d.1987/1/Paris.
DE LUCIA, Giuseppe/b. 1926-a.Brescia/1/Venus.
DE NIGRIS/b. ?-c1700,1749-d. ?/1/Mercury.
DENTE da RAVENNA, Marco/b.Ravenna 1493-Roma 1510-d.Roma 1527/ 6/ birth, dolphins, Minerva, Psyche, roses, Vulcan.
DE PAOLI, Elio/b. Pavia 1923-Torino-/1/sea.
DE ROSSI, Alessi/b. ?-c1650-d. ?/1/ birth.
DIAMANTINI, Giuseppe/b.Fossombrone 1621-d.1705/7/Adonis, Bacchus, Cupid, cupids, dolphins, Paris, Saturn.
DIANO, Giacinto/b.Pozzuoli 1731-d.Napoli 1804/1/Cupid.
DI LIONE, Andrea/ b.Napoli 1610-d.1681/1/Adonis.
DIVINI, Cipriano/b. 1618-d.1686/1/dolphin.
DIZIANI, Gaspare/b.Belluno 1689-Venezia 1710-d.1767/5/Cupid, satyr, sea, Vulcan.
Doceno→ GHERARDI, Cristofano
DODDIS, Alfredo/b. Messina 1951-/1/Mars.

DOMENICHINO, Domenico, detto ZAMPIERI/b.Bologna 1581-Roma 1602-Napoli 1631-d.1641/7/Adonis, chariot, satyr, Venus.
DOMENICO VENEZIANO, Domenico di Bartolomeo/ b.c1400-a. Firenze a1438-d.1461/ 1/ Paris.
DONATI, Enrico/b.Milano 1909-/1/Venus.
DOSIO, Giovanni Antonio/b.Firenze or San Geminiano 1533-Roma 1548-d.Roma or Napoli 1609/ 2/Felix, Paris .
DOSSI, Battista de 'Luteri/b.c1497-Ferrara-Roma 1517-d.1548/3/Cupid, cupids, Venus.
DOSSI, Dosso (Giovanni di Nicoli de'Luteri)/b.c1480,90-Ferrara-d.Mantova 1542/ 2/Cupid, Venus.
DREI, Ercole/b.Faenza 1886-d.Roma 1973/2/dolphin, Venus.
DUCCIO, Agostino di/b.1418-d.b1488/1/attributes. *See PASTI(S), Matteo de'*
DURINI, Alessandro/b. Milano 1818 – d.1892/1/Cupid.

F

FABRIANO, Gentile di Niccolo, detto/b.Fabriano c1370-Roma 1427/1/Adonis.
FABRO, Luciano/ b.Torino 1936-d.2007/ 1/birth.
FALDA, Giovanni Battista/b.1640,43-d.1678/1/fountain.
FALDONI, Giannantonio/b.Asolo 1689-d.Asolo or Roma c1770/1/Vulcan.
FANELLI, Francesco/b.1577-London 1632-d.a1641/7/Adonis, Cupid, dolphin.
FANTUZZI, Antonio/b.Bologna c1510-d.Fontainebleau a1550/4/Adonis, bath, Mars, Paris.
FARINATI (FARINATO), Paolo/b.Verona1524-d.Verona 1606/6/Adonis, Cupid, Paris.
FAURO, ?/b.?-neo-classico-d.?/1/toilet.
FERRARESI, Adriano/b.Roma 1851-d.1892/1/sea.
FERRARI, Luca/b. 1605-d.1654/1/Helen.
FERRI, Ciro/ b.1634 Roma-d.1689/1/Cupid.
FERRUCCI, Francesco di Simone/b.Fiesole1437-d.1493/1/cupids.
FIALETTI, Odoardo/b.Bologna 1573-d.Roma 1638/15/Cupid, Venus asleep.
Filipepi, Alessandro→ BOTTICELLI, Sandro
FIORENTINO, Adriano (de Giovanni de)/b. ?-Firenze 1450-d.c1499/1/Venus.
Fiorentino, Domenico→BARBIERI, Domenico de
FOGGINI, Giovanni Battista /b.Firenze 1652-Roma 1673-d.Firenze 1725/ 1/ Adonis.
FOLO, Giovanni/b.1764 Bassano del Grappa-d.1836 Roma/2/sea, Venus. *Eng for TOFANELLI.*
FONTANA, Lavinia/b.Bologna 1552-d.Roma 1614/3/Cupid, Venus.
FONTANA, Pietro/b.1762-d.1837/1/Adonis.
FONTANESI, Francesco/b.1751-d.1795/1/temple.
FONTEBASSO, Francesco/b. Venezia 1709-d. 1769/3/Paris, sea, satyr.
FORMICA, Claudia/b. Nizza Monferrata ?-c1975 ?-/1/Venus.
FRANCESCHINI, Baldassarre detto Volterrano/b. Volterra 1611- Petraia 1637-Roma 1652-d.Firenze 1689/2/Cupid.
FRANCESCHINI, Marcantonio/b.Bologna 1648-d.1729/19/Adonis, Cupid, Mars, Paris, triumph.
FRANCHI, Antonio (Lucchese)/b.Lucca 1638-d.Firenze 1709/2/cupids, temple.
FRANCHI, Pietro/b.1817-Carrara-d.1878/1/Cupid.
FRANCIA, Francesco Raibolini/b.Bologna c1450-d.1517/1/Paris.
FRANCIA, Jacopo/b. ? f1486-d.1557/2/Cupid, sacrifice.
FRANCO, Giacomo/b.Venezia 1550-d.1620/1/Mars.
FRANCO, Giovanni Battista, detto Il SEMOLEI/b. Venezia 1510?-Roma 1530- Firenze 1541-Urbino 1545-d.Venezia 1561/5/Adonis, Cupid, Mars, Paris.
FRASCOLLA, Giuseppe/b. Trinitapoli 1943-/1/Venus.
FREZZA, Giovanni Girolamo/b.1659-d.1728/1/Paris.
FUNI, Achille/b.1890-d.1973/2/Venus.
FURINI, Francesco/b. Firenze 1603-d. 1646/1/Adonis.

G

GAGLIARDI, Pietro/b.Roma 1809-d.Frascati 1890/1/triumph.
GAJONI, Antonio Luigi/b. Milano 1889-d.S.Miniato al Tedesco 1966/1/birth.
GALANTE, Nicola/b. Vasto 1883-d.Torino 1969/1/Venus.
GALEOTTI, Sebastiano/b.1675-d.1741/1/Adonis.
GALESTRUZZI, Giovanni Battista/b.Firenze c1615,19-c1650-d.a1669/7/allegories, Anadyomene, Anteros, Cupid, Marina, Mars, Victrix.
GALLI, Antonio/b.Viggiù 1811-d.Milano 1862/1/Adonis.
GALLINARI, Giacomo/b.?-fc1676-l1685-d.?/1/Cupid.
GANDOLFI, Gaetano/b.S.Matteo d.Decima 1734-d.Bologna 1802/7/Adonis, Aeneas, Cupid, triumph, Vulcan.
GANDOLFI, Ubaldo/b.S.Matteo d.Decima 1728-d.Ravenna 1781/1/Hercules.
GARGIULO, Domenico, detto MICCO SPADARO /b. Napoli 1609-d.1675/3/Anchise, satyr, toilet.
GARNERO, Enzo/b.Torino 1955-/1/Venus.
GAROFO(A)LO (TISI), Benvenuto/b.c1481-d.1559/2/Mars.
GARZI, Luigi/b.Pistoia 1638-d.Roma 1721/5/Adonis, Cupid, Paris, Vulcan.
GATTI, Oliviero/b.Piacenza 1579-l1626-d. ?/3/Aeneas, Bacchus, Paris.
GAULLI (BACICCIO) Giovanni Battista/b. Genova 1639 - d.1709 Roma/6/Adonis, Aeneas.
GEMIGNANI, Giacinto/b.1611-d.1681/1/Aeneas.
GENNARI, Benedetto I/b.1563-d.1658/1/toilet.
GENNARI, Lorenzo/b.Cento 1595-Bologna-d. Rimini c1665 or 1672/1/Cupid.
Gentile da Fabriano→FABRIANO
GENTILESCHI, Artemisia/b.Roma 1593-d.Napoli c1652/1/Venus asleep.
GENTILI, Carlo/b.1958 Tolentino-/1/Venus.
GHERARDI, Cristofano , detto Il Doceno/b.Borgo S.Sepolcro 1506-d.1556/6/Adonis, birth, Mars, sacrifice, Venus, Vulcan. *Worked together with VASARI, Giorgio.*
GHIGI, Pietro/b.?-a.1806-d.?/1/doves.
GHIRLANDAIO, Michele TOSINI, detto di Rodolfo del/b.Firenze 1503-d.1577/ 3/Cupid.
GHISI, Giorgio/b.Mantova 1520-d.1582/9/Adonis, Ceres, cupids, Mars, Paris, rose, Vulcan.
GHISI, Teodoro/b.Mantova 1536-d.1601/1/Adonis. E*ng by GHISI, Giorgio.*
GHISOLFI, Giovanni/b.c1623-d.1683/1/Paris.
GIAMBOLOGNA, Giovanni da Bologna (Jean de Boulogne), detto/b.Douai 1529- Roma 1550-d.Firenze 1608/19/Anadyomene, bath, Cesarini, crouching, Venus, Venus asleep. *Considered as an Italian artist.*
GIANI, Felice/b.S.Sebastiano Curione 1758-d.Roma 1823/6/Adonis, birth, Cupid, Diomedes, Psyche, triumph.
GIAQUINTO, Corrado/b. Molfetta 1703 –a. Madrid- d.Napoli 1766/6/Adonis, Aeneas, Vulcan.
GIMIGNANI, Giacinto/b. Pistoia 1611-d. Roma 1681/10/Adonis, Aeneas, Bacchus, Cupid, cupids, toilet.
Gigiovanni da Brescia→BRESCIA
GIGOLA, Giambattista/b.1769-d.1841/1/Mars.
GIOLITO de FERRARI, Gabriele/b. Torino?-f1536-l1578-d. ?/2/Planet, Venus.
GIORDANO, Luca/b.Napoli 1632- Firenze-Madrid-d.Napoli 1705/30/Adonis, Aeneas, Hercules, Mars, Paris, Psyche, Venus asleep, Vulcan.
GIORGIO MARTINI, Francesco di (Francesco Maurizio di Giorgio Martino Pollaiuolo)/b. Siena 1439-d.1501/2/Paris.
GIORGIONE da Castelfranco, Giorgio Barbarelli (Zorzo)/b. Castelfranco 1477-d.Venezia 1510/5/Adonis, Cupid, Paris, Venus asleep.
GIOVANNI di TOMMASO, Apollonio di/b.c1415,1417-d.1465/3/Aeneas, worship.
GIROLAMO di BENVENUTO, Giovanni del Guasta/b.Siena 1470-d.1524/ 4/ Cupid, Paris.
GIULIANI, Giovanni/b.1664-d.1744/1/Anadyomene.

GIULIANO, Anna/b.Torino ?-c1977-/1/Venus.
GRANACCI, Francesco/b.Firenze 1477-d.1543/1/Cupid.
GRASSI, Nicola Maria/b.Formeaso 1682-d.Venezia 1748/1/Vulcan.
GRASSINI, Carlo/b. ?-New York c1999-/1/Venus.
GRAZIANI, Ercole/b.1688-d.1765/1/Mercury.
Grechetto→CASTIGLIONE, Giovanni Benedetto
GRECHI LUCCHESE, Michaeli/b. Lucca c1520-Roma-d. ?/1/satyr.
GREGORI, Fernando/ b.Firenze 1743-d.1804/1/Adonis.
GRIMALDI, Giovanni Francesco, detto Il Bolognese/b.Bologna 1606-Roma c1621-Paris 1648- d.Roma 1680/3/Cupid, sacrifice, satyr.
GUALTIERO, Padovano?/b. ?-f1539-l1549-d. ?/1/Cupid.
GUARANA, Jacopo or Giacomo/b.1720-d.1808/2/Paris, triumph.
GUARDI, Francesco de'/b.Venezia b1712-d.1793/1/Paris.
GUARIENTO di ARPO/b.c1310-d.c1368/1/Planet.
GUERCINO, Giovane Francesco Barbieri, detto/b.Cento 1591-Roma-d.Bologna 1666/22/Adonis, chariot, Cupid, cupids, Mars, Saturn, sea, toilet, Venus.
GUIDI, Giovanni Citosibio/b.?- f 1628-l 1655-d.?/1/Cupid.
GULLO, Carmine/b.Lattarico 1935-Torino-/2/Venus.

H-I

HAMILTON, Gavin/b. Lanarkshire 1723-Roma 1748-d.Roma 1798/1/Paris. *Active in Roma.*
HAYEZ, Francesco/b.Venezia 1791-d.Milano 1882/1/doves.
INDIA, Bernardino (Bernardo)/b.Verona 1528-d. 1590/2/Cupid, triumph.

L

LANDINI, Taddeo/ b. c1550-d.1596/1/Paris.
LANFRANCO, Giovanni/b.Parma 1532-d.Roma 1647/1/music.
LAPIS, Gaetano, detto CARRACCETTO/b. ?-a.Roma 1770-d. ?/1/birth.
LAUDANI, Gaetano/b.Pedara 1949-/1/sacrifice.
LAURI, Filippo/b.1623-d.1694/1/Adonis.
LEONARDIS, Giacomo/b. ?-c1762-d.?/1/sacrifice.
LEONBRUNO, Lorenzo/b.1489-d.c1537/1/Vulcan.
LEONE, Andrea di/b.1596,1610-d.1685/1/Adonis.
LIBERI, Marco/b.Padova 1640-d.Venezia c1725 ?/2/Anteros, Cupid.
LIBERI, Pietro, detto Il Libertino/b.Padova 1605 ?1614 ?-Roma 1643-d.Venezia 1687/ 11/Cupid, Graces, satyr, toilet, Venus asleep.
LICINIO, Bernardino/b.Bergamo c1485-Venezia d.Venezia c1550,60/2/doves, Venus.
LIGORIO, Pirro/b.Napoli c1510-d.Ferrara 1583/1/crouching.
LIPPI, Filippino/b.Prato 1457-Roma 1488-d.Firenze 1504/1/swans.
LOCATELLI, Andrea/b.Roma 1695-d.c1741/1/Paris.
LOCATELLI, Pietro (LUCATELLI or LUCATTELLI)/b.Roma c1634-d.Roma 1710/1/Paris.
LODOLA, Marco/b.?-c2003-/1/Urbino.
LOMBARDO, Antonio/b.Venezia c1458-d.Ferrara 1516/3/Anadyomene, Marina, Venus.
LOMBARDO, Tullio/b. c1455 – d.1532/1/Venus.
LORENZETTI, Pietro/b. Sienna c1280,1285-Arezzo-Firenze-Assisi-d.1348?/1/sacrifice.
LORENZI, Battista di Domenico (di Benedetto ?), detto Battista Giovanni del Cavaliere /b.Settignano 1527,28-a.1563-d.Pisa 1594/2/bath, Cupid. *Working together with VASARI, Giorgio.*
LORENZI, Lorenzo/b.Volterra ?-a.c1775-d.?/1/toilet.
LORENZINI, Giovanni Antonio (Fra Antonio)/b.1665-d.1740/2/Adonis, cupids.
Lorenzo→COSIMO, Piero di

LOTTO, Lorenzo/b. Venezia c1480-d.Loreta 1556/3/allegories, Cupid, Venus.
LUCA, Araldo de/b.?-c1600?-d.?/1/Venus.
Lucchese→FRANCHI, Antonio
LUINI, Bernardino/b. Luino c1475-d.1532/5/Europa, Paris, Venus, Vulcan.
LUTI, Benedetto/b. Firenze 1666-Roma 1691-d.1724/4/Adonis, Cupid, Mercury.
LUZZI, Luzzio detto ROMANO/b.1528-d.1576/1/birth.

M

MACCHIETTI, Girolamo/b.Firenze 1535-d.1592/1/Adonis.
MAESTRI, Michelangelo/b.?-fb1802-d.c1812/2/Cupid, Vulcan.
MAESTRO B nel Dado/b.Malaspina c1512-Roma 1532-d.1550/ 3/ Psyche, sacrifice. *Eng for Coxie, Michiel/b. Mechelen 1499-Roma 1532,1539-d.1592.*
MAESTRO I.B. con la Colomba/b.?-1500, 1516-d. ?/1/Vulcan.
MAESTRO del GIUDIZIO di PARIDE/b.?-c1410-1460-d.?. *Also identified as → CECCHINO da Verona*
MAGGESI, Dominique Fortuné/b.Carrara 1801-d.Bordeaux 1892/1/Venus.
MAGNASCO, Allessandro, detto Il LISSANDRINO/b. Genova 1667-Milano 1678-d.1749/2/triumph, Vulcan.
MAGNAVACCHI, Walter/b.Massalombarda 1912-Ravenna-/1/Venus.
MAîTRE de la Prise de TARENTE/b. ?-c1425-d. ?/1/triumph.
MAîTRE de SAINT MARTIN (MAESTRO di SAN MARTINO alla PALMA ?)/b. ?-a.1310-35, 1360-d. ?/1/triumph. *Also known as RAINIERI or RAINERIO, RAINERIUS, RANERIO of UGOLINO/ a.Pisa 1260,1270/ Benezit 2006.*
MALFATTI, Cesare/b. ?-a.Padova 1626-d. ?/2/Graces, sea.
Malosso→TROTTI, Giovan Battista
MANARA, Milo/b.?-a.1980-/2/mirror, musician.
MANFREDI, Bartolomeo/b.Ostiano 1587-d.Roma 1620,21/1/Cupid.
MANIGLIO, Carlo/b.Soleto 1952-Torino-/1/Paris.
Mannozzi, Giovanni→SAN GIOVANNI
MANNOZZI, Vincenzo/b.Firenze 1600-d.1658/1/Mars.
MANTEGNA, Andrea di Biagio/b.Isola di Cartura 1431-d.Mantova 1506/4/Diana, Graces, Mars, Minerva.
Mantovana, Diana→SCULTORI
MARATTA/MARATTI, Carlo/b.Camerano 1625-d.Roma 1713/4/Aeneas, cupids, sacrifice, satyr.
MARCHEGIANI, Elio/b. 1929 Siracusa-a. Roma-/1/Venus.
MARCHESI, Pompeo/b.Saltrio (Co) 1783-d.Milano 1858./3/Venus.
MARCHETTI, Domenico/ b.1780-d.1844/1/Cupid.
Marchetti, Marco→MARCO da FAENZA
MARCO da FAENZA (MARCHETTI, Marco)/b.Faenza c1526-d.1588/5/bath, Cupid, sea, toilet.
MARCOLA, Marco/b.Verona 1740-d.1798/1/Hercules.
MARIANI, Carlo Maria/b.Roma 1931-/1/Venus.
MARINALI, Orazio/b.1643-d.1720/1/Paris.
MARINARI, Onorio / b.1627 Firenze-d.1715/1/Victrix.
MARINI, Antonio(?)/b.Prato 1788-d.Firenze 1861/1/birth.
MARINI, Marino/b.Pistoia 1901-d.Forte dei Marmi 1980/2/Venus.
MARMORELLI, Liborio/b. 1724,25-d.1794/1/Vulcan.
MAROTTA, Gino/b. Campobasso 1935-/1/Cupid.
MARTINI, Arturo/b.Treviso 1885-d.Vadoligure 1947/2/Venus, Victrix.
MASTER IO.FF/b.?-a.c1480-1515-d.?/1/Paris.*Various names have been proposed for this artist.*
MASTER of FLORA/b.?-Fontainebleau c1575-d.?/3/Cupid, cupids, Graces. *Suggested name: RUGGIERO de RUGGIERI.*
MASTER of PARIS/b.?-a.late 15th century-d.?/1/Paris.

MASTER of SANTO SPIRITO/b.?-a. late 15th century-d.?/1/allegory.
MASTER of the ARGONAUT Panels/ b.?-a.1468 Firenze-d.?/1/Psyche. *Also BIAGIO di ANTONIO*
MASTER of the DIE/b.?-Roma c1525-1560-d.?/11/Cupid, rose, Psyche. Engraver, suggested identification: DADDI, Bernardo, Marcantonio RAIMONDI's natural son.
MATTEIS, Paolo di/b. 1662-d. 1728/1/Aeneas.
MATTIOLI, Ludovico/b.Crevalcore 1662-d.Bologna 1747/2/allegory, cupids.
MAURO, Domenico/b.1669-d.1710/1/temple.
MAZZA, Giovanni Giuseppe/b. Bologna 1633-d. c1741/1/Venus.
Mazzola, Girolamo Francesco→PARMIGIANINO
MAZZONI, Giulio/b. Piacenza 1542,43-d.1589/2/Adonis, sea.
MAZZONI, Sebastiano/b.c1611-d.1678/1/Paris.
MEDICI, Adrian/b. ?-c2006/1/Venus.
Mecarino→ BECCAFUMI
MEHUS, Livio/b.Oudenaarde 1627-Milano c1630-d.Firenze 1691/2/Medici, toilet. *Living from early in Italy.*
Meldolla, Andrea→SCHIAVONE
MELONE, Altobello/b.? Cremona-a.1497-1517-d.?/1/Cupid.
MELONI, Francesco Antonio/b.Bologna 1676-d.Wien 1713/1/Cupid.
MEUCCI, Vincenzo/b.Firenze 1694 or 1696-Firenze-d.1766/1/Adonis.
MICHELANGELO, Buonarrotti, Michelangelo di Lodovico, detto/b.Caprese 1475-Roma 1496-d.Roma 1564/6/Cupid, Venus.
MICHELI, Parrasio/b.c1516-d.1578/3/Cupid, music.
Michieli, Andrea→VICENTINO
MIOZZO, Franco/ b.1909 Padova -d.1996/1/birth.
MIRETTO or MIRETTI, Nicolo (Zuan?)/b.Padova 1375-a.1424-d.c1450/2/Planet, zodiac.
MITELLI, Giuseppe Maria/b.Bologna 1634-d.1718/2/Aeneas, chariot.
MODENA, Nicoletto da/b.?-c1500-d.?/5/attributes, Cupid, Paris.
MODIGLIANI, Amedeo/b.Livorno 1884-Firenze 1902-Wien 1903-Paris 1906-d.1920/2/Medici, Venus.
MOLA, Pier Francesco/b.Coldrerio 1612-d.Roma 1666/3/Adonis, satyr, Vulcan.
MOLINARI, Antonio/b.1665-d.a1727/1/Adonis.
MONOGRAMMISTA CpP/b.?-c1650-d. ?/1/Mars.
MONTANARI, Giuseppe/b.Osimo 1889-d.Varese 1976/1/Paris.
MONTELATICI, Francesco, detto CECCO BRAVO/b.Firenze 1601-d.1661/1/Cupid.
MONTELLA, Vincenzo/b. Benevento 1952-Napoli-/2/Milo.
MONTEMEZZANO, Francesco/b.c1540-d.c1602/1/cupids.
MONTI, Gaetano/b. Ravenna 1776 – d. Milano 1847/1/Adonis.
MONTI, Niccolo/b.Pistoia 1780 or '83-d.Cortona 1853/1/Cupid.
MONTRONE, Vincenzo/b.?-a.1974-/1/Venus.
MORO, Giulio del/b.1555-d.a1615/1/Adonis.
Moro dell'Angelo, Marco→ANGELI, Marco d'
MOSCA, Francesco (MOSCHINI, detto)/b.Firenze? c1527-d.Pisa 1578/1/Cupid.
Moschini→MOSCA
MULINARI, Stefano/b.Firenze c1741-d.c1790,1795/3/Mars, toilet, Vulcan.
Musi, Agostino→VENEZIANO
MUSSINI, Cesare/b.1804 Berlin-d.Lucca 1874/1/triumph.

N-O

NARDO, Mariotto di/ b.?-f.1394-1431-d.?/1/Graces.
NEGRO, Roberto (Groven)/b.Torino 1955-/1/Venus.
NELLI, Nicolo/b.c1530-d. ?/1/Adonis.
NIGRONE, Giovanni Antonio/b. ?-a.1575-1608-d. ?/5/Bacchus, Cupid, cupids, Paris.

NOCCHI, Bernardino/b Lucca, 1741; d ?Rome, 1812/1/sea. *(eng by FOLO, G.).*
NOVELLI, Pietro Antonio/b.1729-d. 1804/2/Cupid, Psyche.
NUNZIANTE, Antonio/b. ?-a.2006-/1/temple.
OGGIONO, Marco d'/b.c1467-d.1524/1/Venus.
ORONZIO, Lelli/b. ?-c1894-d. ?/1/Venus.
ORSI, Lelio/b.Novellara 1511-d.1587/3/Cupid, toilet, Vulcan.
Osella/Osello→AVIBUS, Gaspar
OTTAVIANNI, Giovanni/b. 1735 – d.1808/1/Mars.

P

Pacecco, Francesco→ROSA
PACETTI, Camillo/b. Roma 1758 – d. Milano 1822/1/Cupid.
Padovanino, Alessandro→VAROTARI
PAGANO, Luisa/b. Voghera 1895-d. ?/1/Venus.
PAGGI, Giovanni Battista/b.Genova 1554-Firenze-d.Genova 1627/2/Cupid.
PALLADIO, Andrea/b.1508-d.1580/1/temple.
PALMA Il GIOVANE, Jacopo Negretti, detto/b. Venezia 1544-Roma 1567-d.Venezia 1628/11/Adonis, Cupid, Graces, Mars, Paris, satyr, toilet, Vulcan.
PALMA Il VECCHIO, Jacopo Negretti, detto/b.Bergamo c1480-d.Venezia 1528/ 6/Cupid, Mars, Venus.
PALUMBA, Giovanni Battista/b ?-c1500-1525-d. ?/1/Vulcan. *Also known as MASTER IB with the Bird.*
PALUMBO, Onofrio/b. ?-a.1650-d. ?/1/Adonis.
PAMPALONI, Luigi/b.Firenze 1783 or '91-d.1847/1/Venus.
PANDOLFI, Giannantonio : *with CIRCIGNANI, Niccolo*
PANDOLFINI, Emanuele/b. Palermo 1929-/2/birth.
PAN(N)INI, Giovanni Paolo/b. Piacenza 1691-Roma-d.1765/1/Callipyga.
PAOLINI, Giulio/b. Genova 1940-/3/Medici, Mars.
PAOLO, Giovanni di/b.Sienna 1399-d.1482/1/Paris.
PARENTINO, Bernardo/ b.1437-d.1531/1/Cupid.
PARIGI, Giulio/b.1571-d.1635/1/Paris.
Paris Master →MASTER of PARIS
PARISI, Carlo/b.Cava de'Tirreni 1924-d. Milano 1961/2/Callipyga, Venus.
PARMIGGIANI, Claudio/b.1943-/1/Capitolina.
PARMIGIANINO, Girolamo Francesco Maria MAZZOLA, detto/b. Parma 1503-Roma 1524-d.Castelmaggiore 1540/ 15/ bath, chariot, Cupid, cupids, Jupiter, Mars, Venus asleep, Vulcan.
PARODI, Domenico/ b.1668-d. 1740/1/Bacchus.
PARODI, Filippo/ b.1630-d.1702/1/Venus.
PASQUALINI, Giovanni Battista/b.Cento 1585-l1634-d. ?/1/Adonis.
PASSAROTTI, Bartolomeo/b.1529-d.1592/1/Adonis.
PASTI(S), Matteo di Andrea/b.Verona c1420-d.Rimini a1467/1/chariot.
PAZZI, Antonio/b.Firenze 1706-d.a1766 or'68/1/Marina.
PECHEUX, Lorenzo/b. Lyon 1729-Roma 1753-d.Torino 1821/1/Venus.
PEDRETTI, Giuseppe Carlo/b.Bologna 1679-d.1778/1/Cupid.
PEDRINI, Filippo/b.1758-d.1844/2/Graces, triumph.
PEDRO, Francesco del/b.1749-d.1806/2/chariot, Paris.
PELAGI, Pelagio/b.1775-d.1860/1/birth.
PELLEGRINI, Carlo/b.Carrara 1605-d.1649/1/Mars.
PELLEGRINI, Domenico/b.Galliera 1759-Venezia-Roma London 1792-Lisboa-d.Roma 1840/2/ Adonis, Cupid.
PELLEGRINI, Giovanni Antonio/b.1675-d.1741/ 8/ Adonis, Cupid, Paris, satyr, triumph.
Pennacchi, Girolamo→TREVISO

PENNI, Giovanni Francesco/b.c1496-d.a1528/2/Vulcan.
PENNI, Lorenzo/b. ?-fl551-d. ?/1/Adonis. *Son of Luca PENNI.*
PENNI, Luca/b. Firenze 1500,04-d.Paris 1556/ 1/Paris. *Copies known.*
PERINO DEL VAGA, Pietro (Piero di Giovanni) Bonaccorsi (Piero de'Ceri), detto/b.Firenze 1501-Roma 1517- Genova 1527-d. Roma 1547/ 15/Adonis, Cupid, Paris, Psyche, Venus, Vulcan.
PERO(A)I, Giovanni Battista & Francesco & Stefano/b. ? Genova-a.1569-1623 Spain-d. ?/2/Adonis, sea.
PERUGINO, Pietro Vannucci, detto/b. Perugia 1445,50-d.1523/1/chariot.
PERUZZI (Perucci), Baldassare Tommaso/b.Sienna 1481-d. Roma 1536/5/Cupid, Jupiter, Paris, zodiac.
PERUZZINI, Domenico/b.Pesaro 1601 or '02- d.Ancona a1671/1/Vulcan.
PETAZZI, Elio/b.Varese 1912-/1/Paris.
PETERZANO, Simone/b.Bergamo c1540-d. Milano c1596/1/satyr.
PIAMONTINI, Giuseppe/b. Firenze 1663-d.1744/2/Cupid.
PIAZZETTA, Giambattista/b. Venezia 1682-d.1754/3/chariot, Mars.
Piccinelli, Andrea→ BRESCIANINO
PICCINI, Jacopo (Giacomo?)/b.1617-d.c1669/2/Cupid, Venus.
Piccio, Giovanni→CARNOVALI
PIETRI, Pietro di (de' or da)/b.1663-d.1708/5/Psyche.
PIGNATELLI, Luca/b.1962-/1/Venus.
PIGNONE/PIGNONI, Simone/b.1614-d.1698/2/Jupiter, Mars.
PINELLI, Batolomeo/b.Roma 1781-d.1835/4/Aeneas, Cupid, Jupiter.
PINTUCCI, Niccolo/b. ?-c1740-d. ?/1/cupids.
PINTO(U)RICCHIO, Bernardino di Betto, detto/b.Perugia 1454-d.Sienna 1513/3/Cupid, Paris, planet.
PIOLA, Domenico/b. Genova 1627-d.1703/4/ Bacchus, Cupid, Hercules, Vulcan.
PIOMBO, Sebastiano Luciani, detto Sebastiano del/b. Venezia c1485-Roma 1511-d. Roma 1547/3/Adonis, Cupid, zodiac.
Pippi, Giulio→ROMANO, Giulio
PIRANESI, Francesco/b.Roma 1758-d.Paris 1810/1/Callipyga.
PIRANESI, Giovanni Battista/b. Maiano di Mestre 1720-d.Roma 1778/2/temple.
PIROLI, Tommaso/b.1752-d.1824/3/Helen, Mars.
PISANELLO, Antonio di Puccio di Giovanni (Vittore Pisano), detto/b.Pisa c1380- Verona c1400-Venezia 1409-Mantova 1422-Roma 1426-d.Mantova ? c1455)/5/Adonis, birth, Venus.
PISANI, Giovanni/b.Pisa c1248-d.Sienna c1314/1/Capitolina.
PISANI, Giovanni & Brothers/b. ?-a.1816-d.?/1/Italica.
PISANI, Louis/b. ?-c1850-d. ?/1/Cupid.
PISANO, Andrea (da Pontedera)/b.Pontedera c1295-Firenze 1330-Pisa 1343-d.Orvieto a1348/1/Planet.
PISTOLETTO, Michelangelo/b.Biella 1933-/1/Venus.
PITTONI, Giambattista/b.Venezia 1687-d.1767/1/ Mars.
PO, Pietro del/b.Palermo 1610-d.Napoli 1692/1/Vulcan.
POCK, Giovanni/b. Starno 1780 –d. 1842 Milano/1/Venus asleep.
PODESTA, Giovanni Andrea/b.Genova c1608-Roma c1630-d. c1674/2/Adonis, cupids, sacrifice.
PODESTI, Francesco/b. Ancona 1800-d. Roma 1895/6/birth, Paris, sea, toilet, triumph.
POLIDORO da LANCIANO, Polidoro de Renzi, detto /b.Lanciano 1515-d.Venezia 1565/1/Venus asleep.
POLLAI(JU)OLO, Antonio Benci/ b.Firenze c1431-d.Roma 1498/1/Mars.
Pomarancio→ CIRCIGNANI, Niccolo
POMEDELLI(O), Giovanni Maria/b. Villafranca d'Asti c1478-Verona-d.c1537,42/1/Venus.
POMPIGNOLI, Luigo/b.1800-d.1840/1/Cupid.
Pontormo→CARUCCI, Jacopo
PONZONI, Matteo/b.1583-d. a1663/1/Cupid.

PORDENONE, (Giovanni?) Antonio (Licinio?) de Sacchis/b.Pordenone c1484-d.Ferrara 1539/2/Cupid, Mars.
PORTA, Fra Bartolommeo della/b.1472-d.1517/ 2/crouching, sacrifice.
PORTA, Guglielmo della/b.Como c1500-Roma 1537-d.Roma 1577/3/Adonis, Mars, Medici.
POZZI, Stefano/b.Roma 1707-d.1768/1/toilet.
PRADELLA, Vinicius/b.Verona 1926-S.America 1951-Verona 1971-/1/temple.
PRAMPOLINI, Enrico/b.Modena 1894-d.Roma 1956/1/Venus.
PREDIS, Cristoforo de/b. Modena ? c1440-d. Milano c1486/2/Planet.
PRIMATICCIO, Francesco/b.Bologna 1504-Mantova 1526-Fontainebleau 1532-d.Paris 1570/16/ Adonis, Cupid, cupids, Graces, Knidos, Mars, Pluto, Psyche, Vulcan, zodiac. *Many copies were made by others.*
PROCACCINI(O), Camillo/b.c1555-d.1629/1/Paris.
PROCACCINI(O), Giulio Cesare/b. Bologna 1574-d.Milano 1625/1/crouching.
PUGI, G?/b.?-f1900-d.?/2/Cupid, Italica.
PU(I)P(P)INI, Biagio dalle Lame, detto/b.1511-Bologna 1530,40-d.1575/2/Adonis, Vulcan.

Q-R

QUADRONE, Giovan Battista/b. Mondovi 1844-d.Torino 1898/1/Paris.
RAFFAELLO, Sanzio (Santi)/b. Urbino 1483-Roma 1507-d. Roma 1520/ 25/Adonis, birth, Cupid, Minerva, Paris, Psyche, Pudica, toilet, Venus, Vulcan.
Raibolini →FRANCIA
RAIMONDI, Marcantonio/b.Bologna c1480-Venezia 1506-Roma 1510-d.1527,34/27/ Adonis, Aeneas, Anadyomene, bath, birth, Cupid, Mars, Mazarin, Paris, rose , triumph, Venus, Vulcan.
RASOLA, Maria/b. Roma ?-c1995-/1/Venus.
REGONA, Antonio/ b. Bassano 1760-d.1853/1/allegory.
RENI, Guido/b.Calvenzano 1575-d. Bologna 1642/5/Bacchus, Cupid, toilet.
RHO, Manlio/b.Como 1901-d.1957/1/Venus.
RIBERA, Jusepe de, detto Il Spagnoletto/b.Jàtiva 1591-Roma 1615-d.Napoli 1652/2/Adonis. *Born in Spain, but working in Italy.*
Ricamatore →UDINE, Giovanni da
RICCI, Marco/b.1676-d.1729/2/Cupid, triumph.
RICCI, Sebastiano/b.Belluno 1659-d.Venezia 1734/27/Adonis, Cupid, cupids, Graces, Mars, Pygmalion, satyr, triumph, Vulcan.
RICCIARELLI da Volterra, Daniele/ b.Volterra b1509-d.Roma 1566 /2/Cupid, cupids.
Riccio, Andrea→BRIOSCO
RIGHETTI, Francesco/b.1749-d.1819/1/Medici.
RIZZO, Vincenzo/b.Catania 1941-/1/Venus.
ROBAZZA, Benedetto/ b.1934 Roma-/1/Venus.
ROBERTI, Ercole (d'Antonio dei Roberti Grandi)/b. Ferrara c1450-d.1496/1/Mars.
ROBETTA, Christofano di Michele Martini/b.Firenze b1462-d.a1534/2/cupids, Hercules.
ROBIGLIARD, Vincenzo/b. ?-a. Wörlitz 1770,1771-d. ?/1/Bacchus.
Robusti→TINTORETTOROCCA, Michele/ b. 1666 Parma, d. c1751, Venezia/2/Adonis, Mars.
ROCCATAGLIATA, Niccolo/b. Genova 1539-Venezia 1593-d.1636/3/Cupid, Venus.
ROMANELLI, Giovanni Francesco/b.Viterbo 1610-d.Viterbo 1662/7/Adonis, Aeneas, birth, chariot, cupids, Mars, Venus.
ROMANELLI, Pasquale/b.Firenze 1812-d.1887/2/Cupid.
ROMANINO, Girolamo di Romano, detto/b. c1484,87 Brescia– d.a1562/2/Cupid, cupids.
ROMANO, Giulio PIPPI, detto/b.Roma 1492,1499-d.Mantova 1546/28/Adonis, birth, Cupid, cupids, Mars, Paris, Psyche, sacrifice, Venus, Victrix, Vulcan.
ROSA, Francesco de, detto PACECCO/b.Napoli 1607-d.1656/2/Adonis, Paris.
ROSASPINA, Francesco/b.Rimini 1762-d.Bologna 1842/2/Cupid.

Rossi→SALVIATI, Francesco
ROSSI, Mariano/b.Sciaccia 1731-Roma 1750-d.1807/1/Adonis.
ROSSO FIORENTINO, Giovanno Battista Rosso, detto/b.Firenze 1495-Roma 1524-Fontainebleau 1530-d.1540/7/Adonis, Bacchus, birth, chariot, Cupid, Mars.
ROTA, Martino (Kolunic-Rota, Martin)/b.Sebenico c1520 or 1532-d.Wien 1582/1/Adonis.
ROTARI, Pietro/b.Venezia 1707-d.1762/1/Aeneas.
RUGGERI, Antonio Maria/b. ?-c1700-d. ?/1/attributes.
RUSCA, Bartolomeo/ b.1680-a.Madrid-d.1745/2/ Aeneas, Vulcan.
RUSCHI, Francesco/ b.Roma c1600-d.Treviso 1661/2/Adonis.
RUSCONI, Camillo/b. 1658-d.1728/1/Cupid.

S

SALVIATI, Francesco (Cecchino del Francesco de'Rossi, detto)/b.Firenze 1510-d. Roma 1563/4/bath, Cupid, Saturn, Vulcan.
SAN GIOVANNI, Giovanni (Mannozzi) da/b. San Giovanni Valdarno 1592-d.Firenze 1636/5/allegories, Cupid, Paris.
SANSOVINO, Jacopo Tatti, detto/ b.Firenze 1486-Roma 1506-Venezia 1527-d.Venezia 1570/1/Cupid.
SANTI, Giuseppe/ b. Bologna 1761 -d.Ferrara 1825/2/Cupid, Mars.
Santi, Raffaello→RAFFAELLO
SANTINI, Amilcare/b. 1910 Firenze-d. 1975/1/crouching. *Developed the process of combining marble, alabaster and resin for making popular copies.*
SANUTO, Giulio (SANNUTUS)/b.?-Venezia f1540, l1580-d.?/1/Adonis.
Sanzio, Raffaello→RAFFAELLO
SARACENI, Carlo/b.Venezia 1580-d.Roma 1620/2/Mars.
SAVINIO, Alberto (De Chirico, Andrea)/b. Athene 1891-Paris 1910-Ferrara 1917-d.Roma 1952/12/Aeneas, birth, Paris, Venus.
SAVOLDO, Giovanni Gerolamo/ b. Brescia c1480-d.Venezia a1548/1/Venus asleep.
SAVONANZI, Emilio/b.Bologna 1580-Roma 1620-d.Camerino 1660/1/Adonis.
SBISA, Carlo/b.Trieste 1899-d.1964/1/Venus.
SCACCIATI, Andrea/b. Firenze 1726-d.1771/1/Adonis.
SCARAMUCCIA, Luigi Pellegrino, detto Il Perugino/b. 1616-Milano 1680/2/Adonis, Vulcan.
SCARSELLINO, Ippolito Scarsella, detto Lo/b. Ferrara c1550-d.1620/4/Adonis, bath, Cupid, Paris.
SCHIAVO, Paolo (Paolo di STEFANO BADALONI)/b.1397-d.1478/1/Cupid.
SCHIAVONE, Andrea Meldolla, detto/ b.1522 Dalmata-d.1563 Venezia/9/Adonis, bath, dolphins, Paris, Vulcan.
SCHIAVONI, Natale /b.1777-d.1858/1/Venus.
SCIUTI, Giuseppe/b. Catania 1834-d. Roma 1911/ 1/ temple.
SCORZA, Sinibaldo/b.Voltaggio 1589-d.Genova 1631/1/Apollo.
SCULTORI, Diana, detto MANTOVANA/b. Mantova 1547-d.Roma 1612/1/Psyche.
SCULTORI, Giovan Battista/b. Mantova 1503-d.1575/2/Mars.
Sebastiano del Piombo→PIOMBO
SEGANTINI, Giovanni/b.1858-d.1899/1/Venus.
SELLAIO, Jacopo del/b.c1441 Firenze-d.1493/4/Psyche.
SEMINO, Andrea/b. Genova c1526-d.1594/2/Cupid, Mars. . *Collaborated with his brother Ottavio (c1520-1604).*
SEMINTENDI da PRATO, Arrigo/b. ?-a.1350-d. ?/1/Adonis.
SERANGELI, Gioacchino Giuseppe/b.Roma 1768-d. Torino 1852/3/Cupid, Graces.
SERBALDI da PESCIA, Pier Maria/b.c1455-d.c1520/1/Cupid.
Sermoneta→SICIOLANTE, Girolamo
SESTO, Cesare da, detto Il Milanese/b. Sesso Callende 1477-d.Milano 1523/1/Adonis.
SFICCO, Alfredo/b. Polla 1907-Torino-d.?/1/Venus.

SICIOLANTE, Girolamo, detto SERMONETA/b.Sermoneta 1521-d.Roma 1580/1/tortoise.
Simolei→FRANCO, Battista
SIRANI, Elisabetta/b.1638-d.1665/2/Cupid, cupids.
SIRONI, Mario/b.Sassari 1885-d.Milano 1961/2/Venus.
SOCRATE, Carlo/ b.Mezzana Bigli 1889-d. Roma 1967/1/Venus asleep.
Sodoma→BAZZI
SO(E)NS, Giovanni/b. s'Hertogenbosch c1547-d.Parma 1611,1614/1/Mars
SOLDANI-BENZI, Massimiliano/b.Montevarchi 1656-Roma 1678-Firenze 1682-d.Galatrona 1740/7/Adonis, Cupid, Medici, Paris.
SOLIMENA, Francesco/b.Canale di Serino 1657-d. Napoli 1747/2/Vulcan.
SPINAZZI, Innicenzo/b.1726-d.1798/1/Medici.
SPINOCCIA, Pippo/b. Siracusa 1928-/1/Venus.
SPRINGOLO, Nino/b. ?-a.1972-/1/Urbino.
STANGALINO, Laura/b. Vigevano ?-a.1997-/1/attributes.
STRADA, Jacopo/ b.Mantova 1515-d.Wien 1588/3/Genetrix, Medici, Pudica.
SUSINI, Antonio (del SUSINA)/b.?-a.Firenze 1572-d.1624/3/Callipyga, Cesarini, crouching.
SUSINI, Giovanni Francesco (Gianfrancesco)/b.Firenze 1585-d.1653/4/crouching, Cupid.

T

TADOLINI, Adamo/b.Bologna 1788-Roma 1813-d. Roma 1868/1/Victrix.
TASSI, Agostino/ b. c1579-d.1644/1/Adonis.
Tatti, Jacopo→SANSOVINO
TEMPESTA, Antonio/b. Firenze 1555-d. Roma 1630/7/Adonis, Aeneas, Genetrix, Mars, Pluto.
TENERANI, Pietro/b. Torano 1789-d.Roma 1869/1/Cupid.
TESTA, Pietro, detto Il LUCCHESINO/b.Lucca 1612-Roma 1629-d.1650/9/Adonis, Aeneas, allegories, garden.
TIBALDI, Pellegrino, detto Il Pellegrini/b.Como 1527-d.Milano 1596/1/Minerva.
TIEPOLO, Giambattista/b.Venezia 1696-Würzburg 1750-Madrid 1762-d. Madrid 1770/20/Adonis, Aeneas, Apollo, attributes, Cupid, Mars, Olympian goddesses, Saturn, triumph, Venus asleep, Vulcan.
TIEPOLO, Giandomenico/b.Venezia 1727-Würzburg 1750-Madrid 1762-Venezia 1770-d.1804/2/Saturn, Vulcan.
TIEPOLO, Lorenzo/b.Venezia 1736-Würzburg 1750-Madrid 1762-d.1776/1/triumph.
TINTORETTO, Domenico Robusti, detto/b.Venezia 1560-d.1635/2/Adonis, Cupid.
TINTORETTO, Jacopo Robusti, detto/b.Venezia 1518-d.1594/9/Adonis, Bacchus, Cupid, Mars, Minerva, toilet, Vulcan.
Tisi, Benvenuto→GAROFALO
TITO, Ettore/b. 1859-d. 1941/1/birth.
TITO, Santi di/b.Sansepolchro 1536-d. Firenze 1603/1/Adonis.
TIZIANO, Vecellio/b. Pievi di Cadore c1488-d. Venezia 1575/35/Adonis, allegories, Anadyomene, attributes, Cupid, Mars, Mercury, musician, sacrifice, satyr, Urbino, Venus, Venus asleep.
TODESCHINI, Tommaso/b.?-f1801-d.?/1/Cupid.
TOFANELLI, Stefano/b.1752-d.1812. *See FOLO, Giovanni.*
TOMMASI FERRONI, Riccardo/b.Pietrasanta 1934-/2/Cupid, Mars.
TOMMASO (? →GIOVANNI di TOMMASO)/b. ?-a15°century Firenze-d. ?/2/Adonis. *May be CIANFANINI, Giovanni/b.1462-d.1542.*
TORELLI, Lodovico/b.?-c1550-d. ?/1/Cupid.
Tosini→GHIRLANDAIO, Michele di Rodolfo del
TRABALLESI, Giuliano/b.Firenze 1725-Milano 1775-d.1812/2/Cupid, Olympian goddesses.
TREVISANI, Francesco/b.Capodistria 1656-d.Roma 1746/1/Adonis.
TREVISO, Girolamo Pennacchi (di Tommaso) da, Il Giovane/b.Treviso 1497-d.Bologna 1544/1/Venus asleep.

TROTTI, Giovan(ni) Battista, detto Malosso/b.Cremona 1555-d.Parma 1619/ *See SCACCIATTI.*
TURCHI, Alessandro/b.Verona 1578-Roma 1616-d.1650/ 4/Adonis, Cupid, satyr.

U-V

UDINE, Giovanni da (di Ricamatore)/b.Udine 1487-d.Roma 1561/3/Cupid, Mars, Paris.
USSI, Stefano/ b.1822 Firenze-d.1901/1/Cupid.
Utile da Faenza →BIAGIO di Antonio
VACCARO, Nicola/ b.Napoli 1634 -d.1709 (?)/1/Adonis.
VALADIER, Luigi/b. Roma 1726-d. 1785/1/Callipyga.
VALERIANI, Giuseppe/ b. ?-a.Russia-d.1761/1/triumph.
VALESI, Dionigi/b.?-c1750-d.?/1/Venus asleep.
VALESIO, Giovanni Luigi/b.1579 or 1583-d.1633/5/Adonis, Cupid, dolphin, Venus.
Vannucci, Pietro→PERUGINO
VANVITELLI, Luigi/b.Napoli 1700-d.Caserta 1773/2/bath, cupids.
VAROTARI, Alessandro, detto Il PADOVANINO/b. Padova 1588-d. Venezia 1649/13/Adonis, Cupid, cupids, Hymen, Mars, sacrifice, Venus asleep.
VAROTARI, Dario/b. ?-f1660-d. ?/1/Cupid. *False attribution.*
VASARI, Giorgio /b.Arezzo 1511-Firenze 1524-Roma 1531-d. Firenze 1574/10/birth, Cupid, toilet, Vulcan.
VECCHIA, Pietro della/b.1603-d.1678/2/Bacchus, Venus.
VELLANI, Francesco/b.1688-d.1768/1/Adonis.
VENDRI, Antonio da/b.c1485-d.1545/1/Paris.
VENEZIANO, Agostino Musi (De Musis)/b.Venezia 1490-d. Roma 1536,38/9/Adonis, armata, attributes, Cupid, Paris, Psyche, Vulcan.
VENTURINI, Giovanni Francesco/b.1650-d.a1710/2/bath, temple.
VENZO, Gaetano/b. Bassano 1770-d. 1843/1/satyr.
VERONESE, Bonifazio de'Pitati, detto/ b.1487 Venezia-d.1553 Venezia/1/Cupid.
VERONESE, Paolo Caliari (Paolo di Gabriele di Piero Caliari)/b.c1528-d.1588/25/Adonis, allegory, Anteros, Apollo, Cupid, Jupiter, Mars, Mercury, Saturn, satyr, toilet.
VERROCCHIO, Andrea del (di Francesco di Cione, detto)/b. Firenze 1435-d.Venezia 1488/1/Cupid.
VERSETTI, Giorgio/b. ?-c1998-/1/sea.
VIANI, Antonio Maria/b. Cremona c1555-60 – d.1629 Mantua/1/allegories.
VIANI, Domenico Maria/b. Bologna 1668-d. 1711/1/cupids.
VICENTINO, Andrea Michieli, detto il/b.Vicenza 1542-d.1617/1/Vulcan.
VICO, Enea/b.1523-Roma 1541-Firenze 1545-Venezia-Ferrara 1563-d.1567/5/Cupid, Mars, toilet, Vulcan.
VINCENZI, Mario/b. Roma 1921-/1/Venus.
VITALI, Pietro Marco/b.Venezia c1755-d.c1810/3/Adonis, attributes, satyr.
VITTON, Daniele/b.Domodossola 1963-/1/Venus.
VITTORIA, Alessandro/b.Trento 1525-d. Venezia 1608/3/Venus.
VOLTERRANI, Egi/b. Torino 1937-/1/birth.
Volterrano→FRANCESCHINI, Baldassare
VON RIEGER, Federico/b. Ingolstadt 1903-Milano-d. ?/1/birth. *Well known in Italy.*

W- Z

WAGNER, Giuseppe/b.Thalendorf 1706-Venezia 1736-d. Venezia 1786/1/Bacchus. *Disciple of Jacopo AMIGONI, eng in Venezia.*
Zampieri→DOMENICHINO
ZANGUIDI, Jacopo, detto BERTOJA/b.Parma 1544-d.Roma 1573/4/Adonis, Paris.
ZELOTTI, Gian Battista/b.Verona 1526-d.Mantova 1578/3/Adonis, Mars, Vulcan.
ZETTI, Italo/b.Milano 1913-d.1978/1/Venus.

ZOPPO, Marco/ b.Ferrara 1433-d.Venezia 1478/3/Cupid, Victrix (armata).
ZUCCARO, Federico/b.c1540 Sant'Angelo in Vado-d. 1609 Ancona/1/Mars.
ZUCCARO(I), Taddeo/b.?-c1550-d.?/1/Paris.
ZUCCHI, A.R.A./b.1726-d.1795/1/triumph. *Together with BORGNIS, Pietro Maria.*
ZUCCHI, Jacopo/b.Firenze 1541-d.1589,91/3/Adonis, Cupid, sea.
ZUGNO, Francesco/b.Venezia 1708-d.1787/1/Cupid.

Directory of Owners

The following information is given in sequence: **city name** in alphabetical order in the language(s) of the country/ country acronym/ abbreviation of the owner used in the catalogue/ name of the owner in the language of the country/ number of works/ topics identified in the catalogue.

A

Aix-en-Provence, FR/MuG/Musée Granet/1/Adonis.
Altrincham (Cheshire), UK/DM/ Dunham Massey/1/Saturn.
Amsterdam (A'dam), NL/CHR/Christie's Auctioneer/1/crouching.
RMu/Rijksmuseum/5/Cupid, Minerva, Paris, Venus.
RPK/Rijksprentenkabinet/4/Adonis, bath, Mars, rose.
SOT/Sotheby's Auctioneer/1/Adonis.
Arezzo, IT/MCV/Museo di Casa Vasari/1/Adonis.
Auckland, AU/AGa/Auckland Art Gallery/3/Adonis, crouching, Cupid.
Augsburg, DE/SGK/Staatsgallerie in der Katharin/1/Adonis.
Auxerre, FR/MAH/Musée d'Art et d'Histoire/1/Cupid.

B

Baden-Würtemberg, DE/ ScW/Schloss Wolfegg/1/Adonis.
Baltimore, USA/WAG/Walters Art Gallery/1/Adonis.
Barcelona, ES/LL/La Lonja/1/Adonis.
Bassano del Grappa, IT/MuC/Museo Civico/11/Adonis, Cupid, Graces, Italica, Mars, Medici, Victrix
Bassano Romano, IT/ViVG/Villa Vincenzo Gustiniani/3/Cupid, Psyche, toilet.
Bayonne, FR/MuB/Musée Bonnat/2/Adonis, Aeneas.
Bergamo, IT/AcC/Accademia Carrara/2/Cupid, sacrifice.
Berlin, DE/BAS/Bassenge Auctioneer/5/Adonis, Aeneas, sea, Vulcan.
GSM/Gemäldegalerie Staatliche Museen/19/ attributes, Cupid, cupids, Europa, Mars, musician, Paris, Psyche, satyr, Venus.
KSK/Kupferstichkabinett/21/Adonis, Anchise, Cupid, cupids, Felix, Mars, Paris, Saturn, toilet, Vulcan.
LS/Leo Spik Auctioneer/2/Cupid, satyr.
NSM/ Nationalgalerie Staatliche Museen/1/Italica.
Besançon, FR/MBA/Musée des Beaux-Arts/1/Adonis.
Bloomington (IN), USA/IUAM/ Indiana University Art Museum/1/Helen.
Bologna, IT/AFAF/Arte Fiera Arte First/1/Venus.
CdR/Casa di Risparmio/2/Aeneas, chariot.
MDB/Museo Davia Bargellini/1/Graces.
PaM/Palazzo Monti/1/Paris.
PNa/Pinacoteca Nazionale/6/Adonis, Cupid, Saturn, toilet.
VAT/Villa Albergati Theodoli/1/Saturn.
Bonn, DE/PrC/Private Collection/1/Venus.
Bordeaux, FR/MBA/Musée des Beaux-Arts/2/Adonis, Venus.
Borgo S. Sepolchro, IT/ViB/Villa Bufalini/1/Venus.
Boston, USA/MFA/Museum of Fine Arts/5/Aeneas, Cupid, Jupiter, Psyche.
Braunschweig, DE/HAU/Museum Herzog Anton Ulrich/8/Adonis, bath, crouching, satyr, toilet, Venus, Vulcan.

Bremen, DE/KuH/Kunsthalle/1/Marina.
Brescia, IT/ MAS/ Musei civici di Arte e Storia/2/Mars, Venus.
MuR/Museo Romano/2/Cupid, Mars.
PTM/Pinacoteca Tosio-Martinengo/1/toilet, Venus.
Brühl Köln, DE/ ScAB/ Schloss Augustusburg/1/Cupid.
Brussel-Bruxelles, BE/KMSK-MRBA/Koninklijke Musea voor Schone Kunsten-Musées Royaux des Beaux-Arts/1/Apollo.
Bucharest, RO/MNA/Museul Nat. de Artà/1/Cupid.
Budapest, HU/MFA/Museum of Fine Arts/15/Adonis, Bacchus, Cupid, cupids, Felix, Minerva, music, Pudica, satyr.
Buenos Aires, AR/MBA/Museo Nacional de Bellas Artes/1/Paris.
Burghley House (Cambridgeshire), UK/PrC/Private Collection of Marquess of Exeter/1/Adonis

C

Caen, FR/MBA/Musée des Beaux-Arts/3/Adonis, garden, Graces.
Cambridge, UK/FWM/Fitzwilliams Museum/5/Aeneas, Jupiter, musician, Psyche, Venus asleep.
PrC/ Private Collection/ 1/ Venus.
Cambridge (Boston), USA/FAM/Fogg Art Museum/9/Adonis, Aeneas, crouching, Cupid, Paris.
Canton, (Ohio) USA/MuA/Museum of Art/1/Vulcan.
Caserta, IT/PeP/Palazzo e Parco/2/bath, cupids.
Castiglione del Lago (Trasimeno), IT/PdC/Palazzo della Corgna/2/Aeneas, Paris.
CH ?, CH/PrC/Col. Patrick de Charmant/1/Adonis.
Chambéry, FR/MBA/Musée des Beaux-Arts/2/toilet, Vulcan.
Chantilly, FR/MuC/Musée Condé/5/Mars, Venus, Venus asleep.
Chapel Hill, USA/AAM/Ackland Art Museum/2/Cupid.
Chatsworth, UK/DCo/Devonshire Collection/9/Adonis, Bacchus, Cupid, cupids, Venus., Vulcan.
Cheshire, UK/DMC/Dunham Massey Collection/1/Saturn.
Chicago, USA/AIC/Art Institute of Chicago/13/Cupid, cupids, Mars, Psyche, Venus.
Christchurch, NZ/ AGTPW/Art Gallery Te Puna o Waiwhetu/1/Venus asleep.
Cincinnati, USA/ULPC/ University Library Poole Collection/1/Adonis.
Como, IT/GAL/Bassorilievo Italiano/1/Italica.
Corliano (Pi), IT/VAS/Villa Agostino della Seta/1/Cupid.
Cleveland, USA/MuA/Museum of Art/9/Adonis, bath, chariot, Paris, Venus.
Crema, IT/MCC/ Museo Civico di Crema e del Cremasco/1/Paris.
Cremona, IT/ MAP/ Museo Civico Ala Ponzone/1/Paris.
Christchurch, NZ/AGTPW/ART Gallery Te Puna o Waiw/ 1/Adonis.

D-E

Dallas, USA/MMu/Meadows Museum/1/Adonis.
Darmstadt, DE/ HLM/ Hessisches Landesmuseum/1/Adonis.
Den Haag, NL/MaH/Mauritshuis/1/musician.
NKB/Nederlands Kunstbezit/1/Mars. *Works are restituted to rightful owners.*
Denver, USA/DAM/Denver Art Museum/1/Cupid.
Dessau, DE/ScW/Schloss Wörlitz/1/Venus.
Detroit, USA/DIA/Detroit Institute of Arts/4/Aeneas, Cupid, rose, Vulcan.
Dijon, FR/MuM/Musée Mangin/1/Adonis.
Dresden, DE/KSK/Kupferstichkabinett/2/Paris, Vulcan.
SKS/Staatliche Kunstsammlungen, Gemäldegalerie/17/Adonis, attributes, Cupid, Mars, musician, Paris, satyr, Venus asleep, Vulcan
Dublin, IRL/NGI/National Gallery of Ireland/2/Cupid.
Durham, UK, TBM/ The Bowes Museum/2/Aeneas, Vulcan.

Düsseldorf, DE/KuM/Kunstmuseum/1/crouching.
Ecouen, FR/MuR/Musée de la Renaissance/ 3/Cupid, Paris.
Edenbridge, UK/PrC/Archibald Werner/1/Adonis.
Edinburgh, UK/NGS/National Gallery of Scotland/5/Adonis, Anadyomene, Mars, Medici.
El Paso, USA/MuA/Museum of Art/1/Mercury.
El Viso –Ciudad Real, ES/PaM/Palacio del Marqués/2/Adonis, Neptun.
Eton (Windsor), UK/ECL/Eton College Library/1/Marina.

F

Ferrara, IT/PaS/Palazzo Schifanoia/2/Mars, triumph.
Firenze, IT/BiR/Biblioteca Riccardiana/1/Aeneas.
BNC/Biblioteca Nazionale Centrale/2/Adonis, worship.
CaB/Casa Buonarroti//1/Venus.
GaC/Galleria Corsi/1/Mars.
GAM/Galleria d'Arte Moderna/1/sacrifice.
GdA/Galleria dell'Accademia/3/Cupid, Pudica, Urbino.
GdU/Galleria degli Uffizi/36/Adonis, Anteros, bath, birth, Cupid, cupids, Flora, Hercules, Mars, Paris, sacrifice, satyr, toilet, Venus, Venus asleep, Victrix, Vulcan.
GiB/Giardino Boboli/1/Venus.
Gip/Gipsoteca/1/Venus.
IAP/Istituto d'Arte di Porta Romana/1/Italica.
MdC/Museo del Cenacolo di Andrea del Sarto a S. Salvi/1/Adonis.
MMM/Museo Marino Marini/1/Venus.
MNB/Museo Nazionale del Bargello/9/crouching, Paris, Venus, Venus asleep.
MuB/Museo Bardini/1/Cupid.
MuH/Museo Horne/4/crouching, Cupid, Mars.
PaD/Palazzo Davanzati/1/Cupid.
PaP/Palazzo Pitti; Galleria Palatina-Museo degli Argenti/13/Adonis, Cupid, cupids, Hercules, Italica, Minerva, Paris, toilet, Vulcan.
PaV/Palazzo Vecchio/16/Adonis, Anadyomene, bath, birth, Cupid, cupids, Juno, Mars, sacrifice, sea, toilet, Venus, Vulcan.
PGC/Palazzo e Galleria Corsini/1/attributes.
PMF/Palazzo Marucelli-Fenzi/1/Cupid.
PMR/Palazzo Medici-Riccardi/1/Adonis.
PrC/Private Collections/5/Adonis, Cupid, Paris, Vulcan.
SMF/Santa Maria del Fiore/1/Planet.
UFEC/Università, Facoltà di Economia e Commercio/1/triumph.
UN/Unknown/4/birth, Cupid, cupids, Venus.
VMP/Villa Medici at Petraia/2/Anadyomene, Venus.
Fontainebleau, FR/MNC/Musée national du Château /11/Adonis, Capitolina, Cupid, Graces, Mars, Psyche, Vulcan.
Forli, IT/PrC/ Private Collection/1/cupids.
Frankfurt a/Main, DE/GAL/Wudy's Kunst und Graphik/3/Adonis.
SKI/Städelsches Kunstinstitut/5/Adonis, Aeneas, garden, Mars, Venus asleep.
LHM/Liebieghaus Museum Alter Plastik/2/crouching, Pudica.
Frascati, IT/ViF/Villa Falconieri/1/sacrifice.

G-H-K

Genève, CH/MAH/Musée d'Art et d'Histoire/1/Cupid.
VLG/Villa La Grange/1/Adonis.
Genova, IT/BaC/Banca Carige/1/Cupid

GPB/Galleria del Palazzo Bianco/2/Adonis, Cupid.
PDP/Palazzo Doria del Principe/2/Cupid, Venus.
PaRe/Palazzo Reale/2/Bacchus, Venus.
PaRo/Palazzo Rosso/4/Adonis, Cupid.
PDP/Palazzo Durazzo Pallavicini/1/Adonis.
PrC/PrivateCollections/2/Cupid, Vulcan.

Gent, BE/PrC/1/crouching.
Glasgow, UK/HMAG/Hunterian Museum and Art Gallery, University of Glasgow/*many PR.*.
GAGM/ Glasgow Art Gallery & Museum/ 1/ Paris.
ULi/University Library/1/Hymen.
Gorizia, IT/MuP/Musei Provinciali/1/Bacchus.
Göttingen, DE/KSU/Kunstsammlung der Georg-August Universität/1/Adonis.
Gravelines, FR/MDE/Musée du dessin et de l'estampe originale/1/Venus asleep.
Grenoble, FR/MdP/ Musée de Peinture/1/Venus asleep.
Guadalajara, ES/Pal/ Palacio del Infantado/3/Mars, sea, Venus.
Haarlem, NL/TMu/Teylers Museum/4/Cupid.
Hanover, USA/HMA/Hood Museum of Art/11/Cupid, garden, Helen, Mars, Neptun, Paris, temple, Vulcan.
Hildesheim, DE/Mu/Museum/1/Venus.
Houston, USA/MFA/Museum of Fine Arts/1/Italica.
Kassel, DE/SKS/Staatliche Kunstsammlung/3/Adonis, toilet, Vulcan.
Köln, DE/MAK/Museum für Angewandte Kunst/1/Venus.
WRM/Wallraf-Richartz Museum/3/attributes, dolphin, Paris.
Kopenhagen, DK/NCG/Ny Carlsberg Glyptotek/1/Adonis.
SMK/Statens Museum for Kunst/6/Cupid, Paris, rose, toilet.
Krakow, PL/WRC/Wawel Royal Castle/1/Mars.

L

Leeds, UK/CAG/City Art Gallery/1/Italica.
Lille, FR/MBA/ Musée des Beaux-Arts/ 4/Psyche, satyr.
Lisboa, PT/BNP/Biblioteca Nacional de Portugal/2/Cupid, sacrifice.
MNAC/Museu Nacional de Arte Contemporanea/1/Adonis.
PrC/Col.Ferreira Pinto-Basto/1/Saturn.
Liverpool, UK/WAG/Walker Art Gallery/1/Venus.
Ljubljana, SI/NGa/Narodna Galerija/1/Cupid.
London, UK/BON/Bonhams, Auctioneer /2/birth/toilet.
BPa/Buckingham Palace/1/Mars.

BMu/British Museum/84/Adonis, Aeneas, allegories, bath, birth, Ceres, Cupid, cupids, Felix, Genetrix, Graces, Mars, Paris, Planet, Pluto, Psyche, Venus, Victrix (armata), Vulcan.
CHo/Chiswick House/1/Cupid.
CHR/Christie's, Auctioneer/27/Adonis, Aeneas, allegories, birth, chariot, crouching, Cupid, dolphin, Mars, Medici, Mercury, Milo, satyr, temple, triumph, Venus.
CIA/Courtauld Institute of Art/4/Adonis, Cupid, toilet, Venus.
GAL/Galleries/3/Adonis, Anadyomene, cupids.
GAC/Government Art Collection/1/Victrix.
HC/Hampton Court/1/Cupid.
NGa/National Gallery/13/Adonis, Aeneas, allegory, Mars, Mercury, Minerva, sacrifice, Saturn, toilet.
PrC/Private Collections/5/Mercury, Paris, satyr, Venus.
RAA/Royal Academy of Arts/2/cupids, Graces.

RoC/Royal Collection/1/Venus asleep
SOT/Sotheby's, Auctioneer/31/Adonis, Aeneas, attributes, Bacchus, birth, Callipyga, Cupid, Marina, Mars, Milo, temple, toilet, triumph, Venus, Victrix.
VAM/Victoria & Albert Museums/17/Adonis, Anadyomene, Callipyga, Cupid, cupids, Mars, satyr, Venus, Venus asleep.
WaC/Wallace Collection/3/allegory, Cupid, cupids.
WMu/Wellington Museum/1/Cupid.
Los Angeles (LA), USA/CMA/County Museum of Art/10/Adonis, Cupid, Mars, rose, triumph, Vulcan.
JPG/J. Paul Getty Museum/11/Adonis, chariot, Cupid, Mars, Paris, triumph, Venus, Vulcan.
Lucerne, CH/FIS/Fischer, Auctioneer/1/Cupid.
Lugano, CH/PrC/Private Collection/1/Adonis.
Luxembourg, LU/MHA/Musée nationale de l'Histoire de l'Art/1/Bacchus.
Lyon, FR/BiM/Bibliothèque Municipale/4/Adonis, Aeneas, Ceres, garden.

M

Maastricht, NL/BMu/Bonnefantenmuseum/1/birth.
Macerata, IT/PaB/Palazzo Buonaccorsi/2/Vulcan.
Madrid, ES/ASF/Academia di Belle Arte San Fernando/3/Adonis, Aeneas, Cupid.
MLG/Museo Lazaro Galdiano/3/Cupid.
MNP/Museo Nacional del Prado/12/Adonis, musician, Paris, sacrifice, satyr, toilet, triumph, Venus, Vulcan.
MTB/Museo Thyssen Bornemisza/1/Mars.
PaR/Palacio Real/4/Adonis, Aeneas, Vulcan.
PaRA/ Palacio Real de Aranjuez/2/Cupid, Minerva.
Malmaison, FR/MuC/Musée du Château/1/Venus.
Mantova, IT/PaD/Palazzo Ducale/2/Paris, Vulcan.
PdT/ Palazzo del Te/10/ Mars, Paris, Psyche.
Marano di Castenaso, IT/PrC/Col. Molinari Pradelli/1/Bacchus.
Marseille,-FR/MGL/Musée Grobet-Labadié/1/Mars.
Maser (Treviso), IT/ViB/Villa Barbaro/2/Apollo, Cupid.
Melbourne, AU/SOT/Sotheby's Auctioneer/1/Cupid.
Milano, IT/BiA/Biblioteca Ambrosiana/34/Adonis, allegories, Aeneas, Anteros, attributes, birth, crouching, Cupid, Marina, Mars, Olympian goddesses, Paris, satyr, toilet, Venus asleep, Victrix, Vulcan.
CaS/Castello Sforzesco/4/Adonis, dolphins, Juno, Jupiter.
CHR/Christie's Auctioneer/1/Venus.
CRA/ Civiche Raccolte d'Arte, Casa Boschi Di Stefano/1/Venus.
CRB/Civica Raccolta Stampe A. Bertarelli/1/Venus.
FiA/Finarte Auctioneer/2/Adonis, Paris.
GAL/Gabrius Art Market; Alcole/2/Aeneas, Paris.
GAM/Galleria d'Arte Moderna/5/Apollo, Mars, Venus, Vulcan.
MMM/Museo Marino Marini/1/Venus.
PAB/Pinacoteca- Accademia di belle arti di Brera/7/Adonis, Mars, satyr, toilet, Vulcan.
PCS/ Pinacoteca del Castello Sforzesco/1/Hymen.
PiA/Pinacoteca Ambrosiana/1/triumph.
POR/Porro & Co Auctioneers/7/Adonis, Cupid, Jupiter, Mars.
PrC/Private Collections/5/Aeneas, attributes, crouching, Paris, Venus.
SdC/Sala del Collezionista/2/birth, Venus.
SOT/ Sotheby's Auctioneer/3/Bacchus, Cupid, Medici.
TaS/Teatro alla Scala/1/Venus.

VBB/Villa Belgiojoso Bonaparte/9/Adonis, Cupid, Mars, Venus.
Modena, IT/BiE/Biblioteca Estense/2/Planet.
GaE/Galleria Estense/3/Adonis, Cupid, Mars.
MMA/MODENANTIQUARIA/1/Adonis.
PrC/Private Collection/2/rose, satyr.
Molfetta, IT/PrC/Private Collection/1/Vulcan.
Montauban, FR/MuI/ Musée Ingres/1/allegory.
Monte Carlo, FR/GAL/Gabor Kekko/2/Cupid.
Montpellier, FR/MuF/Musée Fabre/1/Cupid.
UFM/ Université Faculté de Médicine/1/Cupid.
Montréal, CA/MBA/Musée des Beaux-Arts/1/Capitolina.
Moscow, RU/ACM/Arkhangelsk Cathedral Museum/1/Cupid.
PrC/Ambasciata Italiana/1/Adonis.
München, DE/APk/Alte Pinakothek/3/Adonis, Cupid, Mars.
BNM/Bayerisches Nationalmuseum/2/Adonis, toilet.
BSBi/Bayerische Staatsbibliothek/1/Mars.
HAM/Hampel Auctioneer/2/Cupid, cupids.
PrC/1/doves.
ScS/Schloss Schleissheim/1/Vulcan.
SGS/ Staatliche Graphische Sammlung/ 2/Anadyomene, Paris.

N-O

Napoli, IT/BiN/Biblioteca Nazionale/6/Bacchus, crouching, Cupid, cupids, Paris.
IOB/Istituto Suor Orsola Benincasa/2/Cupid.
MdC/Museo di Capodimonte/5/Adonis, Mars, satyr.
MSM/Museo di San Martino/1/Adonis.
PrC/Private Collection/1/Adonis.
Newcastle u/Tyne, UK/LAG/Laing Art Gallery, University/1/Adonis.
New Haven, USA/YAG/Yale University Art Gallery/2/Aeneas, birth.
New Orleans, USA/MuA/Museum of Art/1/Vulcan.
New York (NY), USA/BON/Bonhams Auctioneer/1/Cupid.
BMu/Brooklyn Museum/1/Mars.
CHM/Cooper Hewitt Museum/1/Cupid.
CHR/Christie's Auctioneer/12/Adonis, bath, Cupid, cupids, Italica, Mars, Medici, Mercury, sea, Venus, Vulcan.

GAL/Gallery Bonino/1/Venus.
MMA/Metropolitan Museum of Art/27/Adonis, Anchises, Cupid, garden, Jupiter, Mars, Medici, musician, Paris, roses, sacrifice, Saturn, Vulcan.
PML/Pierpont Morgan Library/4/Adonis, Aeneas, Cupid, sea.
PrC/ Coll.Janos Scholz; Ian Woodner; Heinemann; others/4/Adonis, Apollo, Cupid, Psyche.
PuL/Public Library/6/Anadyomene, Aeneas, Bacchus,cupids, Paris.
SOT/Sotheby's Auctioneer/20/Aeneas, Callipyga, Capitolina, Cupid, Mars, Paris, satyr, toilet, Venus, Vulcan.
Northwestern (Ill), USA/BMu/Block Museum/1/Hercules.
Novara, IT/BPN/Banca Popolare di Novara/1/Aeneas.
Nürnberg, DE/GNM/Germanisches Nationalmuseum/1/toilet.
Oberlin (Ohio), USA/AMAM/ Allen Memorial Art Museum/1/Adonis.
Omaha, USA/JAM/ Joselyn Art Museum/1/toilet.

Orléans, FR/MBA/ Musée des Beaux-Arts/1/Adonis.
Ottawa, CA/MBA-NGC/Musée des Beaux-Arts de Canada-National Gallery of Canada/8/Adonis, Aeneas, Cupid, Mars, Minerva, pudica, Saturn, Venus.
Oxford, UK/AMu/Ashmolean Museum/4/Adonis, chariot, Mazarin, pudica.
CCh/ Christ Church/ 1/ Vulcan.
BPa/Blenheim Palace/2/Medici.

P-Q

Padova, IT/ChE/Chiesa Eremitani/1/Planet.
MuC/Museo Civico/3/Adonis, Cupid, Vulcan.
PaM/Palazzo Mussato/1/Cupid.
PdR/Palazzo della Ragione/2/Planet, zodiac.
PEC/Palazzo Emo Capodilista/1/Mars.
Palermo, IT/GRS/Galleria Regionale della Sicilia/1/Adonis.
Palma de Mallorca, ES/PaCV/Palacio de Can Vivot/4/Adonis, Paris.
Palm Desert (CA), USA/GAL/ The Hart Gallery/1/Venus.
Paris, FR/BNF/Bibliothèque Nationale de France/8/attributes, birth, Cupid, cupids, Mars, Planet, Psyche.
CHR/Christie's Auctioneer/4/Adonis, Cupid, Venus.
DRO/Drouot Auctioneer/3/birth, Vulcan.
ENSBA/Ecole Nationale Supérieure des Beaux-Arts/1/Aeneas.
FoC/Fondation Custodia/1/Psyche.
MAD/Musée des Arts Décoratifs/1/Adonis.
MdC/Musée de Cluny /1/Cupid.
MdL/Musée du Louvre/114/Adonis, allegories, Anchise, Aeneas, birth, Callipyga, chariot, Cupid, cupids, dolphin, Graces, Hymen, Mars, Medicis, Minerva, Paris, Pluto, Psyche, Saturn, satyr, , toilet, triumph, Venus, Venus asleep, Victrix, Vulcan, zodiac.
PIA/Piasa Auctioneer/1/sea.
PrC/Ambassade de Peru/1/birth.
PrC/Private Collector; Flameng/2/Mars, Milo.
TAJ/Tajan Auctioneer/2/bath, Vulcan.
Parma, IT/BiP/Biblioteca Palatina/9/Cupid, Mars, toilet, Vulcan.
GaN/ Galleria Nazionale/4/Cupid, Jupiter, Paris.
PdG/Palazzo del Giardino/1/triumph.
Passadena, USA/NSAM/Norton Simon Museum of Art/1/Venus.
Pavia, IT/MuC/Musei Civici/3/Paris, Planet, Vulcan.
Perugia, IT/CdC/Collegia del Cambio/ 1/chariot.
Pescia, IT/MuC/Museo Civico/3/Aeneas, Cupid, cupids.
Philadelphia, USA/MuA/Museum of Art/4/Adonis, Cupid, Venus, Vulcan.
PrC/Col. Nelson Shanks/1/Cupid.
Piacenza, IT/GAL/Galleria d'Arte M.Ricci Oddi/1/Paris.
Pisa, IT/DUO/Duomo/1/Capitolina.
Pistoia, IT/MCR/Museo Clemente Rospigliosi/2/Adonis.
Plymouth, UK/CM&AG/City Museum & Art Gallery/1/Vulcan.
Pommersfelden, DE/ScW/Schloss Weissenstein/3/Adonis, Mercury.
Possagno, IT/CdC/Casa del Canova/13/Adonis, attributes, Cupid, Graces, Mars, mirror, satyr, Victrix.
Princeton, USA/UAM/ University Art Museum/1/Cupid.
Puerto Rico, USA/MAP/Museo de Arte de Ponce/1/Adonis.
Quimper, FR/MBA/Musée des Beaux-Arts/1/Venus.

R

Ravenna, IT/PrC/ Private Collection/1/satyr.

Rennes, FR/MBA/Musée des Beaux-Arts/5/Aeneas, Cupid, Mars, Paris, Vulcan.
Rho, IT/PrC/Col.Vittorio Sgarbi/1/Venus.
Richmond, USA/MFA/Virginia Museum of Fine Arts/1/Venus asleep.
Riggisberg, CH/AS/Abegg-Stiftung/1/Psyche.
Rimini, IT/TeM/Tempio Malatestiano/1/chariot.
Rivoli, IT/CMA/Castello Museo d'Arte/1/Venus.
Roma, IT/BAL/Biblioteca Accademia nazionale Lincei/1/Marina.
BiH/ Biblioteca Hertziana/7/Cupid, cupids, dolphin, doves, Hymen, Venus.
CdD/Camera dei Deputati/1/satyr.
CSA/Castel San Angelo/5/birth, Cupid, Mars, Psyche.
GaB/Galleria Borghese/24/Adonis, allegories, bath, Cupid, cupids, Jupiter, Paris, Psyche, satyr, toilet, Venus, Venus asleep, Victrix, Vulcan.
GaC/Galleria Colonna/2/Cupid, satyr.
GAM/Galleria nazionale d'Arte Moderna/2/temple, Venus.
GaP/Palazzo Pallavicini/4/Adonis, Cupid, Paris.
GASL/Galleria dell'Accademia di San Luca/2/Cupid, Vulcan.
GCAMC/Galleria Comunale d'Arte Moderna e Contemporanea/3/Adonis, sea, Venus.
GCi/Galleria Corsini/5/Adonis, cupids, swans, Vulcan.
GDP/Galleria Doria Pamphilj/5/Anadyomene, Mars, sacrifice, satyr, toilet.
GNB/Galleria Nazionale d'Arte Antica, Palazzo Barberini/9/Adonis, allegories, cupids, Mars, music, Venus asleep.
ING/Istituto Nazionale per la Grafica/72/Adonis, Aeneas, allegories, birth, chariot, Cupid, cupids, garden, Graces, Hymen, Jupiter, Mars, Medici, Minerva, Olympus, Paris, Psyche, roses, satyr, temples, Venus, Vulcan.
MuA/Museo Altemps/1/birth.
MuC/Musei Capitolini/4/Adonis, chariot, sacrifice, triumph.
MuV/Musei Vaticani/8/Adonis, Cupid, Paris, Planet.
PaA/ Palazzo Altieri/2/Psyche, triumph.
PaBo/Palazzo Borghese/4/Adonis, bath, birth, Minerva.
PaBr/Palazzo Braschi/18/attributes, Calipso, Cupid, Diomedes, Paris, satyr, sea, toilet, triumph, Vulcan.
PaDC/Palazzo De Carolis/1/Adonis.
PadE/Palazzo delle Esposizioni/2/satyr, toilet.
PaDP/Palazzo Doria-Pamphilj/7/Adonis, Aeneas, Bacchus, Mars.
PaFa/Palazzo Farnese/5/Adonis, allegories, Anchises, sea, Vulcan.
PaFi/Palazzo Firenze/1/sea.
PaLR/Palazzo Lante delle Rovere/3/chariot, cupids, Mars.
PaM/Palazzo Magnani/1/Venus.
PaMa/Palazzo Margherita/1/Cesarini.
PaMo/Palazzo Montecitorio/5/Adonis, Graces, Mercury, Mars..
PaQ/Palazzo Quirinale/1/Aeneas.
PaRo/Palazzo Rospigliosi Pallavicini/ 1/allegories.
PaRu/Palazzo Ruspoli/1/Vulcan.
PaS/Palazzo Spada/2/Adonis, sea.
PaSC/Palazzo Santa Croce/1/birth.
PaV/Palazzo Venezia/7/Cupid, Mars, Marina, Venere.
PrC/Confederazione d'Agricultura/1/Venus.
PrC/Crediop/1/Cupid.
PrC/?/8/Aeneas, birth.
ViF/Villa Farnesina/9/Psyche, zodiac.
ViM/Villa Medici/1/Cupid.
ViMa/Villa Madama/ 1/ cupids.

VDP/Villa Doria-Pamphilj/1/garden.
Rotterdam, NL/BBM/ Boymans-van Beuningen Museum/1/Venus.
Rouen, FR/MBA/Musée des Beaux-Arts/2/Cupid, Mars.
Rovigo, IT/PaR/Palazzo Roverella/1/Cupid.
Ruvigliano (Lugano), CH/PrC/Private Collection Heinemann/1/Pygmalion.

S-T-U

Salzburg, AT/BMu/Barockmuseum/1/Aeneas.
San Francisco(SF), USA/BON/Bonhams, Auctioneer/4/Adonis, Cupid, Mars.
FAM/Fine Art Museum/57/Adonis, Aeneas, attributes, birth, chariot, Cupid, cupids, dolphins, Genetrix, Graces, Mars, Minerva, Psyche, rose, satyr, temple, Venus, Vulcan.
San Gregorio da Sassola, IT/CaB/Castello Brancaccio/2/Adonis, Mars.
Sao Paulo, BR/MASP/Museu de Arte de Sao Paulo/ 1/Mars.
Sarasota, (FL) USA/RMA/Ringling Museum of Art/5/Cupid, Mars, Paris, satyr, Vulcan.
Savona, IT/PcC/Pinacoteca Civica/1/Mars.
Seattle, USA/AMu/Art Museum/1/Adonis.
Segovia, ES/GSI/La Granja de San Ildefonso/2/Aeneas, Vulcan.
Siena, IT/CaB/Castello Belcaro/1/Paris.
Stamford, UK/BH/Burghley House/2/Adonis, satyr.
St.Louis, USA/AMu/Art Museum/1/Minerva.
St.Petersburg, RU/HMu/Hermitage Museum/6/Adonis, chariot, Flora, Paris, Venus, Vulcan.

Stockholm, SE/BUK/Bukowski Auctioneer/1/Cupid.
NMK/National Museum for Kunst/8/Adonis, Callipyga, chariot, Cupid, cupids, Paris.
Stra (Veneto), IT/VNP/Villa Nazionale Pisani/1/Paris.
Stuttgart, DE/SGa/Staatsgalerie/6/Aeneas, Graces, Paris, satyr, toilet.
Surrey, UK/HCP/Hampton Court Palace/2/Mars, Venus.
Toledo (Ohio), USA/MuA/ Museum of Art/1/Cupid.
Torino, IT/BiR/Biblioteca Reale/1/Adonis.
GAM/ Galleria Civica d'Arte Moderna e Contemporanea/2/Venus.
GaS/Galleria Sabauda/8/chariot, Cupid, Hercules, Mars, Paris, toilet, triumph, Venus.
PaR/Palazzo Reale/2/Paris, triumph.
PrC/Private Collection/1/Adonis.
Toronto, CA/AGO/Art Gallery of Ontario/1/Medici.
Tours, FR/MBA/Musée des Beaux-Arts/1/Paris.
Trento, IT/CaB/Castello del Buonconsiglio/1/Cupid.
CRT/Cassa di Risparmio di Trento/1/doves.
Treviso, IT/MuC/Museo Civico/2/Venus, Vulcan.
Trieste, IT/CMR/Civico Museo Revoltella/1/Venus.
Troyes, FR/ MBA/Musée des Beaux-Arts/1/Paris.
Tucson, USA/UAM/University of Arizona Museum/1/Adonis.
Udine, IT/PrC/Private Collection/1/sacrifice.

V

Vaduz, LT/LMu/Liechtenstein Museum/3/Adonis, crouching, Hercules.
LSK/ Liechtensteinischen Staatlichen Kunstsammlung/ 1/ Mars.
Valenciennes, FR/MBA/Musée des Beaux-Arts/1/Cupid.
Venezia, IT/CaR/Ca' Rezzonico Museo/14/Adonis, Aeneas, Bacchus, bath, birth, Cupid, Mars, Paris, satyr.
CdO/Casa d'Oro/4/attributes, Cupid, Venus, Venus asleep.

FGC/Fondazione Giorgio Cini/13/chariot, Cupid, Hercules, Paris, satyr, temple, triumph, Venus.
FQS/Fondazione Querini Stampalia/2/Adonis, Paris.
GAM/ Galleria d'Arte Moderna di Ca' Pesaro/1/birth.
GdA/Galleria dell' Academia/2/Adonis, cupids.
MuC/Museo Correr/ 11/ Adonis, allegory, Cupid, Paris, sacrifice, triumph, Venus.
PaB/Palazzo Boldù/1/Paris.
PaD/Palazzo Ducale/3/Bacchus, Mars, Vulcan.
PaG/ Palazzo Grassi, Biennale Antiquariato SIMA/1/cupids.
PPM/Palazzo Pisano-Moretta/1/Mars.
PrC/Private Collections/2/Adonis, Cupid.
SEM/SEMENZATO, Auctioneer/3/Adonis, Mars, Paris.
SMCA/San Marco Casa d'Aste/1/Adonis.
Vercelli, IT/MFB/Museo Francesco Borgogna/1/Venus asleep.
Verona, IT/ MdC/Museo di Castelvecchio/1/Hercules.
Vez, FR/Donjon/ 1/Milo.
Vicenza, IT/MuC/Museo Civico/3/Aeneas, Graces, Paris.
PaT/Palazzo Thiene/6/Adonis, Cupid, cupids, Paris, Victrix.
VGM/Villa Godi Malinverni/1/Cupid.
ViC/Villa Caldogno/1/Vulcan.
ViV/Villa Valmarana/ 3/Aeneas, Mars, Vulcan.
Vittorio Veneto,IT/PrC/Collezione Piaia/1/Venus.

W

Washington, DC/USA/LoC/Library of Congress/1/Cupid.
NGA/National Gallery of Art/26/Aeneas, Anadyomene, attributes, birth, Cupid, dolphins, Graces, Paris, roses, Venus, Vulcan.
Weimar, DE/NMu/ Neues Museum/ 1/ Medici.
Wellesley, (Massachusetts) USA/DMCC/ Davis Museum and Cultural Center/ 1/Cupid.
Wetzlar, DE/GAL/Galerie am Dom/2/Venus.
Wien, AT/ABK/Akademie der bildenden Kunst/5/Adonis, Cupid, Mars, Paris.
ALB/Albertina/51/Adonis, Anadyomene, Bacchus, bath, birth, Cupid, cupids, dolphins, Graces, Hercules, Jupiter, Mars, Mazarin, Paris, Psyche, roses, satyr, triumph, Urania, Venus, Vulcan.
DOR/Dorotheum Auctioneers/12/Adonis, allegories, Anteros, Cupid, cupids, Paris, rose, Venus asleep, Vulcan.
GaBW/ Galery Boris Wilnitsky/1/Vulcan.
KHM/Kunsthistorisches Museum/15/Adonis, attributes, Felix, Hymen, Marina, Mars, Medici, satyr, Vulcan.
KNB/Klosterneuburg/1/Cupid..
LMu/Liechtenstein Museum/11/Adonis, Aeneas, Anadyomene, cupids, Mars, Medici, Paris, Venus.
NBi/National Bibliothek/3/ Genetrix, Medici, Pudica.
ScR/Schloss Rohrau/1/Paris.
ScS/ Schloss Schönbrunn/ 1/ satyr.
Wiesbaden, DE/PrC/Private Collection/1/Satyr.
Windsor, UK/RCo/Royal Collection/23/Adonis, birth, Cupid, Hymen, Mars, Paris, Psyche, toilet, Venus, Vulcan.
Wörlitz, DE/ScG/Schlossgarten/1/Bacchus.
Würzburg, DE/MWM/Martin von Wagner Museum der Universität/1/Cupid.

Y-Z

Yerevan, AM/NGA/National Gallery of Armenia/1/triumph.
York, UK/AGa/Art Gallery/1/Venus.
Zürich, CH/ETH/Graphische Sammlung/1/Vulcan.
GAL/Koller/1/satyr.
KuH/ Kunsthaus/1/satyr.

WEB & UNKNOWN LOCATIONS

WEB/ Absolutearts/3/Milo, Venus.
Arsmundi/3/birth, Venus.
Artabus/1/birth.
Artbrokerage/1/Venus.
Artprice/6/Adonis, bath, Italica, Mercury, Urbino, Venus.
Aspireauctions/1/Venus.
Corbis/2/Cupid, sacrifice.
eBay/6/Graces, sea, temple, Venus.
MiloManara/2/attributes, musician.
Trendart/1/Venus.
UN=unknown locations or lost or looted(LO)/Artist Collections?/80/Adonis, attributes, armata, bath, birth, Callipyga, Cupid, dolphin, Mars, Olympian goddesses, Paris, sacrifice, satyr, sea, temple, Urbino, Venus, Venus asleep.
PrC/Private Collections/32/Adonis, Aeneas, birth, Cesarini, crouching, Cupid, Graces, Mars, Paris, satyr, temple, toilet, Urbino, Venus, Venus asleep, Vulcan.

Selected Bibliography

About the meaning of Venus (Aphrodite)

Arscott C&SK (2000) Manifestations of Venus - Art and sexuality. Manchester University Press,Manchester.

Atallah W (1966) Adonis - dans la littérature et l'art grecs. Librairie C. Klincksieck,Paris.

Budin SL (2003) The Origin of Aphrodite. CDL Press,Bethesda, Maryland.

Cavallini E (2000) Il fiore del desiderio-Afrodite e il suo corteggio fra mito e letteratura. Argo,Lecce.

D'Anna G (2004) Apuleio: La favola di Amore e Psiche. Newton Compton, Roma.

Friedrich P (1978) The meaning of Aphrodite. University of Chicago Press,Chicago.

Hard R (1998) Apollodorus : The Library of Greek Mythology. Oxford University Press, Oxford.

Havelock CM (1995) The Aphrodite of Knidos and her Successors - A historical review of the female nude in Greek art. University of Michigan Press,Ann Arbor.

Hinz B (1998) Aphrodite- Geschichte einer abendländischen Passion. Carl Hanser Verlag, München.

Langlotz E (1954) Aphrodite in den Garten . Carl Winter,Heidelberg.

Leis M (2000) Mythos Aphrodite - Texte von Hesiod bis Ernst Jandl. Reclam Verlag,Leipzig.

Lucas FL (1948) Aphrodite - The Homeric Hymn to Aphrodite and The Pervigilium Veneris. University Press,Cambridge.

Paris G (1985) La renaissance d'Aphrodite. Boréal Express,Montréal

Pirenne-Delforge V (1994) L'Aphrodite grecque. Centre international d'étude de la réligion grecque antique,Athènes-Liège.

Prittwitz und Gaffron H-Hv (1988) Der Wandel der Aphrodite. Dr. Rudolf Habelt Gmbh,Bonn.

Rendel Harris J (1999) The Origin of the Cult of Aphrodite. Holmes Publishing Group,Edmonds, WA., USA.

Rudhardt J (1999) Eros e Afrodite nelle cosmogonie greche. Bollati Boringhieri,Torino.

Säflund G (1963) Aphrodite Kallipygos. Almquist & Wiksell,Stockholm.

Schilling R (1955) La réligion romaine de Vénus depuis les origines jusqu'au temps d'Auguste. E. de Boccard,Paris.

Simon E (1959) Die Geburt der Aphrodite. Walter De Gruyter & Co,Berlin.

West ML (1999) Hesiod: Theogony and Works and Days. Oxford University Press,Oxford.

Selected References

Alamillo A (2003) El juicio de Paris a través de la imagen. Universidad Completense de Madrid,Madrid.

Anonymous (1975) Storia della pittura italiana dell'ottocento. 2 Vol. Bramante editrice, Milano.

Anonymous (1989) Subject catalogue of paintings in public collections ; Vol.I London: National Gallery, Wallace Collection, Wellington Museum. Visual Arts Publ., London

Anonymous (1996) Due secoli di incisioni- Academia di Belle Arte di Brera. G.Mondadori.

Anonymous (1998) Il Seicento e Settecento Romano nella Collezione Lemme. Edizioni De Luca,sd.

Anonymous (1998) Stefano Della Bella 1610-1664. Réunion des Musées Nationaux,Paris.

Anonymous (2005) Encyclopédie de l'Art. Garzanti,Paris.

Antetomaso E&MG (2004) La Collezione del Principe da Leonardo a Goya - Disegni e stampe della raccolta Corsini. Istituto Nazionale per la Grafica, Libreria dello Stato,Roma.

Arasse D (1997) Le sujet dans le tableau. Essais d'iconographie analytique. Flammarion,Paris.

Astrua P&SCE (2000) Galleria Sabauda. Guida breve. Electa,Milano.

Avery C&HM (1999) Giambologna (1529-1608) La sculpture du Maître et de ses successeurs. Collection de Michael Hall. Essais et catalogue. Somogy Editions d'art,Paris.

Bacci M (1966) Piero di Cosimo. Bramante Ed. Milano

Bailey CB (1991) Les amours des dieux - La peinture mythologique de Watteau à David. RMN,Paris.

Baini, L (2006) BRERA - Guida alla Pinacoteca. Electa, Milano.

Baker C & Henry T Eds (2001) The National Gallery complete illustrated catalogue. London.

Bardon H (1960) Le Festin des dieux, essai sur l'humanisme dans les arts plastiques. PUF,Paris.

Bartsch 13 (7 4) (1981) Sixteenth Century Artists. Abaris Books,New York.

Bartsch 24 (13 1) (1980) Early Italian Masters.

Bartsch 24 C(Part 1) Commentary, Part 1: Early Italian Masters. 1993,

Bartsch 24 C(Part 4) (1988) German and Netherlandish Masters of the 15th-16th Century.

Bartsch 25 (13 2) (1980) Early Italian Masters.

Bartsch 25 C (13 2) (1984) Early Italian Masters.

Bartsch 26 (14 1) (1978) The works of Marcantonio Raimondi and of his school.

Bartsch 27 (14 2) (1978) The works of Marcantonio RAIMONDI and his school.

Bartsch 28 (15 1) (1985) Italian Masters of the 16th Century.

Bartsch 28 C (15 1) (1995) Italian Masters of the 16th Century.

Bartsch 29 (15 2) (1982) Italian Masters of the 16th Century.

Bartsch 30 (15 3) (1985) Italian Masters of the 16th Century. Enea VICO.

Bartsch 31 (15 4) (1986) Italian Masters of the 16th Century.

Bartsch 32 (16 1) (1979) Italian Artists of the 16th Century-School of Fontainebleau.

Bartsch 33 (16 2) (1979) Italian Artists of the 16th Century - School of Fontainebleau.

Bartsch 34 (17 1) (1982) Italian artists of the 16th century.

Bartsch 36(17 3) (1983) Antonio Tempesta. Italian Masters of the 16th century.

Bartsch 38 (17 5) (1983) Italian Masters of the 16th Century.

Bartsch 39 (18 1) (1980) Italian Masters of the 16th Century.

Bartsch 39 C Part 1 (18 1) (1995) Italian Masters of the 16th Century: Agostino CARRACCI.

Bartsch 39 C Part 2 (18 1) (1996) Italian Masters of the 16th Century: Agostino CARRACCI.

Bartsch 40 (18 2) (1982) Italian Masters of the 16th and 17th Century.

Bartsch 40 C 1(18 2 (1987) Italian Masters of the 16th and 17th Century.

Bartsch 41 (19 1) (1981) Italian Masters of the 17th Century.

Bartsch 42 (19 2) (1981) Italian Masters of the 17th Century.

Bartsch 43 (19 3) (1982) Italian Masters of the 17th Century.

Bartsch 45 (20 2) (1982) Italian Masters of the 17th Century.

Bartsch 45 C (20 2) (1990) Italian Masters of the 17th Century.

Bartsch 46 (21 1) (1982) Italian Masters of the 17 th Century.

Bartsch 46 C (1985) Italian Masters of the 17 th Century.

Bartsch 47 (21 2) (1983) Italian Masters of the 17th Century.

Bartsch 47 C P1 (22) (1987) Italian Masters of the 17th Century.

Beck H (1985) Bildwerke des Klassizismus. Führer durch die Sammlungen. Liebieghaus - Museum alter Plastik, Frankfurt a/M.

Beguin S (1989) 'New evidence for Rosso in France' Burlington Magazine 131 : 828-838.

Bellini P (1998) L'opera incisa di Giorgio Ghisi. Tassotti, Bassano del Grappa.

Benati Deal (1999) The drawings of Annibale CARRACCI. NGA,NY.

Benezit (2006) Dictionary of Artists. 14 Volumes. Gründ, Paris.

Berenson B (1938) The drawings of the Florentine painters. Chicago.

Berenson B (1958) Pitture Italiane del Rinascimento - Elenco dei principali artisti e delle loro opere con un indice dei luoghi -La Scuola Veneta in due volumi. Phaedon/Sansoni, London/Firenze.

Berenson B (1963) Italian pictures of the Renaissance florentine School I + II. Phaidon, London.

Berenson B (1967) The Italian painters of the Renaissance. Phaidon, London.

Berenson B (1968) Italian pictures of the Renaissance - Central Italian and North Italian Schools. Phaidon, London.

BIBLIOGRAPHICAL REFERENCES

Berenson Beal (1963) Palladio, Veronese and Vittoria at MASER. Aldo Martello Editore,Milano.

Berti L (1979) Gli Uffizi – Tutti le pitture esposte. Becocci, Firenze.

Bettagno A (1959) Disegni e dipinti Giovanni Antonio Pellegrini 1675-1741. Neri Pozza, Venezia.

Bettucchi N (1991) Canova all'Ermitage. Le sculture del museo di San Pietroburgo. Marsilio,Venezia.

Bisschoff U (1995) Die "Cassonebilder" des Pietro di Cosimo - Fragen der Ikonografie. Peter Lang, Frankfurt a/M.

Bjurström P (1995) Nicola Pio as collector of drawings. Svecoromana II,Stockholm.

Bjurström P (2001) Italian drawings from the collection of Giorgio Vasari. Nationalmuseum, Stockholm.

Blunt A (1971) The German drawings in the collection of Windsor Castle with supplement on Italian and French drawings. Phaidon, London.

Bober PP&RRO (1986) Renaissance artists and antique sculpture - A handbook of sources with 526 ill. Harvey Miller Publ.,London.

Boccardo P ed. (2004) L'Età di Rubens-Dimore, commitenti, e collezionisti genovesi. Skira,Milano.

Bolaffi Giulio Editore (1979) Dizionario degli artisti italiani del XX secolo. Vol I Voci bibliografiche e bibliografico-critiche di 1336 artisti. Torino.

Bonfait O Ed. (2004) La description de l'oeuvre d'art. Académie de France à Rome.

Bononi G (1973) Arte Bresciana oggi. Ed. F. Sardini, Brescia.

Borea E&GC (2000) L'idea del bello - Viaggio per Roma nel Seicento con Giovan Pietro Bellori. Edizioni de Luca.

Brugerolles E (2001) Le dessin en France au XVII° siècle dans les collections de l'Ecole des Beaux-Arts. Ecole Nationale Supérieure des Beaux-Arts,Paris.

Bury (1990) Giambologna's Fata Morgana rediscovered. Apollo, 96-100.

Calabrese O (2003) Tiziano, la Venere di Urbino. SilvanaEditoriale, Milano.

Calabrese O et al. (2003) Venus ontsluierd. De Venus van Urbino van Titiaan. Brussel: BOZAR, Snoeck/Silvana Editoriale, Gent/Milano.

Calasso R (2006) Il Rosa Tiepolo. Adelphi, Milano.

Campbell SJ (2006) The cabinet of Eros: Renaissance mythological painting and the Studiolo of Isabella d'Este. New Haven.

Canal VL (1989) 'The art collection of the ninth Duke of Medinaceli' Burlington Magazine 131 :108-115.

Caramel L (2001) Batacchi - Nova Venus Italica. Editore Mazzotta.

Casazza O&GR (2005) Mythologica et Erotica - Arte e cultura dall' antichità al XVIII secolo. Sillabe,Livorno.

Catelli Isola M (1976) Immagini da TIZIANO -Stampe del sec. XVI al sec. XIX dalle collezioni del Gabinetto Nazionale delle Stampe. De Luca, Roma.

Cavicchioli S (2002) Eros et Psyché - L'éternelle félicité de l'amour. Flammarion,Paris.

CEDE (1993-2001) Centro Editoriale Europeo. Enciclopedia « Arte Italiana per il Mondo ». Torino.

CELIT (1974-1991) Centro Librario Italiano. Enciclopedia « Arte Italiana per il Mondo ». Torino.

Chiari M (1982) Incisioni da Tiziano-catalogo del fondo grafico a stampa del Museo Correr. Venezia.

Cicinelli A & Vasco Rocca S (1978) Dipinti dei Musei e Gallerie di Roma.-Repertorio delle fotografie del Gabinetto fotografico nazionale. Roma.

Clark K (1969) Le Nu .Tome I et II. Le Livre de Poche,Paris.

Clayton M (1999) Raphael and his circle. Drawings from Windsor Castle. Merrell Holberton,London.

Contini R (1985) Bilivert, saggio di ricostruzione. Firenze.

Cordelier D&PB (1992) Inventaire général des dessins italiens au Louvre. Tome V: Raphaël, son atelier, ses copistes.Paris.

Cresti & Rendina (1998) Palazzi of Rome. Könemann, Köln.

Czére A (2002) L'Eredità Esterhazy.Disegni italiani del Seicento dal Museo di Belle Arti di Budapest. Akademiai Kiado,Budapest.

Czére A (2004) 17th Century Italian Drawings in the Budapest Museum of Fine Arts. Budapest.

Damian V (2005) Autour de Titien – Tableaux d'Italie du Nord au XVI° siècle. Galerie Canesso, Paris.

Damisch H (1997) Le jugement de Pâris.Iconologie analytique 1. Flammarion,Paris.

De Liedekerke MC et al. (1995) Fiamminghi a Roma 1508-1608. Brussel.

De Tolnay C. Sur des Vénus dessinées par Michel-Ange. Gazette Des Beaux-Arts 1967; 193-200.

De Vesme A (1971) Stefano Della Bella - Catalogue raisonné. Collectors Ed.,New York.

De Witt A (1938) La Collezione delle Stampe, Galleria degli Uffizi.Roma.

Dempsey C (2001) Inventing the Renaissance Putto. North Carolina University Press.

Di Castro D&FSP (1983) Disegni dall'antico dei secoli XVI-XVIII. Istituto per la Grafica,Roma.

Di Genova G (1990) Storia dell'arte italiana del '900. Generazione Anni Trenta. Bologna.

Di Genova G (1991) Storia dell'arte italiana del '900. Generazione Anni Venti. Bologna.

Di Genova G (1993) Storia dell'arte italiana del '900. Generazione Maestri Storici. Tomo Primo. Bologna.

Di Genova G (1994) Storia dell'arte italiana del '900. Generazione Maestri Storici. Tomo Secondo. Bologna.

Di Genova G (1995) Storia dell'arte italiana del '900. Generazione Maestri Storici. Tomo Terzo. Bologna.

Di Genova G (1996) Storia dell'arte italiana del '900. Generazione Primo Decennio. Bologna.

Drouot (1990) L'art et les enchères en France. Cie des Commissaires et Priseurs de Paris,Paris.

Duboucher V (1992) Monographie du tableau d'Alessandro ALLORI "Vénus et l'Amour" conservé au musée Fabre à Montpellier. Université de Montpellier III,Montpellier.

Duca J (1966) Erotique de l'Art. La jeune Parque,Paris.

Dunand L & Lemarchand P (s.d.) I Les Amours des Dieux.L'art érotique sous la Renaissance.Les compositions de Jules Romain, gravées par Marc-Antoine Raimondi. Institut d'Iconographie Arietis,Lausanne.

Dunand L & Lemarchand P (s.d.) II Les Amours des Dieux.Les compositions de Titien, gravées par Gian-Jacopo Caraglio, selon les dessins préparatoires de Rosso Fiorentino et Perino del Vaga. Institut d'Iconographie Arietis,Lausanne.

Dunand L & Lemarchand P (s.d.) III Les Amours des Dieux. Les compositions de Augustin Carrache, gravées par Pierre De Jode l'Ancien: Le Lascivie. Institut d'Iconographie Arietis,Lausanne.

BIBLIOGRAPHICAL REFERENCES

Eco U, sous la direction de. Histoire de la Beauté. Paris: Flammarion, 2004.

Enciclopedia (2006) Enciclopedia del Museo del Prado, 6 Vol. Madrid.

Enggass R (1964) The painting of Baciccio - Giovanni Battista Gauli (1639-1709) .Pennsylvania University Press.

Faietti M&OK (1988) Bologna e l'Umanismo 1490-1510. Nuova Alfa Ed.,Bologna.

Faietti M&ZA (1998) Figure - Disegni dal '500 all '800 nella Pinacoteca Nazionale di Bologna. Electa,Milano.

Falletti F&NJK (2002) Venere e Amore: Michelangelo e la nuove bellezza ideale. Giunti,Firenze.

Fels F (1968) Eros ou l'Amour peintre. Editions du Cap,Monte-Carlo.

Ficacci L (2000) Giovanni Piranesi – The complete etchings. Taschen, Koeln, London.

Fleischer Meal (2005) Gemäldegalerie der Akademie der bildenden Künste. Scala,London.

Flemming HT (1978) Bruno Bruni. Ed.Volker Huber, Offenbach a/Main.

Gallwitz KL (1999) The handbook of Italian Renaissance painters. Prestel,Munich.

Gamba C. La Venere di Giorgione reintegrata. Dedalo 1928; 9(4):205-9.

Ginzburg Carignani S (2000) Annibale Carracci a Roma - Gli affreschi di Palazzo Farnese. Donzelli,Roma.

Giorgi R (1990) TIZIANO.Venere, Amore e il Musicista in cinque dipinti . Gangemi Editore,Roma.

Gli Uffizi (1979) Catalogo Generale. Centro Di, Firenze.

Gli Uffizi (1984) La Nascita di Venere e l'Annunciazione del Botticelli restaurate. Centro Di, Firenze.

Gnann A (2007) On a drawing attributed to Giovanni Francesco Penni, in Master Drawings 45,2:229-235.

Godwin J (2005) Hypnerotomachia Poliphili - The strife of love in a dream of Francesco Colonna. Thames & Hudson, London.

Goffen R (1997) Titian's women. Yale University Press,New Haven & London.

Gombrich EH (1951) Hypnerotomachiana. Journal of the Warburg and Courtauld Institutes, 14:119-125.

Gombrich EH (1972) Symbolic images -Studies in the art of the Renaissance. Phaidon.

Gould C (s.d.) The School of Love and Correggio's mythologies. National Gallery, London.

Gould C (1975) The 16th Century Italian Schools . National Gallery Catalogs. London.

Gould C (1994) Parmigianino. Abbeville Press, NY.

Grafton CB (2003) Great drawings of nudes. Dover Art Library,NY.

Greer G (2003) Les garçons, figures de l'éphèbe. Hazan,Paris.

Guillaud M (1990) La Femme chez TITIEN. Guillaud Editions,Paris/New York.

Habert J (1989) ' Italian Baroque painters' Burlington Magazine 131:58-59.

Healy, F (1997) Rubens and the Judgement of Paris - A question of choice. Brepols, Turnhout.

Himmel A (2000) Die Venus von Urbino und Guidobaldo della Rovere- Ein Beitrag zum Herrscherverständnis in Italien im 15.16. Jahrhundert. Peter Lang,Frankfurt a/Main.

Holtman M (1997) The J. Paul Getty Museum-Handbook of the Collections. The J. Paul Getty Museum,Los Angeles.

Howard K (1987) The Metropolitan Museum of Art - GUIDE. MET,New York.

Hutter H. Original-Kopie-Replik-Paraphrase. Bildhefte Der Akademie Der Bildenden Künste in Wien 1980; Doppelheft 12/13:60.

Impelluso L (2003) Eroi e Dei dell'antichità. Electa,Milano.

Jaffé M (1993) Old Master drawings from Chatsworth . British Museum, London.

Jaffé M (1995) Renaissance and Baroque drawings from Chatsworth - a great heritage. National Gallery of Art, Washington, DC.

Jatta B (1995) Francesco Bartolozzi, incisore delle grazie. Artemide,

Joannides P (1996) Michelangelo and his influence. Drawings from Windsor Castle. Lund Humphries Publ.,London.

Joyce H 'The ancient frescoes from the Villa Negroni and their influence in the eighteenth and nineteenth centuries' in Art Bulletin (1983): 423-440.

Kahmen, V (1972) Erotic Art Today. New York Graphic Society Ltd. Greenwich, Connecticut.

Kerber, B 'Giuseppe Bartolomeo Chiari' in Art Bulletin (1968): 75-86.

Kolb C&BM. The sculptures on the Nymphaeum of the Villa Maser. Artibus Et Historiae 1997; 18(35):15-33,35-40.

Kultermann U (1967) Neue Dimensionen der Plastik. Verlag Ernst Wasmuth, Tübingen.

Labrot G (1992) Collections of paintings in Naples 1600-1780 - Italian Inventories 1. Saur, Munich. *Some 55 works with iconography of Venus of identified artists are listed and many more of un-identified artists.*

Lambrichs Ceal (1973) La Vénus de Milo ou les dangers de la célebrité. Musée des Arts décoratifs,Paris.

Landon J (1912) The Education of Cupid.or Mercury Instructing Cupid in the Presence of Venus The famous painting of Antonio Allegri da Correggio Rescued after three centuries of obscurity. Jesse Landon,Watford.

Lawner L (1988) Le Cortigiane-Ritratti del Rinascimento. Rizzoli,Milano.

Lecchini Giovannoni, S (1991) Alessandro Allori. Umberto Allemardi, Torino.

Leithe-Jasper M (2002) 'Venus Este: eine Marmorskulptur aus dem Umkreis des Guglielmo della Porta' Jahrbuch KHM, 4/5 :136-163, Wien.

Levi d'Ancona M (1992) Due quadri del Botticelli eseguiti per nascite in casa Medici Nuova interpretazione della Primavera e della Nascita di Venere. Leo S. Olschki Editore,Firenze.

Leydier R (2003) Pour l'amour de Vénus. Donjon de Vez,Vez.

Llorens T et al (1997) El triunfo de Venus - La imagen de la mujer en la pintura veneciana del siglo XVIII. Museo Thyssen-Bornemisza, Madrid.

Loisel C (2004) Inventaire général des dessins italiens. Tome VII: Ludovico, Agostino, Annibale Carracci. RMN,Paris .

Lomartire S (2003) Andrea Mantegna e l'incisione italiana del Rinascimento nelle collezioni dei Musei Civici di Pavia. Electa,Milano.

Lowenthal A (1995) Joachim Wtewael: Mars and Venus surprised by Vulcan. Getty Museum, Malibu.

Mai E Editor(2001) Venus, vergeten mythe. Voorstellingen van een godin van Cranach tot Cézanne. Koninklijk Museum voor Schone Kunsten.Snoeck-Ducaju & Zonen,Antwerpen.

Mallé L&SF (1968) L'incisione Europeo dal XV al XX secolo. Galleria civica d'arte moderna,Torino.

Marinelli S&MG (1999) Disegni. Electa,Milano.

Martini E (2002) Pinacoteca Egidio Martini a Ca' Rezzonico. Marsilio,Venezia.

Massari S (1993) Giulio Romano pinxit et delineavit - Opere grafiche autografe di collaborazione e bottega. Fratelli Palombi Ed.,Roma.

Massari SeSPVR (1989) Tra Mito e Allegoria.Immagini a stampa nel '500 e '600. Istituto Nazionale per la Grafica (ING),Roma.

Massinelli AM&TF (1992) Treasures of the MEDICI. Thames and Hudson, London.

Matile M (2003) Italienische Holzschnitte der Renaissance und der Barock. Bestandskatalog der Graphischen sammlung der ETH Zürich. Schwabe & Co, Basel.

McParland E (1989) 'Edward Lowett Pearce and the Parliament House in Dublin' Burlington Magazine 131 : 91-100.

Miller D (1991) Marcantonio Franceschini and the Liechtensteins - Prince Johann Adam Andreas and the decoration of the Liechtenstein Garden Palace at Rossau-Vienna. Cambridge University Press

Mochi Onori L&VR (2001) Capolavori della Galleria Nazionale d'Arte Antica, Palazzo Barberini. Ministerio per i Beni Culturali,Roma.

Monbeig-Goguel C (1972) Vasari et son temps-Maîtres toscans nés après 1500, morts avant 1600.Paris.

Moreno P & Stefani c (2004) Galleria Borghese. Touring Club Italiano, Milano.

Morselli, R (1998) Collezioni e quadrerie nella Bologna del Seicento Inventari 1640-1707 - Italian Inventories 3. P Getty Trust, Los Angeles. (*Some 50 works with the iconography of Venus of identified artists are listed and more of un-identified artists.)*

Munoz A (1957) Antonio Canova – Le opere. Ed. Palombi, Roma.

Muraro M&RD (1976) Tiziano e la silografia veneziana del '500. Neri Pozza Ed.

Murphy CP (2003) Lavinia Fontana – A painter and her patrons in 16th century Bologna. Yale University Press, New Haven-London.

Mussini M&DRGM (2003) PARMIGIANINO tradutto. La fortuna di Francesco Mazzola nelle stampe di riproduzione fra il '500 e '800. Silvana,Milano.

Navarrete Orcera AR (2005) La mitologia en los Palacios Españolas. Universidad Nacional de Educacion a Distancia. Madrid.

Negro A (2001) Venere e Amore di Michele di Rodolfo del Ghirlandaio.Il mito di una Venere di Michelangelo fra copie, repliche e pudiche vestizioni. Campisano,Roma.

Nesbitt J (1994) Venus re-defined.Sculpture by Rodin, Matisse and contemporaries. Tate Gallery Liverpool,Liverpool.

Nichols, T (1999) Tintoretto, Tradtion and Identity. Reaktion Books, London.

Nordmann M (2004) Eros invaincu.La bibliothèque Gérard Nordmann. Fondation Martin Bodmer/Editions Cercle d'Art,Genève/Paris.

Oberhuber K&GA (1999) Raphael und der klassische Stil in Rom 1515-1527. Electa,Milano.

Panofsky E (1967) Studies in iconology: humanistic themes in the art of the Renaissance. Harper & Row, New York.

Paraskos S 2000 Aphrodite, the mythology of Cyprus. Interworld Pub. New Barnet.

Pedrocco F (2002) Giambattista Tiepolo. Flammarion, Paris.Pellegrino F, Poletti F (2003) Episodi e personnagi della letteratura.

Electa,Milano.

Penta MT&JB (2002) Incisioni del'700 in Italia nella raccolta d'arte pagliara dell'Istituto Suor Orsola Benincasa.Napoli.

Perez Sancho AE (1977) I grandi disegni italiani nelle collezioni di Madrid. Silvana,Milano.

Pérouse de Montclos J-M (1998) Fontainebleau. Ed. Scala,Paris.

Petrioli Tofani Aeal (1996) Gli Uffizi-Storia e collezioni. Giunti,Firenze.

Pignatti T (1977) I grandi disegni italiani nelle collezioni di Oxford Ashmolean Museum e Christ Chuch Picture Gallery. Silvana,Milano.

Pinto S (1957) Arte di corte a Torino da Carlo Emanuele III a Carlo Felice.Torino.

Pinto S (2002) A history of Italian art in the 20th century. Skira,Milano.

Planischig L. Venere flagillifera: una nuova statuetta di Andrea RICCIO. Bolletino Del Museo Civico Di Padova 1925; (1-3):43-8.

Pocino W (1996) Le fontane di Roma. Newton & Compton, Roma.

Pontiggia E (2004) Carlo Carra - I miei riccordi - l'opera grafica 1922-1964. Medusa,Milano.

Pope-Hennesy J (1964) Catalogue of Italian sculpture in the Victoria & Albert Museum. HMSO, London.

Pope-Hennesy J (1996) An introduction to Italian sculpture. Vol.II Italian Renaissance sculpture. Phaidon, London.

Pope-Hennesy J (1996) An introduction to Italian sculpture. Vol.III Italian High Renaissance and Baroque sculpture. Phaidon, London.

Popham AE & Pouncey P (1950) Italian drawings in the department of prints and drawings of the British Museum - The 14th and 15th centuries. British Museum, London.

Porcheron-Felsing M-D (1983) Vénus et Diane en Italie et en France 1528-1598. Université de Paris I,Paris.

Prater A (2002) Venus at her Mirror.Velazquez and the Art of Nude Painting. Prestel,Munich.

Precerutti-Garberi M (1969) Andrea Appiani, pittore di Napoleone. Milano.

Primatice (2004) Primatice, Maître de Fontainebleau. RMN,Paris.

Quignard P (1982) Blasons anatomiques du corps féminin, suivi des Contreblasons. Gallimard,Paris.

Redig de Campos D (1981) Architecture, peinture, sculpture du Vatican. VNU Books Int. Amsterdam.

Reid JD (1993) The Oxford Guide to Classical Mythology in Arts, 1300-1990s. 2Vol. Oxford University Press, NY.

Relouge IE (1958) Les chefs-d'oeuvres du Nu - Les beautés féminines chantées par la couleur. Ed. du Pont royal,Paris.

Rich A (1987) Dictionnaire des antiquités romaines et grecques accompagné de 2,000 gravures d'après l'antique représentant tous les objets de divers usages d'art et d'industrie des Grecs et des Romains. Henri Veyrier,Paris.

Rizzoli, Editore (1968) Giambattista Tiepolo. Milano.

Rizzoli, Editore (1970) L'Opera completa del Tintoretto.Milano.

Roberts J (1986) Master drawings in the Royal Collection - from Leonardo da Vinci to the present day. Collins Harvill, London.

Rochelle M (1991) Mythological and classical art index. A locator of paintings, sculptures, frescoes, manuscript illuminations, sketches, woodcuts and engravings executed 1200 BC to AD 1900 with a directory of the institutions holding them. McFarland & Cy,Jefferson & London.

Rodino SPV (1994) Da Leonardo a Volterrano - disegni fiorentini dal XV al XVII secolo. de Luca, ING Roma.

Rodino SPV (1997) Pietro da Cortona e il disegno. Electa,

Roettgen S (2001) Mengs - die Erfindung des Klassismus. Hirmer Verla, München.

Romanelli G Editor (1997) Venice, Art and Architecture. 2 Vol. Könemann, Köln

Romanelli Geal (1998) Il mondo di Giacomo Casanova, un Veniziano in Europa 1725-1798 . Marsilio,Venezia.

Rosenberg P (1987) Fragonard. Réunion des Musées nationaux,Paris.

Royalton-Kisch M (1996) Old master drawings from the Malcolm Collection. British Museum, london.

Rozman K (2005) Giuseppe Tominz: Venere e Cupido. Un motivo desunto da un dipinto di Marc'Antonio Franceschini. Slovensko umetnostnozgodovinsko društvo — Filozofska fakulteta,Ljubljana.

Safarik EA (1996) Collezione dei dipinti Colonna (Famiglia) Inventari 1611-1795 - Italian Inventories 2. Saur, Munich. (*Some 58 works with the iconography of Venus of identified artists are listed and many more of un-identified artists.)*

Safarik EA (2002) Galerie Doria Pamphilj - Chefs-d'oeuvre de la peinture. Scala,Firenze.

Salmon D (2000) La Vénus de Milo. Un mythe. Gallimard/Réunion des Musées Nationaux,Paris.

Sauer (1999) Allgemeines Künstler Lexikon – Bio-bibliographischer Index. München-Leipzig.

Scarpa A (2006) Sebastiano RICCI – Catalogue raisonné. B. Alfieri, Milano.

Schwartz E&GA-M (2004) Dieux et Mortels. Les thèmes homériques dans les collections de l'Ecole nationale supérieure des beaux-arts de Paris. Ecole nationale supérieure des beaux-arts,Paris.

Serra R M (1993) L'Ottoocento, Catalogo delle opere esposte – Galleria Civica d'arte Moderna e Contemporaneo Torino. Fabbri Editori.

Serra R M & Passoni R (1993) Il Novecento, Catalogo delle opere esposte – Galleria Civica d'arte Moderna e Contemporaneo Torino. Fabbri Editori.

Seznec J (1961) The survival of the pagan gods.The mythological tradition and its place in Renaissance humanism and art. Harper & Row,New York.

Sframeli M (2003) The Myth of Venus / Il mito di Venere. Silvana,Milano.

Sgarbi V (2002) Giorgio di Chirico: della metafisica alla Metafisica - Opere 1909-1973. Marsilio.

Sisi C (2005) L'Ottocento in Italia – Il Neo-classismo 1789-1815. Electa, Milano.

Schmidt D (1978) Untersuchungen zu den Architektur-ekphrasen in der Hypnerotomachia Poliphili; Die Beschreibung der Venus-Tempel. R.G. Fischer.

Spinosa N (1994) Museo Nazionale di Capodimonte. Electa, Napoli.

Staccioli Seal (1985) Il museo e la Galleria Borghese, Roma. Federico Garolla Editore,Milano.

Städelsches Kunstinstitut (1982) Jean-Antoine Watteau : Einschiffung nach Cythera. Frankfurt a/Main.

Stefani O (2003) CANOVA La statuaria. Electa, Milano.

Stefani O (2004) CANOVA Pittore – Tra Eros e Thanatos. Electa, Milano.

Stillman WJ (1898) Venus and Apollo in painting and sculpture. Bliss, Sands & Co.,London.

Succi D (1983) Da Carlevarijs ai Tiepolo. Incisori veneti e frulani del '600. Albrizzi Ed..

Tinkle T (1996) Medieval Venuses and Cupids.Sexuality, hermeneutics and english poetry. Stanford University Press,Stanford.

Tiziano (1995) Tiziano Vecellio, Amor sacro e Amor profano. Electa,Milano.

Todts H (2001) Vénus, mythe oublié. Ludion/Beaux Arts,Gand/Amsterdam.

Trottein G (1993) Les enfants de Vénus. Art et Astrologie à la Renaissance. Lagune,Paris.

Turner J Ed. (1996) The Dictionary of Art (34 vol.). Grove, NY.

Ubeda de los Cobos A (2005) CARRACCI,Annibale 'Venus, Adonis y Cupido'. Muceo Nacional del Prado,Madrid.

Verdi R (1986) Venus and Mercury. Dulwich Picture Gallery,London.

Vezzosi M (2003) Un capolavoro della pittura fiorentina Venere e Adone di Vicenzo Meucci. Edizioni Polistampa,Firenze.

Viatte FTI (1974) Inventaire général des dessins italiens. Tome II: Les dessins de Stefano DELLA BELLA. Musées nationaux,Paris.

Viatte FTI (1988) Inventaire général des dessins italiens. tome III: Dessins toscans, XVI-XVII siècles.Paris.

Virno C (2004) Roma Galleria Comunale d'Arte Moderna e Contemporanea-Catalogo generale delle collezioni – Autori dell'Ottocento Vol I (A-F). Palumbi Editori, Roma.

Vivarelli P (1996) Alberto Savinio-Catalogo generale. Electa, Milano.

Warburg Institute (2002) The Photographic Collection Index. London.

Ward-Jackson P (1979) Italian drawings. Vol.I & II. Victoria & Albert Museum, London.

Weddingen E (1994) Des Vulkan Paralleles Wesen-Dialog über einen Ehebruch mit einem Glossar zu Tintorettos "Vulkan überrascht Venus und Mars". Scaneg,München.

Weichardt W (s.d.) Die Venus in der Italienischen Malerei. Einhorn Verlag, Dachau.

Wind E (1980) Pagan mysteries in the Renaissance. Oxford University Press.

Wittkower R (1952) The drawings of the CARRACCI at Windsor Castle. Phaidon, London.

Wundram M&PT (1988) Andrea Palladio 1508-1580. Architect tussen Renaissance en Barok . Taschen/Librero,Köln.

Zerner H (1969) Ecole de Fontainebleau-Gravures. Arts et Métiers Graphiques, Paris.

Zentai L (2003) Sixteenth century Northern Italian drawings. Museum Fine Arts, Budapest.

Zuffi S (2001) Arte e erotismo. Electa,Milano.

www.ingramcontent.com/pod-product-compliance
Lightning Source LLC
Chambersburg PA
CBHW081052170526
45165CB00006B/2253

* 9 7 8 1 4 0 9 2 6 5 6 2 7 *